The Materiality of Freedom

The Materiality of
FREEDOM

Archaeologies of Postemancipation Life

Edited by Jodi A. Barnes

The University of South Carolina Press

Published by the University of South Carolina Press
Columbia, South Carolina 29208

www.sc.edu/uscpress

Manufactured in the United States of America

20 19 18 17 16 15 14 13 12 11
10 9 8 7 6 5 4 3 2 1

Library of Congress Cataloging-in-Publication Data
The materiality of freedom : archaeologies of postemancipation life / edited
by Jodi A. Barnes.
     p. cm.
  Includes bibliographical references and index.
  ISBN 978-1-61117-034-4 (cloth : alk. paper)
  1. African Americans—History—1863–1877. 2. African Americans—History—1877–1964.
3. African Americans—Material culture. 4. African Americans—Antiquities. 5. Social
archaeology—United States. 6. Reconstruction (U.S. history, 1865–1877) 7. United
States—Antiquities. I. Barnes, Jodi A.
  E185.2.M38 2011
  973.8—dc22

                                2011015291

This book was printed on a recycled paper with 30 percent postconsumer waste content.

CONTENTS

ILLUSTRATIONS

TABLES

FOREWORD

Charles R. Cobb

This wonderful volume edited by Dr. Jodi Barnes strikes both professional and personal chords for myself. I was a graduate student at Southern Illinois University, Carbondale, in the 1980s when the Visiting Scholar program was established by the Center for Archaeological Investigations. That program was incredibly exciting, as was the opportunity for rubbing shoulders with some of the top archaeologists in the world.

One of my dreams has always been to carry that model to another university. Dean Mary Anne Fitzpatrick and the College of Arts and Sciences at the University of South Carolina graciously afforded me that opportunity when I arrived in 2007. Dr. Barnes is our first postdoctoral scholar, and she generated all of the electricity and enthusiasm that I remembered from my graduate school days. So I have to thank her, as well as SIUC. The Department of Anthropology and the South Carolina Institute for Archaeology and Anthropology are well known for their strengths in historical archaeology and diaspora studies. In addition, individuals such as Dr. Leland Ferguson at the university have been at the forefront of the archaeology of the African American experience. We are extremely lucky to have Dr. Ferguson represented in this volume. We were just as fortunate to have what I believe is the cream of the crop of scholars who are pursuing the archaeology of the African American diaspora in the United States. As Dr. Barnes points out in her introduction, the importance of these particular studies lies in their emphasis on African American history following emancipation. Historical archaeologists since the 1960s have conducted a number of path-breaking studies on the African diaspora from the viewpoint of plantations and enslavement, a period for which personal written narratives are scarce. But even written histories never tell the whole story, and the field of historical archaeology has amply demonstrated that there is much that has escaped the volumes of descriptions of African American life in the postbellum era. Lying under the ground is yet another narrative about the past—one found in broken pots, the charred remains of meals, and other remains. That material record unraveled by archaeologists broadens our understanding of the micro-histories of everyday life, including those of the postemancipation experience.

The histories represented in this volume are particularly pertinent to a generation that has witnessed changes ranging from the passage of the Civil Rights Act over forty years ago to the election of a black president of the United States in the twenty-first century, because they inform us about the foundations of the pivotal changes that we have witnessed in our lifetime. I could not help but revisit some of the scenes from my childhood in Arkansas in the 1960s while reading the essays in this volume: a neighborhood theater with segregated ticket booth entrances and seating areas and a local clinic where black people waited one on side of the building to see the physician while white people waited on the other side to be tended by the very same doctor. Despite the notoriety Little Rock gained from its integration efforts in the 1950s, my elementary school in rural Arkansas did not integrate until the 1966–1967 school year. And that involved one black child per classroom. As these examples from my own life indicate, we may be horrified by the violence of racism represented by such acts as lynching, but the real power of institutionalized oppression derives from—to borrow a notion from Hannah Arendt—its very banality. What in hindsight appears to defy our imagination was in fact a wide-reaching system of taken-for-granteds for a significant portion of the population. Historical archaeology is a discipline uniquely suited to examining the material expressions of the pervasiveness of that inequity and exploitation.

But my personal digression is a very narrow perspective on the themes addressed by *The Materiality of Freedom*. As Dr. Barnes points out, postemancipation was much, much more than a history of victimization. While race is inextricably bound into the history of the United States, the African American experience is tied into other major issues as well: massive migrations from south to north, the birth of organized labor, industrialism, major world wars, the florescence of new churches, and a litany of other topics of central importance to an anthropology of the recent past. As Dr. Barnes emphasizes in her introduction, the gaps and silences in that past are commonplace despite its historical proximity. We are fortunate to have her and her colleagues bring voice through the archaeological record to those silences.

JODI A. BARNES

Introduction

The Materiality of Freedom—Archaeologies
of Postemancipation Life

Now, there are some who question the scale of our ambitions—who suggest that our system cannot tolerate too many big plans. Their memories are short. For they have forgotten what this country has already done; what free men and women can achieve when imagination is joined to common purpose, and necessity to courage.

Barack Obama (2009)

For many who experienced and remember segregation and the civil rights movement, the election of Barack Obama as president was a momentous day. It demonstrates that the actions of men and women with courage and common purpose can create change. The lunch counter strikes, marches, and sit-ins of the 1960s are reminders of what ordinary women and men accomplished through imagination and necessity. Yet the building of African American churches, schools, communities, and neighborhoods—which were also constructed by ordinary men and women and physically mark our landscapes—are often taken for granted in the historical narratives of U.S. history. In his inaugural address, President Obama encouraged us to look to history for inspiration, while reminding us that remembering and forgetting has contemporary social and political implications. In a 2008 speech on race in Philadelphia, Obama stated, "As William Faulkner once wrote, 'The past isn't dead and buried. In fact, it isn't even past.' We do not need to recite here the history of injustice in this country. But we do need to remind ourselves that so many of the disparities that exist in the African American community today can be directly traced to inequalities passed on from an earlier generation that suffered under the brutal legacy of slavery and Jim Crow" (Obama 2008).

President Obama's success, then, does not mean that the long struggle for racial equality finally has been won or forgotten. Instead his election provides the basis for new conversations about race relations and new strategies to remember the legacies of America's color line—strategies that bring the struggles for equality in the recent past to the present and provide a basis for social change in the future.

Archaeologies of Postemancipation Life

Archaeologists are increasingly recognizing that changes in the recent past are connected to contemporary conditions (for example, Barnes and Gadsby 2008; Rathje and Murphy 1992) and that remembering and forgetting are political acts. Carol McDavid (1997: 1) defines politics as "the many ways people compete with each other for power and leadership, in community settings, in workplaces, and in social situations. The position here is that, if archaeological work influences how people in the present negotiate power, then it is political, whether or not the archaeologist chooses to engage in the political process."

The recognition that archaeology is not "value-free" has its impetus in feminist and post-processual archaeologies (for example, Conkey and Gero 1997; Gero 1983; Tilley 1989; Trigger 1984). For some archaeologists, recognizing that the past is political has meant recognizing that the sociopolitical analyses of archaeology involve exposing and critiquing the connections between archaeological knowledge claims and how they are "constituted" by the social and political contexts that directly shape the practice of archaeology through the inclusion of women and people of color in the practice of archaeology (for example, Franklin 1997a, 1997b; Gero et al. 1983; Nelson et al. 1994; Watkins 2001; Wylie 1989) and by arguing for better wages for archaeological work, (for example, Paynter 1983; Shanks and McGuire 1996). Archaeologists have also challenged the authority of academic knowledge claims (for example, Zimmerman 1994, 2005) and the need to actively involve descendant groups in archaeological endeavors (Pyburn and Wilk 1995; Spector 1993).

No longer neutral, archaeologists are advocating for an archaeology that is "emancipatory" (Duke and Saitta 1998), contributes "Power to the People" (Franklin 1997a) and "true acts of inclusion" (Edwards-Ingram 1997), and one that consists of "transformative democratic action" (Wood 2002), "partnerships" (Derry and Malloy 2003; Shackel and Chambers 2004), "civic engagement" (Little and Shackel 2007), and "community service" (Perry 1997). As the authors in this volume demonstrate, archaeology has the potential to present a different view of the past and challenge popular conceptions of how African Americans dealt with the oppression of slavery and its aftermath. This requires that archaeologists recognize that the descendants of the people being studied archaeologically live in the same community in which their ancestors were enslaved, in which descendants of their enslavers still live, and in which both groups of descendants continue to negotiate issues of power and control (McDavid 1997: 1).

Yet Randy McGuire (2008: 14) notes that from "a political sense, the discipline of archaeology is at once trivial and significant. Paradoxically, the significance of archaeology for political action springs from its triviality. Archaeology by and large does not directly engage in the key political struggles of the modern world. Archaeologists do not in any noteworthy way direct armies, shape economies, write laws, or imprison or free people from bondage."

But as archaeologists have noted, archeology has been "put to overt political use" (McGuire 2008: 14; for example, Arnold 1996; Kohl and Fawcett 1995; Trigger 1984). And the ideological products of archaeology have most commonly "sustained, justified, and legitimated the dominant ideological values of capitalism . . . by venerating stability and disparaging change, by equating social change with progress, by biologizing the social, and by rationalizing the economic" (McGuire 2008; Tilley 1989). Archaeologists studying the African diaspora have taken action to create change in two different ways: changing consciousness and direct action (Gadsby and Barnes 2010).

Many archaeologists are exploring the historical construction of supposedly "natural" structures to combat some of the inequality that resides in capitalism (for example, Epperson 2004; Leone 1995, 2005; Little 1984; Spencer-Wood 1996), a system of inherent inequality that sustained and reproduced itself by rendering its structures (family, church, and state) "natural" and "right" (Althusser 2001). With the use of historical and archaeological records, historical archaeologists are able to explore the origins and evolutions of power structures and even occasionally to point out that some, such as race, actually have origins and are not merely part of the natural world (Epperson 1990; Gadsby and Barnes 2010; Wilkie 2000: xix). By "piercing" ideology, one can change consciousness and bring about social change if one communicates archaeological research effectively to the public (Gadsby and Barnes 2010).

A number of archaeologists have also taken approaches to change that include direct action. For instance archaeologists have assisted in the attainment of cultural capital by identifying and consulting with stakeholders, cultivating positive local ownership of heritage, and methodically transferring authority of the research from the scholar to the community while not denying the interests of archaeologists that are involved. In the case of the New York African Burial Ground Project, African Americans would not allow themselves to be denied their ancestry. When Howard University became involved and regarded the descendants as collaborators, a choice became available that allowed African Americans to redress racism and claim control of the community's cultural construction (Blakey 1997: 143; LaRoche and Blakey 1997).

These methods of direct and indirect action help remedy what Michael Blakey (1994: 39) notes as "an ethnic bias that 'whitens' national heritage and identity" in American archaeology. Because many archaeologists have not been interested in the poorer, African communities, there are numerous historical narratives about African American life in the United States that have been forgotten. This forgetting of the recent African American past reflects the ways in which history has been whitewashed to create a unified narrative of American history.

In African American history, images of victimization spring to mind as readily as notions of progress. Hope has frequently bred disappointment and disillusionment. In the early twentieth century, black Americans shared in the aspirations and expectations of their fellow citizens but did so as a people with a unique history and set of barriers to overcome (Grossman 2005: 67). In this volume, historical archaeologists emphasize the ways in which the actions of everyday people—their experiences, material culture, and beliefs—may help us gain insight into larger historic events, particularly Reconstruction, Jim Crow, and urban renewal projects of the 1940s and 1950s. Historical archaeologists have only recently addressed the ways people responded to emancipation, as archaeology has begun to shift "away from enslavement to freedom, away from oppression toward resistance, and away from passivity toward agency" (Leone et al. 2005: 577). Historical archaeology is relevant for the study of this period, particularly because "it illuminates how material objects utterly complicate historical narratives, identities, and experiences" (Mullins 2008: 157).

Through an analysis of varying places and scales, the authors weave concerns about race and racism through these chapters in two interconnected ways: (1) What can archaeology reveal about the role of race and racism in the ways sites are valued, deemed significant, interpreted, and memorialized? and (2) What can archaeology reveal about the historicity of race and racism? The case studies in this volume draw upon historical archaeological data to demonstrate the ways material culture can complicate historical narratives and contribute to the study of people's everyday lives and the landscapes they transformed.

The essays in this volume concentrate mainly on the experiences, identities, and historical narratives of people of African descent, particularly in the United States, with the exception of Wilkie and Farnsworth ("Living Not So Quietly"), who discuss postemancipation life in the Bahamas. The volume fits within research on the archaeology of the African diaspora (Agorsah 1996; Orser 1998; Singleton 1985, 1995, 1999), yet it veers from studies in which plantations and slavery have been the defining diasporic experiences (for example, Babson 1990; Farnsworth 2000; Singleton 1985). Most archaeological research on the African diaspora focuses on the material identification of African identity (for example, Farnsworth 2001; Fennell 2000, 2003, 2007; Ferguson 1980, 1992; Franklin 2001; McCarthy 1997), the archaeology of freedom at Maroon sites (for example, Agorsah 1994; Orser and Funari 2001; Weik 1997), and the archaeology of race and racism (for example, Epperson 2004; Garman 1994; Mullins 1999, 2003; Orser 1999, 2001, 2004). While the study of the diaspora has become more global in scope (for example, Franklin and McKee 2004; Haviser and MacDonald 2006; Ogundiran and Falola 2007), most of these studies investigate enslavement (for example, Armstrong 2003; Ferguson 1992; Singleton 1995, 1999).

This volume places an emphasis on post–Emancipation Proclamation sites or sites occupied following the end of the Civil War, while recognizing that in the northeast there were variable dates of emancipation. In the northeast archaeologists have conducted extensive investigations on African American sites that date to the late eighteenth and early nineteenth centuries, such as the African Meeting House in Boston (Bower and Rushing 1980), the African Baptist Meeting House on Nantucket (Beaudry and Berkland 2007), Black Lucy's Garden (Baker 1980; Bullen and Bullen 1945), the Parting Ways settlement (Deetz 1996), Skunk Hollow (Geismar 1982), Weeksville (Bridges and Salwen 1980) and the W. E. B. DuBois homesite (Muller 1994; Paynter et al. 1996). Yet in the southeast, postemancipation studies tend to concentrate on tenancy (for example, Brown 1994; Orser 1988; Wilkie 2000).

Increasingly, archaeologists are conducting research on the archaeology of the more recent past in the African diaspora (for example, Barnes 2008a, 2008b; Cox 2007; Hicks 2006, 2007; Palus 2009; Praetzellis and Praetzellis 2001, 2008). The African diaspora is a historic process, tracing Africans through the slave trade to homes outside of Africa; yet many archaeologists have neglected the idea of the diaspora as a modern identity with a historical and material context. This volume demonstrates that historical archaeologists, with the focus on time and materiality, have something to contribute to the study of places, sites, and things whose creation is remembered and whose form and character continue to influence our everyday lives (Barnes 2008b; Bradley et al. 2004).

The archaeology of the African diaspora is enhanced when researchers build upon the work of scholars in African and African American Studies. As Maria Franklin (1997a: 44) points out, the archaeology of postemancipation life "must be seen as not only an extension of the disciplines of archaeology and anthropology but also of the vast body of scholarship on black American history and culture, much of it conducted by blacks themselves." The work of W. E .B. DuBois, Zora Neale Hurston, Manning Marable, Frederick Douglass, bell hooks, and other African diaspora scholars complements and expands our understandings of African American life in a racialized society (Mullins 2008).

The emphasis on postemancipation life, or the recent past, with its increased temporal proximity, follows trends in contemporary archaeology in the United Kingdom (for example, Bradley et al. 2004; Buchli and Lucas 2001; Schofield et al. 2002). The archaeology of the contemporary past found a place in the New Archaeology as a parallel effort to historical archaeology. The volume edited by Richard Gould and Michael Schiffer (1981), *Modern Material Culture: The Archaeology of Us,* documents the various means by which its contributors discovered contemporaneous applications for the material culture that archaeologists celebrate. Building on this work, Buchli and Lucas (2001) argue that the archaeology of the contemporary past connects temporal proximity and materiality. It is also a way to constitute the unconstituted, or to take the familiar and make it unfamiliar, and to help individuals and communities cope with painful contradictions that otherwise would remain unarticulated.

For example, for many African Americans the memories of struggle and opportunity that are connected to the Jim Crow and civil rights eras are prolific, yet "the lack of historical places on our contemporary landscape that remind all persons of the omnipresence of African Americans throughout U.S. history . . . helps create a cultural amnesia and contributes to the recreation of racism" (Paynter et al. 1996: 314). Historical archaeology, with an emphasis on the recent past, is in a good position to make these historical places more visible and to reduce the cultural amnesia by addressing the painful histories of Reconstruction and Jim Crow or the more hopeful histories of the building of black communities and neighborhoods. These hopeful historical narratives, such as the building of New Philadelphia in Illinois (see Fennell,"Examining Structural Racism," this volume) or the material life of Harriett Tubman (see Armstrong,"Excavating Inspiration," this volume) have been silenced within the constraints of everyday retelling of American history.

Remembering and Forgetting the Recent African American Past

Plantations—the architecture, gardens, slave cabins, and the consumption of tangible goods and services—have been a significant focal point of archaeological research. Yet sites connected with the postbellum African American past have been understudied because people were poorer, had fewer material goods and less substantial housing, and left more ephemeral archaeological remains (Barile 2004; Palmer, "Archaeology of Jim Crow," this volume). In addition, the opportunities of African Americans were seen to be curtailed because of prejudicial legal and social restrictions. Yet as the authors in this volume demonstrate, African Americans created opportunity despite the struggles.

Although the archaeology of the African diaspora is on the rise, few African American sites have been preserved and interpreted, and many have been razed for economic, social, and/or political reasons. Eric Larsen (Matthews and Larsen, "Black History as Property," this volume) provides one of several examples: the Contrabands and Freedmen's Cemetery in Alexandria, Virginia. The cemetery was established during the Civil War and was thought to have been abandoned in 1927. A gas station was built upon part of the cemetery in 1955, and the Washington Beltway (Highway 495) further disturbed the cemetery in the 1960s. Yet Larsen found evidence that the cemetery was maintained and not abandoned, as the historical narrative appeared to account. Today the cemetery is in the process of being made into a public memorial by the City of Alexandria. Yet the official story of the cemetery does not reference the decades of unofficial regular maintenance or its continuing life after its official closing and abandonment. The memorial narratives seem to have the intent of rectifying the cemetery's desecration by twentieth-century developments. The bodies of the dead have been identified and preserved physically, but symbolically they have been made available for mainstream appropriation. The story presented is of a cemetery built, abandoned, forgotten, and then, by good fortune and good public works, rediscovered for current consumption (Matthews and Larsen,

"Black History as Property," this volume). Although it is important that the cemetery is remembered, Matthews and Larsen, as well as others in this volume, emphasize the significance of what is being forgotten.

Archaeology is a social process in which archaeologists intellectually and physically produce knowledge through reports, papers, books, museum displays, and television programs (Shanks and McGuire 1996). It is an engaged practice and, as such, it is shaped by the questions archaeologists ask and what archaeologists deem to be significant. Significance can be shaped by the social background, training, and experience of individual archaeologists. Until recently, few archaeologists have deemed postemancipation sites worthy of archaeological research. Yet this is not the only reason postemancipation sites are understudied. Interpretations of these sites are influenced by a lack of documentary sources as well as the everyday discourse that influences our perceptions of the past. Leland Ferguson (*Gottesacker,* this volume) discusses how Moravians in Winston-Salem, North Carolina, have struggled with a variety of issues that included dealing with slavery and racism as well as changes within their faith community. Ferguson found that the interpretive variations used to describe a burial site appeared to strip the religious connotations from the place and overlay twentieth-century social and racial perceptions on eighteenth- and nineteenth-century Moravian culture.

Research on the social construction of race can be and has been used to ignore or conceal race behind the rhetoric of colorblindness (Epperson 2004; Babiarz, "White Privilege and Silencing"; and Palmer, "Archaeology of Jim Crow," this volume). Jennifer Babiarz ("White Privileging and Silencing," this volume) builds upon critical race theory (for example, Harris 1998; Lipsitz 1998; Marable 2002) and argues that by examining whiteness and white privilege, archaeologists have the potential to unsilence discussions of race and legitimize diasporic racial identities and communities. Similarly Kelly Dixon (2005, "Place of Recreation," this volume) addresses the ways in which traditional historiography has omitted the stories of African American peoples. Dixon excavated the Boston Saloon, which was operated by people of African ancestry between the 1860s and the 1870s in the mining boomtown of Virginia City, Nevada. She argues that the existence of an archaeological site that once held an African American saloon has the power to revise more traditional Eurocentric historical stories of the West.

Since the archaeology of the recent African American past is concerned with race and racism, one concern is whether the facts found through archaeology and the ways in which they are presented to the public help to counter the overwhelmingly negative perception of African American history. David Babson (1997: 5) states, "If white Americans are to work through their denial of issues of white racism and black oppression, among the many examples of unequal interethnic relations in our past, as discussed by Blakey (1997), then we must have, accept, and understand historical and archaeological information that challenges and repudiates these prejudices."

The authors of many of the case studies in this volume work to involve local and descendant community members in their archaeological research. They use their research to combat racism and uncover "the basic facts of how African Americans created and continue to create lives as complete human beings in the face of severe oppression" (Babson 1997: 5; McKee 1994: 6; see also Agbe-Davies, "Reaching for Freedom," this volume). For example, Chris Fennell ("Examining Structural Racism," this volume) uses community archaeology to provide insight into the ways African American communities combated various forms of structural and aversive racism that diverted economic opportunities. Conducting research in three communities in Illinois—New Philadelphia, Brooklyn, and the Equal Rights settlement outside of Galena—Fennell engages multiple stakeholders, including members of descendant and local communities, in the archaeological research. Fennell shows how our understanding of how racial ideologies, social networks, and developing economic structures influenced the ways in which individuals made choices in shaping their social and built environments and in developing economic strategies and cultural practices. Through community archaeology, he shows how archaeology can significantly aid the members of current-day communities to enhance the visibility of their African American heritage and accomplishments and to combat facets of structural racism they experience today (Fennell, "Examining Structural Racism," this volume).

Major events during the twentieth century have significantly altered our lives today. The study of the recent past is necessary in order to move away from historical narratives that privilege the period of enslavement while enforcing silences about postemancipation life. Therefore, the archaeological record can serve as a crucial information source pertaining to material change in American culture (Cabak et al. 1999; Henry 1995). Archaeological research at postemancipation sites has the potential to highlight the complex relationships between archaeologists, the state, the official public sphere, and local communities (McManamon et al. 2008) as well as the shifting contours of prejudice and discrimination.

The Historicity of Race and Racism

Race is usually conceptualized as a social construct used to define an "other," often through physical characteristics but also through knowledge of lineage and kinship (Harrison 2002; Leone et al. 2005: 580). Defining race as a social construct does not mean that the ramifications of racialization do not exist (Leone et al. 2005: 580; Omi and Winant 1994). Archaeologists, particularly those conducting research on the African diaspora, increasingly have grown concerned with racism as a means of creating and upholding the social inequalities that characterize American society (Orser 1999). Through history and personal experiences, African Americans have learned that their positions in U.S. society cannot be understood without understanding racism. David Babson (1990) argued that historical archaeologists should examine the ways in which racist beliefs have defined identity in relations of power. Since racist ideology structures how people treat one another, racism leaves identifiable traces in archaeological deposits (for example, Babson 1990; Epperson 1990; Mullins 1999; Shackel and Larsen 2000).

During the first decade of the twentieth century, the concept of race became an increasingly important way of categorizing people and cultures. But race was not the only basis for discrimination in American life or the only way Americans defined themselves (for example, Crenshaw 1991; Delle et al. 2000; Hill Collins 2000; Scott 1994). Class and gender, along with religion, ethnicity, and age, also shape lives, ideas, and dreams (Grossman 2005: 67). As W. E. B. DuBois (1990 [1903]) points out, "the problem of the Twentieth Century is the problem of the color line." The significance and the composition of the color line cannot be reduced to the biology of skin pigmentation. DuBois recognizes that it is impossible to understand the meaning of race without understanding class, since the place of African Americans in society is inseparable from their place in the economy (Garman 1994; Grossman 2005: 67; Mullins 1999, 2003). The meaning of race and the practice of racism are tightly intertwined with labor systems, ideas about family life, and assumptions about the relationship between manhood and citizenship. The chapters in this volume place these institutions, systems, and relationships into social, historical, and geographical context. They demonstrate how African Americans sought freedom despite racist legislation and policies by building communities and moving or staying.

Freedom and Its Limitations: Black Codes and Racial Violence

Emancipation reshaped the lives of former enslaved laborers. Freedom meant struggle but also optimism. Anna Agbe-Davies ("Reaching for Freedom," this volume) builds upon the writings of pragmatist philosopher John Dewey (1966 [1922]) to provide a framework for using "freedom" and "responsibility" as analytical concepts for historical archaeology. Agbe-Davies discusses the three main components of freedom: the ability to carry out plans without being thwarted, the ability to vary one's plans, and desire or choice as factors in those plans and variations. Therefore one does not have to execute the wishes of others or "act along lines predetermined to regularity" (Dewey 1966 [1922]: 81–82). The chapters in this volume ask: Were former enslaved laborers able to enact their plans? Where did they enact them? How is freedom, which is often intangible and ephemeral, manifested materially? What role did race and racism play?

Newly freed men and women sought to create a civil society in which the role of government was to provide land for landless ex-slaves, protect all of its citizens from violence and exploitation, make education and basic public services available to all irrespective of race or economic status, ensure that all adult males enjoyed unfettered voting rights, and work actively to achieve full equality for all. As a result of this vision of democracy, Congress passed the Thirteenth Amendment (1865) to the

Constitution, abolishing slavery; the Fourteenth Amendment (1868), granting black people citizenship and fundamental rights; and the Fifteenth Amendment (1870), enabling black men and poor white men the right to vote without property qualifications. All of this happened, in part, because former slaves ran for political office at the local, state, and national levels; promoted legislation that continued to expand the definition of democracy (Kelley and Lewis 2005: vii); and were aided by right-thinking white people.

Yet African Americans quickly learned through their dealings with southern white people that freedom could not be easily attained but would involve struggle. The former political and economic elite sought to regain their accustomed positions and limit the impact of the changes the Civil War brought to their communities. To some white southerners, African American freedom and opportunity was a threat to white supremacy. Many southerners responded with increased levels of intimidation and restrictions. Along with the passage of Black Codes, white vigilante groups sprang up throughout the South to terrorize African Americans and keep them from exercising their vision as free people. The Ku Klux Klan, which was formed in Tennessee in 1866, targeted Euro- and African American men and their families who were active in the Republican Party as well as white and African American schoolteachers (see Palus, "Infrastructure," this volume). The result was an epidemic of lynching in the South (Brooks 2009; Grossman 2005: 81). They also attacked black landowners and African Americans refusing to behave in a manner subservient to white people (Frankel 2000: 243).

Yet lynchings drew the attention of the North, and intimidation had to be accomplished in other ways to keep black people in their place. Across the South, state constitutions, state legislation, and city ordinances were rewritten to enshrine within the law the subordination of black people. As Noralee Frankel (2000) points out, Black Codes bestowed certain legal rights to former slaves, such as the right to enter into contracts legally, which permitted freed people the right to marry (although not interracially) and acquire personal property. Yet most states passed vagrancy laws, which meant that African Americans had to prove they were employed or risk arrest. To further ensure that African Americans were available for employment by white people, the states passed strict rules enforcing yearlong labor contracts so that workers could not change employers for at least a full year, even for higher wages (Frankel 2000: 242–43). Black male southerners would no longer vote or serve on juries, and the separation of the races would be required by law.

Between 1890 and 1915, legislators across the South, as far west as Texas and Oklahoma, enacted Jim Crow laws that ensured black people and white people would not inhabit the same public spaces. In most cases the trains and railroad stations were the first targets of Jim Crow laws. One waiting room was marked "colored," the other "white." Next, rules of conduct were passed for streetcars—white people were seated from front to back, black people from back to front. The legislation quickly extended into nearly all aspects of public life—hotels, restaurants, restrooms, drinking fountains, parks, schools, libraries, saloons, telephone booths, theaters, doorways, prisons, cemeteries, and brothels (Grossman 2005: 83–84). Jim Crow laws and the color line are written upon the American landscape in the building of African American neighborhoods and communities (for example, Weyeneth 2005).

The disenfranchisement that resulted from the enactment of Jim Crow laws was an attack not only on black political influence—of which there was little by the turn of the twentieth century—but also on black manhood, since nineteenth-century Americans tied manhood and citizenship closely together. Both hinged on independence. Cast as naturally docile, unable to control their sexual passions, and economically dependent, black men were labeled unfit for citizenship. For example, Megan Teague and James Davidson ("Victorian Ideals," this volume) use mortuary data from the Freedman's Cemetery to examine the connections between economic opportunity, race, and gender in postemancipation Dallas, Texas. Since African American women worked in much greater numbers than black men during Reconstruction and the immediate post-Reconstruction era, the dynamics between men and women's relationships were altered, as masculinity is often represented as everything that women are not. Denying African American men the ballot further reinforced their exclusion from civic community (Grossman 2005: 83).

Despite the hardships, African Americans living during this time period did more than just survive. They lived their lives, had families, and maintained communities and their dignity. As David Palmer ("Archaeology of Jim Crow," this volume) points out, in popular narratives of history, African Americans have been incorrectly characterized as being passive until outside civil rights workers came to lead them. Historical and archaeological research has demonstrated that this was not the case, and that resistance, in different forms, took place in many areas prior to the 1960s (for example, De Jong 2002; Ferguson 1992; McKee 1992; Weik 1997). Former enslaved laborers were often self-sufficient and connected to the global economy (see Wilkie and Farnsworth, "Living Not So Quietly," this volume). By examining postemancipation life, archaeologists have found evidence of the creative and resourceful ways that families created lives as citizens and freed peoples as they sought land and opportunities and built communities (for example, see Palmer, "Archaeology of Jim Crow"; Steen, "From Slave to Citizen," this volume). Archaeologists working with descendant communities are showing how African Americans actively worked toward democracy and equality.

Staying or Going: Land and Opportunity

After emancipation, land and the economic opportunities connected with landownership were important in people's decisions about where to go and what to do. Some freed people left their former masters in search of family members who had been sold away, to find better opportunities, or simply to find out what it felt like to be free. Freedom meant new opportunities but also new decisions. Wartime redistribution of land by the Union army and the Freedmen's Bureau promised to settle former slaves on plots of their own. Yet in most cases, the Euro-American planter class that controlled the land in the antebellum period continued to retain title to the region's most valuable resource, the land, even when they no longer had a reliable source of labor (Barnes 2008b; Steinberg 2004). Some former slaves assumed the land of their former masters belonged to them (Kelley and Lewis 2005: vii), and some squatted on unused land (see Steen, "From Slave to Citizen"; Wilkie and Farnsworth, "Living Not So Quietly," this volume). A small number of African Americans became landowners with small, family farms, but those who became landowners and business owners were the exception (Barnes 2008b; Frankel 2000: 254; see Dixon, "Place of Recreation"; Fennell, "Examining Structural Racism," this volume). Not all former slaves reacted so boldly to the achievement of freedom. Tens of thousands throughout the South stayed close to the plantations, afraid of starvation and of severing deep family and community ties (see Palmer, "Archaeology of Jim Crow," this volume).

Many emancipated black people found themselves working for white landlords under conditions reminiscent of slavery. In general planters divided their plantations into thirty- to fifty-acre farms and rented them to freedmen (Steinberg 2004), while others sold parcels of land. There were various forms of tenancy arrangements such as cash tenancy, share tenancy, and sharecropping (for example, Barnes 2008b; Orser 1988; Wilkie 2000; also see Palmer, "Archaeology of Jim Crow," this volume). These rural folk had to rent their land, grow the crops the market demanded, and give half or more of what they produced to their landlords. These systems of tenancy kept most African Americans in debt and in poverty. Yet it did not destroy their fighting spirit. African Americans were more than victims of Jim Crow laws and racial violence. They organized, fought back, moved around, thought, wrote, and created works of art (for example, De Jong 2002; Fairclough 2001; Kelley 1993).

After the Reconstruction experiment "ended" in 1877, thousands of former enslaved people left the South and sought the opportunities of the West (Bugarin 2009; see also Dixon, "Place of Recreation"; Fennell, "Examining Structural Racism"; Teague and Davidson, "Victorian Ideals," this volume) or the North (Wall et al. 2008; Palus, "Infrastructure," this volume). According to James Grossman (2005), in most cases patterns of migration conformed to lines of longitude, largely because of railroad routes. North and South Carolinians went to New York, Philadelphia, and other eastern seaboard cities. Pittsburgh's African American newcomers were likely to come from Alabama, Georgia, or Kentucky. From Mississippi, Louisiana, Tennessee, and parts of Georgia and Alabama, people headed for Chicago—an especially popular destination because of the influence of the *Chicago Defender* and the long tentacles of the Illinois Chicago Railroad (Grossman 2005: 110–11; see also Agbe-Davies, "Reaching for Freedom," this volume).

Around the start of World War I, over a million southern black people left. Scores moved from the countryside to cities such as New Orleans, Atlanta, Birmingham, and Dallas (see Teague and Davidson, "Victorian Ideals," this volume). With the wartime economy booming and European immigration at a virtual standstill due to the conflict, the demand for labor attracted hundreds of thousands of black folks to northern metropolises such as New York, Philadelphia, Milwaukee, Cleveland, Detroit, Annapolis (see Babiarz, "White Privilege and Silencing"; Palus, "Infrastructure," this volume), Baltimore, Washington, D.C., and Chicago (see Agbe-Davies, "Reaching for Freedom," this volume).

In the North, black men and women enjoyed the same legal rights as white people, but a color line still set the races apart, limiting where black people could work, live, and send their children to school. In the West patterns somewhat resembled the North. In both regions African Americans lived mainly in cities. Because the black populations in western states remained small, however, there tended to be greater flexibility and fewer restrictions. Black people not only were barely visible in the West; in many cases, they attracted less hostility than Asian and Mexican immigrants (Grossman 2005: 68; see also Dixon, "Place of Recreation," this volume). Everyone, whether they stayed in the South or joined the Great Migration, confronted a society in flux. The world during World War I was a world marked by destruction; international migrations; rapid industrialization; a wave of anticolonial uprisings in Africa and the Caribbean; revolutions in Germany, Mexico, Russia, Ireland, and elsewhere; and racial violence at home. Race solidarity and racism shaped African Americans' experiences as they built new communities.

Building Communities and Institutions

For African Americans the task of organizing communities was only one element of the larger need to create new lives—to reunite families, to find jobs, to establish churches, to gain education, and to figure out what it would mean to live in the United States as citizens. As Carl Steen ("From Slave to Citizen," this volume) notes, citizenship is a set of social practices that defines the relationships between peoples and states and among peoples within communities. Archaeology provides a lens through which to examine how former enslaved laborers materially sought citizenship in order to mobilize limited resources and build community institutions such as churches (for example, Cabak et al. 1995; Jones 2009; McCarthy 1997), schools (for example, Agbe-Davies 2001; Comer 1996; Sprinkle 1994), lodges (for example, Jones 2009; Mullins 1999), and women's groups (see Agbe-Davies, "Reaching for Freedom," this volume).

Black men and women were determined to become educated. Between 1870 and 1910, the literacy rate among black southerners increased from 19 percent to 61 percent (Grossman 2005: 81). The school was one of the major institutions to emerge after emancipation, since building a school was "to participate in the struggle for equality" (Grossman 2005: 88).

The church was another significant African American institution. By the beginning of the twentieth century, the church brought together African Americans as no other institution possibly could. African American churches were not merely places where people went for relief from the burdens of everyday life. As W. E. B. DuBois (1899) points out, "The social life of the Negro centres in his church." Yet freedom also provided for a space for the reclamation of traditional African beliefs. As Ken Brown ("Bakongo Cosmograms," this volume) notes, the turn of the twentieth century resulted in an ethnogenic bricolage (Fennell 2007) of spiritual beliefs as African traditional beliefs were brought back into practice and joined with Christian ones.

In towns and cities, institutions such as churches and schools were joined with women's clubs, fraternal societies, businesses, and social service organizations to shape African American community life and provide the basis for activism (Grossman 2005: 89). Black women's clubs were a type of institution with roots in African American fraternal societies (lodges) and mutual benefit associations. Lodges were typically places for recreation for their members, and membership in a lodge was considered a badge of social responsibility. Mutual benefit associations, by contrast, were likely to concentrate more on insurance functions, especially death benefits (Grossman 2005: 91–92; see Teague and Davidson, "Victorian Ideals," this volume).

The women's club movement grew from the Woman's Convention of the National Baptist Convention in 1900. The National Association of Colored Women (NACW) grew quickly from five thousand members in the late 1890s to a hundred thousand a decade later. Membership in the NACW came mainly from the urban elite—generally teachers and wives of professionals, ministers, and businessmen. These women shared with their white peers a concern with upholding traditional standards of morality and respectability amid the turmoil of movement from country to city and changes in employment from farm to factory (see Agbe-Davies, "Reaching for Freedom"; Armstrong, "Excavating Inspiration"; Teague and Davidson, "Victorian Ideals," this volume). And like black men, they organized to challenge the increasing racism at the turn of the twentieth century (Grossman 2005: 91).

For African Americans in the early twentieth century, the struggle had two related and mutually supportive components. One was to build community institutions such as schools, businesses, clubs, and lodges within the African American world. For instance, black club women recognized that their destiny was inextricably intertwined with less-privileged African Americans. If they could elevate other black women to their standards of morality and manners, then the overall population would be lifted up from the gutter of poverty and degradation. At the same time, they would win from the white people of America the acceptance that they deserved as a result of their middle-class values and position (Grossman 2005: 91; see also Agbe-Davies, "Reaching for Freedom," this volume). The other was to fight for integration into American institutional life by integrating schools, workplaces, residential neighborhoods, public accommodations like hotels and restaurants, and especially councils of government. Yet the quest for integration did not always reflect a desire to mix with white people. Despite the ruling of the United States Supreme Court in *Plessy vs. Ferguson* (1896) that separate institutions were constitutional only if they were equal, African Americans recognized that, in practice, separate always meant unequal. Thus black people frequently fought for integration into white institutions in order to gain access to better services and commodities (Grossman 2005: 88).

The development of a consumer society in the mid- to late nineteenth century was seen as a means for Americans to display or improve their class and status (Mullins 1999: 24). Unfortunately, the consumer market was embedded in a socially and racially unjust system. Historical archaeologists such as Paul Mullins (1999) have examined the intersection of consumerism and racism by considering how African Americans attempted to achieve status and wealth while participating in and, at the same time, resisting the racist consumer system. In places where black businesses were not available, many African Americans turned to national brands and national market chains that offered known quality and quantity, which may have helped avoid some racism in the marketplace (Mullins 1999: 25–26, see also Wilkie and Farnsworth, "Living Not So Quietly," this volume).

In the North and the South, there was a noticeable rise in black business enterprises during the beginning of the twentieth century. To a certain extent, this business activity was the result of increasing segregation, but it was also part of a broader change in the social and economic life of urban black America (Grossman 2005: 93). Black communities were diverse and included small business and professional classes. Yet the business class remained small. Postal workers, porters, and servants employed by the best hotels and wealthiest white families constituted much of the middle class (Cox 2007; Mullins 1999; Praetzellis and Praetzellis 2001). Other workers with stable incomes and some education could also claim middle-class status. What often mattered most was property ownership, preferred leisure activities, and membership in an appropriate club, lodge, or church (Grossman 2005: 95–96). Yet as African Americans resisted racist practices and built communities and institutions, governmental practices and legislation at national, state, and local levels continued to enforce the color line that played a role in shaping their lives.

Placing the Color Line: Governmentality, Displacement, and Urban Renewal

Matthew Palus (2009, "Infrastructure," this volume) builds upon Michel Foucault's (1991) concept of governmentality to discuss the role of local and state governments in promoting the racial identification of people. Governmentality involves "the intensification of relations of power and a flourishing of operations that make families and individuals more and more the subject of governmental authority, while seeming to act through the liberties of the governed" (Palus, "Infrastructure," this volume). Palus documents the structural inequalities created between black and white households during the installation of sanitation infrastructure in Eastport, a neighborhood of Annapolis, Maryland, specifically municipal water in 1927 and sanitary sewers after 1934. He shows that access to these services broke down upon racial lines and that access to sanitary services in Eastport could even be termed a privilege for white people and placed among those other privileges that convinced working-class white people that they were different from their economic peers who were black people.

This was not an uncommon practice, since black neighborhoods showed little evidence of the outpouring of services undertaken by cities of this era. African Americans generally lived on unpaved streets where such standard urban services as police, fire protection, garbage collection, and sewers were rare (Grossman 2005: 77). As late as the mid-1920s, Monroe Work, director of research at Tuskegee Institute in Alabama, could describe most of the southern urban place population as living under "country conditions . . . just beyond the zones for water, lights, and other conveniences" (quoted in Grossman 2005: 77).

In the 1940s and 1950s, federal funding made rapid expansion possible for many ambitious institutions, particularly universities (see Mullins and Jones, "Race, Displacement," this volume). Some municipalities seeking federal funds partnered quite aggressively with universities, and in some cases those institutions rapidly leveled broad swaths of neighboring communities and targeted other spaces for eventual growth. As Paul Mullins and Lewis Jones ("Race, Displacement," this volume) state, "Urban renewal legislation expanded the power of eminent domain to secure properties in the service of slum clearance, and for some newly born universities and their expanding peers, such codes allowed administrators and city leaders to engineer surrounding communities in ways that conformed to their own preconceptions of an appropriate university climate." Urban renewal was a way to revitalize aging and decaying inner cities. Yet the practice also uprooted neighborhoods, and displaced African Americans received little benefit from the programs. As with the building of infrastructure, urban renewal deployed a color line that typically deemed African American neighborhoods as insignificant.

Struggles for Equality: Remembrance of the Recent Past

The displacement of African American families as a result of urban renewal and the destruction of African American neighborhoods by riots during the civil rights movement, in addition to other causes that led to the abandonment of places in which African Americans built communities and institutions, leaves a plethora of sites that hold great significance to the history of the African diaspora. While the lives of the enslaved have been studied intensively, it is only recently that historical archaeologists have begun to study the "afterlives" of plantations (Hicks 2007; Steen, "From Slave to Citizen"; Wilkie and Farnsworth, "Living Not So Quietly," this volume) or investigate the communities and neighborhoods in which former enslaved laborers sought freedom. This volume documents only the beginning. We hope these first steps are the beginning of unsilencing the history of postemancipation life in the United States as well as the rest of the African diaspora.

The long struggle for racial equality in the United States and elsewhere has not been won or forgotten. The building of communities and institutions and the racial and social strife that people of African descent experienced while seeking civil rights are important aspects of American history that need to be remembered and commemorated. Just as President Obama reminds us, history is built upon the shoulders of earlier generations, so it is that contemporary archaeology is built upon the shoulders of previous research. Contemporary social issues such as poverty, education, and violence are best understood from a historical perspective. In his 2008 speech, Obama pointed out that the history of "legalized discrimination—where blacks were prevented, often through violence, from owning property . . . [led to] lack of economic opportunity among black men, and the shame and frustration that came from not being able to provide for one's family, contribute[d] to the erosion of black families . . . and lack of basic services in so many urban black neighborhoods—parks for kids to play in, police walking the beat, regular garbage pick-up and building code enforcement—all helped create a cycle of violence, blight and neglect that continue to haunt us." Historical archaeology has the potential to uncover the corpus of a largely unknown past, to involve descendants and interested communities in the research process, and to provide the basis for new conversations about race relations and new strategies to remember the recent African diasporic past.

Acknowledgments

This volume would not have been possible without the support of Charlie Cobb, the South Carolina Institute of Archaeology and Anthropology (SCIAA), and the Department of Anthropology at the University of South Carolina. The work leading up to this volume was a collaborative effort and couldn't have been done without the help of Emily Bikowski, Marshall Bogue, Claudia Carriere, Joanna Casey, Jake Crockett, Audrey Dawson, Chester DePratter, Helena Ferguson, Kevin Fogle, Cat Keegan, Ken Kelly, Susan Lowe, Melanie Neal, Jeff Norwood, Andrea Palmiotto, Lisa Randle, Nena Powell Rice, David Rigtrup, Stephanie Sapp, Carl Steen, John Sherrer, Amy Kinard and the Historic Columbia Foundation, Dan Littlefield and the Institute for African American Research, Stephanie Mitchem and the African American Studies Program, and Lana Burgess, Ja-Nae Epps, Jason Shamus and the McKissick Museum. I would like to thank all who were involved, including the scholars represented in this volume and those who are not. I am honored to have had the opportunity to organize this work and to collaborate with the great scholars who have contributed to this collection of essays. Special thanks to Tamala Conner, Kelly Ernst, Chris Fennell, Dave Gadsby, Madeline Konz, Carl Steen, and Kirsti Uunila for reading drafts of this introduction.

References

Agbe-Davies, A. 2001. Archaeology of the Old Eliot School. Old Eliot School Trust.

Agorsah, K. 1996. Archaeology of the African Diaspora. *African Archaeological Review* 13(4):221–224.

———. 1994 (editor). Archaeology of Maroon Settlements in Jamaica. In *Maroon Heritage: Archaeological, Ethnographic, and Historical Perspectives,* pp. 163–187. University of West Indies Press.

Althusser, L. 2001. Ideology and Ideological State Apparatus (Notes towards an Investigation). In *Lenin and Philosophy and Other Essays,* pp. 85–126. New York: Monthly Review Press.

Armstrong, D. A. 2003. *Creole Transformation from Slavery to Freedom: Historical Archaeology of the East End Community, St. John, Virgin Islands.* Gainesville: University Press of Florida.

Arnold, B. 1996. Past as Propaganda: Totalitarian Archaeology in Nazi Germany. In *Contemporary Archaeology in Theory: A Reader,* edited by R. Preucel and I. Hodder, pp. 549–569. Oxford: Blackwell Publishers.

Babson, D. W. 1997. Introduction. Thematic issue. In the Realm of Politics: Prospects for Public Participation in African American and Plantation Archaeology. *Historical Archaeology* 31(3):5–6.

———. 1990. The Archaeology of Racism and Ethnicity on Southern Plantations. *Historical Archaeology* 24(4):20–28.

Baker, V. G. 1980. Archaeological Visibility of Afro-American Culture: An Example from Black Lucy's Garden, Andover, Massachusetts. In *Archaeological Perspectives on Ethnicity in America: Afro-American and Asian American Culture History,* edited by R. L. Schuyler, pp. 19–37. Farmingdale, N.Y.: Baywood Publishing.

Barile, K. S. 2004. Race, The National Register, and Cultural Resource Management: Creating an Historic Context for Postbellum Sites. *Historical Archaeology* 38(1): 90–100.

Barnes, J. 2008a. Wilderness: A Contemporary Archaeology of an Appalachian Landscape. *African Diaspora Archaeology Newsletter,* March. Electronic document, www.diaspora.uiuc.edu/news0308/news0308.html#7, accessed March 31, 2008.

———. 2008b. *From Farms to Forests: The Material Life of an Appalachian Landscape.* Ph.D. dissertation, Department of Anthropology, American University, Washington, D.C.

Barnes, J., and D. Gadsby 2008. The Archaeology of Ten Minutes Ago: Material Histories of the Burgeoning Past and the Vanishing Present. Symposium co-organized for the Society for Historical Archaeology Annual Meetings, Albuquerque, N.Mex.

Beaudry, M. C., and E. P. Berkland 2007. Archaeology of the African Meeting House on Nantucket. In *Archaeology of Atlantic Africa and the African Diaspora,* edited by A. Ogundiran and T. Falola, pp. 395–412. Bloomington: Indiana University Press.

Blakey, M. L. 1997. Commentary: Past is Present: Prospects for Public Participation in African American and Plantation Archaeology. *Historical Archaeology* 31(3):140–145.

———. 1994. American Nationality and Ethnicity in the Depicted Past. In *The Politics of the Past*, edited by P. Gathercole and D. Lowenthal, pp. 38–48. One World Archaeology Series. London: Routledge.

Bower, B. A., and B. Rushing. 1980. The African Meeting House: The Center for the 19th Century Afro-American Community in Boston. In *Archaeological Perspectives on Ethnicity in America: Afro-American and Asian American Culture History*, edited by R. L. Schuyler, pp. 69–75. Farmingdale, N.Y.: Baywood Publishing.

Bradley, A., V. Buchli, G. Fairclough, D. Hicks, J. Miller, and J. Schofield 2004. *Change and Creation: Historic Landscape Character, 1950–2000*. London: English Heritage.

Bridges, S. T., and B. Salwen. 1980. Weeksville: The Archaeology of a Black Urban Community. In *Archaeological Perspectives on Ethnicity in America: Afro-American and Asian American Culture History*, edited by R. L. Schuyler, pp. 38–47. Farmingdale, N.Y.: Baywood Publishing.

Brooks, C. 2009. Challenges and Limitations in African-American Cemetery Studies: An Archaeological Perspective from the Carolinas. Paper presented at the First Annual Postdoctoral Fellows Conference, The Archaeology of the Recent African American Past, South Carolina Institute of Archaeology and Anthropology, Columbia, S.C.

Brown, K. L. 1994. Material Culture and Community Structure: The Slave and Tenant Community at Levi Jordan's Plantation, 1848–1892. In *Working toward Freedom: Slave Society and Domestic Economy in the American South*, edited by L. E. Hudson, Jr., pp. 95–118. Rochester, N.Y.: University of Rochester Press.

Buchli, V., and G. Lucas (editors) 2001. *Archaeologies of the Contemporary Past*. London: Routledge.

Bugarin, F. T. 2009. Nicodemus, an Inspiration beneath the Poppy Mallows. Paper presented at the First Annual Postdoctoral Fellows Conference, The Archaeology of the Recent African American Past, South Carolina Institute of Archaeology and Anthropology, Columbia, S.C.

Bullen, A. K., and R. P. Bullen. 1945. Black Lucy's Garden. *Bulletin of the Massachusetts Archaeological Society* 6(2):17–28.

Cabak, M. A., M. D. Groover, and M. M. Inkrot. 1999. Rural Modernization during the Recent Past: Farmstead Archaeology in the Aiken Plateau. *Historical Archaeology* 33(4):19–43.

Cabak, M. A., M. D. Groover, and S. J. Wagers. 1995. Health Care and the Wayman A.M.E. Church. *Historical Archaeology* 29(2):55–76.

Comer, E. A. 1996. Phase I Archaeological Investigation at the Ellicott City Colored School, Ellicott City, Maryland. Submitted to Howard County Department of Recreation and Parks.

Conkey, M. W., and J. M. Gero. 1997. Programme to Practice: Gender and Feminism in Archaeology. *Annual Review of Anthropology* 26:411–437.

Cox, B. R. 2007. The Archaeology of the Allensworth Hotel: Negotiating the System in Jim Crow America. *African Diaspora Archaeology Newsletter*, September. Electronic document, www.diaspora.uiuc.edu/news0907/news0907.html#6, accessed March 31, 2008.

Crenshaw, K. 1991. Mapping the Margins: Intersectionality, Identity Politics, and Violence against Women of Color. *Stanford Law Review* 43(6):1241–1299.

Deetz, J. 1996. *In Small Things Forgotten: An Archaeology of Early American life.* 2nd ed. New York: Anchor Books/Doubleday.

Delle, J. A., S. A. Mrozowski, and R. Paynter (editors) 2000. *Lines That Divide: Historical Archaeologies of Race, Class and Gender.* Knoxville: University of Tennessee Press.

De Jong, G. 2002. *A Different Day: African American Struggles for Justice in Rural Louisiana, 1900–1970.* Chapel Hill: University of North Carolina Press.

Derry, L., and M. Malloy (editors) 2003. *Archaeologist and Local Communities: Partners in Exploring the Past.* Washington, D.C.: Society for American Archaeology.

Dewey, J. 1966 [1922]. What Is freedom? In *John Dewey on Education,* edited by R. D. Archambault, pp. 81–88. New York: Modern Library.

Dixon, K. J. 2005. *Boomtown Saloons: Archaeology and History in Virginia City, Nevada.* Reno: University of Nevada Press.

DuBois, W. E. B. 1990 [1903]. *The Souls of Black Folk.* Reprint ed. New York: Vintage.

———. 1899. *The Philadelphia Negro: A Social Study.* Boston, Mass.: Ginn & Co.

Duke, P., and D. J. Saitta. 1998. An Emancipatory Archaeology for the Working Class. Electronic document, www.shef.ac.uk/assem/4/4duk_sai.html, assessed November 7, 2006.

Edwards-Ingram, Y. 1997. Toward "True Acts of Inclusion": The "Here" and the "Out There" Concepts in Public Archaeology. *Historical Archaeology* 31(3):27–35.

Epperson, T. W. 2004. Critical Race Theory and the Archaeology of the African Diaspora. *Historical Archaeology* 38(1):101–108.

———. 1990. Race and Disciplines of the Plantation. *Historical Archaeology* 24(4):29–36.

Fairclough, A. 2001. *Teaching Equality: Black Schools in the Age of Jim Crow.* Athens: University of Georgia Press.

Farnsworth, P. 2001. Beer Brewing and Consumption in the Maintenance of African Identity by the Enslaved People of the Bahamas, 1783–1834. *Culture & Agriculture* 23(2):19–30.

———. 2000. Brutality or Benevolence in Plantation Archaeology. *International Journal of Historical Archaeology* 4(2):145–159.

Fennell, C. 2007. *Crossroads and Cosmologies: Diasporas and Ethnogenesis in the New World.* Gainesville: University Press of Florida.

———. 2003. Group Identity, Individual Creativity, and Symbolic Generation in a Bakongo Diaspora. *International Journal of Historical Archaeology* 7(1):1–31.

———. 2000. Conjuring Boundaries: Inferring Past Identities from Religious Artifacts. *International Journal of Historical Archaeology* 4(4):281–313.

Ferguson, L. 1992. *Uncommon Ground: Archaeology and Early African America, 1650–1800.* Washington, D.C.: Smithsonian Institution Press.

———. 1980. Looking for the "Afro" in Colono-Indian Pottery. In *Archaeological Perspectives on Ethnicity in America: Afro-American and Asian American Culture History,* edited by R. L. Schuyler, pp. 14–28. Farmingdale, N.Y.: Baywood Publishing.

Foucault, M. 1991. Governmentality. In *The Foucault Effect: Studies in Governmentality,* edited by G. Burchell, C. Gordon, and P. Miller, pp. 87–104. Chicago: University of Chicago Press.

Frankel, N. 2000. Breaking the Chains, 1860–1880. In *To Make Our World Anew: A History of African Americans to 1880,* edited by R. D. G. Kelley and E. Lewis, pp. 227–280, Vol. 1. Oxford: Oxford University Press.

Franklin, M. 2001. The Archaeological Dimensions of Soul Food: Interpreting Race, Culture, and Afro-Virginian Identity. In *Race and the Archaeology of Identity,* edited by C. Orser, pp. 88–107. Salt Lake City: University of Utah Press.

———. 1997a. Power to the People: Sociopolitics and the Archaeology of Black Americans. *Historical Archaeology* 31(3):36–50.

———. 1997b. Why Are There So Few Black American Archaeologists? *Antiquity* 71:799–801.

Franklin, M., and L. McKee (editors) 2004. Transcending Boundaries, Transforming the Discipline: African Diaspora Archaeologies in the New Millennium. Thematic issue. *Historical Archaeology* 38(1).

Gadsby, D., and J. Barnes 2010. Activism as Archaeological Praxis: Engaging Communities with Archaeologies That Matter. In *Archaeologists As Activists: Can Archaeologists Change the World?* edited by J. Stottman. Jacksonville: University Press of Florida.

Garman, J. C. 1994. Viewing the Color Line through the Material Culture of Death. *Historical Archaeology* 28(3):74–93.

Geismar, J. H. 1982. *The Archaeology of Social Disintegration in Skunk Hollow: A Nineteenth-Century Rural Black Community.* New York: Academic Press.

Gero, J. 1983. Gender Bias in Archaeology: A Cross-cultural Perspective. In *The Sociopolitics of Archaeology,* edited by J. Gero, D. M. Lacy, and M. L. Blakey, pp. 51–58, Research Report No. 23. Amherst: Department of Anthropology, University of Massachusetts.

Gero, J., D. M. Lacy, and M. Blakey (editors). 1983. *The Socio-politics of Archaeology.* Research Report No. 23. Amherst: Department of Anthropology, University of Massachusetts.

Gould, R., and M. Schiffer. 1981. *Modern Material Culture: The Archaeology of Us.* New York: Academic Press.

Grossman, J. R. 2005. A Chance to Make Good: 1900–1929. In *To Make Our World Anew: A History of African Americans,* Vol. 2, edited by R. D. G. Kelly and E. Lewis, pp. 67–130. Oxford: Oxford University Press.

Harris, C. 1998. Whiteness as Property. In *Black on White: Black Writers on What it Means to be White,* edited by D. Roediger, pp. 103–118. New York: Random House.

Harrison, F. V. 2002. Subverting the Cultural Logics of Marked and Unmarked Racisms. In *Discrimination and Toleration: New Perspectives,* edited by K. Hastrup and G. Ulrich, pp. 97–125. The Hague: Martinus Nijhoff.

Haviser, J. B., and K. C. MacDonald (editors) 2006. *African Re-genesis: Confronting Social Issues in the Diaspora.* One World Archaeology Series. Walnut Creek, Calif.: Left Coast Press.

Henry, S. L. 1995. The National Register and the 20th Century: Is There Room for Archaeology? *CRM* 18(6):9–12.

Hicks, D. 2007. *The Garden of the World: A Historical Archaeology of Eastern Caribbean Sugar Plantations, AD 1600–2001.* BAR International Series 1632. Oxford: British Archaeological Reports.

———. 2006. From Material Culture to Material Life. *Journal of Iberian Archaeology* 9/10:245–255.

Hill Collins, P. 2000. *Black Feminist Thought: Knowledge, Consciousness, and the Politics of Empowerment.* New York: Routledge.

Jones, A. 2009. Gibson Grove: A Segregated Community Integrated by Archaeology. Paper presented at the First Annual Postdoctoral Fellows Conference, The Archaeology of the Recent African American Past, South Carolina Institute of Archaeology and Anthropology, Columbia, S.C.

Kelley, R. D. G. 1993. We Are Not What We Seem: Rethinking Black Working-Class Opposition in the Jim Crow South. *Journal of American History* 80(1):75–112.

Kelley, R. D. G., and E. Lewis (editors) 2005. Preface. In *To Make Our World Anew: A History of African Americans since 1880,* vol. 2, pp. vii–xiii. Oxford: Oxford University Press.

Kohl, P. L., and C. Fawcett (editors). 1995 *Nationalism, Politics, and the Practice of Archaeology.* Cambridge: Cambridge University Press.

LaRoche, C., and M. Blakey. 1997. Seizing Intellectual Power: The Dialogue at the New York African Burial Ground. *Historical Archaeology* 31(3):84–106.

Leone, M. P. 2005. *The Archaeology of Liberty in an American Capital: Excavations in Annapolis.* Berkeley: University of California Press.

———. 1995. A Historical Archaeology of Capitalism. *American Anthropologist* 97(2):251–268.

Leone, M. P., C. La Roche, and J. J. Babiarz 2005. The Archaeology of Black Americans in Recent Times. *Annual Review of Anthropology* 34:575–598.

Little, B. 1984. "She was . . . an example to her sex": Possibilities for a Feminist Historical Archaeology. In *Historical Archaeology of the Chesapeake,* edited by P. Shackel and B. Little, pp. 189–204. Washington, D.C.: Smithsonian Institution Press.

Little, B., and P. Shackel (editors) 2007. *Archaeology As a Tool of Civic Engagement.* Lanham, Md.: Altamira Press.

Lipsitz, G. 1998. *The Possessive Investment in Whiteness: How White People Profit from Identity Politics.* Philadelphia: Temple University Press.

Marable, M. 2002. The Souls of White Folk. In *Souls: A Critical Journal of Black Politics, Culture, and Society* 4(4):45–51.

McCarthy, J. P. 1997. Material Culture and the Performance of Sociocultural Identity: Community, Ethnicity, and Agency in the Burial Practices at the First African Baptist Church Cemeteries, Philadelphia, 1810–1841. In *American Material Culture: The Shape of the Field,* edited by A. S. Martin and J. R. Garrison, pp. 359–379. Winterthur, Del.: Henry Francis du Pont Winterthur Museum.

McDavid, C. 1997. Introduction. Thematic issue: In the Realm of Politics: Prospects for Public Participation in African-American and Plantation Archaeology. *Historical Archaeology* 31(3):1–4.

McGuire, R. 2008. *Archaeology As Political Action.* Berkeley: University of California Press.

McKee, L. 1994. Is It Futile to Try and Be Useful? Historical Archaeology and the African-American Experience. *Northeast Archaeology* 23:1–7.

———. 1992. The Ideals and Realities behind the Design and Use of 19th Century Virginia Slave Cabins. In *The Art and Mystery of Historical Archaeology: Essays in Honor of James Deetz,* edited by A. E. Yentsch and M. C. Beaudry, pp. 195–214. Boca Raton, Fla.: CRC Press.

McManamon, F. P., A. Stout, and J. Barnes (editors) 2008. *Managing Archaeological Resources: Global Context, National Programs, Local Actions.* One World Archaeology. Walnut Creek, Calif.: Left Coast Press.

Muller, N. L. 1994. The House of the Black Burghardts: An Investigation of Race, Gender, and Class at the W. E. B. DuBois Boyhood Homesite. In *Those of Little Note: Gender, Race and Class in Historical Archaeology,* edited by E. M. Scott, pp. 81–94. Tucson: University of Arizona Press.

Mullins, P. 2008. Excavating America's Metaphor: Race, Diaspora and Vindicationist Archaeologies. *Historical Archaeology* 42(2):104–122.

———. 2003. Engagement and the Color Line: Race, Renewal, and Public Archaeology in the Urban Midwest. *Urban Anthropology* 32(2):205–229.

———. 1999. *Race and Affluence: An Archaeology of African America and Consumer Culture.* New York: Kluwer Academic/Plenum Publishers.

Nelson, M. C., S. M. Nelson, and A. Wylie (editors) 1994. *Equity Issues for Women in Archaeology.* Archeological Papers of the American Anthropological Association, Vol. 5. Washington, D.C.: American Anthropological Association.

Obama, B. 2009. President Barack Obama's inaugural address. The White House: The blog. Electronic document, http://www.whitehouse.gov/blog/inaugural-address/, accessed July 2, 2009.

———. 2008. Remarks of Senator Barack Obama: A More Perfect Union, in Philadelphia, 18 March. Obama News and Speeches. Electronic document, http://www.barackobama.com/2008/03/18/remarks_of_senator_barack_obam_53.php, accessed April 3, 2010.

Ogundiran, A., and T. Falola (editors) 2007. *Archaeology of Atlantic Africa and the African Diaspora.* Bloomington: Indiana University Press.

Omi, M., and H. A. Winant 1994. *Racial Formation in the United States: 1960–1990.* London: Routledge.

Orser, C. E., Jr. 2004. *Race and Practice in Archaeological Interpretation.* Philadelphia: University of Pennsylvania Press.

———. 1999. The Challenge of Race to American Historical Archaeology. *American Anthropologist* 100(3):661–668.

———. 1998. The Archaeology of the African Diaspora. *Annual Review of Anthropology* 27:63–82.

———. 1988. *The Material Basis of the Postbellum Tenant Plantation: Historical Archaeology in the South Carolina Piedmont.* Athens: University of Georgia.

Orser, C. E., Jr. (editor).2001. *Race and the Archaeology of Identity.* Salt Lake City: University of Utah Press.

Orser, C. E., Jr., and P. P. A. Funari 2001. Archaeology and Slave Resistance and Rebellion. *World Archaeology* 33(1):61–72.

Palus, M. M. 2009. *Materialities of Government: A Historical Archaeology of Infrastructure in Annapolis and Eastport, 1865–1951.* Ph.D. dissertation, Columbia University, New York.

Paynter, R. 1983. Field or factory?: Concerning the Degradation of Archaeological Labor. In *The Socio-politics of Archaeology,* edited by J. Gero, D. M. Lacy, and M. L. Blakey, pp. 17–30. Department of Anthropology, University of Massachusetts, Amherst.

Paynter, R., S. Hautaniemi, and N. Muller 1996. The Landscapes of the W. E. B. DuBois Boyhood Homesite: An Agenda for an Archaeology of the Color Line. In *Race*, edited by S. Gregory and R. Sanjek, pp. 285–318. Brunswick, N.J.: Rutgers University Press.

Perry, W. R. 1997. Archaeology As Community Service: The African Burial Ground Project in New York City. *North American Dialogue: Newsletter of the Society for the Anthropology of North America* 2(1):1–5.

Praetzellis, M., and A. Praetzellis 2008. Remaking Connections: Archaeology and Community after the Loma Prieta Earthquake. Paper presented at the Society for Historical Archaeology Annual Meeting, Albuquerque, N.Mex.

———. 2001. Managing Symbols of Gentility in the Wild West: Case Studies in Interpretive Archaeology. *American Anthropologist* 103(3):645–654.

Pyburn, K. A., and R. R. Wilk 1995. Responsible Archaeology Is Applied Anthropology. In *Ethics in American Archaeology: Challenges for the 1990s*, edited by M. Lynott and A. Wylie, pp. 71–76. Washington, D.C.: Society for American Archaeology.

Rathje, W. L., and C. Murphy 1992. *Rubbish! The Archaeology of Garbage: What Our Garbage Tells Us about Ourselves*. New York: Harper Perennial.

Schofield, J., W. G. Johnson, and C. M. Beck 2002. *Matériel Culture: The Archaeology of Twentieth-Century Conflict*. London: Routledge.

Scott, E. M. (editor).1994. *Those of Little Note: Gender, Race, and Class in Historical Archaeology*. Tucson: University of Arizona Press.

Shackel, P. A., and E. J. Chambers (editors) 2004. *Places in Mind: Public Archaeology As Applied Anthropology*. New York: Routledge.

Shackel, P. A., and D. L. Larsen 2000. Labor, Racism, and the Built Environment in Early Industrial Harpers Ferry. In *Lines That Divide: Historical Archaeologies of Race, Class, and Gender*, edited by J. A. Delle, S. A. Mrozowski, and R. Paynter, pp. 22–39. Knoxville: University of Tennessee Press.

Shanks, M., and R. McGuire 1996. The Craft of Archaeology. *American Antiquity* 61(1):75–88.

Singleton, T. A. 1995. The Archaeology of Slavery in North America. *Annual Review of Anthropology* 24:119–140.

Singleton, T. A. (editor). 1999. *I, Too, Am America: Archaeological Studies of African-American Life*. Charlottesville: University of Virginia Press.

———. 1985. *Archaeology of Slavery and Plantation Life*. New York: Academic Press.

Spector, J. 1993. *What This Awl Means*. St. Paul, Minn.: Historical Society Press.

Spencer-Wood, S. M. 1996. Feminist Historical Archaeology and the Transformation of American Culture by Domestic Reform Movements, 1840–1925. In *Historical Archaeology and the Study of American Culture*, edited by L. A. De Cunzo and B. L. Herman, pp. 397–445. Winterthur, Del.: Henry Francis du Pont Winterthur Museum.

Sprinkle, J. 1994. *Relocating the Foundations of Jennie Dean's Vision: Archaeological Investigations at the Manassas Industrial School, 44PW505*. Report prepared by Louis Berger and Associates, Inc.

Steinberg, T. 2002. *Down to Earth: Nature's Role in American History*. New York: Oxford University Press.

Tilley, C. 1989. Archaeology as Socio-political Action in the Present. In *Critical Traditions in Contemporary Archaeology: Essays in the Philosophy, History, and Socio-politics of Archaeology*, edited by V. Pinsky and A. Wylie, pp. 104–116. Cambridge: Cambridge University Press.

Trigger, B. 1984. Alternative Archaeologies: Nationalist, Colonialist, Imperialist. *Man* 19(3):355–370.

Wall, D. D., N. A. Rothschild, and C. Copeland 2008. Seneca Village and Little Africa: Two African American Communities in Antebellum New York City. *Historical Archaeology* 42(1):97–107.

Watkins, J. 2001. *Indigenous Archaeology: American Indian Values and Scientific Practice.* Walnut Creek, Calif.: AltaMira Press.

Weik, T. 1997. The Archaeology of Maroon Societies in the Americas: Resistance, Cultural Continuity, and Transformation in the African Diaspora. *Historical Archaeology* 31(2):81–92.

Weyeneth, R. R. 2005. The Architecture of Racial Segregation: The Challenges of Preserving the Problematical Past. *The Public Historian* 27(4):11–44.

Wilkie, L. A. 2000. *Creating Freedom: Material Culture and African American Identity at Oakley Plantation, Louisiana 1840–1950.* Baton Rouge: Louisiana State University Press.

Wood, M. C. 2002. Moving Towards Transformative Democratic Action through Archaeology. *International Journal of Historical Archaeology* 6(3):187–198.

Wylie, A. 1989. Introduction: Socio-political Context. In *Critical Traditions in Contemporary Archaeology,* edited by V. Pinsky and A. Wylie, pp. 93–95. Cambridge: Cambridge University Press.

Zimmerman, L. J. 2005. Public Heritage, a Desire for a "White" History for America, and Some Impacts of the Kennewick Man/Ancient One Decision. *International Journal of Cultural Property* 12:265–274.

———. 1994. Sharing Control of the Past. *Archaeology* 47(6):65–68.

CHRISTOPHER N. MATTHEWS
AND ERIC L. LARSEN

Black History as Property

A Critique of the Making of a Post–Civil Rights Landscape

While some of us debate what history is or was, others take it into their own hands.
Michel-Rolph Trouillot (1995: 153)

For better or for worse, (as in some of the old marriage ceremonies,) the negroes are evidently a permanent part of the American population. They are too numerous and useful to be colonized, and too enduring and self-perpetuating to disappear by natural causes. Here they are, four millions of them, and, for weal or for woe, here they must remain. Their history is parallel to that of the country; but while the history of the latter has been cheerful and bright with blessings, theirs has been heavy and dark with agonies and curses. What O'Connell said of the history of Ireland may with greater truth be said of the negro's. It may be "traced like a wounded man through a crowd, by the blood."
Frederick Douglass (1867: 112–117)

The election of Barack Obama is cause for reflection on the making of African American history and on if and how things are different in the way the African American past is expressed and experienced now that he is in office. President Obama embodies the aspirations of African American history. His background and upbringing; his education and accomplishments; his family, staff, and supporters; and his opinions and policies now stand as a way to know black history both in what it *actually* is and, more important, what knowing about the African American past means for moving ahead. Obama has repeatedly "made" black history in his life, and his election places an African American within the elite sectors of the American historical canon. His image, and perhaps one day his statue—that is, a permanent public memorial of a *named* black man—will soon inhabit the now entirely white halls of power. From one perspective on history, his election establishes beyond doubt African Americans as viable agents in the making of American history *from now on.*

Post–Civil Rights

Journalist Gwen Ifill (2009) has written about this phenomenon as a "break-through" in which African American political leaders of the "post–civil rights" generation are now emerging. Their success is due in no small part to their support among white voters. No longer simply "black" candidates, these leaders speak of a single or at least theoretically unifiable America. They often elide race by speaking of social justice and responsibility, though none is careless enough to avoid race altogether. Rather, their presentation of race is that it is a problem for all Americans, which is fair enough, but implicit is an assumption that one day we will all walk away from race and racial injustice without a radical transgression of the structure of American society. That racism will end without at least a cognitive revolution is perhaps where we begin to see the limits of anyone who may claim to be "post-racial" or "post–civil rights," of anyone who can look at the civil rights era as something that is past (Hall 2005).

A critique of this stance is voiced by legal scholar Richard Thompson Ford (2008). Ford makes a distinction between what may be called easy and difficult ways of addressing racism in the United States. Ford argues that playing the race card, or the assertion of racial bias based on limited and decontextualized evidence, typifies an easy sort of racial justice because it elicits without reflection the buried yet present tensions that mark most interracial conflicts. So following this easy route, if we ferret out the racists who walk among us, we will eliminate racism. By reading the words and actions of potential racists carefully and in the right light, that is, we will see that individual bias and bigotry underlie most all racial conflict. Ford argues that easy forms of addressing racial injustice fail in many ways. Playing the race card, for example, supplants reflection by inserting instances of racial bias as the subject of our concern. This approach is easy because it calls out an embodied perpetrator whose actions are inviolably racist. Among the most well-known examples is Detective Mark Fuhrman, whose latent racism was brought out in the 1996 O. J. Simpson murder trial. However, the defense case that shifted the blame to Fuhrman essentially absolved the rest of the Los Angeles Police Department (LAPD) and those who fell in line behind them. Moreover, it did nothing at all to address the long history of LAPD violence against black people or the conditions that sustained Fuhrman's racism in a comfortable institutional setting.

Ford (2008) argues that playing the race card and similar easy ways to confront bias undermine other efforts to combat racism and racial inequality. Seeking out racist individuals and specific acts of racial prejudice, we look past the structural racism perpetrated largely unwittingly by the majority of Americans every day. This, for example, is the racism of residential segregation (Lipsitz 2006; Massey and

Denton 1993), which promotes among other ills unhealthy inner-city environments, failing schools, disproportionately high inner-city costs of living, and figures showing significantly higher percentages of African Americans living below the poverty line and spending time in prison than other groups in the United States. Most Americans are aware of these problems yet for the most part do nothing about them. In fact it can be argued that the American middle-class majority (no matter their color) gains substantial material benefits from the suppression and isolation of the underclass (Wilson 1987), prominent among these benefits being the opportunity to be ignorant of the complexities and structures of racial problems altogether (Wise 2005). "One rationale for this inaction derives from history," Ford (2008: 29) writes, "just as the cotton gin replaced manual cleaning of the raw crop, so too American moral ingenuity eventually developed superior replacements for slavery, sharecropping, and Jim Crow segregation. The civil rights movement—once a marginal and suspect political radicalism—has been neatly woven into this tale of inexorable national progress. Now racial justice is among the most touted achievements of American society." With civil rights legislation in place and a civil rights history in hand, Americans now conceive of matters like poverty, failing schools, and incarceration without also referring to race, and since modern American morality does not tolerate racism, these problems are not about racial justice, and to say that they are is to play the race card.

The construction of a "post–civil rights era" establishes a way of thinking and acting that delimits efforts to address the structural causes of racism and racial inequalities that have real historical origins (Bonilla-Silva 2003; Grant-Thomas and powell 2006; Kubisch 2006). These include unfair practices that disproportionately barred African Americans from enjoying the benefits of the New Deal social relief programs or the de facto racist practices by federal housing agencies that enabled the redlining of black neighborhoods and complicated African Americans' access to the subsidized loans that fueled the post–World War II suburban boom (Jackson 1985; Katznelson 2005). Addressing these matters of racial injustice is obviously more difficult, but leaving them be reinforces them as unanswered failings of the American project or, worse, credits racism's beneficiaries for their gumption and blames racism's victims for their failings.

To draw Ford's (2008) ideas together with archaeology, we borrow and alter slightly the concept of "racism without racists" (also see Bonilla-Silva 2003; Orser 2007). Considering issues like racial residential segregation, Ford proposes that we struggle to confront this as a racial problem because "we can't find a bigot to paste to the dartboard"; that is, we do not know who and what to blame and therefore have no idea who or what to fix. The solution is to consider the broader relational context and to realize for example that suburban prosperity and urban poverty go hand in hand, the one benefiting from the other. In this way of thinking no one living in the suburbs need be necessarily racist, but we can and must conceive that their choice to live there and their way of life are complicit in a structural racism that defines the broader spectrum of social relations in American life.

A Landscape without Racists

We narrow this focus to apply Ford's thinking to archaeological practice and its connection to the making of memorials, specifically to the creation of sites connected to the African American past. In this instance we propose that archaeologists operate in a "landscape without racists" such that in the making of historic sites, the agents involved employ a post–civil rights perspective. In the making of the African American historical sites discussed below we see the potential to create sites that silence ongoing sorts of African American commemoration and use that were once possible until a post–civil rights approach to the site was developed. We show that assumptions about what African American "sites" are and how they are thought to exist in a post–civil rights perspective disconnect historically racist structures from the landscapes on which they operate. In their place many African American memorials are built in spaces imagined to be cleansed of racial bias and thus foster reflections on race and racism that segregate past and present in the name of celebrating current dreams of racial harmony and justice.

We focus on the creation of such landscapes without racists through some recently planned and built monuments constructed to commemorate emancipation in Virginia and New York. These monuments seek to speak to reconciliation and memory but potentially miss addressing the forgetting and silencing that the making of monuments inherently involves (Hayden 1995; Savage 1997; Trouillot 1995). We argue, in fact, that the memorialization of black history need not rely solely upon these new voices since it can be already heard in places across the country without them. Black history is quite alive in African American communities, where the stories of families, neighborhoods, work, migrations, and leaders are widely known and shared as part of the everyday grassroots practice of building community. Rather, in the instances explored in this chapter, black history appears missing because it is being interpreted through the lens of white America, which suffers from a blindness toward the presence of people of color, especially in their imagination of public space and culture (Wise 2005; see also Babiarz, "White Privilege and Silencing," and Palmer, "Archaeology of Jim Crow," this volume). This is not to deny that African American history is in need of protection. In fact one problem is that often white America does not see or hear about black history until it is under threat from bulldozers, subdivisions, and other active forces of destruction and denial inherent in the creation of new spaces typically planned and often designated as white (Epperson 2004; LaRoche and Blakey 1997). Yet while these actions call in academics, contractors, activists, civil servants, and other outsiders, they less often call on the makers and keepers of black history, who notably persist in making history despite the destruction and reinvention of their sites from the past (Trouillot 1995).

History, Heritage, Sites, and Property

The process of developing a landscape without racists is found in the making of African American places into "sites." Notably, "sites," as envisioned by archaeologists, museum professionals, planners, and other heritage professionals, do not lie at the root of "black" or any other substantive history. It is communities that do: people rather than places; relationships rather than the record. So the recent hurried efforts to identify and mark black historical sites, especially those located within otherwise symbolically white public spaces, necessarily produces some ambivalence. Past events and places that were part of the lives of African diaspora peoples and the making of African America should certainly be recognized on an even par with those related to European and Euro-American people and achievements. Preserved and interpreted African American places tell a more complete story of the many people and pasts that made the American present. Yet making memorials involves assumptions about the meaning of history and the process of history-making that need to be addressed in order to avoid whitewashing African American sites or, worse, creating a "history in blackface" that appropriates and mocks those whose recognition underwrites a site's significance and distinction.

Necessary here is a reflection on property and ownership as a formal part *and* an essential practice in the making of heritage sites in the modern American capitalist context. Legal scholar Susan Scafidi (2005: 161) concludes that "property is, in essence, a social system." Whether through exclusion, transfer, or in its use and occupation, property mediates relationships. The marking of property is simultaneously a creation of the self as a property owner and the exclusion of those denied free access by virtue of the designation of something as owned. Places, sites, ideas, objects, and persons have distinct and separate meanings in propertied settings such that whatever else they may be (for example, earth, dwellings, concepts, neighbors) functions in relationship with their being owned and thus representative of their owner(s) in specific social contexts. The most extreme of propertied settings is late capitalism in which the very foundations of social meaning are fused to the notion of property through the process of commodification. To become commodities, objects of any sort are stripped of qualities separate from their function in the market. Thus a hammer becomes a commodity when its usefulness has a demand in the market, a socialization of value that shifts the hammer from being a tool to being also and primarily a source of profit. In late capitalism nothing is exempt from commodification, including such unexpected "things" as culture, history, and heritage. While many have written critically about the commodification of history (for example, Carman 2005; Handler 1985; Handler and Gable 1997; Kirshenblatt-Gimblett

1998; Lowenthal 1998; Smith 2006; Trouillot 1995; Wallace 1996), a thrust in much of this critique has been to recover and promote an underlying kernel of historical value that resists commodification. This value of history is often translated as heritage, or the truly meaningful relationships people have with the past that inform them about identity and history.

John Carman (2005: 44) reminds us, however, that "property is theft": far from a neutral or natural claim of individual rights, it is a taking of resources from the community for the sake of private gain. Moreover, Carman (2005: 73) concludes, "value only accrues to things that are in some sense, and in some way, *owned*." Following this line of thought calls for a more nuanced sense of heritage in light of the critique of property. If heritage is the relationships between people and their past, then how is heritage not in some way owned by those people? It is difficult to think of heritage without also thinking it belongs to someone. This problem forces us to conclude with Carman that it is only through *things* (objects *and* objectified ideas and persons) that modern communities find expression—unless, that is, they are based on values that operate outside arenas dominated by property. Discovering these values and understanding how they work, however, demands the use of a very different lens on history than we normally get when sites serve as the medium to the past.

This different lens is well described by Laurajane Smith (2006). Smith regards heritage as a process we go through rather than a thing we have. Simply put, instead of an object, a site, or the histories objects and sites might relate or evoke, heritage is the socially informed and directed actions we undertake in order to occupy sites; it is "what goes on at . . . sites" (Smith 2006: 44). Following David Harvey (2001: 347), Smith sees "heritage as a verb." She continues, "Heritage . . . is a cultural process that engages with acts of remembering that work to create ways to understand and engage with the present, and the sites themselves are cultural tools that can facilitate, but are not necessarily vital, for this process" (Smith 2006: 44). This approach shifts attention from the establishment of sites to their use in the application and construction of memory, a movement that reconnects people with history and with each other in ways less mediated by the materiality of history produced by artifacts, remains, and sites. History is what went on, our interest in history is what is going on, and our thinking about and remembering history is what will go on. Together these temporal exchanges construct heritage as an active engagement with a history in which we are enfolded and in which we enfold ourselves (see also Sider 1994; Sider and Smith 1997; Trouillot 1995). Moreover, the role of scholarship in this approach is not to produce history to inform heritage but to provide a deeper consciousness of the way we make history by folding together our experiences into relationships with others in the present and the past.

To explain this approach from an African American standpoint we turn to historian David Blight (2006: 27–30), who draws from comments made at the 1885 commencement proceedings at West Virginia freedmen's school, Storer College, by

Alexander Crummell and Frederick Douglass. Crummell, born free and a minister and African nationalist, urged the graduates to embrace their present by avoiding "recollections" of slavery. He accepted that the *memory* of slavery was not under their control, but by recalling and retelling the stories of slavery they actively brought it forward where it impeded their otherwise prideful and natural growth, duty, and prosperity. So while they could not forget slavery, they could choose not to remember it. Though his words were not recorded, accounts tell that Douglass, a former slave and later abolitionist, publicly challenged Crummell's position at Storer. Drawing on Douglass's published works, Blight suggests Douglass most likely urged graduates and others to embrace slavery's *living history*. For Douglass the legacy of slavery could be "traced like a wounded man through a crowd, by the blood" (Douglass 1867). It was not something that could be overcome by a force of will, since the blood spilled by slavery was inseparable from the blood flowing in freedmen and their descendants. Slavery was a part of them, and to choose to ignore it was essentially to cut off a significant part of their historical bodies. Blight (2005: 29) concludes that for Douglass "emancipation and the civil war were truly *felt* history, a moral and legal foundation from which to demand citizenship and equality." The unyielding heritage of slavery, not its historical injustice and especially not its legal abolition, informed the political subjectivity Douglass hoped to instill among the graduates and their families. To Douglass, the construction of slavery as in the past rather than a *living* history or heritage was the essence of the white-told story of emancipation. For obvious reasons, this politics failed to resonate among Douglass and his supporters.

Crummell and Douglass present a forked road in the African American relationship to slavery. It is a familiar divide. Herzfeld (1991) called it monumental versus social time, it is Linenthal's (1996) distinction between history and memory, and it is Matthews' (2002) contrast between tradition and history. These distinctions are efforts to contrast the way the past functions in the living world. On the one hand, the past is the official transcript of what happened. These are the monuments, the archives and historical narratives, and the traditions that connect contemporaries to the past. On the other hand, the past is the way people understand and make meaning. This past is the one that affiliates us closer with some people than others and leads us to value some stories more than others and to see ourselves awash in the flow of events to which we have contributed and will naturally contribute. Crummell sought to instill a detached relationship with the slavery that he saw as a history the graduates needed to know but not internalize or reproduce. Douglass argued that detachment was impossible and that instead they should work harder to know more about what slavery *still* means.

Michel-Rolph Trouillot (1995) complicates this debate further, reminding us that these distinctions do not relate to what actually happened in the past but only to what is said to have happened, a process that informs history in subtle yet powerful ways. Trouillot begs us to consider the historicity of our histories, to appreciate how past histories establish, change, remark on, and otherwise influence the structures and processes by which our lives are framed and thus the way we interpret our own and others' experiences. For Trouillot it is easy to see we make history, but it is actually quite difficult, especially when histories of slavery and racism contribute to our structural makeup, to see how we do.

We illustrate this thought in two recent examples of African American commemoration highlighting especially how archaeology identifies the making of black history yet struggles to contribute to what is said to have happened at these sites. The point is that the effort to tell new stories aimed to foster a critical consciousness failed to develop since the stories of slavery and freedom actually produced emerged not from the material conditions of their historical legacy but from the abstract imaginations of the propertied class about the meaning and authority of history and archaeology in speaking about the African American past.

Alexandria's Contrabands and Freedmen's Cemetery

Our first example comes from a recent study of the Contrabands and Freedmen's Cemetery in Alexandria, Virginia (City of Alexandria 2008). Initial efforts at the site began in the late 1980s during early planning stages for the joint federal and state Woodrow Wilson Bridge Improvement Project. At the time, the land was in use by a gas station and an office building. The cemetery's existence had largely been forgotten. Once the location of the cemetery was established, subsequent bridge work avoided the site. An effort to memorialize the cemetery was taken up by private citizens and a community group known as the Friends of Freedmen's Cemetery. Their highly successful long-term efforts resulted in the cemetery becoming a local initiative by the City of Alexandria with support from the Federal Highway Administration, Virginia Department of Transportation, and Virginia Department of Historic Resources. The goal for the project was the reclamation of the site and the creation of a memorial honoring the contrabands and freedmen buried in the cemetery.

At the outbreak of the American Civil War, the city of Alexandria found itself on the boundary between the North and the South. Because it was just across the river from the federal capital, the city was almost immediately occupied by Union forces. The occupation would last the duration of the war, and the city's wharf and railroad depot became vital to the Union's war efforts. Washington, D.C., and Alexandria soon became a draw for enslaved individuals seeking freedom. The military came to refer to these refugees as "contraband." Contrabands, later called "freedmen," provided a pool of labor that was tapped to aid the Union's war effort. Alexandria became one of many collection points for this population, and thousands of African Americans made their way to the city during the war years. Shelter and services for these escapees were limited. Barracks were hastily built along with a hospital and, in 1864, a cemetery.

A record book begun by the military appointed "Superintendant of Contrabands" has the names of more than 1,800 men, women, and children buried in this cemetery during its four years of active operations. The cemetery was officially abandoned in 1869 with the closing of the Freedmen's Bureau and the cemetery property's returning to private ownership. When the Freedmen's Cemetery was established, the property was marginal to much of Alexandria's everyday proceedings. In the 1930s the Mount Vernon Parkway (later incorporated into the larger George Washington Memorial Parkway) provided a new north-south transportation route that ran right in front of Freedmen's Cemetery. With the commercial potential enhanced, the cemetery lands were rezoned in the late 1940s, and the site was developed as a gas station in 1955. In the 1960s Interstate 495 (the Washington Beltway) and a new office building further disturbed the site. The landscape and land use of the site changed, and memory of the cemetery faded. In examining the changing landscape of the site, archaeologists found a 1927 aerial photo that seemed to contradict the story of the cemetery's abandonment and neglect. The photo shows the grounds to be clear and open space—not overgrown as might be expected from 58 years of neglect—which may suggest that the property saw continued use in an unofficial way.

Several newspaper accounts printed in the 1890s also suggest a continued use of the cemetery after its official abandonment (*Washington Post* 1892a, 1892b, 1894). These accounts specifically mention "mounds" rising "six to twelve inches above the level of the ground" (*Washington Post* 1894). This detailed description comes more than 20 years after formal operations at Freedmen's Cemetery had ended—far longer than one would expect an exposed small mound of earth would remain noticeable or noteworthy. The presence of mounds suggests either an informal continuation of burials at the cemetery and/or they may be evidence of continued maintenance of the old burial grounds.

Visible burial mounds and cleared spaces decades after the last known burial suggest the cemetery remained in use. It is possible that burials continued, but Larsen thinks the evidence also speaks to maintenance: "Studies of southern folk practices . . . noted the . . . community maintenance of burial grounds. In the nineteenth century this practice included the 'scraping' of earth around graves (keeping plant and weed growth down around graves) and 'mounding' of earth over the graves themselves" (Larsen 2009: 5; see also Jeane 1989; Jordan 1982).

No archaeological evidence of mounds remains. In fact most of the cemetery's original surface was graded away during the commercialization of the property in the twentieth century. Only a small section of the original surface was found intact. In sampling this portion of the site, city archaeologists were fortunate in finding a concentration of oyster shells associated with a grave. The surviving incident of grave decoration suggests that such burial practices were a normal part of the cemetery's use. However, it represents practices that are not found in the official records of cemetery operations.

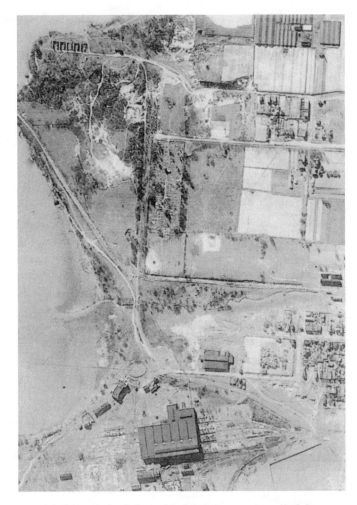

Aerial photograph of Alexandria, Virginia, 1927. Arrow points
to cleared area of former Contraband's and Freedmen's Cemetery.
Courtesy of the National Archives, Cartographic Records, Washington, D.C.

Shell and other grave decorations contrast with the descriptions of operations in
place during the active years of the Contrabands and Freedmen's Cemetery (Pippenger
1992: 10, 1995). Moreover, a maintained cemetery years after burial operations ceased
contradicts the other story line—of gradual decline and mild neglect—suggested by
the documents and largely embraced by the modern Alexandria community until recent years (Larsen 2009: 5). It also describes a different sort of active, ongoing memorialization that draws out a hitherto-unknown history from behind the documents

and the traditions of the site and memories lost behind official histories. While the social or public memory of the cemetery was cut off from the physical site when the gas station was built, there is (as yet) no official evidence that the site was still part of anyone's consciousness. We do know, however, that an awareness of the cemetery and a sense of duty to its maintenance were part of the lives of some in the Alexandria community long after the cemetery itself was officially abandoned. This duty has now been taken up by the Friends of Freedmen's Cemetery.

Today the gas station and office building have been removed, and the cemetery is in process of becoming a public memorial. The entire project is exemplary of today's "best practices," in that community involvement and direction are central to the reclamation and memorial process. We see that the very process of memorializing the site has done an enormous service to the community by reversing the overt erasure of an African American presence in Alexandria that occurred just over 50 years ago.

A design competition was held in 2008 (City of Alexandria 2008). Prizes were to be awarded for the top three submissions with the intention of implementing the winning design (design as framework), with the designer having an advisory role in developing the concept through construction documentation. More than 200 submittals from around the world were received. The winning design clearly reclaims the site for the remembrance of those African Americans who escaped slavery and

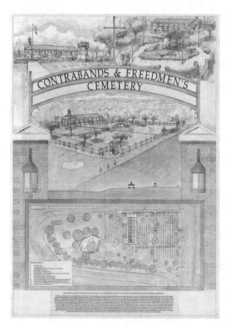

Winning submission from the Freedmen's Cemetery Design Competition. This concept by C. J. Howard (2008) will be used as a framework for a detailed site design for the Contrabands and Freedmen's Cemetery Memorial. Courtesy of the City of Alexandria, Virginia.

were buried there. We praise this design and the many others as a successful step in recapturing the value of the site to history and remembrance.

The declaration of awards, however, provides a logical point at which to pause, evaluate, and reflect upon the project. The Freedmen's Cemetery memorial project has done just that, and the final design for the memorial is still in development as this essay is going to press. Many of the competition's designs clearly had the intent of "making things right"—of rectifying the cemetery's desecration by twentieth-century developments. However, seemingly small decisions (such as the amount of parking, the presence of a pavilion or other gathering place) have myriad seen and unforeseen implications for the site. For us it is absolutely important to recognize that none of the top designs references the story of the cemetery's decades of unofficial regular maintenance, its continuing life after its official closing and abandonment.

In this case, archaeology was deployed to record the site. Five hundred thirty-four graves were "identified, left in place, and protected" (Larsen 2009: 6). These graves are prominent in the winning memorial plan, a design that reminds visitors of the cemetery below their feet. While the bodies of the dead have been identified and preserved physically, they are symbolically made available for mainstream appropriation. This is because the meta-story presented by the winning design is of a cemetery built, abandoned, forgotten, and then by good fortune and good public works rediscovered for current consumption. We think this story is incomplete, and thinking of Ford and Douglass, we should see that it is too easy in terms of how it can be put to use in the critical memorial discourse about American slavery. In fact the historic struggle to preserve this space, its unrecorded but likely once well-known history of memory, may be erased in favor of a preference for the shorter story of American freedom. It would be unfortunate if the memorial (once completed) enabled us to actively forget a powerful historic story of memory—one that the making of the memorial itself actually helped to illuminate. It is this material agency of how memorials are as much places of forgetting as they are for remembering that we need to be most critically aware (see also Ferguson, "*Gottesacker*," this volume).

It is essential to make clear that the Friends of Freedmen's Cemetery (Friends) made enormous strides in protecting the site from destruction. Without their effort and organization the site would have been entirely lost. Since the completion of the excavation, the Friends have identified and connected with several descendants of the freedmen buried at the site.[1] These new relations will invigorate the meaning of the site in powerful new ways, and we think will likely establish the Freedmen's Cemetery as a prominent national site for reflecting on the African American struggle against slavery and their role in bringing it to an end. The laudable efforts by the

---

1. We thank Pam Cressey for informing us about the postexcavation accomplishments of the Friends.

Friends illustrate the best strengths of not only preservation activism but also the necessary social action of memorialization that will turn a cemetery lost to history into a compelling story about African American struggles for recognition in both the past and the present.

Still, we hope that by reflecting at this point in the memorialization process that subsequent planning will consider the impact of the Freedmen's Cemetery Memorial not only in terms of its history but also of its place as a site of memory. It is certain that the memorial space will provide for a wide array of experiences, some official and some not. As such, it is important that the planning and design consider how each and all of these experiences may contribute to the way the memorial addresses the structural makeup of Alexandria's and the nation's racial future. That the cemetery has a documented "unofficial" African American history makes this site an especially apt place for exploring how history is told and how experiences are remembered in public space. The point is that this site is potentially larger than the freedmen, their descendants, and the Friends. It is a site where the very processes of making and telling history collide with foundational American practices of creating and preserving memories. We believe that it is vital that the unofficial story of memorialization be prominent in the memorial itself, for how the cemetery *was* remembered before needs to be part of how it *is* remembered now. Our second case study provides some cautionary observations on how this sort of memorial project can fail significant communities that it may have had the chance to serve if the roles of memory and experience versus propertied and vested interests were more carefully considered.

Fences and Fill at King Manor

Another example draws from research at Rufus King Manor in Jamaica, Queens, New York. King Manor is named for the federalist, anti-slavery politician Rufus King, who moved to the site in 1805. The property was in the King family for three generations before the remaining 11-acre parcel was purchased in 1896 by the village of Jamaica to be used as a park. In 1898, after the consolidation of Queens with New York City, the property became part of the New York City Parks Department (Parks). In 1900 a community women's group, the King Manor Association of Long Island (KMA), took curatorial responsibility for the house museum. The site has remained under the care of Parks and the KMA since.

Under the legal protection of New York City preservation laws, three archaeological investigations of the site were completed in the 1990s (Grossman 1991; Stone 1997, 1998). Among the capital projects cleared for completion by archaeology were a major water-control and landscaping effort and the construction of a fence enclosing a space for a yard behind the manor house. The fence secured a section of the public park for exclusive use by the museum for outdoor educational programs. The success of this fence and the space it enclosed was noticed, and in 1996 a second fence

King Manor today, showing
1998 perimeter fence. Courtesy
of Chris Matthews.

was designed and archaeologically cleared to enclose the entire house, providing
even more security and exclusive space for museum use (Stone 1998). The need to
recreate and secure the museum has thus generated a great deal of archaeological
history about the site that the museum makes limited use of through an archaeology
education program and a small display on archaeology inside the house. Still, questions should be posed about the nature of this history and the possibility that in the
remaking of the museum, as much history-making has been forgotten as has found
its way into the story the museum has to tell.

Current museum interpretation draws virtually nothing at all from the archaeology that has been done at the site. The story is dominated by Rufus King's family and
political life, the operation of the Jamaica farm, aspects of what rural life in Jamaica
was like in contrast to the densely settled urbanized present, and a little bit about the
people who worked there (though not about the slaves who lived at the site before
the Kings arrived). The archaeology that is presented focuses on archaeological research techniques rather than the interpretation archaeologists have made or that
their work would support. While it is by no means incumbent upon the museum
to use the archaeological information generated at the site in their interpretation,
contradictions between the rationale for doing archaeology and the absence of a
substantive and available archaeological history in the interpretation detail an interesting story about the modern museum landscape at King Manor.

Archaeology provided the go-ahead for creating the yard that currently embell-
ishes the Manor House, giving it a homelike, rural, and therefore historic distinction
from the surrounding city park and community. Given this separation, it is not a surprise to learn that those outside the fence do not know much about the site that lies
within it, nor for the most part did we find that people were even all that interested.
Students in the 2004 and 2005 Hofstra University archaeological field schools were
trained to talk to inquisitive onlookers, explain our reasons for doing archaeology at

King Manor, and invite them to pass through the gates to see the excavations up close. Like us, the museum staff was eager to see such connections made, so we were especially emboldened to succeed. Unfortunately, these invitations were largely declined. Rather, those most likely to pass through the fence to see the excavations were lawyers and staff working at the family courthouse across Jamaica Avenue, who learned about the dig in the newspaper. It seems archaeology at King Manor appealed to people who lived far from the site and learned about it from an abstract media source rather from direct personal contact.

The lack of a local interest in the site is not a passive reaction due to limited accessible information about King Manor. It is one that has been actively created by persistent museum-making efforts, which have not only placed King Manor behind a barrier but buried historic components of the site under fill and even dismantled some of the most enduring aspects of the site in the name of history.[2] One example of these landscape-making efforts best captures the intersection of heritage, property, and racism.

This effort involved the removal in the 1980s of a Civil War memorial erected in front of the house between 1914 and 1922 (Evans 2002: 83). The memorial consisted of two Civil War cannons, a carved granite slab with a bronze memorial plaque, and a flagpole, the base of which was discovered in the ground in the 2004 excavations. The space is now occupied by the current perimeter fence and a shrub and flower garden. Anecdotal evidence suggests the memorial was removed because the site's historic focus is Rufus King, who died 35 years before the Civil War began. Nevertheless a set of 1936 images of the Civil War memorial shows that the front porch of the manor was occupied by what were presumably local park-goers. Given that these visitors are sitting on a historic porch and within the confines of a Civil War memorial, it is hard to imagine that they did not understand that the site itself is a historic place, despite its potentially awkward historical associations.

We draw your attention to the African Americans seated on the front porch of the manor house behind the Civil War cannon. It is this active use of the site as a place for black recreation and the very likely understanding that the site is a historic monument to Rufus King and American freedom that has been lost. The ramifications of this loss are significant for understanding the site today. Jamaica, Queens, is a majority minority community and has had a substantial African American population since

2. Two of the most productive belowground features discovered archaeologically were the remains of an eighteenth-century privy shaft and the foundation trench of an eighteenth-century outbuilding. Both structures stood and were in use into the twentieth century and were only removed in an effort to modernize the park and better situate the historic house in an appropriate landscape. The fact that these structures are likely among the oldest sections of the actual historic landscape adds a layer of irony worth consideration (see Matthews 2008).

Civil War Memorial cannon in the front yard of King Manor Museum showing multiracial community members on the front porch of the manor house, 1936. Courtesy of City of New York Department of Parks and Recreation.

the mid–nineteenth century. Modern park-goers are also almost entirely African American, Afro-Caribbean, and Hispanic, the very people who most often inquired about our ongoing project but who also chose not to enter the site. These residents may be contrasted with white court employees who felt at ease entering the site.

The 1936 photograph suggests that the building of the fence, an action that follows from a particular engagement with the official heritage of King Manor, eliminated other uses of the site. This elimination of other uses has consequences that should be of interest to remaking of all sites, like the work underway at Contrabands and Freedmen's Cemetery Memorial. In both instances, the sites were once part of an existing and active local relationship with past people and memories of place that operated off the official record of the site. While in Alexandria this connection may very well have been between ancestors and descendants, at King Manor this was not the case. Nevertheless in both instances the occupation and use of the site was done with an awareness of the presence of historical associations and the making of meanings derived from African American access and control. At King Manor, it is certain that African Americans had little to no control over the official interpretation of the site, yet this was not necessarily their interest. It was as likely that they accepted and used the official stories of the site in their own making of unofficial stories that produced an affiliation with the park, the historic house, and their membership in the local community. They were not barred from the site, and it was part of their heritage inasmuch as they might recall that nice day when they sat on the porch of the old house in the park.

Conclusion

This chapter has read evidence of structural racism in the making of some recent African American historical sites. Situating dominant conceptions of heritage as wed to the interests of property in late capitalism, we highlighted, following Laurajane Smith (2006), that barriers to heritage are not only about material access but may be located within mainstream conceptions that treat heritage as property rather than process. We show here that efforts to memorialize significant historic sites in Alexandria, Virginia, and Jamaica, New York, can unwittingly deploy racist practices by eliminating and ignoring unofficial African American historic uses that are now part of their documented site histories. In their place and in the name of preservation and memorialization, official uses are promoted as available to African Americans who are treated as "just like" all other potential users. It is in the isolation of the meaning and use of sites as solely in the terms of those who directed their making that we find teeth of structural racism in these instances. For one, by insuring the marking of African American heritage sites and insuring that African Americans have access, sites like these construct what we have termed a "landscape without racists," a landscape that insulates their mainstream owners from charges of exclusion and racism. In practice, though, these sites are racist for they continue to exclude and now have in fact a history of eliminating unofficial African American and other minority group use,[3] thereby not only silently restricting unofficial access and use but quashing the practice of African American heritage that these sites once sustained. Memorials, that is, make history both in providing spaces to reflect on their stories as well as in their other "unofficial" modern uses as sites for recreation, relaxation, memory, or protest.

We suggest, therefore, that there is a great deal more to think about in terms of race and the making of sites in practical terms. Whether they are literally fenced off or not, making sites brings about a re-signification of place. Ultimately, we think that sites emphasize places as property, since their meaning is as much a result of the fact that these spaces *belong to someone,* whether this is a private person, activist group, descendant community, and/or the state. Too often, however, the making of historic sites, especially those designated as African American, suffers from the barriers that

---

3. One criticism by some staff at King Manor was aimed at Hispanic park users who played soccer in the field in front of the manor house. When a playing field was constructed on the other side of the park, the use of the front field was banned to the relief of the museum staff, who could once again enjoy the historic house in its appropriate landscape setting.

such propertied associations impose, barriers that separate social and monumental time and history from the past. Speaking in 2005 about the controversial excavation and proposed memorial at the New York African Burial Ground, city councilman and former Black Panther Charles Barron captured this thought: "They disrespected our ancestors when they excavated our bones, they disrespected us when they took them out of the ground, and now they're disrespecting us by turning our grave site into some kind of a museum" (Confessore 2005). The point is that "sites" are always already signified as foundations for making history and have potential in everybody's hands. The opportunity we are often presented with in African American history is the chance to record these significations in *unconventional* ways as we explore what happens to sites as their meaning and use move across the color line, and to see historical meanings as they stand now rather than simply what they may have stood for then that can be recaptured now. The cases we presented show that African American meaning-making was ongoing at these sites almost until archaeology silenced and recast them in monumental terms. We suspect no archaeologist would want his or her work to foster these results. However, archaeologists alone cannot change this trend; it is only in collaboration, in building communities in the present, and in presenting the ongoing history-making that collaboration involves that we can shift the basis of meaning from sites themselves to what there is new to say about them given what's changed in the world around us and what has not. This was Frederick Douglass's point about coming to understand African American history in the 1880s. Despite the fact that African Americans are "evidently a permanent part of the American population," too much still remains to be done in order to bring African Americans into equal public standing to support the idea of putting slavery into history. This essay has sought to guide archaeologists and heritage planners to consider more seriously their place in this process.

Acknowledgments

We wish to thanks Jodi Barnes for her editorial excellence and the invitation to participate in this volume. We also thank Pam Cressey and Carol McDavid for their close reading of the text. We are certain their suggestions have improved the paper. We also thank Mary Anne Mrozinski and the King Manor Museum staff for inviting Matthews to conduct fieldwork at King Manor. Of course, any and all errors are the sole responsibility of the authors.

References

Blight, D.W. 2006. If You Don't Tell It Like It Was, It Can Never Be As It Ought to Be. In *Slavery and Public History: The Tough Stuff of American Memory*, edited by J. O. Horton and L. E. Horton, pp. 19–33. New York: New Press.

Bonilla-Silva, E. 2003. *Racism without Racists: Color-Blind Racism and the Persistence of Racial Inequality in the United States.* Lanham, Md.: Rowan and Littlefield.

Carman, J. 2005. *Against Cultural Property: Archaeology, Heritage, and Ownership.* London: Duckworth.

City of Alexandria 2008. Call for Entries, Contrabands and Freedmen's Cemetery Memorial. Electronic document, http://www3.alexandriava.gov/freedmens/pdf/CallforEntries .pdf, accessed April 28, 2010.

Confessore, N. 2005. Design Is Picked for African Burial Ground, and the Heckling Begins. *New York Times* 30 April, B1.

Douglass, F. 1867. An Appeal to Congress for Impartial Suffrage. *Atlantic Monthly* 19 (111):112–117. Electronic document, http://eserver.org/race/impartial-suffrage.html, accessed May 17, 2009.

Epperson, T. 2004. Critical Race Theory and the Archaeology of the African Diaspora. *Historical Archaeology* 38(1):101–108.

Evans, J. 2002. *Rufus King Manor, King Park, Jamaica, Queens, Cultural Landscape Inventory.* Prepared for Historic House Trust, New York City. Manuscript on file, King Manor Museum, Queens, N.Y.

Ford, R. T. 2008. *The Race Card: How Bluffing about Bias Makes Race Relations Worse.* New York: Farrar, Strauss, and Giroux.

Grant-Thomas, A., and j. a. powell 2006. Towards a Structural Racism Framework. *Poverty & Race* 15(6):3–6.

Grossman, J. W. 1991. *Archaeological Tests and Artifact Analysis Results from Rufus King Park, Jamaica, Queens, New York.* Prepared for Land-Site Contracting Corp. Manuscript on file, King Manor Museum, Queens, N.Y.

Hall, J. D. 2005. The Long Civil Rights Movement and the Political Uses of the Past. *Journal of American History* 91(4):1233–1263.

Handler, R. 1985. On Having a Culture: Nationalism and the Preservation of Quebec's Patrimoine. In *Objects and Others: Essays on Museums and Material Culture,* edited by G. W. Stocking, Jr., pp. 192–217. Madison: University of Wisconsin Press.

Handler, R., and E. Gable 1997. *The New History in an Old Museum: Creating the Past in Colonial Williamsburg.* Durham: Duke University Press.

Harvey, D. 2001. *Spaces of Capital: Towards a Critical Geography.* New York: Routledge.

———. 1995. *The Power of Place.* Cambridge: MIT Press.

Herzfeld, M. 1991. *A Place in History: Social and Monumental Time in a Cretan Town.* Princeton: Princeton University Press.

Howard, C. J. 2008. Winners. Contrabands and Freedmen's Cemetery Memorial, City of Alexandria, Virginia. Electronic document, http://www3.alexandriava.gov/freedmens/ winners.php, accessed April 8, 2010.

Ifill, G. 2009. *Breakthrough: Politics and Race in the Age of Obama.* New York: Doubleday.

Jackson, K. T. 1985. *Crabgrass Frontier: The Suburbanization of the United States.* New York: Oxford University Press.

Jeane, D. G. 1989. The Upland South Folk Cemetery Complex: Some Suggestions of Origin. In *Cemeteries and Gravemarkers: Voices of American Culture,* edited by R. E. Meyer, pp. 107–136. Logan: Utah State University Press.

Jordan, T. G. 1982. *Texas Graveyards: A Cultural Legacy.* Austin: University of Texas Press.

Katznelson, I. 2005. *When Affirmative Action Was White: An Untold Story of Racial Inequality in 20th Century America.* New York: Norton.

Kirshenblatt-Gimblett, B. 1998. *Destination Culture: Tourism, Museums, Heritage.* Berkeley: University of California Press.

Kubisch, A. C. 2006. Why Structural Racism? *Poverty & Race* 15(6):1–3.

LaRoche, C., and M. L. Blakey 1997. Seizing Intellectual Power: The Dialogue at the New York African Burial Ground. *Historical Archaeology* 31(3):84–106.

Larsen, E. 2009. Self Measure of a Community: Examining the City of Alexandria Virginia through the Contrabands and Freedmen's Cemetery. Paper presented at the Society for Historical Archaeology Annual Meeting, Toronto, Ontario.

Linenthal, E. T. (editor).1996. *History Wars: The Enola Gay and Other Battles for the American Past.* New York: Metropolitan Books.

Lipsitz, G. 2006 [1995]. The Possessive Investment in Whiteness: Racialized Social Democracy and the "White" Problem in American Studies. In *The Suburb Reader,* edited by B. M. Nicolaides and A. Wiese, pp. 341–344. New York: Routledge.

Lowenthal, D. 1998. *The Heritage Crusade and the Spoils of History.* Cambridge: Cambridge University Press.

Massey, D. S., and N. A. Denton 1993. *American Apartheid: Segregation and the Making of the Underclass.* Cambridge: Harvard University Press.

Matthews, C. N. 2008. *Draft Report of 2004–2006 Archaeological Investigations at the Rufus King Manor Site (81.01.11) in Jamaica, Queens, New York.* Submitted to King Manor Association of Long Island, Inc. Manuscript on file, Center for Public Archaeology, Hofstra University, Hempstead, N.Y.

———. 2002. *Archaeology of History and Tradition: Moments of Danger in the Annapolis Landscape.* New York: Kluwer/Plenum.

Orser, C. E., Jr. 2007. *The Archaeology of Race and Racialization in Historic America.* Gainesville: University Press of Florida.

Pippenger, W. E. 1995 *Alexandria, Virginia, Death Records 1863–1869 (The Gladwin Record), and 1869–1896.* Westminster Md.: Family Line Publications.

———. 1992. *Tombstone Inscriptions of Alexandria, Virginia.* Vol. 3. Westminster, Md.: Family Line Publications.

Savage, K. 1997. *Standing Soldiers and Kneeling Slaves: Race, War, and Monument in Nineteenth-Century America.* Princeton: Princeton University Press.

Scafidi, S. 2005. *Who Owns Culture? Appropriation and Authenticity in American Law.* New Brunswick. N.J.: Rutgers University Press.

Sider, G. M. 1994. Identity as History: Ethnohistory, Ethnogenesis, and Ethnocide in the Southeastern United States. *Identities* 1(1):109–122.

Sider, G. M., and G. Smith (editors) 1997. *Between History and Histories: The Making of Silences and Commemorations.* Toronto: University of Toronto Press.

Smith, L. 2006. *Uses of Heritage.* New York: Routledge.

Stone, L. 1998. *Report of Archaeological Testing in Advance of Improvements Associated with the Drainage and Termite Project at Rufus King Park, Jamaica Avenue and 150–153 Streets,*

Jamaica, Queens, New York. Prepared for Fredante Construction Corporation. Manuscript on file, Center for Public Archaeology, Hofstra University, Hempstead, N.Y.

———. 1997. *Report on Archaeological Testing in Advance of Improvements Associated with the Fence Project at Rufus King Park, Jamaica Avenue and 150–153 Streets, Jamaica, Queens, New York.* Prepared for Gazebo Contracting Inc. Manuscript on file, Center for Public Archaeology, Hofstra University, Hempstead, N.Y.

Trouillot, M. 1995. *Silencing the Past: Power and the Production of History.* Boston: Beacon Press.

Wallace, M. 1996. *Mickey Mouse History and Other Essays on American Memory.* Philadelphia: Temple University Press.

Washington Post. 1892a 29 March.

———. 1892b. 2 October.

———. 1894. 5 January.

Wilson, W. J. 1987 *The Truly Disadvantaged: The Inner City, the Underclass, and Public Policy.* Chicago: University of Chicago Press.

Wise, T. 2005. *White Like Me: Reflections on Race from a Privileged Son.* Brooklyn, N.Y.: Soft Skull Press.

Jennifer J. Babiarz

White Privilege and Silencing within the Heritage Landscape

Race and the Practice of Cultural Resource Management

Manning Marable (2002: 49) has said, "What whites also need to understand is that white privilege operates so well because *nobody talks about it.*" I take direction from black feminist scholars who have demonstrated the relationship between power and representation and who argue that one's positionality influences the way we see the world around us (for example, Hill Collins 2000; hooks 1995). Black feminist scholars also emphasize that we must merge our scholarly work with our politics, a politics of social justice. Thus I begin the conversation with how my personal experiences within the field of archaeology have brought me to this moment and to the belief that it is critical that we, as archaeologists, scholars, and citizens, continue to seriously discuss and contend with white privilege.

Some of the most important moments of my awareness of issues regarding whiteness in the field occurred during my public archaeology work with Archaeology in Annapolis (AiA). AiA is a collaborative educational and research project that exists as a partnership between the Department of Anthropology at the University of Maryland at College Park and the City of Annapolis. The program has had two major goals in mind: "(1) to help reenfrancise people by giving them control over their own consumption of history and (2) to illuminate portions of everyday life that are taken for granted but, when given history, can be questioned or challenged" (Leone et al. 2009: 155–156). Annapolis is a city whose economy relies on tourism, which is focused on sailing and antebellum history. This history is communicated through historic house and local history museums, walking tours within Annapolis and suburbs of the city, as well as public lectures and published books and articles.

One of the projects that I worked on in 2006 came about after an African American descendant community approached AiA directly to work in partnership to draw local attention to their postbellum neighborhood, called Parole. Parole, located on the west edge of Annapolis, was named for a Civil War prisoner-of-war camp (Camp Parole) that had been constructed on farmland next to the railroad tracks, and at that time outside of the city. After the Civil War, this area became a large African American farm community that continued into the twentieth century, containing a self-actualized economic, spiritual, and educational infrastructure. Families within the community shared food (including communal gardening and slaughtering areas), jobs, and educational support of children, who grew up to be members of city and state government, lawyers, doctors, and professionals in Parole and Annapolis into the present. Today Parole is being severely impacted by development. After beginning the project in the neighborhood it became clear that the members of the community held a depth of shared memories of the area. In fact, on the public days that we held behind the Mount Olive A.M.E. Church in a field that had once been a communal gardening, food preparation, and gathering space, community members were able to help analyze features as we were digging them. That is not to say that there weren't questions posed by the residents during Community History Days that only archaeology could answer (Lisa Kraus, personal communication 2009), specifically: why did members of the Parole community seek archaeologists to collaborate with in the first place?

The context for this collaboration began in the 1950s, when a section of U.S. Highway 50 was built that connected the District of Columbia to the City of Annapolis. One of its exit ramps bisected and destroyed a whole swath of the oldest section of Parole, including the original location of the Mount Olive A.M.E. Church. By the time of our field school in 2007, a new mixed-use condo/commercial space was about to break ground. In fact the area where we did archaeology was to be the site of a community center paid for by developers in compensation for the development's impacts on the Parole neighborhood. In 2006 and 2007, the exit ramp from U.S. 50 was greatly widened to allow for access to a new, large county hospital complex; this physically destroyed most of what was left of the oldest part of Parole. The City of Annapolis had pioneered the use of archaeology and historic preservation to build tourism in order to create a viable local economy and allow the survival of a small city with no agriculture or industry. Community members of Parole, including elected city officials, were using the same tools to draw attention to the neighborhood's importance in the city's history, which had been ignored by historians and local, state, and federal governments. There was little interest in our work outside of the neighborhood and our partnerships; the general consensus seemed to be that Parole was slowly dying due to development and in fact had lost its authenticity when impacted by development starting in the early 1980s. The unspoken message was that a truly vibrant, important community would not have been so easily paved over. It took me a while to start to understand the great many deliberate choices being made in this situation relating to transportation and development going back 50 or 60 years. It wasn't until I got out of academic archaeology and into CRM that the connections between African American disenfranchisement, institutionalized racism, and local, state, and federal infrastructure became clearer—more specifically, how white archaeologists have rarely talked about either white privilege and racism within the profession or archaeology's economic and social dependence on the very institutions that are instrumental in the perpetuation of white supremacy (but see Barnes 2008; McDavid 2007; Zimmerman 2005).

What happened in Parole has happened in black communities across the African diaspora: the silencing of historical narratives that could place African Americans within an everyday retelling of history. It's been stated that "The lack of historical places on our contemporary landscape that remind all persons of the omnipresence of African Americans throughout U.S. history . . . helps create a cultural amnesia and contributes to the recreation of racism (Paynter et al. 1996: 314). Public archaeology is one of the solutions to try to correct this gap in the presentation of the historical record. Although ideas in how to sweep back the veil that separates the experiences of those who have been "othered" from what is considered mainstream American culture have been argued over, very little discussion has revolved around the mechanisms of this erasure. Keeping the lives of individuals and communities invisible or even physically erased from the landscape requires constant, literal action. Many of these actions are so built into the quotidian workings of our civil institutions that they will not cease without direct action because, as George Lipsitz (1998: vii) says, "white Americans are encouraged to invest in whiteness, to remain true to an identity that provides them with resources, power, and opportunity" (see also Palmer, "Archaeology of Jim Crow," this volume). This is an investment into what Eduardo Bonilla-Silva (2001) calls "the new racism," which he defines as social systems of racial domination. These social systems are reflected in everything from mortgage rates to the industrial prison complex and are too myriad and complex to detail fully here. So I'll start off by talking about two examples of social systems where archaeologists, who are nearly all white, have become invested in whiteness: the employment of archaeologists within the CRM field, particularly as part of state and federal legislation requiring the assessment for the cultural resource potential of land before infrastructural building, and the training of archaeologists in graduate school.

The first historical archaeology excavations in the United States were celebrations through preservation of individuals and events that were considered most important to the country's history. In 1935 the Historic Sites Act declared the federal responsibility "to preserve for public use historic sites, buildings, and objects of national significance for the preservation and benefit of the people of the United States" (United States Congress 1935: 1). One of the first archaeological sites to gain national attention was Jamestown, Virginia, where excavations began in 1934. Jamestown was one of the many archaeological sites to be excavated with support from federal agencies during the Great Depression, including the Emergency Conservation Work Group and the Civilian Conservation Corps (Orser and Fagan 1995). This was the beginning of a long relationship between federal legislation and the economy of archaeology, culminating in the birth of modern CRM archaeology from the head of the National

Historic Preservation Act of 1966 (United States Congress 2006). This Act worked to preserve properties significant to local, state, and federal history and culture. It was also during the 1950s and 1960s that city and infrastructure planning changed dramatically with the growth of the suburbs. This growth was linked to white flight from the inner cities with the aid of racist implementing of Federal Housing Authority–subsidized mortgages. In order for the white residents of the suburbs to get to their jobs in the city, federal and state governments subsidized the building of a vast network of highways across the country. African American neighborhoods were weakened by the inflation of housing costs, mortgage foreclosures, and, during much of this time, a lack of voting rights. It seems a foregone conclusion that governments would choose black communities rather than white communities when taking land for the purpose of building prisons, waste dumps, and highways.

One example of this infrastructural building was the construction of the Cross Bronx Expressway (CBE) in the 1950s. The CBE was part of a multicomponent plan toward the reorganization of New York City led in part by the builder Robert Moses. Along with the displacement of 60,000 residents came the construction of massive public housing units in the South Bronx and East Brooklyn at the same time as the explosion in the building of New York–area whites-only suburbs. Frightening in its

Truss Structure at 3rd Avenue Line, Cross Bronx Expressway, View Northwest. Courtesy of Historic American Engineering Record, American Memory, the Library of Congress, Washington, D.C., 1968.

efficiency, the CBE "would allow people to traverse the Bronx from the suburbs of New Jersey through upper Manhattan to the suburbs of Queens in fifteen minutes" (Chang 2005: 10). Manufacturing jobs vanished from the Bronx, slumlords realized more money could be made from insurance collection after the destruction of their buildings, and the expressway made it all too easy to isolate and ignore entire sections of the city that could be driven over on elevated freeways (Chang 2005). This was one of the main arguments of community groups during their successful three-decade fight against the South Midtown Freeway (SMF) in Kansas City, Missouri. In the freeway plans, there were no exits within the African American sections of the city, so that not only was that part of the city to be fully bypassed, it was to be purposely cut off (Gotham 1999). The building of freeways across the country worked in tandem with many other factors to identify and quarantine poor and minority populations.

In 1976 the National Historic Preservation Act was amended to give more detail as to how and when the federal government would be responsible for upholding the 1966 preservation law; most state governments eventually followed suit with similar legislation. Section 106 and Section 110 (the sections of the amendment relating to archaeology) became the primary economic support for the archaeological profession, as it made all federal agencies consider any potential effect on cultural resources before any undertakings. That means before any road can be built or fixed, or even a traffic light can be added to the corner of a state highway, the effect of the proposed project on cultural resources must be established. The vast majority of those individuals working as paid archaeologists today are funded through compliance with this legislation, including myself. It took only a short time working for a state highway administration before I began to notice, and had pointed out to me, a disturbing history that began before the days of contract archaeology in the 1950s and 1960s. This history was a reflection of the glut of highway building that I previously mentioned, and it affected rural African American communities as much as urban ones. During this time, highway bypasses were built around small white country towns and through black towns and even cemeteries (see Matthews and Larsen, this volume). Some of these towns had been so obliterated by highway construction that they no longer existed on a map, although this was also likely a reflection of a historic refusal by white mapmakers of the nineteenth century to label some black towns by name. So how do these actions affect archaeological work now?

Archaeological excavations aren't automatically employed in order to determine whether or not a physical place is significant. An archaeologist has to decide whether or not a place has a great enough *possibility* for significance before excavations are deemed to be warranted. One of the criteria for an archaeological site's eligibility for preservation is that the site still has integrity and that its historical context is clear; it is extremely difficult to get protection for a site that has been greatly disturbed. Kerri Barile's (2004) analysis of the confluence of race, the National Register, and CRM in

Texas presents some of the problems caused by methodologies of interpreting significance. Specifically, she explored the worry that many states have begun to express about the continued collections management and eligibility of late-nineteenth- and twentieth-century sites. In Texas and across the country, the poorest citizens of that period were generally former slaves and immigrants. The majority of African Americans lived rurally as tenant farmers, which would be reflected in the paucity of the architectural and archaeological record. When evaluating significance, CRM firms tend to use "artifact quantity, rather than quality. . . . This approach appears to favor large sites with elaborate architecture and a high quantity of artifacts, rather than lower class sites with vernacular architecture" (Barile 2004: 93). In her study, Barile found that such methodologies led disturbingly to a determination of eligibility for 77 percent of white postbellum sites and only 6 percent of postbellum African American sites (Barile 2004). She believes the solution to this problem lies in a change in the methodology and training of CRM archaeologists toward a multidisciplinary approach to research and in ending the primary reliance on archaeological data in determinations of significance (Barile 2004; see also Matthews and Larsen, "Black History as Property," and Palmer, "Archaeology of Jim Crow," this volume).

It is much harder to get a site recognized and protected if it has been partially destroyed by a highway, if it contains few artifacts or ephemeral architectural features, or if it has been rendered invisible in official histories. This can make it very, very difficult to get archaeological sites important to African American history and memory legally recognized as important to America. Cheryl Harris (1998) has written about how civil law has been used as a tool for racial oppression. She says, "Whiteness has functioned as self-identity in the domain of the intrinsic, personal, and psychological; as reputation in the interstices between internal and external identity; and, as property in the extrinsic, public, and legal realms. . . . The law's construction of whiteness defined and affirmed critical aspects of identity (who is white); of privilege (what benefits accrue to that status); and of property (what *legal* entitlements arise from that status)" (Harris 1998: 104).

The National Historic Preservation Act, the cornerstone of historic preservation legislation, states that part of its purpose as defined by Congress is "the historical and cultural foundations of the Nation should be preserved as a living part of our community life and development in order to give a sense of orientation to the American people" (National Register of Historic Places 1997: Section 1(b) (2)). Therefore, part of the purpose of the protection and recognition of historic sites is to help in the creation of an American identity, and significant sites are those that inform what it means to be an American. American citizenship, and subsequently the protections granted those who are considered citizens, is partly defined by collective identification with a shared history.

If historical sites associated with people of color are less represented on the National Register for Historic Places because it is more difficult for African American sites to be recognized as significant for the reasons mentioned previously, then what is the federal government telling all of its citizens about who is deserving of citizenship? Using shared history to define citizenship is a cunning method of disenfranchisement. This is how archaeology is used as a tool for racial oppression. It is why none of the black residents of Parole were surprised that the highway kept widening through their community and the local and state government did not recognize Parole's significance.

The vast majority of archaeologists are white. Even the lowest-paid field technician in CRM is required to have a college degree before being hired, and almost all of the professors who train archaeologists, most of whom will end up working in CRM, are also white. The number of African American archaeology professors in the United States can practically be counted on two hands. How does this academic training affect the way that archaeologists see and interpret the world around them? Archaeologists train in a sort of apprenticeship, where they are taught how to look at soil and landscape in a very particular way. That way has to do with using experiential learning and empathy to interpret how the landscape may have seemed to those humans in the past who moved across it and changed it for their daily needs, as a place to sleep and eat and settle. If only white archaeologists are teaching you how to think about moving through the landscape, then you are learning from people who have themselves experienced the physical world as a place of possibility and perhaps even neutrality.

These different ways of living and experiencing one's physical surroundings have been written about by bell hooks (1995). For her the landscape held very clear safe places and places of fear, for example, in the terrifying walk that she had to make through a poor white neighborhood to get to her grandparents' house. As hooks (1995: 45) says, "It is useful, when theorizing black experience, to examine the way the concept of 'terror' is linked to representations of whiteness. . . . I learned as a child that to be 'safe' it was important to recognize the power of whiteness, even to fear it, and to avoid encounter."

A large part of CRM historical archaeology is trying to figure out the most likely areas in which a site may be found in order to maximize time in the field with an effective testing strategy. This requires understanding something about how people in the past would have made decisions about movement (such as roads or informal pathways) and the relationship between households within communities, which would have affected the physical layout of neighborhoods and towns. If a white archaeologist is not aware how much a part of everyday life negotiating these terrorisms has been in African American communities, how can the archaeologist possibly interpret and communicate these histories?

Compounding these problems is the continuing division between the labor and the analysis of archaeology as outlined by Shanks and McGuire (1996). They argue that archaeology must be pursued as a craft to remain viable as an act (or series of acts) of cultural production. In order to create a product for the communities being served, an archaeologist must engage in dialogue to understand the practical and emotional needs that archaeology will serve. CRM has, in most cases, effectively routinized the production of archaeology to a point that it has nearly lost its ability to communicate a shared vision of community through history.

I think that there are two fundamental ways that can help change the whiting-out of history through archaeology. The first is a focus on training and hiring more African American archaeologists within academia and CRM. This has been at the forefront of discussion about the future of historical archaeology at conferences and in journal articles for the last decade (for example, Agbe-Davies 1998, 2002; Franklin 1997; McKee 1994). At the very least, this would bring multiple perspectives to bear on interpretations of the past, but it will also challenge and hopefully change the racialized political landscape of archaeology. The second is a change in positionality, in the worldview, of white archaeologists. For me it was cross-disciplinary learning, specifically from black activist scholars within the African Diaspora program at the University of Texas, which led me to understand that I had a particular raced standpoint and that it needed to be repositioned. This change in positionality requires honesty and critical self-reflection on the part of white archaeologists in acknowledging, both inwardly and outwardly, their own white privilege. Students should be required to train cross-disciplinarily, even if just to jolt them out of their worldview long enough for them to realize that the culture of archaeology has a political position that privileges them. The most crucial element of all, however, is white students and professionals taking responsibility for their own repositioning, for example, by educating themselves about the works of black feminist and critical race scholars and by working in collaborations with communities of color. One example of this sort of collaboration is found in the work of Carol McDavid's Community Archaeology Research Institute, Inc. (CARI), in Houston, Texas. Their mission is "to advance research in the field of community based archaeology, to develop educational and public outreach activities related to that research, to provide training for teachers and other archaeologists, and to further the public knowledge and use of archaeology and history" (Community Archaeology Research Institute 2008: paragraph 10).

A main goal of their research activities and outreach is to engage in dialogue toward the destruction of present-day racism, classism, and misogyny. By sharing intellectual and economic power with already-existing community groups, McDavid is actively repositioning herself. This sort of repositioning can also take the form of self-education through scholarship. Robert Paul Wolff, a white Afro-American Studies professor at the University of Massachusetts at Amherst, discusses this approach in *Autobiography of an Ex-White Man: Learning a New Master Narrative for America* (2005). This text traces the profound changes that the reading of foundational texts assigned to first-year doctoral students in the Afro-American Studies Department made in his worldview, particularly in his self-reflection on his white privilege and the difficulties it causes in true attempts at activist collaboration.

Hopefully, for the future of CRM this will mean more practitioners thinking critically about whether the archaeology they are being contracted to do is being used to support social inequality. Although CRM archaeologists may not be able to stop projects from going forward, they do write the reports that are very important to future archaeologists, who use them to determine the potential for archaeological resources in an area. CRM professionals also often have some sway in deciding what interested citizens' groups can be included in the Section 106 process. Perhaps this is where Shanks and McGuire's vision of archaeology as a craft can be particularly useful. They say that "the labor of craft is a constant dialogue between archaeologist and material, archaeologist and community—and expressive and interpretive experience within which the past is created" (Shanks and McGuire 1996: 86). Archaeologists must begin to take responsibility for the connections between their labor (analyses and reportage of historical "facts") and its uses by and within communities creating acts of cultural production. If there is no understanding on the part of white archaeologists about their own white privilege, then collaboration will never truly work. A great example of this, which everyone is familiar with, is the African Burial Ground. White CRM archaeologists were forced to change their methodological positionality only after they completely failed to collaborate with politically powerful black communities (LaRoche and Blakey 1997). These archaeologists were forced to acknowledge their white privilege once, and it is possible that they haven't chosen (or been forced) to acknowledge it again. Have the lessons learned from this and similar projects not been taken seriously by white archaeologists because they actively enjoy their white privilege too much, or because they don't understand its connections to "the new racism"?

Despite the fact that archaeologists have been investigating African American sites since the late 1960s and even though gender politics entered archaeological discussion in the 1980s, it wasn't until the 1990s that a concern with the racial politics of archaeology took shape. As I hope to have demonstrated, archaeologists cannot begin to challenge racism until they first reflect upon how they have been privileged by the ways in which archaeology operates in erasing already marginalized histories. Further, the laws that are meant to protect historic sites are working in exclusionary ways if the criterion of site significance is "integrity" and African American sites generally lack this due to urban renewal and development that have racially targeted and severely impacted them. To date, we have either remained silent on this issue because our white privilege allows us to acknowledge this discrimination or because we recognize it but are at a loss as to how to amend the problem. If it is our intent to challenge racial injustice, however, we need to start by documenting these sites and lobbying for their significance, working with African American stakeholders in doing so, and agitating for changing the laws if need be.

References

Agbe-Davies, A. 1998. Dealing with "Race" in African American Archaeology. *Anthropology Newsletter* 39(5):14.

——. 2002. Black Scholars, Black Pasts. *SAA Archaeological Record* 2(4):24–28.

Barile, K. 2004. Race, the National Register, and Cultural Resource Management: Creating an Historic Context for Postbellum Sites. *Historical Archaeology* 38(1):90–100.

Barnes, J. 2008. Kennewick Man: Critical Whiteness Studies and the Practice of Archaeology. In *Kennewick Man: Perspectives on the Ancient One*, edited by H. Burke, C. Smith, D. Lippert, J. Watkins, and L. Zimmerman. Walnut Creek, Calif.: Left Coast Press.

Bonilla-Silva, E. 2001. *White Supremacy & Racism in the Post Civil Rights Era*. Boulder, Colo.: Lynne Rienner Publishers.

Chang, J. 2005. *Can't Stop Won't Stop: A History of the Hip Hop Generation*. New York: St. Martin's Press.

Community Archaeology Research Institute, Inc. 2008. *CARI's Mission*. Electronic document, http://www.publicarchaeology.org/CARI/, accessed April 19, 2009.

Franklin, M. 1997 Why Are There So Few Black American Archaeologists? *Antiquity* 71:799–801.

Harris, C. 1998. Whiteness as Property. In *Black on White: Black Writers on What It Means to Be White*, edited by D. Roediger, pp. 103–118. New York: Random House.

Hill Collins, P. 2000 *Black Feminist Thought: Knowledge, Consciousness, and the Politics of Empowerment*. New York: Routledge.

Gotham, K. 1999. Political Opportunity, Community Identity, and the Emergence of a Local Anti-Expressway Movement. *Social Problems* 46(3):332–354.

Historic American Engineering Record [HAER] 1968. Truss Structure at 3rd Avenue Line, Cross Bronx Expressway, View Northwest. Library of Congress, Prints and Photographs Division, Historic American Buildings Survey or Historic American Engineering Record, HAER N.Y., 3–Bronx, pp. 13–44.

Hooks, b. 1995. Representations of Whiteness in the Black Imagination. In *Killing Rage: Ending Racism*, pp. 31–50. New York: Henry Holt and Company.

LaRoche, C. and M. Blakey 1997. Seizing Intellectual Power: The Dialogue at the New York African Burial Ground. *Historical Archaeology* 31(3):84–106.

Leone, M., A. Chisholm, J. Babiarz, M. Palus, and L. Kraus 2009. Annapolis Historic Period Archaeology. In *Archaeology in America: An Encyclopedia*, Vol. 1, edited by L. S. Cordell, F. P. McManamon, K. G. Lightfoot, G. R. Milner, pp. 153–156. Westport, Conn.: Greenwood Press.

Lipsitz, G. 1998. *The Possessive Investment in Whiteness: How White People Profit from Identity Politics*. Philadelphia: Temple University Press.

Marable, M. 2002. The Souls of White Folk. *Souls: A Critical Journal of Black Politics, Culture, and Society* 4(4):45–51.

McDavid, C. 2007. Beyond Strategy and Good Intentions: Archaeology, Race, and White Privilege. In *Archaeology as a Tool of Civic Engagement*, edited by B. Little and P. Shackel, pp. 67–88. Lanham, Md.: AltaMira Press.

McKee, L. 1994. Is It Futile to Try and Be Useful? Historical Archaeology and the African American Experience. *Northeast Historical Archaeology* 23:1–7.

National Register of Historic Places 1997. *How to Apply the National Register Criteria for Evaluation.* National Register Bulletin No. 15, National Park Service. Electronic document, http://www.nps.gov/nr/publications/bulletins/nrb15/, accessed April 30, 2009.

Orser, C., Jr., and B. Fagan 1995. *Historical Archaeology.* New York: HarperCollins College Publishers.

Paynter, R., S. Hautaniemi, and N. Muller 1996. The Landscapes of the W. E. B. DuBois Boyhood Homesite: An Agenda for an Archaeology of the Color Line. In *Race,* edited by S. Gregory and R. Sanjek, pp. 285–318. New Brunswick, N.J.: Rutgers University Press.

Wolff, R. 2005. *Autobiography of An Ex-White Man: Learning a New Master Narrative for America.* Rochester, N.Y.: University of Rochester Press.

United States Congress 1935. Historic Sites Act of 1935. Electronic document, http://www.blm.gov/pgdata/etc/medialib/blm/wo/Planning_and_Renewable_Resources/coop_agencies/cr_publications.Par.38648.File.dat/histsite.pdf, accessed April 20, 2009.

———. 2006. National Historic Preservation Act of 1966, As Amended through 2006. Electronic document, http://www.achp.gov/docs/nhpa%202008–final.pdf, accessed April 20, 2009.

Zimmerman, L. J. 2005. Public Heritage, a Desire for a "White" History for America, and Some Impacts of the Kennewick Man/Ancient One Decision. *International Journal of Cultural Property* 12:265–274.

LAURIE A. WILKIE AND PAUL FARNSWORTH

Living Not So Quietly, Not So on the Edge of Things

A Twentieth-Century Bahamian Household

Bahamian historical archaeology, in many ways, is still in its infancy. Although a number of archaeologists have conducted work here since the 1970s (for example, Aarons 1990; Baxter 2007; Baxter and Burton 2005; Farnsworth 1993, 1994, 1996; Farnsworth and Wilkie 1999; Gerace 1982; Turner 1993; Wilkie and Farnsworth 2005), much of this research has focused on a narrow range of site types, especially plantations. This circumstance parallels the historical trajectory of archaeological work in the American South, as well as the rest of the Caribbean, where development of lands that were once agricultural into residential and commercial lots prompted excavations at many historic plantations. Rapid development in all of the Bahamas has led to a similar circumstance—in a very small span of time, countless sites related to the pre-Loyalist and Loyalist plantations of the Bahamas will be lost to development. When possible, archaeologists have attempted to conduct some excavations before the bulldozing begins (for example, Farnsworth 1993, 1994, 1996; Wilkie and Farnsworth 2005).

For the most part, however, there is still a large gap in our knowledge about the archaeological past of the Bahamas following emancipation (1838, the end of the apprenticeship period) to the present. In part this silence is the result of the cultural resource management priorities of the Bahamian government that privilege work at early colonial period sites as well as ways that plantations are conceptualized in the contemporary Bahamas. Again, the Bahamas is typical of other parts of the Caribbean, where postemancipation sites receive less attention than those dating before freedom. Important exceptions like Douglas Armstrong's (1990, 2003) work at Drax Hall Plantation, Jamaica, and the East End Village in the Virgin Islands demonstrate the great potential of such research. Still, the archaeology of the late-nineteenth and twentieth centuries remains understudied in most of the Caribbean (Hicks 2007: 76).

The neglect of later sites may be an artifact of the dominance of plantation landscapes on modern social geographies in the Caribbean, and particularly the Bahamas.

Most Bahamian plantations have been abandoned as centers of large-scale commercial agriculture for close to 200 years, yet these institutions continue to mark the social landscape and geography of the islands. Gated communities take their names from former plantation sites, and localities are often referred to by long-abandoned plantation or planter names. The boundaries of Crown land grants are still recognizable in modern land transactions.

The buildings of the plantation period likewise remain an enduring part of the landscape, particularly on the Family Islands. The better-built stone structures of the old plantations are still occupied, often without the benefit of "modern" conveniences like plumbing or electricity. Plantations commanded large supplies of labor; similar amounts of labor were not available postemancipation to continue to develop and maintain these spaces. In addition, crumbling plantation works have become one of the evocative images of Caribbean tourism, and the narrative of plantation abandonment is a common one repeated in eco-tourism marketing, assuring visitors that they are entering a place where time has stopped—or at least been interrupted.

The illusion is that "progress," in the modernist sense, ceased when plantation industry came to an end. This seeming compression of time on the landscape—the notion that the plantation past is only a step removed from today—has an insidious aspect to it: it erases and renders invisible the ways that generations of Bahamians have remade and reused the landscape since emancipation. Much plantation archaeology in the Bahamas has sought to answer important questions that are relevant to modern Bahamians: questions about how their contemporary culture is related to ancestral populations that came from Africa, Europe, and the Americas, questions about the Bahamas' role in the global colonial market. In a short time, archaeologists have contributed a significant amount of information about the lives of Bahamians from the 1700s through the end of the Loyalist period.

Yet in terms of understanding how Bahamian culture came to be what it is today, the postemancipation period is extraordinarily important. Formerly enslaved Africans and African Bahamians were no longer bound to particular tasks or land parcels. New populations of Africans continued to settle in the Bahamas as a result of Britain's continued naval actions against the Spanish slave trade, and new waves of European immigrant populations, like the Greeks, came to the islands.

Collectively, those of us who have been excavating plantation sites are probably well positioned to begin to fill these chronological gaps with data we have already excavated. As we noted above, many of the structures still standing at plantations were reoccupied at different times, and these reoccupations have left archaeological traces—evidence of what Hicks (2007: 68) refers to as the "afterlives" of plantations. The term *afterlife* is helpful in emphasizing the value of understanding these occupations. Often these "afterlives," which have a more subtle archaeological signature, are ignored, described as "ephemeral" occupations or merely evidence of "squatters" or lumped under the generic title "modern disturbance" (see also Steen, "From Slave to Citizen," this volume). These characterizations are dismissive of the lives lived in these spaces and serve only to reify historical narratives that privilege the period of enslavement while enforcing silences about the postemancipation period. As archaeologists interested in constructing broader understandings of the diaspora, we should be focusing our attention on these seemingly "quiet" and "peripheral" occupations. In this essay we will discuss our efforts to begin to look at the continued uses of Clifton Plantation following emancipation, with particular focus on an early-twentieth-century household occupation.

Clifton Plantation

We have detailed the Loyalist history of Clifton plantation extensively in other publications (for example, Wilkie and Farnsworth 2005), but it is worth providing a brief review of the plantation's Loyalist history. The plantation lands were first developed in the late 1700s, but it was after the acquisition of the land by William Wylly in 1809 during the Loyalist period that the lands of Clifton were most developed. Under Wylly's ownership, as many as 70 enslaved people lived at Clifton. Wylly's ownership ended with his death in 1828, and while a number of additional families owned the plantation, after the burning of the planter's residence in the 1850s attempts to run Clifton as an organized economic venture ended. Ultimately the land came to be owned in 1935 by Harry Oakes, who in the early twentieth century was at one time proclaimed to be the wealthiest man on earth. The Oakes family held the lands of Clifton until just recently, when the government of the Bahamas acquired the property. The Oakes never developed the property themselves. There were several attempts in the twentieth century to develop Clifton into new agricultural ventures and resort housing, but none came to fruition.

Documentation regarding life on Clifton during the Wylly period is relatively rich. After Wylly's ownership, however, there are few references to the property. Located 14 miles from the city of New Providence, even today the western end of the island, where Clifton is located, is seen as remote and distant from the center of island life in the city. Fifteen limestone-block buildings still stand from the Wylly period, and these noticeable landmarks have been utilized in a variety of ways in the over-150 years since the planter residence burned.

During our archaeological research on Clifton Plantation, we uncovered extensive evidence of post-Loyalist occupation of individual structures and reuse of fields. While the occupation of the plantation during the Loyalist period incorporated all the buildings and spaces of the plantation's acreage, the postemancipation period was fragmented, with particular buildings and spaces of the landscape used and then left alone and used again at different times. Clifton has never been abandoned; some part of the lands has been used continuously, whether by fisherman temporarily camping in a building while exploiting the rich resources of the reef, families coming to raise crops in the clearly defined farming plots, or persons harvesting fruit from trees planted during enslavement.

Parts of the landscape have been more extensively exploited. In 1938 Oakes' land company, Nassoak, entered into a legal agreement with 10 individuals who were described as utilizing the lands of Clifton as "tenants." In exchange for continued use of the land, these individuals agreed to make no future claim on the lands. Aerial photographs show that extensive cultivation was evident on the plantation from the 1930s through the end of the 1950s (Bain 1993). At least three of the eight cabins still standing in the main African village have been refurbished and occupied during the postemancipation period, though not necessarily concurrently. Crumbling walls were repaired, new layers of mortar and paint applied, and in one instance, a tin roof added. The two structures located on the beachfront of Clifton were similarly reoccupied, with one modified into a bar (and possible brothel) during the late nineteenth century and the other serving as a domestic residence. The plantation office, located near the planter's residence, according to oral history, served a short stint as a small grocery store/market.

In this essay, we want to discuss more fully the twentieth-century occupation of one of the village houses, a house designated as Locus H. During excavations in 1999, a significant portion of the houseyard associated with this structure was excavated. While the intent of the excavations was to reveal more information about the Loyalist period occupation of the house, we were able to identify a thin lens of midden associated with 1930s to 1950s artifactual materials (Table 1). Glass, ceramic, plastic,

TABLE 1. Datable Glass Artifacts from Second Locus H Occupation

Datable Artifact	Date Range	Minimum Number of Vessels Recovered
"Duraglas" mark of Owens Illinois glass company	1940+	7
Owens Illinois mark from Owen Illinois plant 7	1950	1
Selenium-tinted bottles	1915–1960	7
Hazel-Atlas tumbler	1920–1964	1
Selenium bottle marked "Pat'd 1930"	1930–1960	1
Ketterer's Liver Klenzor	1912+	2
PGCo beer bottle, Portland Glass Company of Greenford, England	1922–1956	1
"Townie" mark of Brockway Glass	1925+	1
Jug wine, Regina company	1934+	1
"Mayfair" (open rose) depression glass plate	1931–1937	1
"American Sweetheart" depression glass plate	1930–1936	1

After Luckey 1986; Toulouse 1971; U.S. General Patent Office 1913.

rubber, metal, and bone artifacts representing a minimum of 161 distinct objects and associated faunal materials were recovered for this period of occupation.

Given the location of Clifton on the island of New Providence and the documentary silences that surround that part of the island, it would be easy to assume that the people living on Clifton existed on the edge of Bahamian society, isolated from goods, services, and amenities and sheltered from the world. An analysis of the materials from the household demonstrates quite the opposite. The family living on Clifton may have been living quietly on the edge of the island, but even there they were most certainly still in the center of the world.

The Material Spaces at Locus H

The eight structures of the Clifton village are mainly arranged in a single line facing the main road that stretches around the west end of the island. The westernmost structures in the line are the driver's house and the village communal kitchen. Locus H is the first house east of these structures. Each house has a yard area extending 10 to 14 meters from the rear of the house and a garden plot behind. During the Loyalist period, yams, benne, maize, sorghum, and okra were among the crops grown in these garden plots. Farming in the Bahamas is no easy task. There are few places where rich "black soil" suitable for agriculture is accumulated, and even in those areas the coral/limestone bedrock is thick in the soil. Each farm plot is dotted with piles of limestone that have been turned up during tilling. Planting takes place between the piles. The labor necessary to prep these fields has been appreciated by later generations who, even when living elsewhere, have returned to grow crops in these old gardens.

The house at H is one of the larger ones built in the village, measuring 27 by 15.5 feet in size. It has a door facing the road and another facing the yard. One window is situated on the southern side of the house. There is no evidence of internal subdivision of the structure; the floor is composed of limestone mortar. The exterior of the house was once painted pink. There is no evidence of internal paint, just plaster. The house has a pitched roofline that, based on the lack of evidence of roofing materials, was probably covered with thatch. Hinges demonstrate that the structure had wood shutters and doors. The house would have appeared much as many of the houses in older Bahamian settlements like Grants and Baintown appear today. Archaeological excavation demonstrates that little use was made of the space in front of the house—not only was there more room in the back of the cabin but also more privacy from the road. Brush grows quickly in the Bahamas, and the five meters between the front of the structure and the road, if left unmaintained, would have sprouted quickly into a natural privacy screen. During excavation, it was clear that most passersby who used the road regularly had no idea that the cabins at Clifton existed. If they chose to, the family at Locus H could have lived quite unnoticed at Clifton.

Even today it is not uncommon to find Loyalist-period slave cabins occupied by contemporary families on the small, less-populated Family Islands of the Bahamian archipelago. The small houses are designed with open floor plans, with doors and windows oriented to catch prevailing winds. The open roofs allow air to circulate throughout the house to create a natural air-conditioning unit. The houses are much more comfortable than would be expected. Still, houses are mainly used for sleeping and storage. Most daytime activities take place outside in the yard (Wilkie 1996). Cooking, childcare, chatting, eating, and laundry all take place in the yard areas of the house. Agricultural fields are usually located a short distance from the house. In buildings that have been powered by gas generators, electric stoves can be found; for other houses, limestone mortar ovens built in the yard are still used.

Excavations in the Locus H houseyard demonstrated that this pattern of space usage is long established in the Bahamas. The yard of H contained the foundation of an oven surrounded by food remains, particularly burnt animal bone and broken ceramics as well as the posts from a sunshade. Food preparation and consumption took place under the shade. After the Wylly period, there is no evidence that any sustained occupation of the house took place until the 1930s. Bottle manufacturing marks, Depression-glass patterns, and the presence of early plastics suggest the house was intensively occupied from the mid-1930s through the end of the 1950s (Luckey 1986; Toulouse 1971; United States General Patent Office 1913). At that time, the Loyalist period oven must have still been recognizable. Food preparation activities continued to be focused in that area.

There are distinct differences between the yard usage in the Loyalist versus post-emancipation period. A much smaller amount of space was utilized around the house in the latter period. While the first occupants of the house utilized at least 10 meters of yard extending back from the rear of the house, the twentieth-century inhabitants concentrated their activities predominantly in the area extending six meters back from the house. Similarly, while the distribution of materials during the Loyalist period suggested extensive yard-sweeping, with highest concentrations appearing in natural solution holes or along the yard perimeter, the trash from the twentieth century was more uniformly distributed across the yard surface. Of course, these differences could represent a difference in the age of the household's occupants. Yard-sweeping is rigorous work, and aging occupants may maintain a smaller yard and be less vigilant about the intensity of their sweeping. The recovery of a magnifying lens from the excavations may suggest that one of the occupants had failing eyesight, requiring the assistance of the lens.

Still, despite these small differences, the yard life of the twentieth century occupants of Locus H would have looked familiar to the families who had lived in the house in the nineteenth century, while being equally recognizable to many of the twenty-first-century Bahamians who have traveled to the out islands or driven through the

"African" villages of Gambier, Baintown, and Grants Town, also on New Providence. Looks can be deceiving, however.

Household Economic Activities and Self-Sufficiency: Material Culture

The material culture from Locus H demonstrates both evidence of self-sufficiency and a remarkable degree of connectedness to the global economy. The lands of Clifton are rich in natural resources. The village of Clifton is located on a ridge above the sea. Cutting along stone fence lines through the bush, it takes about 10 minutes to walk from the house at Locus H to the coast. The lands of Clifton wrap around a calm bay with reefs easily accessible from shore without a boat—the only circumstance where this occurs on the island. In addition, the westernmost edge of the property is characterized by a high outcropping that makes a sheer drop into the water. From this outcropping, one can sit on land and fish in deep waters. Most of the reef species can be caught easily in fishing pots or with nets. Conch, West Indian top shell (known locally as whelk), chiton, and a range of bivalves are available at the shore. Today freshwater swamps dot the property and draw water birds. Raccoons, a species introduced to the islands in the Loyalist period, thrive on the property. Coco plums, seagrapes, and other local fruits are found at the coast edge; and several tamarind trees, planted by previous generations, still provide a sweet and tangy fruit.

It is possible to draw a significant part of one's living from the land, and archaeological materials demonstrate that a number of local species were consumed. Of the shellfish species recovered, lucine (a clam), whelk, chitons, conch, and crab were the most widely utilized shellfish resources. Snappers, grunts, porgies, sea basses, and wrasses, all easily acquired from Clifton's waters, were also recovered. The individuals recovered are all of a size that could be captured from shore using line, net, or pot. None of the larger species like parrot fish or large groupers, which are often acquired with spears, was found. A single brass fishing hook and several lead strips—which are used as weights on both fishing lines and nets—were found archaeologically, demonstrating that the household procured at least some of their own food from the sea.

Land animals represented were raccoons, water birds, some chickens, and some sheep or goats. There is no indication that the family was involved in any large-scale animal husbandry, apart from potentially raising a few chickens and maybe keeping a goat. Goats are able to forage freely and would be helpful in keep down brush but are also damaging to crops. Raccoons are a problem for families tending any number of fruit trees. Mango farmers on the island regularly kill raccoons both for consumption and as a way of protecting their crops.

Sixteen glass food containers were found at the site, including three mason jars, ten commercially packaged jarred foods, and three condiments (vinegar, salad cream, and Worcestershire sauce). The wet environment of the Bahamas causes iron cans to rust quickly, and it is likely if the household was acquiring other commercially prepared foodstuffs that they likely were also using canned goods. Again, as with the beverage bottles, reuse is always a possibility, particularly since almost all of the glass artifacts recovered from the site were broken. Beverage containers included soda bottles, liquor bottles, beer bottles, and wine bottles, as well as a number of unidentified bottles. Any of these bottles may have been reused for water storage. The vast majority of the bottles (30 of 46) originally contained alcoholic beverages, with pint flasks being the most common. One bottle of Gordon's London Dry Gin and one bottle of Meyer's Rum were identifiable based on embossing.

Obtaining fresh water remains one of the greater challenges of daily life in the Bahamas. Much of the rainwater sinks into the bedrock, and wells are often invaded with brackish water. Even in the cities and towns, many families and businesses often supplement public water or wells with water from cisterns or other rain catchment setups. In rural areas, cisterns and wells provide all of fresh water needs. Among the artifacts recovered from the household dump were three large bleach bottles. While bleach is used in laundry and other cleaning, bleach is still commonly added to wells and cisterns today to "purify" water and kill amoebas and other contaminants. There is no well within the village, but a large solution hole in the bush to the west of the village acts as a natural well. While there is no evidence of a cistern system remaining at the house itself, we cannot dismiss that possibility. In addition, the 46 glass bottles from the site need to be considered, not only for the potential uses of their primary contents but also how they may have been reused for water storage and toting. In particular larger liquor bottles, a wine jug, and the Clorox bottles are large and would be useful for both carrying larger amounts of water between the source and the household and for storing it. While smaller bottles are less useful that way, they are also lighter to carry.

A significant number of medicinal products were also acquired from the site, 22 of the 161 identified objects. Included among this subassemblage were "Moroline," a hair pomade; "Vaseline," which has a wide range of cosmetic and first aid uses; two ointment jars; and a toilet water. The rest of the assemblage includes a range of first aid and medical care products: aspirin, iodine, a homeopathic medicine vial, hydrogen peroxide, two examples of "Ketterer's Liver Klenzor," a Northup and Lyman pharmaceutical bottle, and a number of unembossed medicine bottles. Perhaps it is unseemly to mention that one of the uses of Ketterer's Liver Klenzor was to aid in the treatment of alcoholism (United States Patent Office 1913). Certainly we do not have the archaeological evidence to weigh in. The range of products speaks to both the everyday needs of a household and attempts to self-treat more serious conditions.

The toiletries provide some insight into the social lives of the house's inhabitants. Attention was paid to the treatment of the hair and body. Hairpins, a scrimshaw brooch, a brass finger ring, and a range of ornate buttons and ornamental brass clothing rivets were found in addition to snaps and buttons from work pants. The household of Locus H was not merely scratching out an existence on the abandoned lands of Clifton; they participated in social lives outside the home, lives for which they dressed and groomed.

Table and serving wares recovered from the house were modest but extensive enough to convince us during excavation that we were seeing evidence of a longer-term domestic occupation rather than shorter-term camping. Ceramics included a mug, saucers, and two plates. Glassware, including Depression-glass bowls, plates, and tumblers, made up the majority of the tableware. Depression-glass pieces were often given as promotional items with the sales of groceries or laundry detergent in the United States, and it is interesting to ponder whether these items represent similar acquisition histories in the Bahamas. Two marbles and a jaw harp suggest that children were at least visitors to the household, if not fulltime residents.

Connections and Conclusions

Overall, the objects identified to place of origin demonstrate the connectedness of the Bahamas to the broader British commonwealth of which it was a part. Beer bottles from the site included manufacturers based in Canada and Great Britain. Northup and Lyman pharmaceutical products were manufactured in Toronto. Liquor from Jamaica and England, as well as pre-prepared foodstuffs like salad cream and Worcestershire sauce from England, are additional British commonwealth products in the assemblage. However, the Bahamas remained influenced by their nearby American neighbors as well. Glassware, sodas, beer bottles, medicines, and other household wares manufactured in the United States were found as well—but strikingly, there is no evidence of trade with any of the Spanish Caribbean even though, while illegal during the colonial period, such trade was common.

The faunal remains recovered from the site suggest that a significant proportion of the diet could be drawn from the immediate area of the house. The remainder of the archaeological evidence, however, demonstrates that despite evidence of self-sufficiency, the household was also articulated into a range of local and regional economic networks. The west end of New Providence is still thought of by residents as remote from the urban center of Nassau; yet, while modest, there is nothing meager or impoverished or isolated in the lifestyle evidenced in the archaeology.

We do not know the names or identities of the household members who lived at Locus H in the mid–twentieth century, though it might be possible to identify them from the 1938 Nassoake documents. These residents lived on land they did not own (but may have felt an ancestral entitlement to) and did not pay taxes or otherwise participate in activities that allowed their identities to be explicitly tied to a particular space of the plantation at a particular time. On the surface of things, there is a certain irony in the recognition that it is easier to identify the families who lived on Clifton 200 years ago than it is to identify those who lived there a mere 50 years ago. Even though enslaved people appear in the documentary record as part of property transfers, in slave registers, and in newspaper advertisements, their presence is a by-product of being seen as dehumanized objects—not people.

As residents of the former plantation site, the residents of Locus H were able to create a life that was uniquely Bahamian while also drawing upon the resources of the global system. And they did so while maintaining possession of something that previously enslaved generations had been denied—their privacy. As archaeologists, we would be remiss to interpret their desire to maintain a low profile in the documentary record as evidence that their lives are not worthy of our consideration. In the afterlives of plantations, we can find evidence of the creative and resourceful ways that families created lives as citizens and freed peoples. We have learned much about Caribbean life during enslavement; it is time that we spent as much attention on that which followed.

References

Aarons, G. 1990. History through Archaeology in the Bahamas 1984–1990, The Failures and Successes in Interpreting the Post-Columbus Period. *Journal of Bahamas Historical Society* 12(1):3–8).

Armstrong, D. 2003. *Creole Transformation from Slavery to Freedom.* Gainesville: University of Florida Press.

———. 1990. *The Old Village and the Great House.* Urbana: University of Illinois Press.

Bain, R. 1993. Rosetta Bain vs. Nassoak Limited and O'Brien Loans Limited. Commonwealth of the Bahamas Supreme Court, Nassau, New Providence, The Bahamas.

Baxter, J. 2007. 700 Islands, 3 Analogs. Situating Bahamian Historical Archaeology in Comparative Contexts. *Journal of the Bahamas Historical* Society 29:10–16.

Baxter, J., and J. D. Burton 2006. Building Meaning into Landscape: Building Design and Use at Polly Hill Plantation, San Salvador. *Journal of the Bahamas Historical Society* 28:35–44.

Farnsworth, P. 1996. The Influence of Trade on Bahamian Slave Culture. *Historical Archaeology* 30(4):1–23.

———. 1994. Archaeological Excavations at Promised Land Plantation. *Journal of the Bahamas Historical Society* 16(1):21–29.

———. 1993. Archaeological Excavations at Wade's Green Plantation, North Caicos. *Journal of the Bahamas Historical Society* 15(1):2–10.

Farnsworth, P., and L. A. Wilkie 1999. Excavations at Marine Farm and Great Hope Plantations, Crooked Island, Bahamas. *Journal of the Bahamas Historical Society* 20:19–26.

Gerace, K. S. 1982. The Loyalist Plantations of San Salvador Island, Bahamas. *The Florida Anthropologist* 35(4):216.

Hicks, D. 2007. *"The Garden of the World": An Historical Archaeology of Sugar Landscapes in the Eastern Caribbean.* BAR International Series 1632. Oxford: British Archaeological Reports.

Luckey, C. F. 1986. *Depression Era Glassware.* 2nd ed. Florence, Ala.: Books Americana.

Toulouse, J. 1971. *Bottle Makers and the Marks.* New York: Thomas Nelson.

Turner, G. 1993. An Archaeological Record of Plantation Life in the Bahamas. *Journal of the Bahamas Historical Society* 14(1):30–40.

United States General Patent Office (1913). DOC 6427. United States Congressional Serial Set. Digitized November 18, 2005, University of Michigan, Ann Arbor.

Wilkie, L. A. 1996. House Gardens and Female Identity on Crooked Island. *Journal of the Bahamas Historical Society* 15:32–37.

Wilkie, L. A., and P. Farnsworth 2005. *Sampling Many Pots: An Archaeology of Memory and Tradition at a Bahamian Plantation.* Gainesville: University Press of Florida.

ANNA S. AGBE-DAVIES

Reaching for Freedom, Seizing Responsibility

Archaeology at the Phyllis Wheatley Home for Girls, Chicago

The letters of black men, women, and children seeking to leave the South speak so eloquently of the troubles they faced and their hopes for the future. Letter writers explained that conditions were "getting so bad with us black peple down south hear" (Scott 1919: 336). They decried the starvation wages, the bad treatment, and the prejudice that limited their employment opportunities. One man described conditions in Mobile, Alabama, and ended with a plea to his addressee: "There is nothing here for the colored man but a hard time wich these southern [people] gives us. We has not had any work to do in 4 wks. and everything is high to the colored man so please let me hear from you by return mail. *Please do this for your brother*" (Scott 1919: 329, emphasis added). Appeals to race solidarity appear frequently in the letters and reflect an ideology that drew people northward and shaped their experiences in new communities.

Freedom from /Freedom to

In their letters, potential migrants sketched out their vision of a better life. First and foremost, they wanted to work. Writers saw gainful employment as the means to any number of ends. A second writer from Mobile notes, "This is my native home but it is not fit to live in. . . . I am the mother of 8 children 25 years old and I want to get out of this dog hold because I dont know what I am raising them up for in this place and I want to get to Chicago where I know they will be raised and my husband crazy to get there because he know he can get more to raise his children" (Scott 1919: 332).

Many parents mentioned wanting a good education for their young children and better opportunities generally for the young ones. Sometimes the writers were children themselves: a 15-year-old boy from Texas wondered "can a Colored boy be an artist and make a white man's salary up there" (Scott 1919: 297). A girl the same age from New Orleans had more prosaic goals. After explaining that she sometimes had to work for food, she claimed, "if you will sin me a pass [for transportation north] you will not be sorry i am not no lazy girl i am smart i have got very much learning but i can do any work that come to my hand to do"(Scott 1919: 316). Most of the writers whose letters Emmett Scott published in 1919 were men, and some of them express a longing to be treated "like a man," to speak and act freely, to be respected for one's abilities. Men and women alike framed their desires in terms of providing for themselves and their families along with "the betterment of the race."

The letters were addressed to labor agents, employers, and in particular, the editors of nationally circulating black newspapers such as the Chicago *Defender*. Editorials urging people to abandon the South for new homes and lives in the North were a constant feature of the paper. In many cases, people responded directly to the *Defender* or to a person, company, or agency they saw mentioned in its pages. The readership of the paper based on sales was magnified by the fact that it was also passed hand-to-hand, often circulated by men working as Pullman porters on trains that plied the same lines migrants ultimately boarded to head north. Census and other records clearly indicate that the majority of Illinois's (and by extension, Chicago's) immigrants came from states well connected to the city by rail lines.

Of course all was not peaches and cream when they arrived. Industrial employers found ways to pit the new migrants against striking workers (who by and large refused them admittance into their unions). Many migrants found themselves in jobs where conditions were fairer and less invasive than the paternalistic systems they left behind, but a significant number of fields were still off-limits even to people with appropriate skills (Drake and Cayton 1993 [1945]: 252–262). And though black Chicago initially clustered along the southern portion of the State Street corridor, what may have started out as an economic or social decision was ultimately enforced not by Jim Crow laws but by restrictive real estate covenants. Neighborhood associations in communities surrounding the "Black Belt" used these contracts to prevent white homeowners from renting and/or selling to "colored people" (Spear 1967). This meant that landlords in the nonrestricted areas had a captive audience and therefore could afford to allow the housing stock to deteriorate below levels acceptable elsewhere in the city, yet still charge higher rents (Drake and Cayton 1993 [1945]).

Some of the women who joined this "Great Migration" and its subsequent streams spent some time at the Phyllis Wheatley Home for Girls. From 1908 through the 1960s, the Phyllis Wheatley Association ran a series of these homes. In 1920 their facility operated on the 3200 block of Rhodes Avenue. The census reveals that more than half of the 13 roomers then present were born in either Tennessee or Mississippi. Despite being a "home for *girls*," the average age of the clientele was 31 and included a married woman and two widows (United States Bureau of the Census 1920). The anonymous woman who wrote to the *Defender* from New Orleans in 1917 would have fit right in. "I am thinking of coming to Chicago about the first of June and wants a position. I have very fine references if needed. I am a widow of 28. No children, not a relative living and I can do first class work as house maid and dining room or care for invalid ladies. I am honest and neat and refined with a fairly good education . . . because its very trying for a good girl to be out in a large city by self among strangers is why I would like a good home with good people" (Scott 1919: 317). Her letter also highlights the principal justification for the home's existence: the difficulty of making one's way in a new city as a woman alone.

The black club women who funded and operated the Phyllis Wheatley homes identified this particular need in 1906. Elizabeth Lindsay Davis, the founder of the Phyllis Wheatley Association and an active leader in the National Association of Colored Women's Clubs, described it this way: "The object of the Phyllis Wheatley Home Association is to maintain a home which will solve the problem of the colored girl or woman of good character who come to Chicago for the purpose of advancement, often without relatives, friends or money; to surround them with Christian influences, to elevate the standard of employment and to provide a social or community center. . . . There is no endowment to support the institution . . . the only of its kind that has been managed entirely by race women and supported almost entirely by colored people" (Davis 1922: 95). At the time she wrote those words, the association was actively seeking to purchase a new home because they had outgrown the facility on Rhodes. The women of the Phyllis Wheatley Association felt a special responsibility to protect and educate their newly arrived sisters by ensuring that they had the support and infrastructure they needed to find their way in the city and become a credit to their race.

The house the club women settled on was on the 5100 block of Michigan Avenue in a neighborhood that in 1920 was solidly white but by 1930 had become part of an expanding "Black Metropolis." The women who lived there at the time of the 1930 census differed slightly from their sisters a decade earlier. The 28 boarders had an average age of 24, and over a third had been born in the Midwest, perhaps the daughters of an earlier generation of migrants. One 22-year-old resident was a student, but 17 of the "girls" worked in private homes as servants. Five of the women worked in factories, and four had pink-collar jobs in offices and stores (United States Bureau of the Census 1930). St. Clair Drake and Horace Cayton (1993 [1945]), using data from the same year, observed that the majority of black working women in Chicago toiled as servants, while another third worked in skilled or semiskilled industry jobs, whereas less than 5 percent of black women workers held clerical positions. It may be that women with the wherewithal to seek out the home had better employment prospects. Perhaps residence in or training at the home prepared women for "better" employment. A large number of residents were servants, but more worked as skilled factory operatives and at what Drake and Cayton (1993 [1945]) called "clean" jobs than was typical of black women in the city (see Wolcott 2001 on the preference among women migrants for nondomestic work).

Despite the trials and hurdles to be overcome, once settled in Chicago the ideal of "freedom" persisted for the city's migrants. The concept was a common thread running through respondents surveyed by Chicago's Commission on Race Relations in

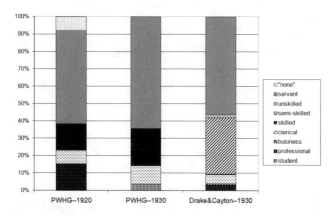

Occupations of black working women in Chicago, Illinois.

the early 1920s (Chicago Commission on Race Relations 1922: 100–101).[1] Twenty-one replies to the question "What do you like about the North?" appeared in the commission's final report:

1) **Freedom** in voting and conditions of colored people here. I mean you can live in good houses; men here get a chance to go with the best-looking girls in the race; some may do it in Memphis, but it ain't always safe.
2) **Freedom** and chance to make a living; privileges.
3) **Freedom** and opportunity to acquire something
4) **Freedom** allowed in every way
5) More money and more pleasure to be gotten from it; personal **freedom** Chicago affords, and voting.
6) **Freedom** and working conditions.
7) Work, can work any place, **freedom**
8) The schools for the children, the better wages, and the privileges for colored people.
9) The chance colored people have to live; privileges allowed them and better homes.
10) The friendliness of the people, the climate which makes health better.
11) Like the privileges, the climate; have better health.
12) No discrimination; can express opinion and vote.
13) **Freedom** of speech, right to live and work as other races. Higher pay for labor.
14) **Freedom**; privileges; treatment of whites; ability to live in peace; not held down.

1. The Commission was convened in response to a riot in 1919 that claimed the lives of 23 black Chicagoans and 15 white Chicagoans (537 injured).

15) **Freedom** of speech and action. Can live without fear, no Jim Crow.
16) More enjoyment; more places of attraction; better treatment; better schools for children.
17) Liberty, better schools.
18) I like the North for wages earned and better homes colored people can live in and go more places than at home.
19) Privileges, **freedom**, industrial and educational facilities.
20) The people, the **freedom** and liberty colored people enjoy here that they never before experienced. Even the ways of the people are better than at home.
21) Haven't found anything yet to like, except wife thinks she will like the opportunity of earning more money than ever before.[2]

People generally reported that they experienced greater freedom in Chicago than they had "at home."

This introduction provides a glimpse into how black Chicagoans of the twentieth century may have regarded the idea of "freedom" and how they viewed their responsibilities. In this essay, I use the writings of pragmatist philosopher John Dewey to provide a framework for using "freedom" and "responsibility" as analytical concepts. Then, the essay turns toward a consideration of how these concepts can be applied to the study of the material record at the Phyllis Wheatley Home for Girls and how that dataset complements other sources of information about the Great Migration. I next compare this analysis of the recent African American past with more traditional approaches to African American "freedom" at more traditional African American archaeological sites, namely those associated with plantation slavery. The essay concludes with a discussion of freedom and responsibility in twenty-first-century Chicago and in archaeological practice more generally.

Freedom as an Analytical Concept and Its Connection with Responsibility

As archaeologists, our understandings of what freedom may consist of at any point in time, or for any person or group, are mediated by the fact that we approach people through their material culture. So we need to think about several issues: (1) how was freedom defined and constructed in the past; (2) what do *we* mean by freedom; and (3) how can material culture speak to both of these issues? Furthermore, I argue that there are intangible or ephemeral, as well as material, manifestations of freedom. These ideas shape the following discussion of the freedom sought by black Americans as they flooded northern cities during the "Great Migration" and the

2. There is little contextual information in the report regarding the circumstances of this questioning, that is, race of interviewer, number of respondents and representativeness of the printed responses, written or oral responses, etc.

ensuing comparison of the freedom sought by the founders of the United States with that of the men and women they claimed to own.

John Dewey's essay "What is Freedom?" (Dewey 1966 [1922]) offers a useful framework for considering some of the notions of freedom that archaeologists might bring to their analyses. He wrote to refute the notion that freedom can be understood and identified in the abstract, exclusively in metaphysical terms. He sought to bring these notions back down to earth and situate them in a real world of experiences, social relations, and things. According to Dewey, "freedom" has three main components: that one be able to carry out plans without being thwarted, that one be able to vary one's plans, and that desire or choice be factors in those plans and variations. Contrariwise, "the slave is a man who executes the wish of others, one doomed to act along lines predetermined to regularity" (Dewey 1966 [1922]: 81–82). So we might ask to what extent were migrants able to carry out their plans, pre- and post-migration, and what role did choice play in the execution of said plans?

These, I would argue, are questions apart from an analyst's evaluation of the autonomy of these people as limited by, for example, structural racism or class exploitation and conflict. While we need not suppress the perspective made possible by our analytical distance from the scene, neither should we ignore the opportunity to evaluate life in the Black Metropolis on its own terms. And as historical archaeologists, we might inquire how texts *and* material culture together illuminate our understanding of the pursuit of freedom in this social context.

As it happens, responsibility is a subtext in both the contemporaneous texts under consideration here and in Dewey's analysis. The testimony of migrants themselves can be used to assess their quest for freedom and the responsibilities they accepted alongside. The letter writers, along with the hundreds of thousands of peers they represent, sought freedom—not in the abstract, not for its own sake, but in order to more fully meet their responsibilities. Men, in particular, described the difficulty of providing for their families in the absence of a living wage. Men and women alike were willing to take on *any* work: skilled and highly educated workers offered to become common laborers; unskilled workers fantasized about opportunities to learn trades that were closed to them at home. Parents wanted to send their children to better schools and rear them in a society that encouraged their ambitions. Strivers sought to demonstrate what members of the race were capable of accomplishing. The survey respondents give us an opportunity to evaluate the results. As far as "intangibles" are concerned, they praised the schools and the lack of discrimination, particularly in terms of employment. They reveled in the opportunity to partake in the social life of the city, to speak their minds, and to vote. As for *material* results, these people emphasized good wages, better homes, and good health as consequences of their migration. To all the world, this sounds like the successful integration of freedom and responsibility on Dewey's terms. He writes, "To forsee future objective alternatives and to be able by deliberation to choose one of them and thereby weight its chances in the struggle for future existence, measures our freedom. *It is assumed sometimes that if it can be shown that deliberation determines choice and deliberation is determined by characteristics and conditions, there is no freedom. . . .* The question is not what are the antecedents of deliberation and choice, but what are the consequences" (Dewey 1966 [1922]: 87, emphasis added).

I emphasize the matter of determination because of the tendency by analysts, even those working contemporaneously with the phenomenon, to evaluate freedom (we might also call it power) in the abstract, neglecting its operation in real social worlds. While we may note, along with the Chicago Commission on Race Relations (1922), deplorable housing conditions as created by the covenants described above, we must also take seriously the assertions of thinking men and women who claim that their efforts have resulted in "good," even "better" housing. Likewise, we can identify the effects of racism in 1920s Chicago, but we also need to acknowledge and attempt to understand statements by black residents describing a lack of discrimination in the city. This is not to say that we should ignore the racial ideologies and other social structures that shaped the experiences of black Chicagoans, but that the fact of those structures cannot negate the possibility of free action. It could be that archaeology's emphasis on the material puts us in a better position to negotiate this tension than analysts who would rely on texts alone.

The Material Correlates of Freedom Struggles

The Great Migration and later flows are inscribed on the Chicago landscape in the form of demographic patterns, buildings, and, of course, archaeological deposits. Though Christopher Reed (2005) rightly asserts, "we have been here since the beginning,"[3] the social landscape of Chicago was remarkably altered by the rapid influx of several hundred thousand people of African descent, many of them in the 1910s and 1920s. Recent migrants were assisted by those who had come before, but they also faced pressure from more-established black Chicagoans to conform to their norms. The Urban League worked to change the city, to make it more receptive to migrants. It also worked to mold the migrants into an image that justified claims to equality and freedoms for *all* black people in the city. An ideology of "respectability" organized the efforts of race leaders to cement their own status and to "uplift" the masses (Drake and Cayton 1993 [1945]: 710; Wolcott 2001); the club women of the Phyllis Wheatley Association were no exception.

The association was an offshoot of the Phyllis Wheatley Club, whose members enjoyed lectures, dances, teas, and the like as membership benefits. Many of those

3. Indeed, Chicago's founding by Jean Baptiste Pointe DuSable, a man of African descent and the first-known nonnative to settle within the current city limits, is well known and oft-repeated by modern residents of the city.

events acted as fundraisers for club projects, such as the home. The activities for club and association members stand in contrast to those offered to home residents and other clients. In addition to room and board for a limited number of women, the Phyllis Wheatley Association also offered employment contacts and instruction designed to enhance the employability of recent migrants (Knupfer 1997). Courses usually emphasized domestic science and in many ways recalled the club's early work to promote effective household management in club members' *own* homes. However, the later courses for home clients prepared them for the "private homes" in which so many recent female migrants were employed.

If the instruction was anything like what was offered by social service organizations in Detroit, part of the home could have served as a laboratory for practicing the techniques taught to the girls. While the impact of such activities on the archaeological assemblage remains to be analyzed, it is certainly clear that the residents practiced what the club women preached when it comes to the exterior spaces of the home. The backyard appears to have a higher artifact density and a more midden-like quality to the deposits: more food and dining refuse, highly fragmented items, and complex stratification. The front yard, however, contains fewer discrete deposits, with fewer artifacts. Black arbiters of respectability were particularly keen that residents in their neighborhoods maintain clean and orderly yards to refute racist expectations of squalor. Elizabeth Lindsay Davis, one of the founders of the club and association, describes greeting newly arrived families with pamphlets "making an appeal for cleanliness, respect for public property, orderly conduct in the street and the best possible upkeep of the household" (Davis 1922: 38). Future directions for comparative analysis include an assessment of how the finds from semi-institutional spaces like the home compare with those from the private residences in which the club women lived.

The home's superintendent, assistant superintendent, cook, and matron all lived on site, acting as agents of the association and no doubt providing plenty of supervision. These women were responsible for the upkeep of the home, to be sure, but also for the virtue of its residents and the reinforcement of the association's ideals. While the girls were not institutionalized in the sense that inmates or patients are (see De Cunzo 2006), the staff would have modeled respectable comportment, enforced home rules, and maintained the material surroundings that supported the association's mission. Information regarding this aspect of life at the home is most likely to come from material evidence, particularly the fabric of the building itself, which is to be the focus of the upcoming season of investigation. This is because the very limited archive of the Phyllis Wheatley Association is restricted to later periods of the home's occupation, when residents were as likely to be students as working women (Anonymous 1908/1967; Joann Tate, personal communication 2006, 2009). Even so, it is clear that in later years the association and its agents continued to feel responsible for the girls entrusted to their care.

Material culture is likewise an underutilized medium for examining the transformation of certain sectors of the South Side from all-white or racially heterogeneous populations to increasingly all-black populations. In 1920 the owner-occupant of the home-to-be was a young widow, living alone. She and all of her neighbors, a mix of native-born and immigrant families, were white (United States Bureau of the Census 1920). Ten years later, the home's neighbors were all Negroes, most of them born in the South. Also, in 1930 a larger proportion of the neighborhood's residents were lodgers—households' response to Depression-era wages and an artificially high demand for housing (United States Bureau of the Census 1930). This marks a rapid change from 1920, or from 1910, when many of the renters had live-in servants, or even 1900, when the houses were nearly new and many of them owner-occupied. To date, most of the deposits uncovered pertain to the home period and later, but there are scattered finds from earlier occupations that will complement what we know about neighborhood transitions from texts, written and oral. Certainly the overwhelming archaeological visibility of later periods signifies the intensification of use that attended the incorporation of this neighborhood into the Black Metropolis during the 1920s.

While club women and newly arrived girls partook of the freedoms associated with their lives in the city, they also had significant responsibilities with material implications. The home was a project to provide for the needs of migrant women, certainly, but it was also a part of a much larger endeavor: to uplift the race (Hendricks 1998; Knupfer 1997, 2006). The women who founded the home used their considerable organizational energies to bring about change in fields deemed appropriate for women: youth, the home, and virtuous living. The women who lodged there had seized the responsibility to change their own lives by moving to a new city. Both groups had to negotiate the difficult terrain of "respectability" and the unique burdens that ideology placed on black women. The racial ideology at work in early-twentieth-century Chicago, as in the rest of the United States, denied the respectability of black women, making them susceptible to sexual harassment and exploitation by employers, a significant hazard of domestic work in private homes whether in the South or North (Powdermaker 1993 [1939]; Wolcott 2001). Though Drake and Cayton (1993 [1945]: 710–714) diagnosed pressures to conform to acceptable standards of behavior as originating in class distinctions, it is also true that middle-class and elite African American women felt that their own position in society was at risk when other members of the race transgressed. Archaeology provides a means to identify the material manifestations of these challenges and also how material culture was used to negotiate this terrain. It furthermore gives us an opportunity to see these issues from multiple perspectives. Texts inform us of the stated desires and standards of the club women—what was the response of their migrant sisters? An initial examination of the artifactual record reveals a concern for appearance: costume jewelry, cosmetics cases, and evidence of quality clothing take on additional meaning given

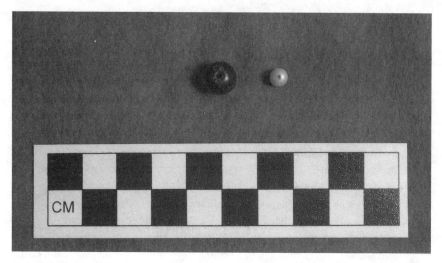

Beads excavated from the Phyllis Wheatley Home for Girls. Courtesy of the author.

the exhortations that even women engaged in domestic work refrain from wearing "boudoir caps" or "bungalow aprons"—their badges of service—on the street (Wolcott 2001). For while the club women supported the home, available records do not document their constant presence there, thus for the time being, we attribute these personal items to the girls themselves.

Previous historical analysis suggests that most of the training provided at the home was geared toward eventual domestic employment (Knupfer 1996). It may be that club women advanced such courses with the idea that the professionalization of domestic work would change employers' perceptions about domestic workers, thus protecting the girls from harassment and abuse. The assemblage recovered from the home does not appear to demonstrate unusual emphasis on modern or scientific principles of household management (Agbe-Davies 2009), but it may be that further comparison with contemporaneous sites or sites with similar agendas (for example, De Cunzo 1995; Spencer-Wood 1987) will reveal such subtle differences.

Degrees of Freedom

One theme I am interested in exploring with additional analysis is a comparison between sites "at home" in places like Mississippi, Tennessee, Alabama, and Georgia, on the one hand, and contemporary sites in the Black Metropolis on the other. When I first started thinking about these issues before starting work at the home, I asked myself what would we learn, really, by comparing and contrasting the material conditions faced by black Chicagoans with those faced by their brothers and sisters in the South. Could we say using those data who had greater freedom? Literally, "Can we—from where we stand—presume to know better than they" (Agbe-Davies 2006)? At the time, I was thinking about the theoretical and critical problems associated with comparisons based on artifact cost, or "status" (see Singleton 1995 for a discussion). Now I see the issue as less a matter of a cost-benefit analysis of some freedom quotient and more to do with providing a context or backdrop for understanding the transformative experience of migration. Comparing freedom at the Phyllis Wheatley Home for Girls with conditions in the South also begs the question of comparison with earlier, pre-emancipation sites, such as the plantation sites I studied in Virginia before commencing fieldwork in Illinois. While the danger in Virginia is failing to capture the true meaning of what it means to deny a population their freedom, the danger in Illinois is an uncritical romanticization of the quest for freedom, pre- or postemancipation, and the exaggeration of that freedom's extent.

Excavations on late-eighteenth-century Virginia plantations must confront the ideology of the time that allowed planters to "declare" their own freedom yet still hold people in bondage. Governor Dunmore exploited this disconnect and countered Thomas Jefferson's Declaration by issuing a Proclamation of his own: freedom for any servant or slave who took up arms in defense of the Crown (Dunmore 1775; Isaac 2004; Morgan 1975). The quarter site at Phillip Ludwell's Rich Neck plantation may well have been abandoned as a result of Dunmore's Proclamation. On the other hand, the residents may have absconded during the chaos surrounding the battle of Green Spring, after which as many as 70 men, women, and children fled the Williamsburg-area plantations owned by the Ludwell family (Franklin 2004: 32, 164). Either way, it seems that Afro-Virginians of the eighteenth century had a pretty clear concept of freedom, and many may have agreed with John Dewey's assertion that "Variability, initiative, innovation, departure from routine, experimentation . . . it is their elimination from the life of a slave which makes his life servile, intolerable to the freeman who has once been on his own, no matter what his animal comfort and security. A free man would rather take his chance in an open world than be guaranteed in a closed world" (Dewey 1966 [1922]: 86). Yet because of archaeologists' reliance on the material record, we often come up with concepts of freedom that would be totally foreign to those people who clearly had occasional access to the trappings of gentility yet did not consider *being* a material possession a price worth paying for their own material possessions.

As noted, archaeologists have tried and rejected perspectives that see freedom in the market or prestige value of goods. Nevertheless we try to approach an understanding of what "freedoms" may have existed in their worlds. For example, Fraser Neiman (1997) has argued that one of the factors determining the arrangement and use of subfloor pits is the degree to which the residents of a quarter dwelling were related to and/or trusted their co-residents. So a reduction in the number of subfloor pits may be a material indicator of the control a household could wield over its internal composition—to what degree they exercised freedom of association. Maria Franklin's (2001) analysis of the faunal remains from Rich Neck and Joanne Bowen's (1996) comparative studies have remarked on the presence of wild fauna from later-eighteenth-century quarters. Can we interpret the spectrum of meat foods eaten as evidence of "varying one's plans"? Do bones that demonstrate hunting and fishing show that one is "able to carry out plans without being thwarted"? Are these varieties of freedom? And is it accurate, or possible, to argue this without trivializing the bondage of the people whose lives we are describing?

Archaeologists have for many years attempted to understand the extent to which people who were owned could or would participate in the "Consumer Revolution" of the eighteenth and nineteenth centuries, with an emphasis on the consumption of increasingly specialized and refined ceramics (see, for example, Moore 1985; Otto 1984). Consider the results obtained by Jillian Galle and Fraser Neiman (2003) when they compared the relative abundance of different categories of ceramics from a range of quarter sites in the Virginia Piedmont and Tidewater: Mount Vernon's House for Families, Stratford Hall's ST 116, and Monticello's Buildings *l, o, r,* and *s,* and Site 8.[4] They discovered that some vessels that archaeologists have argued reflect ceramic sophistication and/or participation in the consumer revolution were present at varying rates on these sites and that the one outlying quarter (Monticello's Site 8) really stood out from the other sites in terms of the occupants' use of tea ware and chamber pots (low) and utilitarian wares (high).

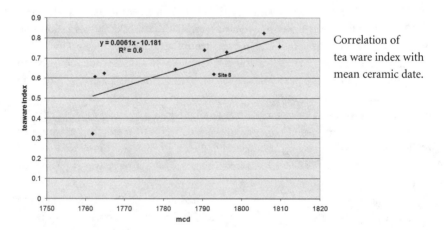

Correlation of tea ware index with mean ceramic date.

4. The recent availability of a large, standardized database of quarter sites in the Digital Archaeological Archive of Comparative Slavery (www.daacs.org) allows us to address this question with a range of quarter sites in relation to one another rather than focusing on only a few at a time or in relation to a written record.

I compared their findings with two additional outlying quarters, Rich Neck and Palace Lands quarters, to determine if proximity to the owner—and all that that entails—could be the principal factor governing access to these wares. When the other two outlying quarters—which also happened to be earlier than the Monticello sites—were included, Site 8 began to look much more like its contemporaries. In fact the prevalence in the assemblages of tea ware, for example, was closely correlated with mean ceramic date and may not have had as much to do with proximity to the owner or access to markets as date of deposit. If *this* is the case, then the acquisition and use of these items may tell us less than we anticipated about choice and capacity to carry out plans on the part of the quarters' residents. While excellent arguments have been made for the use of consumer goods to inculcate or project refinement (for example, Bell 2003; Mullins 1999), it may be that the measures we often use in plantation archaeology speak more to the availability of certain forms over time than to whether or not slaves were free to consume despite their legal/social status. In the analysis summarized above, two interesting exceptions to the correlation with time of deposit were the abundance of chamber pots and of utilitarian wares. *These specific forms,* then, might be an important means to start to understand the diversity of experiences of enslavement, rather than focusing on variables such as cost or decorative style. For archaeologists we need to think critically about what material patterns represent the "choices" central to an approach grounded in Dewey's understanding of freedom.

Freedom and Responsibility in the Twenty-First Century

The covenants that created the Black Belt were finally ruled unenforceable in 1948, but their effect on the city's contemporary racial geography is clear to this day. Chicago is a notoriously segregated city even in the twenty-first century. The racial makeup of the South Side has added resonance because of the recent resurgence of neighborhood property values. The area that has traditionally been the cultural and commercial center of black Chicago is being rapidly overtaken by new construction. The grand greystone homes like the Phyllis Wheatley Home that line the boulevards are being rehabbed for new residents or torn down. The (in)famous projects of the Chicago Housing Authority—Robert Taylor Homes, Stateway Gardens, and others— are now largely demolished, just as earlier neighborhoods such as "the Shacks" and "Federal Street" were to make way for those self-same projects under the guise of urban renewal (for analysis, see Hyra 2008; Pattillo 2007). South Side residents are alarmed by these rapid changes in their neighborhoods and the potential loss of historically and culturally significant landmarks. Should developers, including public housing agencies, have the freedom to purchase and build wherever the market takes them? Will current residents have the freedom to claim the benefits that come along with a more affluent population? Will they be free to stay?

The gentrification process in the Black Metropolis is slightly different from even other areas of Chicago. In this case, both the current residents and the gentrifiers are black, which changes the racial dimensions of the process and foregrounds its class aspects (M. Boyd 2005; M. R. Boyd 2008). While tensions abound, ethnographic work by Mary Patillo (2007: 301–302) indicates that even the incoming "gentry," so easily demonized for displacing those without the power or wealth to remain in their own neighborhoods, feel, and attempt to act on, a great sense of responsibility for their erstwhile neighbors.

Archaeologists must consider questions of freedom and responsibility in our own practice, as well. These issues are often raised by archaeologists who work closely with stakeholder communities, particularly regarding the question of who sets the agenda (for example, Derry 1997; McKee 1994). "Do I study the sites that excite the communities within which I work or the ones that interest me? Do I have any right to consider the work that I do 'public' (or 'applied' or 'activist' or 'engaged,' etc.) if it springs more from my research agenda than the agendas of those I purport to work for and with? What about my freedom?" (Agbe-Davies 2006).

When I wrote these words, I had yet to meet the people who would lead me to the Phyllis Wheatley Home for Girls. In the years since, I have seen what is possible when the archaeologist is truly a collaborating partner within, rather than the driving force behind, a community-based archaeological project. The excavation and analysis is my responsibility, but my coconspirators, Joann Tate and Bobbie Johnson, take the lead on developing community outreach and nonuniversity educational aspects of the project. When we first started, Ms. Johnson told me in no uncertain terms that the old model of community research so familiar to the residents of the Black Metropolis was not going to work—that I was not to come in and get my data but leave my hosts, guides, and mentors with nothing to show for it. I have found a significant amount of freedom within the collaborative framework we have established and hope that I have begun to meet my responsibilities to the partners who have been so generous to me.

The individuals and organizations with whom I have worked to reveal the story of this home for girls are continuing the legacy of the club women of the Phyllis Wheatley Association. They have taken responsibility for the education of the city's youth, the preservation of Chicago's African American history, and, yes, the uplift of the race (Agbe-Davies 2008). Whatever archaeology can contribute to their efforts (Little and Shackel 2007), I believe it is my responsibility to make it happen.

Coda

Dewey claimed that freedom is marked by volition. I would add one more criterion, drawing on the writing of Walter Mosley. Perhaps better known for his Easy Rawlins detective novels and science fiction than political philosophy, Mosley has neverthe-less articulated an interesting next step in the pursuit of freedom. His thesis in *What Next: A Memoir toward World Peace* is that African America has a special role to play in the current geopolitical climate. Mosley argues that we experience freedom only insofar as we build a world in which all others can be free, according to lines very similar to those outlined by Dewey. Mosley (2003) further maintains that, because of our history in this country, black Americans are uniquely equipped to address the problems that face the nation today. Having lived with both exploitation and domes-tic terrorism, we can move in the spaces between the overwhelming hegemony of the United States and its corporations and those global populations who are exploited by the same (Mosley 2003: 138). In his words: "We cannot be quiet. Even if our voices cause conflict and consternation . . . even if there is danger involved, we have to remember our responsibilities. We are the bright sons and daughters of America's tragic beginning. We are at least part of the answer to making it right" (Mosley 2003: 88–89).

The first time I made the connection between Mosley, Dewey, and African dias-pora archaeology, I commented (in a somewhat flippant manner) on the influence of our then current and immediately past secretaries of state: Condoleeza Rice and Colin Powell. As I revisit this topic, we have just witnessed the inauguration of Presi-dent Barack Obama. Having observed the progress of the campaign and the response of my fellow citizens to his election, I give even more credit to Mosley for being able to anticipate the significance of black leadership in our nation's future and our long-ing for security and justice.

Acknowledgments

I am grateful, first of all, for the opportunity to work with such inspiring collabo-rative partners, especially Joann Tate, owner of the former Phyllis Wheatley Home for Girls. The excavations at the site have been sponsored by DePaul University, with artifact analysis in particular facilitated by the Undergraduate Research Assis-tant Program. I have learned a great deal from my two field school co-directors, Rebecca Graff and J. Eric Deetz. Many thanks to Jillian Galle for recalculating the results for the nine quarter sites I was interested in and for talking me through the use of estimated vessel equivalencies (EVEs) and indices as measures of ceramic abundance (Galle, personal communication 2005). The ideas expressed in this chap-ter have benefited from thoughtful comments in a variety of forums, including dis-cussant remarks by Barbara Voss and Neil Silberman. Thanks finally to Jodi Barnes for bringing together such a vibrant group of scholars to think critically about the potential and challenges of using archaeology to explore the recent African Ameri-can past.

References

Agbe-Davies, A. S. 2006. Material Approaches to Freedom in African America. Paper presented at the Society for Historical Archaeology Annual Meeting, Sacramento, Calif.

————. 2008. Community Archaeology in Bronzeville: The Phyllis Wheatley Home for Girls. *Ohio Valley Historical Archaeology* 23:23–30.

————. 2009. Archaeology as a Tool to Illuminate and Support Community Struggles in the Black Metropolis of the 20th and 21st Centuries. Paper presented at the Society for Historical Archaeology Annual Meeting, Toronto, Canada.

Anonymous 1908/1967. Phyllis Wheatley Association Collection. Unpublished collection of papers on file, University of Illinois, Chicago.

Bell, A. 2003. Articulations of Ceramic Use and Socio-Economic Circumstance: Investigations of Late 18th-Century Virginia Sites Using the Digital Archaeological Archive of Chesapeake Slavery. Paper presented at the Society for Historical Archaeology Annual Meeting, Providence, R.I.

Bowen, J. 1996. Foodways in the 18th-Century Chesapeake. In *The Archaeology of 18th-Century Virginia*, edited by T. R. Reinhart, 87–130. Richmond, Va.: Spectrum Press.

Boyd, M. 2005. The Downside of Racial Uplift: The Meaning of Gentrification in an African American Neighborhood. *City & Society* 17(2):265–288.

Boyd, M. R. 2008. *Jim Crow Nostalgia: Reconstructing Race in Bronzeville.* Minneapolis: University of Minnesota Press.

Chicago Commission on Race Relations 1922. *The Negro in Chicago: A Study of Race Relations and a Race Riot.* Chicago: University of Chicago.

Davis, E. L. 1922. *The Story of the Illinois Federation of Colored Women's Clubs.* New York: G. K. Hall & Co.

De Cunzo, L.A. (1995) Reform, Respite, Ritual: An Archaeology of Institutions; The Magdalen Society of Philadelphia, 1800–1850. *Historical Archaeology* 29(3):iii–168.

————. 2006. Exploring the Institution: Reform, Confinement, Social Change. In *Historical Archaeology*, edited by M. Hall and S. W. Silliman, pp. 167–189. Oxford: Blackwell Publishing.

Derry, L. 1997. Pre-Emancipation Archaeology: Does It Play in Selma, Alabama? *Historical Archaeology* 31(3):18–26.

Dewey, J. 1966 [1922]. What is Freedom? In *John Dewey on Education*, edited by R. D. Archambault, pp. 81–88. New York: The Modern Library.

Drake, S. C., and H. A. Cayton 1993 [1945]. *Black Metropolis: A Study of Negro Life in a Northern City.* Chicago: University of Chicago Press.

Dunmore, J. 1775. A Proclamation. Canada's Digital Collections. Electronic document, http://collections.ic.gc.ca/blackloyalists/documents/official/dunmore.htm, accessed December 12, 2005.

Franklin, M. 2001. The Archaeological Dimensions of Soul Food: Interpreting Race, Culture, and Afro-Virginian Identity. In *Race and the Archaeology of Identity*, edited by C. Orser, pp. 88–107. Salt Lake City: University of Utah Press.

————. 2004. *An Archaeological Study of the Rich Neck Slave Quarter and Enslaved Domestic Life.* Colonial Williamsburg Research Publications. Richmond, Va.: Dietz Press

Galle, J. E., and F. Neiman 2003. Patterns of Tea and Tableware Consumption on Late Eighteenth Century Slave Quarter Sites. Paper presented at the Society for Historical Archaeology Annual Meeting, Providence, R.I.

Hendricks, W. A. 1998. *Gender, Race, and Politics in the Midwest: Black Club Women in Illinois.* Bloomington: Indiana University Press.

Hyra, D. A. 2008. *The New Urban Renewal: The Economic Transformation of Harlem and Bronzeville.* Chicago: University of Chicago Press.

Isaac, R. 2004. *Landon Carter's Uneasy Kingdom: Revolution and Rebellion on a Virginia Plantation.* Oxford: Oxford University Press.

Knupfer, A. M. 1996. *Toward a Tenderer Humanity and a Nobler Womanhood: African American Women's Clubs in Turn-of-the-Century Chicago.* New York: New York University Press.

———. 1997. "If You Can't Push, Pull, If You Can't Pull, Please Get Out of the Way": The Phyllis Wheatley Club and Home in Chicago, 1896 to 1920. *Journal of Negro History* 82(2):221–231.

———. 2006. *The Chicago Black Renaissance and Women's Activism.* Urbana: University of Illinois Press.

Little, B. J., and P. A. Shackel (editors) 2007. *Archaeology as a Tool of Civic Engagement.* Lanham, Md.: AltaMira Press.

McKee, L. 1994. Is It Futile to Try and Be Useful? Historical Archaeology and the African-American Experience. *Northeast Historical Archaeology* 23:1–7.

Moore, S. M. 1985. Social and Economic Status on the Coastal Plantation: An Archaeological Perspective. In *The Archaeology of Slavery and Plantation Life*, edited by T .A. Singleton, pp. 141–160. San Diego: Academic Press, Inc.

Morgan, E. S. 1975. *American Slavery, American Freedom: The Ordeal of Colonial Virginia.* New York: W. W. Norton & Company.

Mosley, W. 2003. *What Next: A Memoir toward World Peace.* Baltimore: Black Classic Press.

Mullins, P. R. 1999. *Race and Affluence: An Archaeology of African America and Consumer Culture.* New York: Kluwer Academic.

Neiman, F. D 1997. *Sub-Floor Pits and Slavery in 18th and Early 19th-Century Virginia.* Paper presented at the Society for Historical Archaeology Annual Meeting, Cincinnati, Ohio.

Otto, J. S. 1984. *Cannon's Point Plantation, 1794–1860: Living Conditions and Status Patterns in the Old South.* Orlando: Academic Press.

Pattillo, M. 2007. *Black on the Block: The Politics of Race and Class in the City.* Chicago: University of Chicago Press.

Powdermaker, H. 1993 [1939]. *After Freedom: A Cultural Study in the Deep South.* Madison: University of Wisconsin Press.

Reed, C. R. 2005. *Black Chicago's First Century, Vol. 1, 1833–1900.* Columbia: University of Missouri Press.

Scott, E. J. 1919. Letters of Negro Migrants of 1916–1918. *Journal of Negro History* 4(3):290–340.

Singleton, T. A. 1995. The Archaeology of Slavery in North America. *Annual Review of Anthropology* 24:119–140.

Spear, A. H. 1967. *Black Chicago: The Making of a Negro Ghetto 1890–1920.* Chicago: University of Chicago Press.

Spencer-Wood, S. M. 1987. A Survey of Domestic Reform Movement Sites in Boston and Cambridge, ca. 1865–1905. *Historical Archaeology* 21(2):7–36.

United States Bureau of the Census 1920. *Fourteenth Census of the United States 1920—Population.* Chicago: Department of Commerce, Bureau of the Census.

———. 1930. *Fifteenth Census of the United States 1920—Population.* Chicago: Department of Commerce, Bureau of the Census.

Wolcott, V. W. 2001. *Remaking Respectability: African American Women in Interwar Detroit.* Chapel Hill: University of North Carolina Press.

MEGAN ANN TEAGUE AND JAMES M. DAVIDSON

Victorian Ideals and Evolving Realities

Late-Nineteenth- and Early-Twentieth-Century
Black Dallas and an Engendered African America

Modern perceptions of gender are deeply rooted in the late nineteenth and early twentieth centuries, when contemporary gender roles first began to emerge. During this period, gender roles within African American society were arguably distinct from European American patriarchy. Black urban society in the old American Southwest was additionally distinctive from the Deep South's rural social systems and economies. In this essay, we argue that post-emancipation members of black Dallas transformed their gender and childhood ideologies from previous social models formed under enslavement, using at least some of the ideals of white Victorian life, while simultaneously struggling under the constraints placed on them by white Victorian hegemony.

Barbara Little made the distinction between "an anthropology of gender ... (and) a feminist anthropology" (1994: 190). According to Little, an engendered archaeology would search for and examine the artifacts of women, toward the goal of delineating women's contributions or roles in the past, while a feminist archaeology would rather attempt to illuminate and expose past social constructions of gender roles (and theoretically other social constructions, such as race). By exposing past gender roles as constructions (and not essentialized determinants), feminist archaeology would be active politically in their present-day deconstruction (Little 1994: 190).

Scholars such as Gwendolyn Simmons (2007) and bell hooks (1981) have argued that black women were largely omitted from the women's liberation movement as well as the later historical interpretation of these events. While middle- and upper-class white women were fighting for the right to work outside the home, labor for black women was the norm from the beginnings of enslavement in the 1500s and extending with little exception into the twentieth century. Clearly both an engendered and a black feminist approach are paramount and necessary in African diasporic archaeology, at the very least because the traditional white model simply does not conform to the black experience (for example, Franklin 2001).

While of great significance, observing the formation, or the transformation, of gender roles in American society in the nineteenth and twentieth centuries is difficult archaeologically (cf., Little 1994). With the goal of viewing gender on equal footing with race, ethnicity, and class, gender and the role of women have been examined in brothels, saloons (Seifert 1991; Spude 2005), and even prisons (Nobles 2000), but when attempting to define women's roles and lives in nineteenth- and early-twentieth-century America, researchers most often rely upon household archaeology and artifacts suggestive of feminine domesticity, such as tea ware or thimbles and other sewing tools (Beaudry 2006; Brown 1994; Clements 1993; Fitts 1999; Spencer-Wood 1996, 1999; Wall 1991, 1999). Dallas has seen little in the way of household archaeology, and those rare examples (for example, Juliette Street, see below, and Davidson 2004a) have been disturbed by development and yield limited information. In this research we propose an alternative approach to examine gender roles in black Dallas in the Reconstruction and immediate post-Reconstruction eras using data derived from mortuary contexts. Previous researchers have often ignored historic cemetery excavations in regard to gender, though one preliminary study by Wilson and Cabek (2004) examined gender patterns in six late-nineteenth- and early-twentieth-century cemeteries in the South.

Our primary window into this past is through the mortal remains exhumed from Freedman's Cemetery in Dallas, Texas. Freedman's Cemetery was founded on April 29, 1869, and closed on July 26, 1907. The Freedman's Cemetery Project was necessitated by the expansion of North Central Expressway in downtown Dallas. Research revealed that previous highway-building efforts undertaken in the 1940s had paved over nearly an acre of the site. Excavations occurred for three years—between November 1991 and August 1994—resulting in the exhumation and scientific analysis of 1,150 burials containing 1,157 individuals. The cemetery was the only place of burial available for African Americans for 34 of its 39 years of operation, thus the demography of the cemetery is an inclusive one, simultaneously containing both the poorest members of the community as well as Dallas's African American middle class and elite (Condon et al. 1998; Davidson 1999, 2004b). A diachronic view of the graves was achieved using the burial chronology created by Davidson (1999), who formulated three major time periods termed simply Early, Middle, and Late that subdivide this 39-year interval (see Table 1).

TABLE 1. The periods and corresponding dates
of Freedman's Cemetery, Dallas, Texas

Early Period	1869–1884
Middle Period	1885–1899
Late Period	1900–1907

To examine the agency inherent within the expression or transformation of African American gender roles, we focus on the funds expended upon the death experience, key personal effects placed with the dead, the positioning of the body in the burial container, and health proxies as discernible from the skeletal remains themselves. Within the lens of gender and a focus on the rapidly evolving identities of adult black women, we also examine gender construction in children and the evolving perception of childhood through the use of cultural and social capital, using the funeral event to assess black childhood, African American parental behaviors, and views of sentimentality (Bourdieu 1977, 1980; Coleman 1988; Lareau and Weininger 2003; Portes 1998).

The use of mortuary data as a window into these conditions is not without its perils. One has extreme control over context, being able to associate objects and behaviors to an individual with known age, sex, and health proxies. In addition, burial episodes are relatively well dated in many cemetery contexts. However, it is also true that within the Beautification of Death Movement of the nineteenth century, behavior was highly ritualized, and extremely conscious decisions were represented for display and communication to others (Davidson 2004b: 118–124; Farrell 1980).

In part, what is being communicated is not an individual's true socioeconomic or status position within society but rather a projected economic state of aspired wealth and position. Additionally, the inclusion of certain objects may imply exaggerated connections between material symbols and individuality. However, specific objects do have the ability to elevate an individual's gender identity in burial contexts. This relationship between material culture and individual provides a window into the conscious, cultural construction of gender. Given that, the relative differences within the cemetery population, between men and women and adults and children, will remain relevant and meaningful.

Historical Background

Dallas, Texas, was founded in 1841, and by 1856 the town had a population of 350 (Greene 1973: 7; Holmes and Saxon 1992: 39; McDonald 1978: 10). African Americans were in Dallas County as early as 1842, and by 1859 in the town of Dallas there were 97 slaves out of a population of 775 (12.5 percent of the total population) (Kimball 1927: 25). The most dramatic antebellum event in Dallas occurred in 1860 when the entire business district burned to the ground, supposedly as part of a greater slave rebellion. Three enslaved African Americans were accused of leading the "rebellion" and summarily lynched (Davidson 1998; Greene 1973: 16; Prince 1993: 17–19).

Along with the majority of Texas, Dallas County voted to secede from the Union in 1861. Due to the state's geography marking the western extent of the Confederacy, Texas was the last to hear word of the war's end, with the announcement of Lee's surrender read in the port city of Galveston on June 19, 1865 (Greene 1973: 18). Although Dallas County never saw a battle during the war (Prince 1993: 20), Reconstruction was extremely brutal, with freedmen and -women often the targets of violent acts including rape and murder. The Freedmen's Bureau and federal troops arrived in Dallas in March 1867, but violence continued seemingly unabated, including 13 murders in 1867 alone (Davidson 2004b: 19–21; Smith 1989). In 1868 the same year that black people voted for the first time, the Ku Klux Klan arrived in town (Holmes and Saxon 1992: 58–59).

In the fall of 1865, the Dallas city council passed a vagrants ordinance specifically targeting freedmen and their families, with the express purpose of discouraging black people from settling within the town (Davidson 1999: 22–23). Despite this, literally hundreds if not thousands of black people arrived in the vicinity of Dallas during Reconstruction (McDonald 1978: 17). Instead of settling in Dallas proper, however, most African Americans formed a series of freedmen's towns that ringed the city's limits. The largest of these was Freedman's Town, later known as North Dallas Freedman's Town. Within the broad boundaries of this settlement, Freedman's Cemetery was established in 1869 (Davidson 1999: 18–29).

Reconstruction ended in Dallas in November 1872, with the holding of the first general elections since military rule was imposed (Cochran 1966 [1928]: 221). The Freedmen's Bureau also closed nationally in 1872 (Bergman 1969: 271). With the end of Reconstruction came the restoration of local white political autonomy, with recently freed black people once more relegated to a relatively powerless and subservient position.

Despite some fundamental setbacks, in the 1880s black people in Dallas—like much of the country—actually saw the expansion of some civil rights and a greater tolerance of their presence and achievements than had been displayed in the 1870s, however false this promise of equality would become (Woodward 1974: 72). For example, in 1888 the Dallas *Times Herald* announced it likely that a black man would be voted onto the city council, all with no fanfare or outrage. Perhaps more important, in the early 1890s black and white people worked together in Dallas's local labor unions, even sharing the same Labor Hall for their meetings. In 1891 striking white workers urged black workers to join them in the picket lines, which they did eagerly, presenting a solidarity in class and race that 10 years before or even 10 years after would have been all but impossible (*Times Herald* 1891).

Unfortunately this united labor front in 1891 would be one of the last times that black people and white people would openly mix together until the 1960s. Instead the fragile inroads to equality that African Americans created with extreme diligence and patience in the 1870s and 1880s eroded and collapsed in the early 1890s due to a multiplicity of causes. C. Vann Woodward (1974: 81), one of the preeminent American historians on race, puts it this way: "If the psychologists are correct in their hypothesis that aggression is always the result of frustration, then the South toward the end of the 'nineties was the perfect cultural seedbed for aggression against the minority race. Economic, political and social frustrations had pyramided to a climax of social tensions."

The economic depression of the 1890s (Hoffman 1956) marked the beginning of the end for black civil rights, as black citizens were accused of stealing white jobs, and white anger was on the rise. In retrospect, if a single event or year can serve as the tipping point to mark that moment when African Americans began to rapidly lose those remaining freedoms they had struggled for since emancipation, it would be 1896 and the *Plessy vs. Ferguson* decision. In that case, the United States Supreme Court upheld the state segregation law for railroad cars in Louisiana (Separate Car Act of 1980) and handed down the "separate but equal" doctrine for the country generally, which came to be known euphemistically as "Jim Crow" laws. A year before the Supreme Court decision in *Plessy vs. Ferguson,* the de facto national black leader, Booker T. Washington, speaking in 1895 at the Cotton Exposition in Atlanta, Georgia, stated that African Americans would for the immediate future forgo social integration and social equality for economic advancement. With Washington's acquiescence and the Supreme Court's ruling one year later, the doctrine of segregation would become all but inevitable and serve as the benchmark for defining American race relations in the twentieth century (Woodward 1974: 71).

Juliette Street

Glimpses of those who lived and died during this dynamic period can be seen through a wealth of extant archival materials, including such standard fare as city directories, tax and probate records, newspaper articles, photographs, and death records derived from the city and county, newspapers, and private funeral homes. The archival record for Dallas is impressive, although fundamental gaps do exist, especially for African Americans. Archaeologically, one traditional approach to studying gender relies on "household archaeology" (for example, Barile and Brandon 2004), a concept that can reiterate the historic stereotype that a "woman's place" is within the home.

Household archaeology in Dallas is rare; one pertinent example is the Cole House excavations. In 2002 the University of Texas conducted an archaeological field school in the historic North Dallas Freedman's Town district led by Maria Franklin, James M. Davidson, and Jamie C. Brandon. The excavations focused on a single block of an abandoned street in the center of North Dallas Freedman's Town—Juliette Street (Davidson 2004a).

Founded in the early 1870s, Juliette Street was once a part of a thriving African American community. An archival study conducted by Davidson (2004a) of a single block of Juliette Street (bounded by Routh and Boll streets) between 1900 and 1910 revealed several interesting historic trends. During this period the block contained two churches and black-owned businesses such as a millinery, a meat market, and two grocery stores. There were also 16 residences on the block, all single-family dwellings, which varied in size from 300 to 1,100 square feet. In the 1900 federal census, these 16 homes housed 71 individuals. The largest home on the block belonged to a neighborhood grocer whose salary, according to the 1900 national income averages (see Preston and Haines 1991), would have approximated $1,100 per year. Also living on Juliette Street during the 1900–1910 period were six female heads of household who were employed as laundresses, which had a national average salary in 1900 of only $209 per annum (Preston and Haines 1991).

Household composition on Juliette Street was highly variable in terms of family size, with the number of people living within the houses ranging between two and eight individuals. Long-term residence on the street was also fairly unusual, with only a few families living in the houses for a decade or longer. Typically, the houses on this block of Juliette Street between 1900 and 1910 saw one family move out and another family move in approximately every two and a half years; this was likely a consequence of job instability and a lack of home ownership among African Americans. Families typically moved from Juliette Street into other black enclaves located around the outskirts of Dallas as opposed to leaving the city altogether (Davidson 2004a; Engerrand 1978).

The 2002 archaeological excavations took place on a single house lot (23 feet by 87 feet) that once held a shotgun house, likely with three rooms with no hall to connect them. A series of working-class African American families resided on this property from its initial purchase in 1880 to 1962 when the structure was razed. The longest occupation was by the Cole family from 1886 to 1910, some 25 years. Both Thomas and Nora Cole were born into slavery in Texas during the Civil War, and their four daughters—Henrietta, Della, Sallie, and Viola—were born in the 1880s. Thomas Cole was, depending upon the year, a day laborer, a carpenter, and later owner of a horse feed and fuel business. According to census records and city directories, at least by 1900, Nora never worked outside the home (Davidson 2004a).

The 2002 Cole house excavations project was a modest step toward the goal of understanding some of the societal processes African American families both experienced and created in the earliest stages of building a life for themselves after enslavement. Although under active analysis and interpretation, the artifact assemblage recovered during excavations that date to the late nineteenth century is slight overall, in large part due to a loss of archaeological integrity during demolition and leveling activities on the property in recent decades.

Equally problematic is the site's fractured occupational history. Urban household contexts are typically inhabited by multiple individuals in a single time period and often have multiple occupation periods. The knowledge gained from residential complexes is vast and obviously useful; however, this lack of clarity or resolution regarding gender roles within domestic space makes the archaeological evidence from Freedman's Cemetery even more meaningful and relevant.

Black Women in Dallas

Like Nora Cole in Dallas, according to Peter Kolchin (1972) in a study of the 1870 federal census, between 80 and 95 percent of black women in some districts of Alabama were homemakers. This illustrates the ideal felt by many African American families to feel equal with their white counterparts and (with some success) display their genteel nature. However, Nora Cole and the Alabamian women actually represent an uncommon social position in Reconstruction and post-Reconstruction African America, as the majority of black women were required to work outside the home. While "home-maker" was the prescribed social position for women in Victorian society (Spencer-Wood 1999), the ability to cultivate and maintain such a role was extremely difficult due to social pressures placed on the black community.

As many white women in the late nineteenth century were struggling for the right to vote and other markers of equality, including the right to work outside the home, such labors for black women were hardly a right and largely a necessity. Of course black women had been working both in and out of the home since the beginnings of enslavement, and economic necessity compelled the vast majority to do so well after emancipation. During Reconstruction black men in Dallas County were often denied work, as evidenced by the 1870 federal census manuscript for Dallas County, where most African American men list no occupation (Smith 1989).

In contrast, African American women worked in much greater numbers than black men during Reconstruction and the immediate post-Reconstruction era as laundresses, domestics, cooks, and nursemaids in the homes of wealthy white families. Due to the social and economic instability experienced during and after Reconstruction, the separation of families, and the all-too-common death of husbands, 30 percent of African American women in Dallas were enumerated in the 1880 federal census as heads of households. Thus as much as a third of all African American women in Dallas were de facto single parents, faced with the heavy burden of both raising a family and providing necessities such as clothing, food, and shelter (Davidson 2004b: 273; Engerrand 1978).

Remarkably, this trend of overemployment of black women and underemployment of black men can be seen in the skeletal remains exhumed from Freedman's Cemetery. Osteoarthritis levels in women are at their lowest levels during the Early Period, or for those who died between 1869 and 1884, and then increase sharply in the Middle Period (1885–1899), before exhibiting an overall decline to more moderate levels in the Late Period (1900–1907). The overall increase in osteoarthritis rates in black women, as seen from the Early to the Middle Period, certainly suggests a significant and widespread increase in workloads experienced during the 1870s and early 1880s, with these same women showing unmistakable evidence of increased hard labor on their bones after their deaths in the late 1880s and 1890s. Interestingly, there is a complementary pattern in male skeletal remains with a relative high level during the Early Period, a drop in the Middle Period (perhaps corresponding with their relative lack of jobs in the first decades after emancipation), and then an increase during Freedman's Late Period. The only joints that show a continuous increase in osteoarthritis among black women are the shoulder/elbow, corresponding with the increase of washerwomen in Dallas into the early twentieth century and the requisite scrubbing and wringing of clothes of that profession (Davidson et al. 2002).

The rejection of black men and the inclusion of women within the greater Dallas economy altered the dynamic between men and women's relationships, as masculinity is often represented as everything that women are not (Gutmann 1997: 386). This is a critical concept in the representation of men and women in black Dallas; if the woman acted as the head of household, the breadwinner, and the primary family caregiver, this would likely affect men's identity as "male" and alter perceptions of what "manliness" is (Gutmann 1997: 386). Unfortunately, black men had the ever-constant reminder of male expectations during the Victorian era as exemplified by the middle and upper classes of Dallas. Even today, according to Cazenave (1981, 1983: 343), "Many lower-class black men find themselves in a double bind of having to prove their manhood while being denied the social resources with which to do so." It is easy to see how this alteration of gender roles would skew black gender identity and aid in the black community's further separation from the white Victorian norm.

White Victorian Ideals

Middle- and upper-class, typically white households in Dallas likely ascribed to the Victorian era's ostentatious display of wealth, consumption, and implied morality both within and outside the home (for Texas, see Brandimarte 1991; McDonald

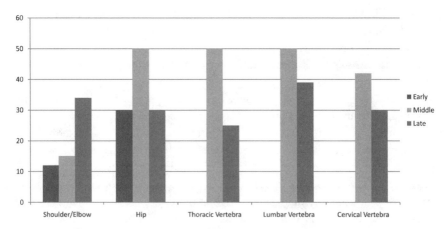

Female osteoarthritis rates by Freedman's Period (Davidson et al. 2002).

1978). Their displays in tableware, furniture, bric-a-brac, and architecture would certainly have been seen and experienced by the many black women who worked inside white houses as domestics and cooks. However, Victorian hegemony left little room for subaltern emulation or easy appropriation, as most aspects of culture, including material culture, were imbued with strict meaning that was inherently class-based (Praetzellis and Praetzellis 2001: 647). One primary pillar of Victorian culture was the prescribed gender role of women, who typically were expected to adhere to the "cult of ladydom" or "true womanhood," which dictated acceptable feminine lifestyles and behaviors.

According to Victorian patriarchy, women were pure, angelic, and in need of protection and aid. Fee (1973: 29) summarized the work of Victorian era author John McLennan, who wrote *Primitive Marriage* (1865) and *The Patriarchal Theory* (1885), by stating that in his opinion he had "demonstrated that women were less useful to society than were men [for] as for all bourgeois Victorians knew, women could not support themselves, nor could they contribute by their labor to the common good." However, the most explicit statement about the status of women in Victorian society was made by Fee (1973: 37) in summation of Social Darwinist Herbert Spencer:

> In the monogamous family, women could finally be placed on the pedestal on which they belonged . . . with settled family life, women lived longer because their husbands continued to support them even after their sexual attractiveness and general usefulness were long dead; in monogamous marriage, women came to be protected, respected, and insulated from the necessity of production and the evils of the marketplace. In primitive societies, Spencer reminded his readers, women had received brutal and cruel treatment; eye-witnesses testified to women's fishing, carrying and pitching tents, digging up roots, planting, plowing and reaping . . . even hunting and going to war. We should, Spencer argued, congratulate ourselves on "the improvement of women's status implied by limitation of their labors to the lighter kinds."

Welter (1966: 152) and Praetzellis and Praetzellis (2001: 646) describe the four principal values for "true women" as piety, purity, submissiveness, and domesticity. This doctrine of gendered inequality and passivity worked hand-in-hand with the existing cultural milieu of intensive mothering and domesticity (Hays 1996; Wilkie 2003; Zelizer 1985). For black women to remain in the home and focus on "mothering," African American men would have to earn a reasonable salary as heads of household; this, however, was not possible for most African American families in Dallas. Thus black women were often perceived as "coarse" and "unladylike" by the white population because they took work outside the home to support their family, often including an underemployed husband (Hill 1996: 130).

According to Welter (1966), all women had the choice of maintaining society's prescribed social role, or they could choose to alienate themselves from that role by seeking work outside the home. However, the dominant classes' opinion of the latter choice is evidenced by a quote from a Reverend Mr. Stearns (quoted in Welter 1966: 173): "Yours [women] it is to determine ... whether the beautiful order of society ... shall continue as it has been or whether society shall break up and become a chaos of disjointed and unsightly elements." Therefore, through no fault of personal choice, working and predominantly black women were seen as the potential downfall of Victorian society itself.

Philosophy of the Child/Childhood Studies

In working to support their families, black women further denied their primary role as full-time mother. The fact that they could not provide full-time supervision and care for their children, however, led many white people to conclude that they cared less about their family and that their absence was the root cause of young African American suffering and mortality (King 1995). Collins (1990: 74) explains how black mothers are often blamed for the failure of their children: "an elite white male standpoint suggests that black children lack the attention and care allegedly lavished on White, middle-class children and that this deficiency seriously retards black children's achievements. Such a view diverts attention from the political and economic inequality affecting black mother's and children and suggests that anyone can rise from poverty if he or she only received good values at home" (in Woodard and Mastin 2005: 271–272).

Daily confrontation with white standards of living likely played a role in the black community's perception of who they were, what a child was, and how a child should be treated. However, without the financial or social capital to imbue their child with the same advantages, African Americans had to transform the prescribed Victorian treatment of children into a realistic goal. In regard to the repositioning of children within the family, Cherlin (1983: 57) asked, "was this [alteration of feelings toward children] because of the emergence of new feelings or because lower child mortality allowed ... parents to express openly the emotions they had had all along but had suppressed as long as many of their children died young?" This question is not easily answered, as there is no universally recognizable shift in the treatment of children as many, both black and white, are abused or forced to labor even into the modern era.

The elite treatment of children as sacred has arguably been traced back to the early teachings of Christianity (Harris 1994) or to the seventeenth century by Philip Aries (1962). Within America however, by the eighteenth and nineteenth centuries, educated, middle- and upper-class women and men were writing manuals describing how to deal with the death of a child (Anonymous 1857; Gammon 2000: 49). Thus the sacralization of children evolved over many centuries so that, according to Zelizer (1985), by the Industrial Revolution women of all socioeconomic classes were striving to fulfill the role of "full-time mother." Black Dallasites would have readily recognized the symbolic alterations of sentimentality toward children displayed in the more economically affluent groups but were on the whole less able to expend the same resources to symbolize their love of a child. Similarly, black families would have been unable to fully mirror middle- and upper-class displays of grief over the loss of a child due predominantly to economic constraints.

The Mortuary Realm

Ceremonies such as funerals manipulate people's thoughts and emotions in intentional ways, ceremonies of which at least some are created and maintained by the upper class (Bourdieu 1980: 69). The prescribed elite rules pertaining to mortuary ritual and grief would have been well known to the lower classes despite their economic disadvantage. The elite's ability to prescribe normative funerary behavior often led to attempts of emulation by the lower classes, and black Dallas was no exception (Cannon 1989). Bourdieu (1977: 40) refers to individuals who cannot afford outright financial wealth displays as the "*irresponsible* man," an appellation that arguably could be applied to the majority of the black community of Dallas, "who, not content with breaking the rules, does nothing to extenuate his infractions, groups make room for the well-meaning rule-breaker who by conceding the appearances or intent of conformity, that is, recognition, to rules he can neither respect nor deny, contributes to the—entirely official—survival of the rule." This description in many ways typifies the black experience in Dallas, with its honorable members striving to give their deceased loved ones the appearance of a grand funeral in the manner exemplified by white Victorian elites, even if it was only a superficial and unreal display of wealth. For all social classes, the living family/community, whether intentionally or unintentionally, objectified their deceased loved ones and used their bodies and funerals to make statements about their own financial and social capital (McGuire 1988).

Funerary displays could then be used, in turn, to obtain even greater social wealth; this accumulation of social wealth may have been particularly important to the African American community as they were constantly struggling to gain equality and respect within both their own peer group as well as the white community. While African Americans tried to show that they could "properly" grieve over the loss of their child, they likely did not garner any respect or social capital from the middle- and upper-class communities, as displays were constantly evaluated on the basis of who was making them (Bourdieu 1977, 1980). This attempt to accumulate social capital can explain how social capital may be responsible for economically irrational behaviors among people (Bourdieu 1980: 121) and may partially explain the presence of elaborate and expensive funeral displays among the poor, black community of Dallas.

Burial Positions, Socioeconomics, and Inclusions

While African American women's place in the public labor force is well established (for Dallas, see Davidson et al. 2002), as are the opinions of white Victorian ideals, we currently do not possess a comprehensive or inclusive textual view of what black families thought of black women in late-nineteenth-century America. One means of insight into the perceptions of black Dallas regarding their wives and mothers, however, is through an examination of the funeral events of black women, to understand how surviving family and community chose to memorialize them.

TABLE 2: Comparison of Female/male Estimated Average
          Wholesale Hardware Cost per Period

	Early (1869–84)	Middle (1885–99)	Late (1900–97)
Male	$0.16	$0.76	$3.09
Female	$0.15	$1.32	$3.61

From Davidson 2004b.

Burial expense can be used as a proxy for both the human value of an individual and the social value of a family or community (Davidson 2004b: 143–233). Not all funerals in the late-nineteenth and early-twentieth centuries were paid for "out-of-pocket" with direct cash payments. While national insurance companies systematically discriminated against black people in their policies until the mid-1900s, other means of obtaining both life and burial insurance became available to African Americans, typically through fraternal/sororital organizations (for example, the Masons, Odd Fellows). Through examining the funeral company daybook records for E. C. Smith Funeral Home (pre-1900), G. W. Loudermilk Funeral Home (1902–1907), and People's Undertaking Company (post-1900) it was possible to discern the frequency of black individuals who received a financial death benefit from their fraternal organization or society upon their death. From a limited archival sample, burial insurance was used in approximately 18 percent of all adult African American funerals between 1900 and 1907 (Davidson 2004b: 192).

If an individual had not obtained burial insurance in life, there were two remaining options for burial. The survivors could allow the city or county to bury the individual as a pauper or could pay for the funeral themselves. Since salaries were so low among black citizens, savings were also minimal; this forced funeral homes to allow payments to be made in weekly or monthly installations, as well as accepting valuable items as collateral. Examples of such items as horses and mules put up for collateral to cover the cost of a black funeral are known in early-twentieth-century Dallas. These latter two options were available only to African Americans who had steady employment and were deemed trustworthy. It was sometimes the case that white employers would pay for all or part of the funeral expenses for their employees; however, Davidson (2004b: 211) found that 74 percent of black funerals paid for by private individuals (and not the city or county) interred between 1900 and 1907 were paid in full by the immediate family or other African Americans within their community.

While burial insurance was available for adults, insurance companies saw the high infant and child mortality rates as a risk. In fact Preston and Haines (1991) document that, at the turn of the century, black children under the age of five years were twice as likely to die as white children. Therefore, few if any policies were ever written for children under the age of one year. Funeral expenses for young children therefore would represent a significant drain on family resources, since African Americans would have had to pay for these burials with whatever finances were available at the time of the child's death. The wholesale burial costs of these infants, as derived from the Freedman's Cemetery excavations, are therefore better indicators of true socio-economic status for black Dallas families generally than those of adults.

Given the typically poor living conditions of African Americans in Dallas, one would expect to see burials with very few or no personal inclusions. In lower-class cemeteries it is uncommon to find personal inclusions such as shoes, jewelry, and toys, as many of these objects are recyclable and could be used by survivors even after the death of the original owner (for multiple examples, see Davidson 2004b: 323–360). This, however, is not the case at Freedman's Cemetery, where personal inclusions are present (albeit in low numbers) and, significantly, most are associated with burials of women and children.

As Sorenson (2007: 4) has stated, "due to some of the obvious characteristics of things and, in particular, their enabling qualities, objects would have been significant means of gender construction. Of prime importance, for example, is the fundamental role of artifacts in the learning, negotiation, and enactment of differences, including differences in gender." This importance is amplified within a mortuary context; the mortuary language of materiality differs from most archaeological contexts in the premeditated inclusion of an object into the archaeological record. In this way, the ideas that are conveyed through artifacts are truly constructed, not created passively by accidental loss. Not all artifacts recovered from a grave context, however, can be considered personal effects/inclusions; archaeologically speaking, "grave goods" can include mortuary-related artifacts such as coffin (for example, handles, thumbscrews) or body preparation devices (for example, embalming paraphernalia).

For the purpose of this study, objects associated with the coffin or casket, objects based within specific mortuary traditions, incidental objects, and items of questionable association are excluded from analysis. Items indicative of mortuary-based traditions include, for example, the last thing touched by the dying (for example, plates, spoons, bottles), or coins that pay for the passage of the spirit (Davidson 2004: 294–321). Objects such as a book of matches would be considered incidental if found alone in a jacket pocket for instance; it is likely that surviving family members or funeral workers failed to notice the object while preparing the body and thus it inadvertently became part of the burial assemblage.

Items found outside of the burial container (that is, in the grave fill) and not located directly on the lid of the coffin/casket were also excluded from the category of personal effect or inclusion, since a direct association was questionable and might stem from previous disturbances and the insults to the graves due to urban development. Finally, at least for the purposes of this specific study, jewelry and shoes were *not* included in the category of personal effects. The elimination of these categories helps to isolate specific, intentional cases of personal inclusions and clarify the messages being communicated by the presence of these objects.

Burial Costs and Personal Effects

Funerals taking place during Freedman's Early Period (n=64 burials) occurred in the years immediately following emancipation (1869–1884). Black Americans faced numerous hardships during this time, as many attempted to locate missing family, move to new areas, and obtain a paying job for the first time in their lives. These trying times and the general instability of the black community can be seen in the Early Period burials, as they are all of minimal cost. As exhibited through investments in the death event, seemingly across the board all members of the black community lived in a relative equality of poverty with no age or gendered group receiving greater or less expense.

For men, the average wholesale coffin hardware cost was 16 cents; for women, 15 cents, while subadults had an average hardware cost of just 9 cents (Table 2). As further testament to the high child and infant mortality rates within the black community, 64 percent of the Early Period burials were subadults (that is, children between birth and 15 years of age) (Table 3). This period also saw the fewest personal inclusions; only two, or 3.1 percent, of these burials held personal effects (excluding shoes and jewelry). The low number of inclusions may be evidence of community recycling, a likely probability given that many African Americans after emancipation lacked a steady income as they tried to rebuild their lives. The only personal inclusions were a pocketknife interred with an adult man and a baby rattle interred with a subadult female less than one year old (Table 4).[1]

Despite the early struggles that most African Americans faced after emancipation, by the mid-1880s many had gained an economic foothold; the Dallas City Directory

---

1. A brief note on the osteological sexing of subadult individuals is necessary here as many physical anthropologists deem this task impossible (though see Rega 2000: 242–243 for a similar methodology). The sex of subadults from Freedman's Cemetery was determined through an analysis on sexual dimorphism of discrete skeletal elements (Condon et

TABLE 2. Population Demography for the Early Period (1869–1884)

General Age Group	Biological Sex	Number	Percent
Subadult (0–15 years)	—	41	64
Adult	Male	11	17
	Female	10	16
	Indeterminate	2	3
TOTAL		64	100

TABLE 3. Early Period (1869–1884) Wholesale
Estimated Hardware Costs Per Age Group

Age	Biological Sex	Wholesale Estimated Hardware Cost		
		Minimum	Mean	Maximum
Subadult		0.00	0.09	0.40
Adult	Male	0.01	0.16	0.42
	Female	0.01	0.15	0.42
	Indeterminate	0.07	0.22	0.36
TOTAL		0.00	0.11	0.42

Adapted from Davidson (2004c).

TABLE 4. Early Period (1869–1884) Burials with Personal
Inclusions and Estimated Wholesale Hardware Cost

Burial Number	Age	Biological Sex	Total Estimated Hardware Cost Wholesale	Inclusion(s)
1330	39.8 years	Male	$0.01	Pocket Knife
1391	7.5 months	Female	$0.10	Bead located at neck; Rattle

al. 1998). The large adult burial population allowed for an unprecedented study of sexual dimorphism within a single population that resulted in statistical significance. Through the analysis of male and female measurements, Condon's work revealed that sexual dimorphism could be used to reliably determine sex with greater-than-50–percent probability for subadults, making sex and gender estimates at least better than simple chance. In addition to statistical evidence, gendered burial materials such as clothing style, jewelry, and gendered objects such as dolls were used as circumstantial evidence for sex/gender estimates. Condon's estimations, while significant, must not be applied heedlessly to other osteological populations without prior consideration of the unique circumstances of Freedman's Cemetery, which made this type of analysis possible.

of 1890 shows that black people were employed in greater numbers in the city. The greater employment and therefore income can be seen in the Freedman's burial population, as the average wholesale costs of coffin hardware associated with Middle Period burials (n= 170) increased by between five and nine times over that seen in the Early Period; for men, average wholesale hardware costs were 76 cents; for women, the average was $1.32; for subadults, 70 cents. During Freedman's Middle Period (1885–1899), subadults again comprise over 50 percent of the burial population, although this number is beginning to decline compared to the Early Period (Table 5). The Middle Period is also when cost discrepancies between men and women first appear: women during this time consistently received greater wholesale funerary costs than men; on average, investment in a woman's funeral was double that of men (Table 6).

The number of personal inclusions was once again low. Three burials contained personal items (as defined for this study); two were adult females, and one was an adult man (Table 7). Burial 1397—an 18-year-old woman—has the maximum funerary expenditure for her age and gender group; she was also interred with a myriad of items such as a lace pin, a hair pin, a pocketknife, a coin purse, and a porcelain doll.

In the turn-of-the-century Late Period (1900–1907), a definitive increase in the relative quality of life experienced by African Americans in Dallas is apparent. Used as an archival correlate to the Late Period, the 1909 Dallas City Directory demonstrates that women are still key in the workplace, while approximately 60 percent of men are working. Additionally the 1909 directory reveals that the occupation of laundress had grown to encompass nearly 40 percent of all working African American women in Dallas.

The Late Period (1900–1907) held the largest number of burials (N = 878, containing 884 individuals) (Table 8). For the first time, the subadult population makes up less than half of the interments, speaking to the greater quality of life experienced by African Americans and indicating increased access to medical care within the black community. Testifying to the greater expendable income that many African Americans now enjoyed, wholesale burial expenditure rose to an average of $2.59 and a maximum expenditure of $13.38 wholesale (Table 9). Despite the number of men now in the workforce, black women continued to have estimated average wholesale hardware costs ($3.61) that were greater than their male counterparts ($3.09), but the disparity between men and women was attenuated compared to the previous Middle Period.

Personal inclusions in the Late Period dropped in relative frequency to 1.8 percent (16 individuals out of 884) (Table 10). Of these, six were interred with females and six with subadult females. The remaining four burials belong to three adult males and one subadult male (interred with a cap pistol, marbles, toy catalogue). In addition to being found typically in association with women and female children, 8 of

TABLE 5. Population Demography for the Middle Period (1885–1899)

General Age Group	Biological Sex	Number	Percent
Subadult (0–15 years)	—	91	53.2
Adult	Male	38	22.2
	Female	32	18.7
	Indeterminate	10	5.8
TOTAL		171	100.0

TABLE 6. Middle Period Average Estimated
Wholesale Hardware Cost per Age Group

Age	Biological Sex	Wholesale Estimated Hardware Cost		
		Minimum	*Mean*	*Maximum*
Subadult	0.00	0.70	4.03	
Adult	Male	0.00	0.76	4.32
	Female	0.00	1.32	4.95
	Indeterminate	0.00	0.59	2.62
TOTAL		0.00	0.82	4.95

Adapted from Davidson (2004c).

TABLE 7. Middle Period (1885–1899) Burials with Personal Inclusions
and Estimated Wholesale Hardware Cost

Burial Number	Age	Biological Sex	Total Estimated Hardware Cost Wholesale	Inclusion(s)
1397	18.5 years	Female	$0.50	Coin purse; Doll; Pocket knife
1026	35.5 years	Female	$0.60	Pocket knife
389	18 years	Male	$0.00	Pocket knife

TABLE 8. Population Demography for the Late Period (1900–1907)

General Age Group	Biological Sex	Number	Percent
Subadult (0–15 years)	—	328	37.1
Adult	Male	233	26.4
	Female	232	26.2
	Indeterminate	91	10.3
TOTAL		884	100.0

TABLE 9. Late Period Average Estimated Wholesale Hardware
Cost per Age Group

Age	Biological Sex	Wholesale Estimated Hardware Cost		
		Minimum	*Mean*	*Maximum*
Subadult		0.00	1.34	9.35
Adult	Male	0.00	3.09	13.38
	Female	0.00	3.61	11.41
	Indeterminate	0.00	3.17	8.49
TOTAL		0.00	2.59	13.38

Adapted from Davidson (2004c).

TABLE 10. Late Period Burials with Personal Inclusions
and Total Estimated Hardware Cost

Burial Number	Age	Biological Sex	Total Estimated Hardware Cost Wholesale	Inclusion(s)
108	32.5 years	Female	$7.82	Brush, Mirror, Comb
110	16.6 years	Female	$1.68	Doll
320	14.5 years	Female	$3.98	Doll
871	38.2 years	Female	$3.95	Pocket knife
264	43.4 years	Indeterminate Female	$4.10	Coin purse
801	28.8 years	Indeterminate Female	$4.90	Coin purse
600	55 years	Male	$0.00	Pocket knife
1422	43.1 years	Male	$7.86	Pocket knife
1285	40.2 years	Male	$6.95	Walking cane
121	1.4 years	—	$0.66	Rattle
85	5.6 years	Female	$4.29	Doll
315	1.18	Female	$0.91	Doll
856	4.8 years	Female	$4.47	Doll
1003	6.3 years	Female	$4.42	Doll
1120	9 years	Female	$0.80	Doll
147	9.6 years	Male	$0.94	Cap gun; Marbles; Perfume bottle; Book

these 12 (67 percent) were found in burials of above-average wholesale cost. Interestingly, all six young girls were interred with porcelain dolls, all of which were depicted with white skin and European features.

Although there is a relatively low occurrence of personal inclusions at Freedman's Cemetery overall, this rarity belies their significance; the members of the deceased individual's family and community must have endowed these objects with meaning. The frequency and form of personal inclusions over time are also interesting; it was not until the Late Period that a broader diversity of objects was found, possibly implying higher degrees of individuality developing at the turn of the twentieth century.

When these personal effects are interpreted through the lens of gender, it becomes apparent that females have the larger share of personal effects interred with them in all but the Early Period. The Middle Period showed the beginning of a gendered disparity not only in cost but also in personal inclusion rates. The pattern becomes even more readily apparent in the Late Period, with 75 percent of personal effects buried with females; it is also the first time that subadults begin to be commonly interred with personal items. While adult women account for 7 of the 16 burials with personal inclusions, subadult females rival that with 6.

Of the toys found in the graves at Freedman's Cemetery, 80 percent are ceramic dolls. Dolls also appear to be gender specific, as all were located inside the burial container of women or female children. The expense of these dolls may or may not be correlated to the socioeconomic standing of the household. An expensive doll found within a below-average-cost burial may indicate parental emphasis on obtaining semi-extravagant items for their daughter. This again can be related to the actual versus "aspired to" existence of black Americans and their evolving concept of an appropriate childhood.

The interment of dolls strictly with females suggests that dolls were being used as an object of gender identity and socialization. The youngest individual to be interred with a doll was a one-year-old child (Burial 315). The presence of a doll with a child too young to realistically play with it indicates that the parents of the child, even at one year of age, were beginning the socialization process, and the idea of an individual at this age with a possession may indicate concepts of gendered personhood.

Body Position and Gender Patterning

Obviously the funeral event was much more than an expedient means to bury the dead. Rather, the dead were placed on display and manipulated in a myriad of ways—with an at-times elaborate and costly burial container and trimmings and personal effects placed with the body and arranged for artistic display within the coffin. Even the position of the body could communicate a great deal about how the dead, as gendered individuals, were viewed within society and how that view changed through time.

In Dallas, the bodies of black women were positioned within the coffin or casket in ways fundamentally different from that of men, typically with the arms crossed over the chest, indicative of femininity, modesty, and Victorian purity; the breasts covered as if in sleep. In the Early Period (1869–1884), arms crossed over the chest was the most common position, seen with 42 percent of women, while men had only one individual in this position (or 8.3 percent of all men with scorable arms). In the Middle Period (1885–1899), this number declines but is still the most common single burial position seen with women (32.1 percent) and is still a minority type used with men (n=2; 6.25 percent). Only in the Late Period does the "arms across the chest" position become a minority type for women, accounting for only 18 individuals, or 8.70 percent.

The lack of personal inclusions with men in the Freedman's graves may be the result of the Victorian paradox that viewed death as sleep (Farrell 1980:58). Men who are typically considered active, public members of the community are likely to be interred without personal effects, simply because "masculine" items would reflect their active lifestyles. For instance, imagine a man who was a carpenter. After his death he might be interred with a hammer, but its presence would imply action, not rest, and seem incongruous if displayed within the coffin or casket. Perhaps personal effects included with men would be redundant, since their idealized roles were active breadwinners, but the identity of women and children were in flux, at odds with past models and Victorian ideals. The ubiquitousness of dolls within the graves may suggest an obvious focus to the constructed gendered role of motherhood and a further projection of this role onto young girls. In addition to granting their children some of the finer things in life, like dolls, African Americans may have been acting in response to what Paul Mullins (2001: 158) has termed "Victorian material moralism": "Rather than reduce goods simply to passive reflections of style, culture, or wealth, genteel Victorians believed the material world actively created, shaped, and reproduced virtuous or degenerate values that either fashioned genteel discipline or bred Victorian society's most pressing dilemmas" (Mullins 2001: 158).

This consumer ideal of the Victorian era may have been partially responsible for the propensity of African Americans and others of low socioeconomic means to purchase beautiful, yet nonessential, objects in order to gain social capital. By illustrating their ability to appreciate and purchase items associated with the upper classes, black communities were openly performing judicious consumption tactics, proving their purchasing power and their genteel taste. These displays were made for communicating not only with the elite white community but also to showcase themselves within the more exclusive world of black Dallas.

In spending large amounts of money on funeral events that may have been otherwise used within the household, African Americans used a symbol of white wealth and beauty to resist their social position and emulate hegemonic ideology. Further, African Americans could prove their genteel tastes and purchasing power by consuming objects that were looked upon favorably by the upper classes. During the Middle and Late Periods (that is, from the mid-1880s to the early twentieth century), this translated to elaborate burials that were extremely similar to those of the white population in appearance (for contemporary middle-class white Dallas graves, see Cooper et al. 2000).

Research by Carlson (1992) has elicited the possibility that black Victoria differed from white Victoria and, therefore, Victorianism should not be judged to have a singular meaning. Carlson (1992: 62) noted that black women of the time held "strong community and racial consciousness . . . [she] was highly esteemed by her community," certainly implying a certain amount of public power that was not available, nor desired, for white women. She stated that this might have been an effect of slavery, where women were forced to work outside the home. By working both in the fields or big house, as well as in their own homes, slave women developed a clear perception that the home was not their only place in society (Carlson 1992: 63). This can be compared to white women, who as a result of the "cult of true womanhood" have been described as "hostages in the home" (Welter 1966: 151).

The burial cost and the body position of black women display an incongruity because, while black women in life were far from "true" womanhood, in death (through the effects of the living community) black women became symbols of Victorian femininity. These details illustrate that black families looked upon women lovingly and did not condemn them for working outside the home, a choice that would result in further divergence from white Victorian society. Interestingly, this burial pattern also indicates that, while black Dallas bought into the Victorian Beautification of Death movement, they were simultaneously rejecting the Victorian patriarchy that the white upper and middle classes actualized. But how do the burials in black Dallas compare to white middle- and upper-class graves or contemporary rural African Americans?

The above-average burial expense directed toward black women and children was in direct opposition to ideals held by the Victorian patriarchy, and the atypical nature of this mortuary treatment is most easily seen by comparison to other contemporaneous burial contexts. For example, the upper-class, semi-urban, and white Vardeman Cemetery in Kentucky had a distinctly different pattern of mortuary display, with males receiving the greatest expenditure, followed by women, and finally children, respectively (Davidson 2004b: 268–271). Most of the pre-1900 interments in the Vardeman Cemetery are substantially earlier than the founding date of Freedman's Cemetery (many dating to the 1840s and 1850s) and thus predate even the common introduction of mass-produced coffin hardware into the marketplace in the United States (Davidson 2004c). Still, those graves with elaboration in this early period are commonly men's, and only men were interred within metallic burial cases, which was the most expensive form of coffin during this period. For the graves at the Vardeman Cemetery that dated between 1900 and 1920, or broadly contemporary with Freedman's Cemetery's Late Period (1900–1907), the pattern is for men on average to have the most investments in their funeral (wholesale hardware costs = $4.46), adult women to have on average attenuated costs ($2.94), while subadults and infants typically had the least investment in their funerals ($1.64).

This patriarchal pattern is echoed in an archival study of funerals for white working-class families in nineteenth-century Pittsburgh, Pennsylvania. Kleinberg (1977) noted that these white, working poor mimicked middle- and upper-class rituals, despite the grimmer reality of their day-to-day existence. Of those who died, the most mourned and publicly bereaved were adult men, and it was for these funerals that the most elaborate mortuary displays and commensurate costs were invested. As the principal breadwinners, men were perceived as having greater social positions relative to adult women. Additionally, in this Pittsburgh study Kleinberg (1977) also noted that, at least as measured by mortuary displays, the least-valued within society were children and especially infants.

In contrast to working-class white people in Pittsburgh, the evidence from the rural and African American Cedar Grove Cemetery in southwest Arkansas is also striking (Rose 1985). A mere 200 miles east of Dallas, these African American tenant farmers were burying their dead in the early twentieth century with minimum monetary expense and typically without personal inclusions, but women did have slightly higher investments in their funerals on average (as measured by the average wholesale cost of associated coffin hardware: men = $1.70; women = $1.98). The Cedar Grove burials are at odds with the Freedman's funerals in Dallas, however, and more in line with the white working poor in Pittsburgh, in regard to the funerals of children and infants. This element of society in rural early-twentieth-century Arkansas actually had very minimal investments in their funeral (average wholesale hardware costs for subadults = 29 cents) compared to the contemporary Late Period in Dallas, which had average costs for children and infants nearly five times greater ($1.34). Finally, the Cedar Grove Cemetery had no inclusions that could be termed as personal effects, save for a rusted tin that may have once held talcum or face powder (Davidson 2004b: 324, 358; Rose 1985).

Finally, it is possible to directly compare white and black graves from the late nineteenth and early twentieth centuries in Dallas, using the Freedman's Cemetery data and a later excavation of the old white City Cemetery (now called the Pioneer Cemetery), which was conducted in the late 1990s. Fifteen middle-class white burials dated variously between 1880 and 1921 were examined archaeologically, and although the wholesale cost of the coffin hardware has not been calculated, it was typical of the more elaborate graves seen in the Late Period burials at Freedman's Cemetery. Further, none of these white graves had any personal effects as grave inclusions, in stark contrast to Freedman's Cemetery.

There are three possible reasons for the economic disparity seen between urban Freedman's Cemetery and the rural Cedar Grove Cemetery in Arkansas. The first is that as tenant farmers, those African Americans who lived in rural Lafayette County and interred their dead at the Cedar Grove Cemetery were simply too cash-poor to pay for an elaborate funeral and accompanying coffin and trimmings. Another possibility is that within the rural economy, local general stores offered only limited choices in mass-produced funerary goods in this area of the state. One final possibility is that within a rural context, a predominantly black population would simply not be exposed to the dominant white ideology on a daily basis. Still, black women in rural Lafayette County, Arkansas, during the early twentieth century had average investments in their funeral event that were at least somewhat greater than their male counterparts. Arguably, however, black residents of Cedar Grove would not have felt the same social pressures as Dallas's black population, simply due to their disassociation with the greater white community. Black Dallas did not have this luxury, as most African Americans had white employers or worked within the homes of the middle- and upper-class white community.

Even the china and porcelain "white" dolls interred with the women and girls in Freedman's Cemetery still manifested aspects of the greater white community. This replication may be couched within images of Victorian beauty and acceptability, because the citizens of black Dallas understood that, contextually, white was beautiful. White standards of beauty were obviously on the minds of black men and women, as evidenced by the myriad of products on the market in the late nineteenth and early twentieth centuries to bleach skin or straighten hair (Davidson 2004a; White and White 1998: 169–172, 187–188).

Interestingly, this may have also been dependent on socioeconomic class. Behind the house that once belonged to Thomas and Nora Cole, the 2002 University of Texas excavations recovered a "High Brown" brass face powder compact within a shallow trash pit. High Brown face powder was one of several black beauty products produced by the black entrepreneur Anthony Overton and his Overton Hygienic Manufacturing Company. The example recovered at the Cole house dated after 1911 and therefore did not belong to any of the Cole women; however, the importance of this artifact is clear. High Brown face powder was a product manufactured not to mask or diminish blackness; rather it was a product to enhance the natural beauty of black women (Davidson 2004a). It may be that the pressure to emulate "white" standards of beauty and social condition was greatest for the poorest elements of black Dallas.

Conclusions

In those initial years after emancipation, large elements of black society in this country emerged as a free people just as the social and moral dictates of the Victorian movement were at their height. The movement was obviously a strong force in mainstream society, but African American men and women in their newfound freedom did not blindly emulate these white traditions, nor did they steadfastly maintain traditional models but rather forged some middle ground bounded by racism and economic limitations.

The initial difficulties faced by Dallas's African American community after emancipation was only partially mitigated through time. In general the improving quality of life for black people in the 1880s and 1890s was the result of increased job stability more than improved employment opportunities or increased salaries. However, life was never easy; African Americans faced constant discrimination, fear of white violence (Davidson 2008), and high infant and childhood mortality. Compounding these distressing factors, African Americans were presented with cultural standards and values within which they could not fully participate or achieve.

While many of the graves in Dallas's Freedman's Cemetery at least by the mid-1880s might seemed to be middle-class on first glance, the simple or direct relationship between real wealth and the cost of burial or grave inclusions is spurious. These investments in many instances created only an illusion of "ideal affluence" that did not exist at the time of an individual's death and burial. It is only when the details of the burials are examined that truer stories are revealed. People with elaborate, expensive funerals often lived in perpetual poverty and poor health—a group of people who were attempting to climb a social ladder even with the odds stacked against them both financially and culturally.

Despite the fact that black women worked outside the home and could not be "intensive" mothers, the greater black community did not condemn them for being visible barriers to their transition into the middle and upper classes. Instead, as demonstrated in Dallas through the Freedman's graves, the black community maintained the Victorian ideal of womanhood even though they failed to adhere to the gendered tenets of Victorian patriarchy. Upon a female's death, she became exemplified in the same way a middle- or upper-class woman would be, elevated even above men within their own society, a point that stands in clear contrast to Victorian patriarchy, where men within white contexts have the most elaborate funerals. In death these women were transformed into something that they had not experienced in life: the quintessential image of womanhood and ladydom.

The partial replication of elite funerary displays by the black community can be interpreted as either strict mimicry of the white population or a more meaningful resistance using emulation to contest the Victorian patriarchy and gender roles. If Carlson (1992) is right, however, the greater expense of female funerary displays—coupled with their body position, clothing, and grave inclusions—could represent an alternative version of Victorianism. It is possible that instead of blindly assigning men the role of default leaders of both households and public spheres, black Americans may simply have been giving credit where it was due.

References

Anonymous 1857. *Agnes and the Key of Her Little Coffin.* Boston: S. K. Whipple and Company.
Aries, P. (1962) *Centuries of Childhood.* New York: Knopf.

Barile, K. S., and J. C. Brandon (editors) 2004. *Household Chores and Household Choices: Theorizing the Domestic Sphere in Historical Archaeology.* Tuscaloosa: University of Alabama Press.

Beaudry, M. C. 2006. *Findings: The Material Culture of Needlework and Sewing.* New Haven, Conn.: Yale University Press.

Bergman, P. M. 1969. *The Chronological History of the Negro in America.* New York: Harper and Row.

Bourdieu, P. 1980. *The Logic of Practice.* Translated by Richard Nice. Stanford, Calif.: Stanford University Press.

———. 1977. *Outline of a Theory of Practice.* Translated by Richard Nice. Cambridge: Cambridge University Press.

Brandimarte, C. 1991. *Inside Texas: Culture, Identity and Houses, 1878–1920.* Fort Worth, Tex.: Texas Christian University Press

Brown, K. L. 1994. Material Culture and Community Structure: The Slave and Tenant Community at Levi Jordan's Plantation, 1848–1892. In *Working toward Freedom: Slave Society and Domestic Economy in the American South,* edited by L. E. Hudson, Jr., pp. 95–118. Rochester, N.Y.: University of Rochester Press.

Cannon, A. 1989. The Historical Dimension in Mortuary Expressions of Status and Sentiment. *Current Anthropology* 30:437–458.

Carlson, S. J. 1992. Black Ideals of Womanhood in the Late Victorian Era. *The Journal of Negro History* 77(2):61–73.

Cazenave, N. A. 1983. Black Male-Black Female Relationships: The Perceptions of 155 Middle-Class Black Men. *Family Relations* 32(3):341–350.

———. 1981 Black Men in America: The Quest for "Manhood." In *Black Families,* edited by H. McAdoo, pp. 176–186. Beverly Hills, Calif.: Sage Publishing.

Cherlin, A. 1983. Changing Family and Household: Contemporary Lessons from Historical Research. *Annual Review of Sociology* 9:51–66.

Clements, J. M. 1993. The Cultural Creation of the Feminine Gender: An Example from 19th-Century Military Households at Fort Independence, Boston. *Historical Archaeology* 27(4):39–64.

Cochran, J. H. 1966 [1928]. *Dallas County: A Record of Its Pioneers and Progress.* Reprint ed. Dallas, Tex.: Aldridge Book Store.

Coleman, J. S. 1988. Social Capital in the Creation of Human Capital. *American Journal of Sociology* 94:S95–S120.

Collins, P. H. 1990. *Black Feminist Thought: Knowledge, Consciousness, and the Politics of Empowerment.* Boston: Unwin Hyman.

Condon, C.C., J. L. Becker, H. J. H. Edgars, J. M. Davidson, J. R. Hoffman, P. Kalima, D. Kysar, S. Mooreland, V. M. Owens, and K. Condon 1998. *Freedman's Cemetery: Site 41DL316, Dallas, Texas, Assessments of Sex, Age at Death, Stature and Date of Interment for Excavated Burials.* Report No. 9. Archaeological Studies Program, Environmental Affairs Division, Texas Department of Transportation, Austin, Tex.

Cooper, J. H., A. L. Tine, M. Prior, C. M. Clow, D. Shanabrook, and E. Salo 2000. *Cultural Resources and Bioarchaeological Investigations at the Dallas Convention Center and Pioneer Cemetery, Dallas, Texas. Miscellaneous Reports of Investigations No. 205.* Plano, Tex.: Geo-Marine, Inc.

Davidson, J. M. 2008. Identity and Violent Death: Contextualizing Lethal Gun Violence within the African-American Community of Dallas, Tex. (1900–1907). *The Journal of Social Archaeology* 8(3):321–356.

———. 2004a. Living Symbols of Their Life Long Struggles: In Search of the Home and Household in the Heart of Freedman's Town, Dallas, Texas. In *Household Choices and Household Chores: Theorizing Domestic Relations and Social Spaces in Historical Archaeology,* edited by K. Barile and J. C. Brandon, pp. 75–106. Tuscaloosa: University of Alabama Press.

———. 2004b. *Mediating Race and Class through the Death Experience: Power Relations and Resistance Strategies of an African-American Community, Dallas, Texas (1869–1907).* Ph.D. dissertation, Department of Anthropology, University of Texas, Austin.

———. 2004c. Holmes-Vardeman-Stephenson Cemetery Analysis: Mortuary Hardware Typology, Burial Chronology, and Socioeconomic Study. Draft Manuscript. Program for Archaeological Research, University of Kentucky, Lexington.

———. 1999. *Freedman's Cemetery (1869–1907): A Chronological Reconstruction of an Excavated African-American Burial Ground, Dallas, Texas.* Master's thesis, Department of Anthropology, University of Arkansas, Fayetteville.

———. 1998. The Old Dallas Burial Ground: A Forgotten Cemetery. *Southwestern Historical Quarterly* CII(2):62–184.

Davidson, J. M., J. C. Rose, M. Gutmann, M. Haines, C. Condon, and K. Condon 2002. The Quality of African-American Life in the Old Southwest Near the Turn of the 20th Century. In *The Backbone of History: Health and Nutrition in the Western Hemisphere,* edited by R. Steckel and J. C. Rose, pp. 226–277. Cambridge, England: Cambridge University Press.

Engerrand, S. W. 1978. Black and Mulatto Mobility and Stability in Dallas, Texas, 1880–1910. *Phylon* 39(3):203–209.

Farrell, J. J. 1980. *Inventing the American Way of Death, 1830–1920.* Philadelphia: Temple University Press.

Fee, E. 1973. The Sexual Politics of Victorian Social Anthropology. Thematic Issue: Women's History. *Feminist Studies* 1(3/4):3–39.

Fitts, R. 1999. The Archaeology of Middle-Class Domesticity and Gentility in Victorian Brooklyn. *Historical Archaeology* 33(1):39–62.

Franklin, M. 2001. A Black Feminist-Inspired Archaeology? *Journal of Social Archaeology* 1(1):108–125.

Gammon, V. 2000. Child Death in British and American Ballads from the Sixteenth to Twentieth Centuries. In *Representations of Childhood Death,* edited by G. Avery and K. Reynolds, pp. 29–51. New York: St. Martin's Press.

Greene, A. C. 1973. *Dallas: The Deciding Years—A Historical Portrait.* Austin, Tex.: Encino Press.

Gutmann, M. C. 1997 Trafficking in Men: The Anthropology of Masculinity. *Annual Review of Anthropology* 26:385–409.

Harris, W. V. 1994. Child-Exposure in the Roman Empire. *Journal of Roman Studies* 84:1–22.

Hays, S. 1996. *The Cultural Contradictions of Motherhood.* New Haven: Yale University Press.

Hill, P. E. 1996. *Dallas: The Making of a Modern City.* Austin: University of Texas Press.

Hoffman, C. 1956. The Depression of the Nineties. *The Journal of Economic History* 16(2): 137–164.

Holmes, M., and G. D. Saxon (editors) 1992. *The WPA Dallas Guide and History.* Dallas Public Library, Texas Center for the Book. Denton and Dallas: University of North Texas Press.

hooks, b. 1981 *Ain't I a Woman: Black Women and Feminism.* Boston: South End Press.

Kimball, J. F. 1927. *Our City Dallas, A Community Civics.* Dallas, Tex.: Kessler Plan Association of Dallas.

King, W. 1995. *Stolen Childhood: Slave Youth in Nineteenth-Century America.* Bloomington and Indianapolis: Indiana University Press.

Kleinberg, S. J. 1977. Death and the Working Class. *Journal of Popular Culture* XI(1):193–209.

Kolchin, P. 1972. *First Freedom: The Responses of Alabama's Blacks to Emancipation and Reconstruction.* Westport: Greenwood Publishing.

Lareau, A., and E. B. Weininger 2003. Cultural Capital in Education Research: A Critical Assessment. *Theory and Sociology* 32(5/6):567–606.

Little, B. J. 1994. "She was . . . an example to her sex": Possibilities for a Feminist Historical Archaeology. In *Historical Archaeology of the Chesapeake,* edited by P. A. Shackel and B. J. Little, pp. 189–204. Washington, D.C.: Smithsonian Institution Press.

McLennan, J. F. 1885. *The Patriarchal Theory.* London: Macmillan.

———. 1865. *Primitive Marriage: The Origin of the Form of Capture in Marriage Ceremonies.* Edinburg: Adam and Clark Black.

McDonald, W. L. 1978. *Dallas Rediscovered: A Photographic Chronicle of Urban Expansion, 1870–1925.* Dallas, Tex.: Dallas Historical Society.

McGuire, R. H. 1988. Dialogues with the Dead: Ideology and the Cemetery. In *The Recovery of Meaning: Historical Archaeology in the Eastern United States,* edited by M. P. Leone and P. B. Potter, Jr., pp. 435–480. Washington, D.C.: Smithsonian Institution Press.

Mullins, P. 2001 Racializing the Parlor: Race and Victorian Bric-Brac Consumption. In *Race and the Archaeology of Identity,* edited by C. E. Orser, Jr., pp. 158–176. Salt Lake City, Utah: University of Utah Press.

Nobles, C. H. 2000 Gazing upon the Invisible: Women and Children at the Old Baton Rouge Penitentiary. *American Antiquity* 65(1):5–14.

Portes, A. 1998. Social Capital: Origins and Applications in Modern Sociology. *Annual Review of Sociology* 24:1–24.

Praetzellis, A., and M. Praetzellis 2001. Managing Symbols of Gentility in the Wild West: Case Studies in Interpretive Archaeology. *American Anthropologist* 103(3):645–654.

Preston, S. H., and M. R. Haines 1991. *The Fatal Years: Child Mortality in Late Nineteenth Century America.* Princeton, N.J.: Princeton University Press.

Prince, R. 1993. *A History of Dallas, from a Different Perspective.* Wichita Falls, Tex.: Nortex Press.

Rega, E. 2000. The Gendering of Children in the Early Bronze Age Cemetery at Mokrin. In *Gender and Material Culture in Archaeological Perspective,* edited by M. Donald and L. Hurcombe, pp. 238–249. New York: St. Martin's Press.

Rose, J. C. (editor).1985. *Gone to a Better Land: A Biohistory of a Black Cemetery in the Post-Reconstruction South.* Research Series 25. Fayetteville: Arkansas Archeological Survey.

Seifert, D. 1991. Within Site of the White House: The Archaeology of Working Women. *Historical Archaeology* 25(4):83–108

Simmons, G. Z. 2007. Mama Told Me Not to Go. In *Time It Was: American Stories from the Sixties,* edited by K. M. Smith and T. Koster. Upper Saddle River, N.J.: Pearson-Prentice Hall.

Smith, T. H. 1989. Conflict and Corruption: The Dallas Establishment v. the Freedman's Bureau Agent. *Legacies, a Historical Journal for Dallas and North Central Texas* 1(2):24–30.

Sorenson, M. L. S. 2007. On Gender Negotiation and Its Materiality. In *Archaeology and Women: Ancient and Modern Issues,* edited by S. Hamilton, R. Whitehouse, and K. I. Wright, pp. 41–51. Walnut Creek, Calif.: Left Coast Press.

Spencer-Wood, S. M. 1999. The World Their Household: Changing Meanings of the Domestic Sphere in the Nineteenth Century. In *The Archaeology of Household Activities,* edited by P. M. Allison, pp. 162–189. London: Routledge.

———. 1996. Feminist Historical Archaeology and the Transformation of American Culture by Domestic Reform Movements, 1840–1925. In *Historical Archaeology and the Study of American Culture,* edited by L. A. De Cunzo and B. L. Herman, pp. 397–445. Winterthur, Del.: Henry Francis du Pont Winterthur Museum.

Spude, C. H. 2005. Brothels and Saloons: An Archaeology of Gender in the American West. *Historical Archaeology* 39(1):89–106.

Times Herald 1891. Untitled. 6 May. Dallas, Tex.

———. 1888. Untitled. 21 July. Dallas, Tex.

Wall, D. D. 1999. Examining Gender, Class, and Ethnicity in Nineteenth-Century New York City. *Historical Archaeology* 33(1):102–117.

———. 1991. Sacred Dinners and Secular Teas: Constructing Domesticity in Mid-19th-Century New York. *Historical Archaeology* 25(4):69–81.

Welter, B. 1966. The Cult of True Womanhood: 1820–1860. *American Quarterly* 18(2):151–174.

Wilkie, L. A. 2003. *The Archaeology of Mothering: An African-American Midwife's Tale.* New York and London: Routledge.

Wilson, K. J., and M. A. Cabak 2004. Feminine Voices from beyond the Grave: What Burials Can Tell Us about Gender Differences among African Americans. In *Engendering African American Archaeology: A Southern Perspective,* edited by J. E. Galle and A. L. Young, pp. 263–285. Knoxville: University of Tennessee Press.

Woodard, J. B., and T. Mastin 2005. Black Womanhood: "Essence" and Its Treatment of Stereotypical Images of Black Women. *Journal of Black Studies* 36(2):264–281.

Woodward, C. V. 1974. *The Strange Career of Jim Crow.* 3rd revised ed. New York: Oxford University Press.

Zelizer, V. A. 1985. *Pricing the Priceless Child: The Changing Social Value of Children.* Princeton, N.J.: Princeton University Press.

KELLY J. DIXON

"A place of recreation of our own"

Archaeology of the Boston Saloon

A gunshot pierced the smoky air in the small, boomtown saloon. It came from the poker table, where all but one of the players sprang to their feet. One of the players writhed on the floor as blood spilled from his leg. The shot was an accident, caused by a pistol falling from someone's lap and discharging when it hit the floor. Although his leg was sore for a while, the victim survived. Except for the man shot in the leg, who happened to be the only white man in the saloon at the moment, all the participants in this scene were of people of color.

Territorial Enterprise (1866)

The accidental shooting summarized above occurred in the Boston Saloon in Virginia City, Nevada, shortly after the American Civil War. Upon telling this story to friends and colleagues, I initially did not indicate that African Americans filled the saloon. I then proceeded to ask these individuals to describe how they imagined the characters in the scene. They gave Hollywood-inspired answers like "Gene Hackman, Clint Eastwood, and John Wayne." Although Hollywood's popular depictions forge a common, monotonous misperception of saloons that ignore their diversity, historical and archaeological records demonstrate the variety of these leisure institutions (for example, Dixon 2005; Hardesty and James 1995; Hardesty et al. 1996; Lord 1883: 377; West 1979: xiv–xv), including saloons that served as "popular resorts" for people of color living in mining communities (*Territorial Enterprise* 1866).

The Boston Saloon represents one such establishment that operated between the 1860s and the 1870s in the mining boomtown of Virginia City, Nevada. Indeed, Hollywood portrayals and western historical literature tend to present saloons and mining boomtowns as sordid places primarily populated by European Americans, with Chinese and Native Americans on the margins. Even though they rarely enter the story of the diverse populations of mining boomtowns, people of African ancestry were there. The mere existence of an archaeological site that once held an African American saloon has the power to revise more traditional, western historical stories

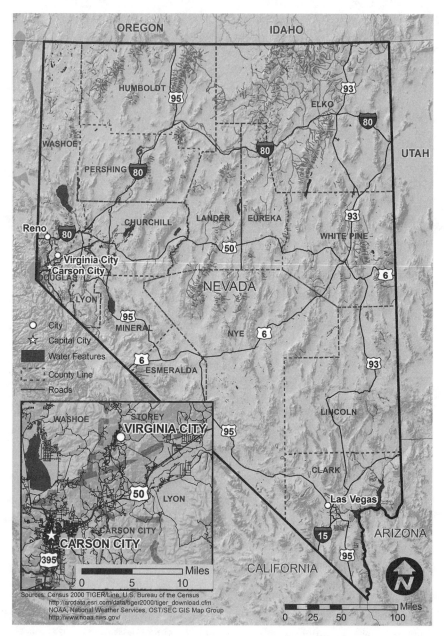

Location of Virginia City in the state of Nevada. Courtesy of Cody Harris.

that are overly Eurocentric and that have focused on the contributions of "English-speaking white men" (Limerick 1987: 58; see also Dixon 2005: 164).

Here I integrate historical and archaeological data to present an abridged story of the Boston Saloon with the intent of both presenting a story linked with an archaeology of freedom and overcoming the prevailing Eurocentric stereotypes of the mining West. I argue that the archaeological remains of the Boston Saloon have the power to combat racist attitudes that were laced throughout the social backdrop of the region. Finally, I draw on literature associated with the history of leisure to consider how saloons—as leisure institutions—harbored cultural identity amid the context of intense cultural contact in cosmopolitan boomtowns of the American West.

Go West, Archaeology of the African American Past

Although the Boston Saloon project certainly contributes to the history of African Americans in the American West, this research is also part of an archaeology of the African diaspora. This field emerged with the excavation of slave cabins in the 1960s and has since encouraged numerous investigations of antebellum and postbellum African Americans in the American South and East, as well as the Caribbean and Africa (for example, Blakey 1998; Davidson 2004; Deagan 1995; Fennell 2007; Ferguson 1992; Galle and Young 2004; Haviser 1999; Mullins 1999; Orser 1988, 1998; Paynter 1992; Schulyer 1980; Singleton 1985, 1999; Singleton and Bograd 1995; Wilkie 1999). There have been only a few examinations of postbellum free African and African American populations in the American West (for example, Cox 2007; Guenther 1988; Praetzellis and Praetzellis 1992, 2001; Wood et al. 1999), that is, the geographic region situated west of the 98th meridian. Until the Boston Saloon project (Dixon 2002, 2005, 2006) there were no archaeological investigations of people of African ancestry in the complex mining communities of the West.

Historians have established a contextual foundation for such archaeological investigations (for example, Billington and Hardaway 1998; Katz 1996; Taylor 1998). Not only did enslaved African Americans move westward with their masters during the nineteenth century, free African Americans also migrated to the West. In fact the most significant unforced migration of people of African descent occurred after 1849 as African Americans moved westward (Captain 1995: 55; Woods 1998: 128). They traveled to the West hoping to elevate their social status and reach the "same economic starting point as others in America," inspired by the word that there was more tolerance in the West for people of color (Captain 1995: 42–44; cf., Taylor 1998). African Americans who moved to this region during the era of slavery tended to find more social and economic opportunity (Billington and Hardaway 1998: 240). Then after the Reconstruction experiment "ended" in 1877, thousands of former enslaved people left the South and sought the opportunities of the West. This historical context, along with the paucity of archaeological investigations of people of African ancestry in the West, influenced the decision to take a closer look at archaeological remains associated with African Americans in the late-nineteenth-century mining West and eventually led to an investigation of the Boston Saloon in Virginia City, Nevada.

Virginia City, Heart of the Comstock

Our search for an archaeological site associated with an African American household or business in the West began in historic Virginia City, Nevada, the heart of Nevada's Comstock Mining District. Founded in 1859, the Comstock Mining District produced millions of dollars in silver and gold and inspired the invention of technologies and mining methods used throughout the world. The popular *Bonanza* television series aired in 1959 and presented Virginia City as a rustic town. Yet the people of the Comstock, particularly those in Virginia City, lived in an urbanized, cosmopolitan, industrial setting. At its peak of about 20,000 to 25,000 people, Virginia City and its sister community, Gold Hill, merged into one of the larger cities west of the Mississippi (James 1998: 143–166; see also Johnson 2000). From around 1860 to the late 1870s, the Comstock's mining wealth captured international headlines, and Virginia City developed a complex, cosmopolitan community, attracting immigrants from all over the globe. People from North, South, and Central America, Europe, Asia, and Africa came to the mining district hoping to harness some of its globally renowned glitter of silver and gold.

The silver and gold did not last, however, and beginning in the late 1870s, the Comstock mines began to fail. The ensuing exodus caused Virginia City to decline to a "ghost town" of fewer than 500 people by the 1930s. Today multi-generation residents—known as "Comstockers"—and several entrepreneurial newcomers operate a series of gift shops, saloons, ice cream parlors, hotels, and restaurants that cater to droves of tourists seeking to experience vestiges of the "wild" West. Virginia City's modern saloons engage the sensationalism of the region's legendarily notorious character, boasting roadside attractions such as the "Suicide Poker Table" at the Delta Saloon and sporting names such as "The Bucket of Blood Saloon." Incidentally, the remains of the African American–owned Boston Saloon lie in a parking lot behind the Bucket of Blood Saloon.

Virginia City Saloons

Saloons were quite common along Virginia City's sprawling urban landscape and usually outnumbered all other retail establishments in this and other mining boomtowns (for example, Duis 1983: 1; West 1979: xiv-xv). Over a hundred saloons reportedly operated in and around Virginia City during the 1870s (Lord 1883: 377). Numerous advertisements in historic newspapers portray the assortment of Virginia

A present-day view of C Street shows a revived Virginia City, Nevada. Courtesy of the author.

City saloons, including those that offered customers billiards, poker games, bowling alleys, reading rooms, meals, Havana cigars, female entertainment, female companionship, dancing, coffee, cock fights, "chicken arguments," dog fights, shooting galleries, and, of course, a range of alcoholic beverages (for example, *Daily Stage* 1880; *The Footlight* 1880; Hardesty and James 1995: 4–5; Hardesty et al. 1996; Lord 1883: 93; *Territorial Enterprise* 1867, 1870; *Virginia Evening Chronicle* 1872). This variety illustrates the myriad ways shrewd entrepreneurs tried to fill niches in a saturated market.

As boomtowns such as Virginia City expanded and became internationally famous, more people arrived from all over the world, amplifying the cultural and ethnic diversity of these communities (James 1998: 143–166; Johnson 2000). Well-established cities therefore supported saloons that filled additional entertainment niches by catering to specific cultural affiliations. Saloons came to reflect the diversity of these and other urban American centers more than any other social institution. As the variety of cultures and subcultures increased, so did the need for drinking houses to service the needs of each group (Duis 1983: 143, 169; West 1979: 43). Upon arrival in the region's bustling boomtowns, immigrants frequently found a foreign, intimidating, and often hostile environment (for example, Captain 1995), comprised of distinct groups of people living, working, and socializing in a setting of intense cultural contact. Saloons owned by a specific cultural group often accommodated customers of similar backgrounds and provided places of refuge and solidarity.

The Boston Saloon and an African American Past in Virginia City

The Boston Saloon operated from the heart of Virginia City, Nevada, during the 1860s and 1870s. Historical records were essential to locate the site of this establishment and to home in on the locations of African American households and businesses in Virginia City. Political scientist and activist Elmer Rusco (1975) started the process by compiling a history of people of African ancestry in Nevada. More recently, historian Ron James (1998) examined a series of historical records, including directories and census manuscripts (for example, Collins 1865; Kelly 1863; *Virginia & Truckee Railroad Directory* 1873–1874) to determine how many people of African ancestry lived in Virginia City during the mining boom and to identify where they were living in that community. Significantly, James discovered that they were not living in a distinct or designated community as did people of Asian ancestry, with their neighborhood of Chinatown. Instead, African Americans were living in locations scattered throughout town and incorporated within Virginia City's diverse international community (James 1998: 152).

People of African ancestry who lived in Virginia City and who visited the surrounding Comstock Mining District during the latter portion of the nineteenth century found themselves amidst a complex political climate. This setting overtly and subtly pervaded many aspects of their lives, demonstrating an intriguing pattern of integration, marginal survival, and success (James 1998: 7, 152–153). On the one hand, they appeared to have more freedom and opportunity there than in many other parts of the country in terms of economic successes and an overall tone of integrated living. On the other hand, they consistently experienced racist undertones and overtly restrictive attitudes and laws (Rusco 1975: 23, 42–44). Their lives were composed of a complex juxtaposition of integration and prejudice and of neighborly acceptance and ill treatment. Such variation in treatment of people of color in the West was common and was experienced by African American soldiers stationed all over that region (Schubert 1971: 411).

Virginia City's context of integration initially hindered attempts to carry out an archaeology of the African American past in that community because of the probability for mixed cultural deposits. That is, integration rendered it impossible to locate archaeological remains that could accurately be linked with people of African ancestry. Furthermore, their business enterprises left few archaeological traces because they, like many boomtown entrepreneurs, frequently changed locations. Given this, it initially appeared to be impossible to locate archaeological remains that could accurately be linked with African American life and work in this community.

Then Ron James correlated several historical references to deduce the historic location of the Boston Saloon. Multiple lines of evidence, including historical newspaper articles from the *Territorial Enterprise* newspaper, the *Virginia & Truckee Railroad Directory* (V&TRR) (1873–1874), and Nevada state census records (1875) all pointed to the location of a saloon that was owned by African American William A. G. Brown and that catered to a clientele comprising people of color (for example, *Territorial Enterprise* 1866). The long-lived Boston Saloon stayed at a single location, the southwest corner of D and Union Streets in Virginia City, for nine years from 1866 to 1875.

William A. G. Brown, from Massachusetts, arrived in Virginia City by 1863, at which time he worked as a street shoe-polisher. By 1864 he went into business for himself and founded the Boston Saloon on B Street. The saloon was located on an upslope location along Virginia City's mountainside, well beyond the center of town. Sometime between 1864 and 1866, Brown moved his saloon from the B Street setting to a second locality at the southwest corner of D and Union streets, where his business thrived until 1875, at which time it disappeared from historical records. The saloon's new and final setting at the corner of D and Union streets was in the heart of Virginia City's entertainment and red-light district. Historical records indicate that in addition to cribs and brothels, this area housed Virginia City's finest opera houses and theaters, and many of the nearby saloons were considered respectable establishments. The Boston Saloon flourished at this location until 1875 (Collins 1865; James 1998: 154; Kelly 1863; *Territorial Enterprise* 1866).

Entrepreneurial enterprises in Virginia City were at the mercy of mining boom and bust cycles—or the mere threat of the latter. Given this economic reality, such business endeavors were fortunate to last a few months. In this context, William Brown's enterprise represents a major success. This success is perhaps even more profound when considering entrepreneurial discrimination of drinking houses in Massachusetts, where Brown was born. He named his Virginia City establishment the "Boston Saloon." Whether the paradox was intentional is unknown, but it is important to point out that in Brown's home state African Americans suffered major entrepreneurial discrimination that "all but eliminated their participation in the Boston liquor business" by the end of the nineteenth and the early twentieth centuries (Duis 1983: 170).

Historical documents describe the Boston Saloon as "the popular resort of many of the colored population," and African American writers lamented the loss of "a place of recreation of our own" in Virginia City after the Boston Saloon closed (*Pacific*

Section of Virginia City as shown in *Bird's Eye View of Virginia City, Storey County, Colorado* (1875).

Appeal 1875; *Territorial Enterprise* 1866). Wording, such as "a place of recreation of our own," in the African American–published *Pacific Appeal*[1] suggests that the Boston Saloon catered to people of African ancestry. African American men and women in Virginia City occupied an array of occupational statuses, including bootblacks, servants, boardinghouse operators, and physicians (for example, James 1998: 97–98, 153–154; Rusco 1975: 73–80). The Boston Saloon likely catered to the socioeconomic range of these individuals, whereas other Virginia City saloons catered to distinct socioeconomic segments of European and European American populations (Hardesty and James 1995: 3–5).

William A. G. Brown disappears from all records until his death in 1893; he died on the Comstock on April 29, 1893, at the age of 63 (Storey County Death Vitals 1882–1911). John Martin, who served as a trustee of the African Methodist Episcopal (A.M.E.) church in Virginia City as early as 1867 and who worked as a bootblack in Virginia City during the mining boom, was among the witnesses to Brown's death (Rusco 1975: 177; V&TRR Directory 1874). Martin was an African American who had been in town as long as William Brown himself.

Archaeology at the Boston Saloon

Historical information on William A. G. Brown's Boston Saloon becomes even richer when archaeological discoveries are integrated into the story. A modern asphalt parking lot covers the Boston Saloon's historic D Street location. This seemed a minor obstacle to carry out the first known archaeological excavation of an African American saloon in the American West, as well as the first known archaeological investigation of an African American site within the state of Nevada. Thanks to a cooperative agreement with the Bucket of Blood Saloon, which owned (and still owns) the parking lot, we were granted permission to use a backhoe to remove the asphalt and fill—and then replace these with a new parking lot at the end of our excavations.

Once the backhoe removed the parking lot's asphalt barrier, the crew used a skid steer to remove additional parking lot fill. Then we commenced with hand excavation to work our way through historic fill layers and to identify the stratigraphic layer containing Boston Saloon deposits. The crew knew they had reached the Boston Saloon's buried deposits by observing a distinct grayish-black-colored layer of ash and charred wood. This layer represented a blatant reminder of Virginia City's Great Fire of 1875. In the case of the Boston Saloon, that ashy temporal marker took on deeper

---

1. The San Francisco-based *Pacific Appeal* was self-proclaimed as "published and ably edited by a colored man of San Francisco, for the worthy purpose of elevating and improving his race . . ." (*Pacific Appeal* 1863) and eventually billed itself as the "Organ of the colored citizens of the Pacific States and Territories" (for example *Pacific Appeal* 1874).

Location of the Boston Saloon, along with the three other saloons noted, amid the urban landscape of Virginia City. From *Bird's Eye View of Virginia City, Storey County, Colorado* (1875).

meaning because, according to information from the historical overview described above, the establishment's proprietor, William Brown, closed his saloon in 1875, just months before the well-documented, devastating blaze. Due to his establishment's nine-year operation at that single location, material traces of the saloon including bottles, glassware, tobacco pipes, and animal bones accumulated in tiny layers until they were capped by the charred wood, ash, and other debris associated with the 1875 fire.

After recording and processing the Boston Saloon collection, it became clear that the project had yielded an impressive array of late-nineteenth-century materials from a bustling corner of Virginia City's entertainment district. Even so, without comparing this collection to other Virginia City saloon assemblages, it would be difficult to make meaningful observations and interpretations about the Boston Saloon's material culture. Due to a series of previous historical archaeological endeavors in Virginia City (for example, Dixon et al. 1999; Dixon 2005; Hardesty and James 1995; Hardesty et al. 1996; James 1998), three other contemporaneous Virginia City saloon collections had been recovered from the following establishments: the Irish-owned O'Brien and Costello's Saloon and Shooting Gallery, the German-owned Opera House's "theater saloon" called Piper's Old Corner Bar, and the Irish-owned Hibernia

Brewery, which was situated in a notorious neighborhood known as the Barbary Coast. Considering the fact that there were at least a hundred saloons operating in Virginia City at one time, these four are too small a sample to develop grandiose statements about the West's public drinking culture and about the Boston Saloon's role in that broader context. Still, this is a start, and the Boston Saloon collection was compared with the materials recovered from these three other establishments. Each archaeological collection—along with their respective histories—provided a comparative framework for a study of saloon diversity in a cosmopolitan western boomtown (see Dixon 2005 for a more thorough examination of this comparative study).

Sidling Up to the Bar: Archaeological Remains of Beverages

Unsurprisingly, archaeological excavations at the Boston Saloon and other Virginia City drinking establishments turned up a profusion of bottles and bottle fragments. The majority of these include dark-green glass wine, champagne, and ale bottles. Mostly recovered in thousands of fragments, these beverage containers were the most common and abundant bottle type represented in the Boston Saloon assemblage, as well as in the other three saloons, suggesting a similarity in basic, mass-produced menu items across cultural and socioeconomic lines.

Artifact quantities provided the best evidence for distinctions among these establishments. For example, the highest quantities of intact bottles unearthed during the Boston Saloon dig were aqua-blue "Essence of Jamaica Ginger" bottles. This product used a certain type of ginger, white ginger, and was prepared in Jamaica (Bradley 1901: 169). Historical newspaper advertisements describe this product as a cure for nausea and other "diseases" of the stomach and digestive organs (*Territorial Enterprise* 1866). It also may have provided a substitute for alcoholic beverages (Kallet and Schlink 1933: 151). Additionally, ginger might have been added to ale to make a flavored beer, or it could have been combined with soda water to make a nonalcoholic ginger-flavored drink. Although it is not currently possible to prove this product's use in such mixtures, there is evidence of soda water bottles and ale bottles at the Boston Saloon, suggesting that all of the above could have been menu options at that establishment. Whether those menu items were mixed in any way, however, is open to speculation. Other beverages represented by the remains recovered from the Boston Saloon include gin and mineral water bottles (see also Dixon 2002: 153–176).

Saloon "Lunches"

Advertisements for saloon lunches in Virginia City were quite common (for example, *Territorial Enterprise* 1867: 4; *Virginia Evening Chronicle* 1872: 1). Meals were common among the various saloon offerings, and the "saloon-restaurant combination was a fixture in the mining camps" (Conlin 1986: 174, 176). Faunal remains, condiment containers, and trace elements of food residues indicate that the Boston Saloon was among those drinking houses that offered meals, and this is where William

Brown's establishment appears to stand out from the other three establishments. For example, a comparative faunal analysis indicated that the Boston Saloon served more expensive cuts of meat than the three other Virginia City saloons, with a much larger percentage of high-quality cuts of beef and lamb associated with the Boston than the others (Dixon 2002: 147–158; Dixon 2005: 87–95).

The story of lunches grew even more intriguing when excavations at the Boston Saloon unearthed fragments of a colorless glass bottle with an embossed label, reading "TABASCO//*PEPPER*//SAUCE." This bottle, with its thin lip, angular shoulder, and label, turned out to be something of a "missing link" in the pepper sauce company's bottle chronology, becoming the only known example of a transitional form of Tabasco bottles from the company's earliest years of operation.[2] In 1868 Edmund McIlhenny produced his first commercial batch of pepper sauce on Avery Island, Louisiana, using the pepper *Capsicum frutescens*, bottled in second-hand cologne

Percentage of Sheep Quality Cuts from Virginia City Saloons

	Boston	Piper's	O'Brien & Costello's	Hibernia
High Quality	67%	38%	4%	20%
Medium Quality	11%	15%	68%	35%
Low Quality	11%	15%	28%	45%
Unknown	10%	31%		

Percentage of Cow/Beef Quality Cuts from Virginia City Saloons

	Boston	Piper's	O'Brien & Costello's	Hibernia
High Quality	64%	17%	36%	32%
High/Medium Quality	—	—	7%	20%
Medium Quality	13%	32%	17%	20%
Medium/Low Quality	—	—	19%	24%
Low Quality	9%	4%	21%	—
Unknown	5%	47%	—	—

The Boston Saloon collection contained the largest percentage of high-quality cuts of sheep and beef when compared to the other three Virginia City drinking houses (Dixon 2005: 88).

2. The bottle's angular shoulder and its embossed basal mark with embossed six-pointed stars were not unusual, but the Boston Saloon's bottle stood out because it had those traits in combination with a relatively thin lip. Up to that point, Tabasco historians believed that the earliest bottles made especially for the pepper sauce had much thicker lips (Shane Bernard and Ashley Dumas, personal communication 2002). http://www.diaspora.uiuc.edu/news0606/news0606–2a.html

A rare Tabasco bottle recovered during archaeological excavations of the Boston Saloon is shown here, with a close-up view of the base mark. Courtesy of Ronald M. James.

bottles (Orser and Babson 1990: 107). By 1869 McIlhenny made bottles especially for his pepper sauce; the bottle type at the Boston Saloon may represent one of the earliest of these specially made containers for the product. The archaeology crew unearthed the bottle from the buried deposits affiliated with the 1875 fire. This provides a chronological control that places the bottle's appearance in the Boston Saloon sometime between 1869 and the Great Fire of 1875. The pepper sauce company, however, has no records of their product being shipped to Nevada during that period.

The Tabasco bottle's presence at the Boston Saloon and absence from the other Virginia City saloons may suggest an affiliation with African American cuisine or beverages, given the evidence for pepper sauces in many traditional African, Afro-Caribbean, and African American dishes (Shange 1998: 29). This cannot be proven, however, and is an example of the ways in which artifacts can lead archaeologists only so far before their interpretations become mere speculation. In certain cases, oral history may be able to shed light on the meanings and uses of certain products (for example, Mullins 1999). Yet oral histories were not an option for the Boston Saloon project, since African American descendants who could provide such insights could not be found. They, like many others living in western boomtowns, moved away from these urban centers once the bustle and commerce associated with mining bonanzas died down.

Despite the uncertainties of interpretations associated with the Tabasco bottle, one fact remained certain: the sauce was actually used in a meat-based meal. This was indicated by gas chromatograph-mass spectrometer (GC/MS) testing on a red-colored stain marking the surface of one of the artifacts recovered during the Boston Saloon excavation. GC/MS testing on that stain detected a mix of this red pepper sauce and lipids from animal fat (Dixon 2006).

Ambience: Swirling Tobacco Smoke, Fancily Clad Women, and Gleaming Gas Lights

Archaeological remains of fine meals and early Tabasco use at the Boston Saloon are only segments of this establishment's story. Other artifacts enrich an understanding of this drinking house's ambience and daily operations. For instance, an array of tobacco pipes reveals an indulgent, smoky complement to the saloon's social atmosphere. While some were made of white clay in Glasgow, Scotland, and represented a common find on nineteenth-century archaeological sites, a handful of others were made of red clay and are unique in that no other pipe styles of their kind have been found from this period for comparison.

Among the various artifacts representative of smoking paraphernalia, one tobacco pipe stem fragment stood out because it was marred with teeth clench marks. Teeth clench marks indicate that this object made contact with the inside of someone's mouth, and this provided the opportunity to carry out DNA tests to see if any microscopic biological remains lingered from the pipe user's saliva. Testing on this item recovered one female DNA profile from the area near the borehole and the tooth marks (Dixon 2006). This provides evidence that a woman used at least one tobacco pipe from the Boston Saloon. While one woman's DNA does not overturn powerful stereotypes, this discovery provides an explicit incentive for rethinking the male-dominated imagery of the western saloon (West 1979: 145).

An array of fancy buttons and dress beads, also unearthed from the saloon, adds more to this story (see Dixon 2005: 124–132). In light of the relatively small amount of women's clothing fasteners found at the other three Virginia City saloons noted above, the quantity, diversity, and vividness of these objects at the Boston Saloon reveal a major distinction that set this place apart. Women—and rather well-dressed women—either patronized or worked in this establishment to a much greater degree than they did at the other places. In addition, perfume bottle stoppers were recovered from the Boston Saloon. Much like the buttons and beads, the stoppers provide indirect evidence of a feminine presence in this establishment. While these may be representative of the courtesan who resided in or near the Boston Saloon (Nevada State Census 1875), they might also have been associated with saloon patrons such as African American women who owned other businesses in Virginia City, including another saloon (Dixon 2002: 306–308).

In addition to women, the saloon's atmosphere included the glow of gas lights. The pipes and fixtures emerged during excavations, but details about the gas lights became evident in the lab with the observation of patent information on one of the light fixture fragments. Associated patent information indicates that the Boston Saloon's lighting represented a new technology that cut down on the fumes typically associated with such lighting (U.S. Patent Records, December 24, 1872). While some visitors to western saloons indicate a stale, fume-filled, dimly lit atmosphere (for example, West 1979: 42), the presence of these lights at least implies an attempt to provide a more clean ambiance within the Boston Saloon.

Other artifacts complement an interpretation that the Boston Saloon had a relatively upscale setting, namely fine crystal stemware. The two Irish-owned establishments did not have as much evidence of fancy glassware, whereas the nicer wares were clearly part of both the Boston Saloon's and the Opera House saloon's ambience. Historical records remind us that Virginia City saloons spanned a range of decors, from simple pine bars to upscale drinking houses with velvet wallpaper and shiny decanters (Lord 1883: 93). When examined collectively and in comparative context, the artifacts strongly suggest that William A. G. Brown's D Street Boston Saloon was on the finer end of this scale.

Discussion

A Virginia City journalist's description of William A. G. Brown's first, early-1860s saloon on B Street depicted it as "a dead fall" (Hoff 1938: 52). Sometime after this, by 1866, Brown moved his establishment to the bustling entertainment district at the intersection of D Street and Union Street. The Boston Saloon's archaeological record indicates that the new location was *anything* but a dead fall, with relatively elegant fixtures. Such remains contradict local descriptions of Brown's establishment and help combat late-nineteenth- and early-twentieth-century racist assumptions about African American saloons (for example, Duis 1983: 160).

The comparatively upscale ambience of the Boston Saloon is not the first instance of relatively ornate archaeological remains associated with African Americans in the West. For example, Adrian and Mary Praetzellis (2001) discovered an array of fancy dinnerware and stemware in the household of African American porters who lived in Oakland during the late nineteenth century. Praetzellis and Praetzellis proposed that these individuals may have been using such high-class goods, above their so-called lower social status, in order to resist the prejudicial system that created that status. They argue that such resistance actually contradicted and combated contemporary racist assumptions about an African American way of life (2001: 651).

A similar interpretation is certainly possible for the Boston Saloon, especially given the frequent instances of prejudice in Virginia City's boomtown setting (for example, James 1998: 153; Rusco 1975: 56). However, it is also quite possible that William A. G. Brown was not necessarily purchasing and displaying goods *above* his status because he had actually attained a relatively high socioeconomic status as a result of his entrepreneurial success.

For example the Boston Saloon operated for nine years at the D Street location and at least another one to two years at its former B Street location (Collins 1865;

James 1998: 154; Kelly 1863; *Territorial Enterprise* 1866). Such longevity indirectly suggests that the Boston Saloon was a rather flourishing business and that William Brown was a successful entrepreneur since he was able to keep his business in operation for so many years despite the difficulty of operating a business amidst the unpredictable boom-and-bust cycles of a mining community. It can be argued, then, that the material record of his saloon reflected his success and sported a setting that could be considered relatively lofty on a socioeconomic scale, including high-quality foods and an array of fancy fixtures. Brown also owned property downslope from the Boston Saloon (Storey County Book of Deeds, 1885, Book 49: 1) despite the fact that he dealt with inevitable instances of prejudice as an African American resident of Virginia City (Rusco 1975: 56).

Whether by default and/or whether by the resistant agency of Brown himself, the ambience of the Boston Saloon certainly combated racist assumptions. The Boston Saloon and the mining West in general were linked with national and international political, social, and economic networks. These networks represented the far-reaching influence of events like the Civil War, Emancipation, and Reconstruction, along with varying degrees of racial prejudice and sympathy toward enslaved and freed people of African descent. These individuals had to deal with the perception among themselves and the dominant society that these places of recreation were certain to detract from the progress of African Americans during the late nineteenth century (Duis 1983: 159–160; Hutton 1993: 158, 169). Such networks fostered attitudes that migrated to Virginia City along with the people moving there (see also Schubert 1971: 410). The attitudes likely affected African Americans such as William A. G. Brown trying to establish new and better lives for themselves. Given this context, whether by intention or by default, the fancy fixtures in Brown's saloon must have, on some level, contradicted the attitudes that were laced throughout the social backdrop of the region and that contradicted the stereotype of African American establishments as dives (for example, Duis 1983: 160). These fixtures also debunk the myth of western saloons in general as rough-and-tumble establishments.

Descriptions of places like the Boston Saloon provide fodder for sanguine conclusions about life for African Americans in the West.[3] Although racial prejudice was not as widespread in the nineteenth century West as it was in the Jim Crow South, it is important to bear in mind that the West was not a "utopian promised land" for

---

3. The Boston Saloon is not the only incidence of a relatively fancy African American saloon in the West. There was an African American "club" in Helena, Montana, that was also considered one of the nicest, if not *the* nicest, places in that community (Lang 1998: 204). Thus the evidence of fancy African American saloons from these two different western boomtowns is noteworthy for its potential to contradict racist assumptions about African American lifestyles at that time and to provide evidence of successful, perhaps resistant, African American entrepreneurship in the mining West.

people of African descent (Woods 1998: 182–183; see also Dixon 2002: 40–41; James 1998: 152–153; Rusco 1975: 56–58; Schubert 1971: 411). Even so, African American families worked together to make better lives for themselves, as did groups or communities of African Americans in the West. The chronicles of these individuals are numerous and complex, and the Boston Saloon is merely one among countless stories providing a unique perspective from what many consider a place of leisure.

Conclusion

Leisure studies call attention to the fact that people tend to express their class-based and/or cultural (or ethnic) identity during their free time, especially when living in a hegemonic, prejudicial, and/or hostile social and economic context (for example, Barth 1980; Cunningham 1980: 10–12; Duis 1983; Handlin 1941; West 1979; see also Captain 1995: 93–94; Murphy 1997; Peiss 1986: 4–10; Rosenzweig 1983: 1, 52, 225). As leisure institutions, saloons, too, likely fostered expressions of identity. By interpreting leisure as a medium for maintaining cultural identity, it is possible to visualize how the saloon—as a leisure institution—also represented a bastion for such identity.

Since leisure activities offered opportunities to socialize with people sharing similar life experiences, they eased the transition for newcomers of various backgrounds to new, and often hostile, social settings and helped those individuals maintain distinctions in those settings (for example, Handlin 1941). As places of leisure, saloons encouraged such identity and became physical places that harbored the American West's cultural diversity and fostered that region's cosmopolitan culture.

People tended to socialize and relax with others of similar backgrounds and/or experiences during their leisure activities, especially in context of contact situations like those common to urban, cosmopolitan mining boomtowns (for example, Emmons 1989: 94–95; James 1994: 32). Many activities were separated and segregated due to prejudicial treatment in such contact situations. Leisure activities therefore provided slates for active expressions of cultural (and socioeconomic) identity in such contexts, which helped foster and maintain such identities among the various groups creating the cosmopolitan character of those boomtowns.

Because its primary role represented a place of leisure, the saloon embodied the diverse social, cultural, economic, and ethnic milieu of mining communities. As mining camps developed into boomtowns, saloons multiplied to cater to the diverse groups making up cosmopolitan settings (for example, Duis 1983: 143, 169). The western saloon therefore reflects the diverse setting of mining boomtowns. Saloons subsequently encouraged a pluralistic society over a society of "indiscriminate social mixing" (West 1979: 91). Thus prejudicial treatment, which either inspired and/or was combined with people's tendency to spend their leisure time with others of similar backgrounds, ultimately harbored the various dimensions of diversity among saloons. The Boston Saloon represented a "resort" for African Americans in Virginia City to relax and socialize with people of similar backgrounds during their leisure time. This establishment's story serves as a reminder of the complexities of an archaeology of freedom and underscores one of several contributions of African American heritage to the history of the mining West.

Today the site of the Boston Saloon is covered by a parking lot, which was replaced after excavations ended in the summer of 2000. A sign describing and dedicated to the Boston Saloon currently hangs on the main street, C Street, in Virginia City, on the south wall of the well-visited Bucket of Blood Saloon. This sign is intended to remind visitors that places like the Boston Saloon lie beneath the streets of this bustling town in the American West and to cultivate a sense of mutual respect for the diverse cultures comprising the history and current character of the United States and of the rest of the modern world (for example, Asante 1998: xi).

Acknowledgments

This project was made possible by the support and cooperation of the following: University of Nevada, Reno, Department of Anthropology's Archaeological Field School, the Comstock Archaeology Center, the Nevada State Historic Preservation Office, the National Association for the Advancement of Colored People (NAACP) Reno-Sparks Chapter, the National Endowment for the Humanities, AmArcs of Nevada, and the Bucket of Blood Saloon. Much of the information presented in this essay was originally presented in the African Diaspora Archaeology Newsletter, June 2006, http://www.diaspora.uiuc.edu/news0606/news0606.html#2.

References

Asante, M. K. 1998. *The Afrocentric Idea.* Revised and expanded ed. Philadelphia: Temple University Press.

Barth, G. 1980. *City People: The Rise of Modern City Culture in Nineteenth-Century America.* New York: Oxford University Press.

Billington, M. L., and R. D. Hardaway (editors) 1998. *African Americans on the Western Frontier.* Niwot: University Press of Colorado.

Blakey, M. 1998. The New York Burial Ground Project: An Examination of Enslaved Lives, A Construction of Ancestral Ties. *Transforming Anthropology* 7(1):53–58.

Bradley, H. 1901. *A New English Dictionary on Historical Principles Founded Mainly on the Materials Collected by the Philological Society,* Vols. IV, F, and G, edited by J. A. H. Murray. Oxford: Clarendon Press.

Captain, G. 1995. Social, Religious, and Leisure Pursuits of Northern California's African American Population: The Discovery of Gold through World War II. Unpublished master's thesis, University of California, Berkeley.

Collins, C. 1865. *Mercantile Guide and Directory for Virginia City and Gold Hill, 1864–1865.* Virginia City, Nev.: Agnew and Deffebach.

Conlin, J. R. 1986. *Bacon, Beans, and Galantines: Food and Foodways on the Western Mining Frontier*. Reno: University of Nevada Press.

Cox, B. R. 2007. The Archaeology of the Allensworth Hotel: Negotiating the System in Jim Crow America. *African Diaspora Archaeology Newsletter*, September. Electronic document, www.diaspora.uiuc.edu/news0907/news0907.html#6, accessed March 31, 2008.

Cunningham, H. 1980. *Leisure and the Industrial Revolution c. 1780–1880*. New York: St. Martin's Press.

Daily Stage 1880. Advertisements listing various saloon activities and offerings between September and October. Virginia City, Nev.

Davidson, J. M. 2004. Rituals Captured in Context and Time: Charm Use in North Dallas Freedmen's Town (1869–1907), Dallas, Texas. *Historical Archaeology* 38(2):22–54.

Deagan, K. 1999. *Fort Mose: Colonial America's Black Fortress of Freedom*. Gainesville: University Press of Florida.

Dixon, K. J. 2006. Survival of Biological Evidence on Artifacts: Applying Forensic Techniques at the Boston Saloon, Virginia City, Nevada. *Historical Archaeology* 40(3):20–30.

———. 2005. *Boomtown Saloons: Archaeology and History in Virginia City*. Reno: University of Nevada Press.

———. 2002. *"A Place of Recreation of Our Own" The Archaeology of the Boston Saloon: Diversity and Leisure in an African American-Owned Saloon, Virginia City, Nevada*. Ph.D. dissertation, Department of Anthropology, University of Nevada, Reno. University Microfilms International, Ann Arbor, Mich.

Dixon, K. J., R. M. James, R. C. Leavitt, D. Urriola, and C. Urriola 1999. The Archaeology of Piper's Old Corner Bar, Virginia City, Nevada. The Comstock Archaeology Center Preliminary Report of Investigations. Report prepared for the Nevada State Historic Preservation Office, Carson City.

Duis, P. 1983. *The Saloon: Public Drinking in Chicago and Boston, 1880–1920*. Chicago: University of Illinois Press.

Emmons, D. M. 1989. *The Butte Irish: Class and Ethnicity in an American Mining Town, 1875–1925*. Urbana and Chicago: University of Illinois Press.

Fennell, C. 2007. *Crossroads and Cosmologies: Diasporas and Ethnogenesis in the New World*. Gainesville: University Press of Florida.

Ferguson, L. 1992. *Uncommon Ground: Archaeology and Early African America, 1650–1800*. Washington, D.C.: Smithsonian Institution Press.

Footlight, The 1880. Advertisement listing various saloon activities, 1 March. Virginia City, Nev.

Galle, J. E., and A. L. Young (editors) 2004. *Engendering African American Archaeology: A Southern Perspective*. Knoxville: University of Tennessee Press.

Guenther, T. 1988. At Home on the Range: Black Settlement in Rural Wyoming, 1850–1950. Unpublished master's thesis, University of Wyoming, Laramie.

Handlin, O. 1941. *Boston's Immigrants, 1790–1865: A Study in Acculturation*. Cambridge: Harvard University Press.

Hardesty, D. L., and R. M. James 1995. "Can I buy you a drink": The Archaeology of the Saloon on the Comstock's Big Bonanza. Paper presented at the Mining History Association Conference, Nevada City, California.

Hardesty, D. L., with J. E. Baxter, R. M. James, R. B. Giles, Jr., and E. M. Scott 1996. Public Archaeology on the Comstock. Report prepared for the Nevada State Historic Preservation Office, Nevada State Historic Preservation Office, Carson City. University of Nevada, Reno.

Haviser, J. 1999. *African Sites Archaeology in the Caribbean.* Princeton, N.J.: Princeton University Press.

Hoff, L. (editor). 1938. *The Washoe Giant in San Francisco: Uncollected Sketches by Mark Twain.* San Francisco: George Fields.

Hutton, F. 1993. *The Early Black Press in America, 1827 to 1860.* Westport, Conn., and London: Greenwood Press.

James, R. M. 1998. *The Roar and the Silence.* Reno: University of Nevada Press.

James, R. M., and C. E. Raymond (editors) 1998. *Comstock Women: The Making of a Mining Community.* Reno: University of Nevada Press.

Johnson, S. L. 2000. *Roaring Camp: The Social World of the California Gold Rush.* New York: W. W. Norton and Co.

Kallet, A., and F. J. Schlink 1933. *100,000,000 Guinea Pigs: Dangers in Everyday Foods, Drugs, and Cosmetics.* New York: Vanguard Press.

Katz, W. L. 1996. *The Black West: A Documentary and Pictorial History of the African American Role in Westward Expansion of the United States.* New York: Simon and Schuster.

Kelly, J. W. 1863. *Second Directory of the Nevada Territory.* Virginia City, Nev.: Valentine and Company.

Lang, W. L. 1998. Helena, Montana's Black Community, 1900–1912. In *African Americans on the Western Frontier,* edited by M. L. Billington and R. D. Hardaway, pp. 198–216. Niwot: University Press of Colorado.

Limerick, P. N. 1987. *The Legacy of Conquest: The Unbroken Past of the American West.* New York: W. W. Norton & Co.

Lord, E. 1883. *Comstock Mining and Miners.* Washington, D.C.: United States Geological Survey, Government Printing Office.

Mathews, M. M. 1985. *Ten Years in Nevada: or, Life on the Pacific Coast.* Lincoln: University of Nebraska Press.

Mullins, P. R. 1999. *Race and Affluence: An Archaeology of African America and Consumer Culture.* New York: Kluwer Academic/Plenum Publishers.

Murphy, M. M. 1997. *Mining Cultures: Men, Women, and Leisure in Butte, 1914–1941.* Urbana: University of Illinois Press.

Nevada State Census 1875. Census manuscripts on microfilm, Nevada Historical Society.

———. 1863. Census manuscripts on microfilm, Nevada Historical Society.

Orser, C.E., Jr. 1998. The Archaeology of the African Diaspora. *Annual Review of Anthropology* 27:63–82.

———. 1988. *The Material Basis of a Postbellum Tenant Plantation.* Athens and London: University of Georgia Press.

Orser, C.E., Jr., and D. W. Babson 1990. Tabasco Brand Pepper Sauce Bottles from Avery Island, Louisiana. *Historical Archaeology* 25(2):107–114.

Pacific Appeal 1875. Untitled. Article describing the effects of the Great Fire of 1875 on a newly constructed saloon owned by an African American, 26 October. San Francisco.

————. 1874a Untitled. Byline and description of newspaper as the "Organ of the colored citizens of the Pacific States and Territories," 10 August. San Francisco.

————. 1874b. Untitled. 10 January. San Francisco.

————. 1863. Introductory article describing the *Pacific Appeal* was self-proclaimed as "published and ably ed. a colored man of San Francisco, for the worthy purpose of elevating and improving his race. . . ." 5 May. San Francisco.

Paynter, R. 1992 W. E. B. DuBois and the Material World of African Americans in Great Barrington, Massachusetts. *Critique of Anthropology* 12(3):277–291.

Peiss, K. 1986. *Cheap Amusements: Working Women and Leisure in Turn-of-the-Century New York.* Philadelphia: Temple University Press.

Praetzellis, A., and M. Praetzellis 2001. Mangling Symbols of Gentility in the Wild West: Case Studies in Interpretive Archaeology. *American Anthropologist* 103(3):645–654.

————. 1992. "We were there, too": Archaeology of an African-American Family in Sacramento, California. Cultural Resources Facility, Anthropological Studies Center, Sonoma State University, Rohnert Park, Calif.

Rosenzweig, R. 1983. *Eight Hours for What We Will: Workers and Leisure in an Industrial City, 1870–1920.* Cambridge, Mass.: Cambridge University Press.

Rusco, E. 1975. *Good Times Coming: Black Nevadans in the Nineteenth Century.* Westport, Conn.: Greenwood Press.

Schubert, F. N. 1971. Black Soldiers on the White Frontier: Some Factors Influencing Race Relations. *Phylon* 32(4):410–415.

Schuyler, R. (editor).1980. *Archaeological Perspectives on Ethnicity in America: Afro-American and Asian American Culture History.* Farmingdale, N.Y.: Baywood Publishing.

Shange, N. 1998. *If I Can Cook/You Know God Can.* Boston: Beacon Press.

Singleton, T. A. (editor).1999. *I, Too, Am America: Studies in African American Archaeology.* Charlottesville: University Press of Virginia.

————. 1985. *The Archaeology of Slavery and Plantation Life.* New York: Academic Press.

Singleton, T. A., and M. D. Bograd 1995. *The Archaeology of the African Diaspora in the Americas.* Columbian Quincentenary Series: Guides to the Archaeological Literature of the Immigrant Experience in America, No. 2. Society for Historical Archaeology, Tucson, Ariz.

Storey County Book of Deeds 1885 Storey County Recorder's Office, Storey County Courthouse, Virginia City, Nev.

Storey County Death Vitals 1882–1911 Death Records. Storey County Recorder's Office, Storey County Courthouse, Virginia City, Nev.

Taylor, Q. 1998. *In Search of the Racial Frontier: African Americans in the American West 1528–1990.* New York: W. W. Norton and Co.

Territorial Enterprise 1870. Advertisements listing various saloon activities and offerings between September and February. Virginia City, Nev.

————. 1867. Advertisements listing various saloon activities and offerings between January and April. Virginia City, Nev.

————. 1866. Untitled. Article describing the accidental shooting in the Boston Saloon, 7 August. Virginia City, Nev.

United States Manuscript Census 1880. Census on microfilm, Nevada State Historical Society.

———. 1870. Census on microfilm, Nevada State Historical Society.

———. 1860. Census on microfilm, Nevada State Historical Society.

United States Patent Records 1872 24 December. Patent records, the Getchell Library at the University of Nevada, Reno.

Virginia Evening Chronicle 1872. Advertisements listing various saloon activities in November. Virginia City, Nev.

Virginia & Truckee Railroad Directory 1874 *Virginia & Truckee Railroad Directory for 1873–1874.* Virginia City, Nev.: John F. Uhlhurn.

West, E. 1979. *The Saloon on the Rocky Mountain Mining Frontier.* Lincoln: University of Nebraska Press.

Wilkie, L. A. 1999. *An Archaeology of Mothering: An African American Midwife's Tale.* Berkeley: University of California Press.

Wood, M. C., R. F. Carrillo, T. McBride, D. L. Bryant, and W. J. Convery III 1999. Historical Archaeological Testing and Data Recovery for the Broadway Viaduct Replacement Project, Downtown Denver, Colorado: Mitigation of Site 5DV5997. Report submitted to the Colorado Department of Transportation, Office of Environmental Services, Denver, Colorado, and Hamon Contractors, Inc., Denver, Colorado. Report submitted by SWCA, Inc., Environmental Consultants, Westminster, Colo.; SWCA Archaeological Report No. 99–308.

Woods, R. B. 1998. Integration, Exclusion, or Segregation: The Color Line in Kansas, 1878–1900. In *African Americans on the Western Frontier,* edited by M. L. Billington and R. D. Hardaway, pp. 128–146. Niwot: University Press of Colorado.

David T. Palmer

Archaeology of Jim Crow–Era African American Life on Louisiana's Sugar Plantations

Archaeology, when used in conjunction with other methods and available data sets, is a valuable approach for the study and interpretation of African American lives in the more recent past. Our understanding of African American life during Reconstruction and the Jim Crow era, although somewhat documented and within the memory of people still living, is incomplete and biased. Archaeology at Alma and Riverlake sugar plantations in Louisiana provide nuanced, local-scale evidence of former enslaved laborers' everyday practices to maintain and express dignity and increase economic independence. It also contradicts the debunked, but still extant, notion that rural southern African Americans of this time were passive until roused by civil rights workers from the Northeast. These everyday practices have histories that extend back to the first enslaved Africans brought to the New World but were also influenced (and reinforced) by early-twentieth-century racial uplift or self-improvement programs such as that promoted by Booker T. Washington and his Tuskegee Institute.

Booker T. Washington was a complex man whose legacy and public image are equally complicated and mixed. His genuine commitment to African American progress is tarnished by both his "accomodationist mask" (most infamously expressed in his 1895 "Atlanta Compromise" speech) and the ruthless political tactics he used to maintain his unofficial position as "the" African American leader in the eyes of the United States government (Ferguson 1998: 34; Harlan 1971). Washington's accomodationism and emphasis on vocational education and economic progress while postponing civil rights most famously put him at odds with W. E. B. DuBois and earned him a reputation as an "Uncle Tom" among some African Americans and others (Bauerlein 2004–2005; DuBois 1989: 36–50; Flynn 1969). Washington's advocacy of separatism and black unity in the pursuit of economic independence, on the other hand, places him in the company of historical figures generally seen in a more positive light, such as Marcus Garvey and Malcolm X, as does his generally overlooked role in assisting black nationalist organizations abroad such as the early African National Congress (Ferguson 1998: 33–34; Marable 1974). The more balanced historical perspective on Washington began to emerge in the late 1950s with August Meier's work and that of later scholars who place the man and his accomplishments and shortcomings in historical and cultural context (Friedman 1974; Harlan 1970, 1971; Meier 1957).

Hard work, thrift, agricultural diversification and improvement, and vocational education were promoted as part of the program of black racial uplift by Washington and his proxies in speeches and publications, through the teaching and outreach work of Tuskegee Institute graduates and through the influence of agricultural outreach by African American agents working for the Negro Cooperative Demonstration Service of Tuskegee or employed in other southern states as U.S.D.A. agricultural extension agents or home demonstrators. The work of the latter, demonstrating gardening and livestock-raising, repairing farm tools, and the like, might seem innocuous today, but in the context of plantation regions of the Jim Crow South in the early twentieth century, "the idea of black agents entering a southern community to teach black farmers to increase their prosperity through greater self-sufficiency was in itself subversive to white eyes," particularly those of plantation owners who relied upon the labor of African Americans (Ferguson 1998: 37).

The African American agents themselves had to appear to accommodate to white supremacist mores in order to perform their work. Ferguson notes that it was not uncommon (in Alabama at least, but it would not be a leap to assume that this was the case in other southern states) for them to appeal to white plantation owners' sense of themselves as benevolent paternalists to gain access to African American plantation farmers and their families (Ferguson 1998: 39). This behavior, along with the wealthier dress and better education of the African American agents, resentment of their imposition of bourgeois values as part of their rural reform mission, and the attendance of meetings by white agricultural agents who presented themselves as in charge, led many African American tenant farmers to distrust African American agents as operatives of the sheriff and planter rather than recognizing them as radical educators (Ferguson 1998: 39–44). Dependence on white benefactors and white-controlled government funds and the lack of farming choices by African Americans who were not working land they owned were other factors militating against the success of African American agricultural extension work (Ferguson 1998:39–44).

After the passage of the Smith-Lever Act of 1914, African American land grant institutions lost not only most of their funding for agricultural education but also their control over that funding, as it was channeled through the white land grant institutions in contradiction of the stipulations for direct funding of the Morrill Act of 1890 (Whayne 1998: 524). A survey of historically black colleges (HBCs) in 1928, which included Louisiana, describes a dependent, segregated, and unequal relationship with white agricultural schools, which in the case of Louisiana would be

Louisiana State University and Agricultural and Mechanical College (LSU) (Whayne 1998: 525).

Agricultural extension work with African Americans—and particularly that by African Americans with African Americans—was primarily in the cotton-growing regions of the South. This was the case in Louisiana, where the first African American agricultural agent, Tuskegee graduate T. J. Jordan, was appointed as an agricultural demonstration agent for work with African Americans in Bienville and Claiborne parishes in 1913 as part of an agreement between the (African American) Farmer's League of those parishes and the United States Department of Agriculture (William-son 1951: 208–209). In 1918 Jordan was appointed as the state club (4–H) agent for work with African American 4–H groups, with his headquarters at Southern University, one of Louisiana's HBCs, located in Baton Rouge. Later, in 1932, the Self-Help League, founded by African American farmers, hosted a training school at another of Louisiana's HBCs, Grambling State University in rural northern Louisiana, which featured demonstration courses on dairying, soil improvement, terracing and drain-age, and similar topics (Williamson 1951: 211).

Pointe Coupee Parish, the south Louisiana home of Alma and Riverlake sugar plantations, was among the parishes to gain a home demonstration agent in addition to an agricultural agent in the official state agency's expansion period of 1918–1928, but these were not African American agents (Williamson 1951: 210). Responses to a 1940 questionnaire by the white home demonstration and agricultural agents for Pointe Coupee Parish (part of an official agency reaction to pressure from African American community and land grant institution leaders for hiring of African American agricultural extension personnel in proportion to the population of African American farmers) indicated that the parish did not have an African American home demonstration or agricultural agent, nor did it have African American 4–H clubs, adult community clubs, agricultural committees, or local leaders (Extension Service 1940: folder 3). However, the white female home demonstration agent stated (within the context of completing a questionnaire designed to gather data in defense of the status quo) that most of the home demonstration work was being done by employ-ees of the Farm Security Administration and that she "cooperates with both the white and negro F.S.A. workers in their negro work" (Extension Service 1940: folder 3). Under the same context, the white male agricultural agent stated in the section for further comments, "For a period of 25 years, I have given our negro population service without regard to color. Of course more service is given to landowners than a share tenant, because of his control of operations and ability to determine his own wants, desires, and agricultural bid" (Extension Service 1940: folder 3).

The lack of control from not owning the land mentioned by this agent was a key element that kept the agricultural outreach efforts specifically—and by extension the Washington program more generally—from having more of an impact (Fergu-son 1998). Not many African Americans were able to become landowners during this period, but nonetheless the racial uplift message, emphasizing racial unity and self-sufficiency (or at least reduced dependency) through increased home production and thrift, arguably allowed some African Americans in the cotton plantation areas, and likely more so those in the wage-labor sugarcane plantation areas, to achieve a greater degree of autonomy in their lives and to have greater hope for a better future.

Direct contact of African American plantation workers at Alma and Riverlake by African American agricultural extension agents seems to be unlikely, but some of the activities promoted by the white agents of the U.S.D.A. were congruent with the Washington program in that they promoted home production and thrift. African Americans at Alma and Riverlake perhaps heard about Washington's program for racial uplift secondhand through contacts with seasonal visitors from cotton-producing areas; visiting ministers, students, teachers, railroad employees, or others; or more directly through publications. Washington himself gave a series of lectures in Louisiana in April 1915, including talks in the public square of Baton Rouge and at Southern University (Vincent 1981).

Archaeology, Bias, and Critical Race Theory: A Theoretical Framework

While there has been steady growth in both the practice and appreciation of the archaeology of the more recent African American past, the work is still hindered by the effects of bias. There are many biases that coalesce and reinforce each other to affect negatively the prospects for the archaeology of the more recent African American past. My discussion of these biases is influenced by the works of some scholars operating within critical race theory, Keri Barile's (2004) work (arguably an example of critical race theory applied to archaeology), and my experience and awareness of issues around rural African American sites of the postbellum to Jim Crow years in the southern United States of America (for example: Crenshaw 1995; Epperson 2004; Gotanda 1995; Jinks 1997; Palmer 2005). These biases are, of course, present in other parts of the United States as well.

Race is a social construct in which points along the continuum of phenotypic traits are selected and associated with nonbiological attributes in an attempt to reify hierarchical categorizations of human beings, with negative consequences for access to resources and human rights for those occupying lower positions in the hierarchy and privileged access to resources for those occupying the upper positions. Although it has been demonstrated that the race concept lacks biological validity, it nonetheless has a continuing social and cultural reality. Although approaching the research from a standpoint that emphasizes human agency, I use the term "race" to apply to African Americans rather than "ethnicity" because African Americans (as distinct from "white ethnics," for example) have little choice as to their racialization (Brandon 2009: 5). Todorov (2009) distinguishes between "racism" as designating behavior and "racialism" as designating doctrines of race and posits that the two are not necessarily linked. In the context of what is now the United States, however, the two are linked, with the doctrine of white supremacy underlying racism (whether actors behaving in a racist manner are fully aware of this or not). The imposition of racialized identities in this context occurred during the early colonial period of what is now the United States, not long after the economic usefulness of a marked category of captive people who could provide unpaid labor (mainly on plantations) converged with the availability of involuntary immigrants from Africa (Epperson 1999, 1997).

Critical race theory (CRT) was founded by legal scholars in the United States, particularly Derrick Bell, Charles Lawrence, Lani Guinier, Richard Delgado, Mari Matsuda, Patricia Williams, and Kimberlé Crenshaw (Taylor 1988: 122). CRT acknowledges the subjectivity of perspective and that, as a consequence of this, perceptions of truth, justice, and fairness reflect the status, mindset, and experience of the knower (Taylor 1998: 122). In a white-dominated society, perspectives coming from African Americans and other "others" are viewed as challenges to cherished normative "truths" held by white people (Taylor 1998: 122). CRT has many different threads but can be roughly defined as a movement to recognize that in the United States and other nations with a history of racialized enslavement, assumptions of white superiority are ingrained in many of the institutions of society, including law (Taylor 1988: 122–123). These assumptions, however, are so ingrained that they generally go unrecognized (even as they harm persons of African descent, Native Americans, and others considered to be "nonwhites"). Thus in the framework of CRT, claims to "race neutrality" or "objectivity" make no sense in a society in which people have historically been, and continue to be, treated differently on the basis of group membership alone (Taylor 1998: 123; for example, Crenshaw 1995; Gotanda 1995). "Race neutrality" or "objectivity" also poses a danger in allowing us to ignore the racial construction (historical contingency) of whiteness, which reinforces the privileged and oppressive position of whiteness (Harris 1995; Taylor 1998: 123). Racism is viewed as a fact of daily life in the United States, not as aberrant or unusual phenomena, and individual racist acts are not isolated instances of bigotry but manifestations or the tip of the iceberg of the larger institutional and structural fact of white hegemony (Taylor 1998: 122–123).

Critical historical examinations of "whiteness" (the social and historical construction or definition of the racial identity of "white") were influenced by CRT and the implosion of the fixed, immutable race concept. Perhaps the most well-known of these historical studies are Noel Ignatiev's (1995) study of the Irish in the nineteenth century United States and Roediger's (1991) study of the laboring sector of persons and how race played a negative role in the making of the U.S. working class. In archaeology Epperson's (1999, 1997) work examines how the identity of "whiteness" came to be in colonial Virginia, putting his findings into the broader context of historical research using CRT in which he exposes "whiteness" as a category, as historically and culturally contingent and created, and a source of privilege for those who could (and do) claim it.

CRT is also a form of oppositional scholarship that challenges the experiences of white people as the normative standard, instead grounding its conceptual framework in the distinctive experiences of people of color (Taylor 1998: 122). Another key part of CRT is the recognition of the significance of the lived experiences of racism by persons of African descent and other minorities as they have been singled out, with wide consensus among white people, as worthy of suppression (Epperson 2004; Taylor 1998: 122). Historical archaeologies of the African diaspora synergize with this aspect of CRT by drawing upon oral histories and related narratives of life under Jim Crow, as well as the fruition of our examinations of material culture. CRT is inherently vindicationist and has been successfully employed in African diaspora archaeology explicitly in this vein (for example, Blakey 2004; Epperson 2004; LaRoche and Blakey 1997; Mack and Blakey 2004; Perry and Paynter 1999).

Oral history has proven to be a particularly apt method for documenting and interpreting the lived experiences of members of the African diaspora. This is demonstrated in a number of studies, examples of which include using the WPA ex-slave narratives to interpret life under enslavement, interviews with women formerly employed in domestic service in Washington, D.C., during the early-twentieth-century "Great Migration" years, and interviews with rural Louisianans about their struggle for civil rights prior to extra-regional activist involvement (for example, Clark-Lewis 1996; DeJong 2002; Genovese 1974). Oral history, of course, comes with its own well-developed methods and theoretical history, the majority of which are, however, convergent with use in a historical archaeology drawing upon CRT and structuration approaches (Henige 1982; Palmer 2005: 64–83; Portelli 1991, 1997; Ritchie 1995; Thompson 1978; Vansina 1985).

Practice theory approaches, also called structuration, work well for the analysis of past human behavior through archaeology, as quotidian activities are the most available material remains of past human behavior, and these everyday activities unconsciously express and reinforce deeply held ideas of how the world should be and is (worldview) (Bourdieu 1977; Giddens 1979, 1984; Lightfoot et al. 1998). In seeking to uncover the histories of African Americans in the Jim Crow era U.S. South, it is important to understand race and racism during this period. The imposition and maintenance of racialized subjectivities and status were accomplished by white people through a myriad of legal and extralegal actions, ranging from infantilizing forms of address used with African Americans to spatial separation and denial of access to resources (including political rights) to torture and murder carried out by individuals or organized terrorist organizations. A structuration approach is appropriate, as Jim Crow–era segregation laws mandating spatial separation of African Americans from white people and limiting the mobility and citizenship rights of African Americans were the expression and reinforcing action of a pernicious *doxa,* or something that is taken for granted in society: that of white supremacy. Critical race theory intersects with structuration approaches in that the *doxa* of white hegemony is expressed and reinforced through the daily actions of white people (*habitus*), including unconscious actions of "microaggression" performed by many white people who do not consider themselves to be racist (Lawrence 1995).

White people invested considerable energy into maintaining and expanding their hegemony. The *doxa* of white supremacy in the Jim Crow era required a *habitus* of daily denigration of African Americans through a host of imposed indignities and violence. Agency is expressed not only in innovation but also in maintaining a status quo (Joyce and Lopiparo 2005: 368), and this latter expression of agency was certainly the case for white people during the Jim Crow era. White people, whether "conscious" racists or not, by behaving within the confines of the racial rules of the Jim Crow South, elided the dignity of African Americans (if not always their humanity) and reinforced the racial system.

Some Obstacles to Archaeologies of the Recent African American Past

Returning to biases that hinder the prospects for an archaeology of the recent African American past, historical archaeologists are familiar with the general bias against archaeological investigations of more recent sites, especially those chronologically within the lifetimes of persons still living. There is also a bias against doing archaeology on controversial topics. As any archaeology of the African American past will elicit questions about race and racism, the potential controversy is enough to discourage many from this field. There is also taphonomic bias. It is widely and unresistingly recognized that people who were poorer and those whose opportunities were curtailed by prejudicial legal and social restrictions had fewer material goods and less substantial housing and thus left us more ephemeral archaeological remains. This handicapped start was then exaggerated by social, legal, and economic barriers to landownership, with few African Americans owning their own land and white landowners and others who did not hesitate to raze, demolish, plow under, and otherwise destroy the physical remnants of African American sites for economic, social, and/or political reasons. Racism, as a cultural taphonomic factor, compounds the destruction of the archaeological record by natural taphonomic processes (these processes are also referred to as "c-transforms" and "n-transforms") (Schiffer 1987: 22).

Decisions about the integrity and significance of more recent (as well as older, for that matter!) African American sites are all too often made without any consideration at all for the taphonomic distortions that are in no small part the result of past racism. U.S. cultural resource laws at the time of writing do not specifically include a consideration of the taphonomic impact of racism. This very lack of specificity in the laws, however, is a space in which alternative solutions could be created, such as sampling strategies in which representation of the cultural diversity of a state's population and historic events is included as a part of the National Register of Historic Places eligibility-consideration process (Barile 2004: 99). Such a solution, however, would doubtlessly be challenged by the same (primarily white and male) interests who so vehemently oppose any perceived threat to their privileges, whether it be history textbook revisions or legal remedies to racial discrimination.

Archaeologists, particularly those working in cultural resources management (as they perform the majority of archaeological work in the United States), are well-intentioned individuals but often make their decisions with these biases (against more recent sites, against controversial sites, against sites with less-than-ideal integrity) as an influence, conscious or not. Although they are likely unaware of it, this failure to explicitly acknowledge racism as a cultural taphonomic factor ignores history and unwittingly reifies past racism and economic bias. Barile (2004: 98) is not writing hyperbolically when she states that if this trend of the vast majority of more recent African American sites not being considered archaeologically significant continues, "the result will be that few late-nineteenth-century African American sites will be federally or locally protected; this era, and those who experienced it and their descendants, will remain 'without history' indefinitely" (see also Babiarz, "White Privilege and Silencing," this volume).

The African American archaeological components of Alma and Riverlake plantations in Louisiana are two such sites where these biases could have precluded archaeological investigation (and in the case of Riverlake, nearly did so: Wilkie 1995) but for the efforts of archaeologists and, in the case of Alma Plantation, an owner amenable to historic preservation and research. Archaeological studies of Africans and African Americans in Louisiana have been extremely limited, especially when the economic and cultural contributions of Africans and African-descended people to the state are considered (Wilkie et al. 2010). The Alma and Riverlake project is one of a recent few that explore the tumultuous postbellum years of Reconstruction, Restoration, and Jim Crow.

An Archaeology of Human Dignity: African American Life at Alma and Riverlake Plantations during the Jim Crow Era

The Compact Oxford English Dictionary (2010) defines *dignity* as "the state or quality of being worthy of respect. Origin: Latin *dignitas,* from *dingus,* 'worthy.'" African Americans living and working on plantations during the postbellum and Jim Crow years often had to contend with employers and others who not too long ago considered them to be a form of property. Although the legacies of enslavement and racism are still with us, it is clear that many African Americans living during this time period were able to do more than just survive; they reunited families and built communities while maintaining their dignity. As stated previously, rural southern African Americans have been incorrectly characterized in popular narratives of history as being passive until outside civil rights workers came to lead them. Historical and archaeological research has demonstrated that this was not the case, and that resistance, in different forms, took place in many areas prior to the 1960s (for example, DeJong 2002; Ferguson 1992; Hall 1992; McKee 1992; Scott 1994; Weik 1997). This resistance, some of the quotidian forms of which may seem quite mundane when considered outside of the Jim Crow context, defied the *habitus* expected of African Americans living under the imposed *doxa* of Jim Crow white supremacy.

Historical archaeology contributes to this research because the material evidence recovered through archaeology is a valuable source of information about everyday life and allows us to consider social and cultural behaviors. Although sometimes dismissed as being merely economic information, data about diet and household goods—when part of a research strategy using all available lines of evidence (oral, ethnographic, archaeological, documentary and ethnoarchaeological) and appropriate interpretive approaches (critical, vindicationist, structurationist) to place the data in its context—are valuable for addressing more broadly humanistic questions. Our findings as archaeologists are often at the local, community, or even household scale, which we could choose to see as limiting. However, when we compare this data with that from other sites and bring it into a broader context, we are able to engage larger historical and cultural issues. Human dignity is one of these issues. Archaeology at Alma and Riverlake plantations provides examples of the maintenance and assertion of dignity by African Americans during the postbellum and Jim Crow eras.

Alma and Riverlake Plantations

Riverlake and Alma plantations are located in Pointe Coupée Parish, Louisiana, about a 30-minute drive from Baton Rouge and within walking distance of False River, a Mississippi oxbow lake. In conducting the research, I used the full range of available data for the Alma and Riverlake project: archaeological, ethnoarchaeological, documentary, and oral historical evidence. The archaeological data from Riverlake Plantation was obtained by salvage excavations in the former workers' housing area in 1993 led by Paul Farnsworth and Laurie Wilkie (Farnsworth 1993; Palmer 2005: 54–55). Farnsworth and Wilkie also conducted limited oral and documentary history research as part of this project. In 2000 I directed archaeological exploratory excavations, followed in 2003 with block excavations of a former workers' house site at Alma Plantation, which were the source of archaeological data from that site (Palmer 2005: 54–64). I also conducted oral history interviews with African American former residents and employees of Alma Plantation, archival research, and, with the assistance of students and volunteers, collected ethnoarchaeological data on house and yard space use (Palmer 2005: 59–62, 77–86).

To understand postemancipation life, it is important to recognize the apparent contradictions in the postbellum-era sugar regions. There were continuities in housing and labor organization, but the agricultural technology and methods from before

Location of Alma and Riverlake plantations within Pointe Coupée Parish, Louisiana.

Alma & Riverlake Plantations

the Civil War contrasted with the fact that African American workers were no longer enslaved and could (at considerable risk) exercise their power to withhold labor in order to gain better wages, conditions, and other benefits (Rodrigue 2001: 1–4). In other words, African American workers were in a strikingly different relationship with their former owners. These changes represented a paradigm shift for the world-views of the planters and formerly enslaved alike. Attitudes of paternalism on the part of many planters conflicted with the new paradigm in which they were not deal-ing with their presumed property but with a group of people with whom they had to negotiate payment and other conditions of labor. Additionally, in many cases relationships with planter families continued, but there were changes and conflicts because much of these relationships was based upon paternalism. Among other results, this shift often resulted in the ending of informal use rights (to tools, live-stock, housing, pasturage, and so on). These changes often did not occur at once but rather in a patchwork fashion. One of the results of this change was that African Americans working on plantations could contemplate a different future—if not for themselves, then for their children and grandchildren.

In Louisiana the technology of field labor for the sugarcane industry did not change significantly from the first crops until the 1940s. Crops were harvested by hand; tractors did not become common until after the 1940s. Thus the period circa 1870–1940 is what I call the postbellum, hand-cutting era (Conrad and Lucas 1995: 69; Palmer 2005: 6). The relatively static technology for harvesting belied the changes that took place during this era, lending a veneer of continuity with the antebellum era.

Both the Alma and Riverlake plantations have records of ownership by Europeans and Euro Americans dating back to the colonial era. Riverlake passed from Creole, or Francophone, Louisianan hands to an Anglophone in 1892, and Alma was transferred to an Anglophone in 1859. With these transfers, there were changes in the organization of labor that hampered African American efforts at self-sufficiency. Under the Creole owners, Africans and African Americans worked under a gang leader from among themselves on a set task. Once they completed this daily task, they could work in their gardens or the plantation provisioning grounds, fish, hunt, work extra jobs such as cutting wood (for pay in some cases), or engage in noneconomic social activities. Of course, they *had* to do these self-provisioning activities, as the planters did not provide them with full rations of food (if they provided any at all). The Anglophone American planters imposed a work regime under which the enslaved worked under an overseer for long, fixed hours (before sunrise to after sunset) and were provided with (minimal) rations of food and clothing. Self-provisioning was still necessary under this "American" plan (as it is known in Louisiana), but opportunities for carrying it out were constrained. The practice of self-provisioning, although made necessary for survival, was an activity that countered the dependent and subservient role imposed upon the enslaved by white people operating under the *doxa* of white supremacy. Eating is a necessity for biological existence, and this fundamental role of eating is no small part of the cultural significance of food and foodways. Self-provisioning, then, can be seen as both a humble, quotidian task related to survival and yet one through which enslaved and later free Africans and African Americans were able to maintain and express their culture and dignity.

Dignity in Daily Life: Self-sufficiency and Self-provisioning

Dignity was nurtured and expressed in a number of everyday activities. Some of these activities were more evident archaeologically than others. Self-provisioning, religious faith and practice, education, health maintenance, glass-knapping, sewing, and changes in ceramic assemblages provide insight into the expression and maintenance of dignity in daily life by African Americans living and working at Alma and Riverlake plantations during the Reconstruction and Jim Crow eras. By using multiple lines of evidence, I was able to find and interpret remains of these activities in contexts at different scales.

Self-sufficiency, especially self-provisioning, served a practical purpose (survival) but was also an avenue for asserting and maintaining a sense of dignity in a broader society hostile to African Americans. These activities, with origins dating to the earliest days of enslavement, were encouraged by African American activists, particularly Booker T. Washington. Self-sufficiency was an avenue for moving away from paternalistic relationships and interactions, which limited their aspirations.

Although not highly visible archaeologically, religious faith and practice and education were cornerstones of preparing and maintaining habits of self-sufficiency within the community. African Americans at Alma and Riverlake, as was typical for plantation communities of the region, established their own churches and schools during the postbellum, hand-cutting era, pooling their funds and providing sweat equity so that their community could have the benefits of these institutions (Antoine 2001; Cooley 2004; Dunn and Dunn 2004; Palmer 2005: 207–208). Church services were (and continue to be) a time of renewal and restoration of spirit and a place for the community to gather together. The church was also a place where the community could organize to help meet the needs of those who were ill, infirm, or otherwise having difficulty.

While limited agricultural and other vocational education for rural African Americans was promoted by some members of the white government and private sector establishment, academic education was discouraged. The school "year" for African American children was considerably shorter than that for white children. Economic pressure for children to quit school and join the workforce continued into the 1970s for many African Americans in plantation regions, and racist white people also used violence to discourage African American education. There are several documented incidences from the postbellum, hand-cutting era of African Americans in Pointe Coupée and nearby West Feliciana parishes being assaulted and murdered by white people for pursuing education or displaying too much proficiency with mental tasks (De Jong 2002: 33; Wilkie 2000: 215–216).

Of the living older members of the Alma African American community whom I interviewed, only one, Mrs. Peggy Sambo, reported having attended school for more than five years (Sambo and Slaughter 2004). Her longer-than-average school attendance is likely a consequence of her being the daughter of Rev. Steve Johnson, minister at Saint Alma Baptist at that time. According to Mrs. Sambo, school for African American children at the time (ca. 1918–1930 in her case) was available only 3 of the 12 months of the year (Sambo and Slaughter 2004). When asked about contact with white children when she was young, Mrs. Sambo bitterly recalled an instance of imposed indignity from her childhood: "White children would pass us in their busses and we poor children would be walking in their dust" (Sambo and Slaughter 2004).

Although not able to attend school for more than a few years, Mr. Eddie Antoine of Alma Plantation did not let this stop him from obtaining knowledge throughout his life. He learned new techniques at work through observation and also picked up some conversational Italian from immigrant agricultural workers in the strawberry fields of Ponchatoula (Antoine 2001). Mr. Antoine also participated in a sheep-shearing program held at Poplar Grove (sugar) Plantation near Port Allen, Louisiana, sponsored in part by Southern University as part of its agricultural extension work. The class included both African American and white men, but the white instructor was not as interested in teaching African Americans (Antoine 2001). The instructor's racist worldview was revealed one day when Mr. Antoine acted outside of the imposed *habitus* of African Americans under Jim Crow. Mr. Antoine was shearing a sheep every 10 or 15 minutes and kept calling upon the white man who was catching sheep for him to bring another, at which point the white instructor accosted Mr. Antoine using racially abusive language ("You know what dirty word he said? 'Nigger what you doing?'") (Antoine 2001). Mr. Antoine had been at the end of the line of about 15 men who had to shear a certain number of sheep and was trying to complete the task so that he could take his lunch break at noon (after beginning at six a.m.) when the incident occurred, and he responded to the white instructor by telling him not to treat him like a dog (and briefly contemplating smashing the man in the head with the sheep shears) (Antoine 2001). If this had not been a government-sponsored program, it is likely that Mr. Antoine's violation of the expected *habitus* for African Americans living under Jim Crow racism could have resulted in a physical assault upon him by the white instructor or other white people. African Americans at Alma and Riverlake pursued educational opportunities despite economic pressures to leave school for the workforce, hostile learning environments (even in government-sponsored programs as was the situation with Mr. Antoine's sheep-shearing experience), and the very real threat of white terrorist violence.

Health maintenance artifacts were also not that visible in the archaeological record at either site (Palmer 2005: 177–178). We know from oral history and ethno-archaeology that more activity related to maintaining or restoring health was taking place than is reflected in the archaeological record, as many of the folk remedies used by African Americans did not require artifacts specifically identifiable as medical products. Several homemade herbal remedies for colds, fevers, and headaches were described to me by former Alma residents (Dunn and Dunn 2004; Sambo and Slaughter 2004). Some of the mass-produced products found were used for multiple purposes, including as ingredients for home remedies. An example of this is petroleum jelly, which was used as hair pomade, on cuts and scrapes, and as a base for homemade salves (Wilkie 1996a).

Alma's workers and residents had access to treatment by an M.D. in the nearby town of New Roads, but they limited their use of his services to illnesses or injuries that could not be treated at home using patent medicines or folk remedies (Antoine 2001; Cooley 2004; Dunn and Dunn 2004; Sambo and Slaughter 2004). Medical problems that were beyond the care of the local physician required a trip to the Charity Hospital in New Orleans (Antoine 2001). Although partly reliant upon home and traditional remedies out of financial constraints, knowing how to resolve certain injuries and illnesses—and doing so within the community—was no doubt a source of pride, as it demonstrated self-sufficiency, knowledge, and mastery, all of which contribute to personal and community dignity.

Flaked-glass tools found at Alma and Riverlake are examples of an economic strategy of self-sufficiency, limiting store purchases and producing things within the community. This strategy allowed African Americans there to maximize their limited resources and to maintain and assert their dignity. Worked glass included an aqua bottle base and a colorless container base from the 1910–1940 Alma subassemblage and a colorless sauce dish from 1910–1940 Riverlake with distinct edge wear. The glass tools are also an example of creative reuse of material culture. Making these tools was not only economically beneficial but was also a source of pride from possessing the skill and mastery needed to make them. Flaked-glass tools were used by enslaved Africans and postbellum African Americans in Louisiana for a number of things including being used as razors for shaving designs into the hair, for shaving the face, and for smoothing axe and hoe handles (Wilkie 1996b: 44–45).

Safety razor blades could also be used for these purposes and were commonly used by rural Louisiana African Americans for whittling, cutting, and scraping (Wilkie 1996a: 46). However, safety razor blades would have been expensive for sugarcane workers during the postbellum, hand-cutting era (Antoine 2001; Reeves 1999; Sambo and Slaughter 2004; Wilkie 1996b: 45–46).

Alma's and Riverlake's African American residents also maximized their financial resources by limiting purchases of ready-to-wear clothing through home manufacture and the reuse of clothing as "hand-me-downs" (Dunn and Dunn 2004). Cloth would be purchased in the plantation store or during the infrequent shopping trip to New Roads or Baton Rouge, or salvaged from old garments. Commodity bags (from bulk staples such as rice, sugar, flour, cornmeal, or animal feed) were also a source of cloth for towels, tablecloths, curtains, and work and informal clothing (Banning 2005). A skilled seamstress from Alma made christening gowns for the infants of the community, contributing to the gift and exchange network in this manner and strengthening intra-community cooperation and connections (Dunn and Dunn 2004). Producing beautiful gowns for this important ritual was a tangible expression of craft mastery. The gowns were also a material projection of dignity onto the infants, who would all too soon have to learn how to negotiate their way in life in a world dominated by white people who viewed them as unworthy of rights, privileges, and dignity.

Sewing was also one of the ways in which extra money could be earned. Others included taking in laundry, gardening for others, moonlighting in the mill, housecleaning, childcare, and cutting firewood. This latter job is documented as being a paid moonlighting job prior to emancipation at several Louisiana sugar plantations, and some of the other tasks may also have been performed for cash at the time.

In addition to working the harvest of other (nonsugar) crops in Ponchatoula, Opelousas, and Mississippi, Mr. Eddie Antoine took the opportunity to earn extra money by working nights in the sugar mill after putting in a 12-hour day in the fields: "So, what we used to do, us would work in the field until six o'clock in the evening, and us would knock off out of the field, and us would go to the sugar house and truck sugar until twelve o'clock at night. And go home at twelve o'clock that night and be ready to go back to work in the field at six o'clock that morning. So us was making a day and a half" (Antoine 2001).

African American cotton farmers from Mississippi (share or tenant farmers) also worked in the sugar mill at Alma during the grinding season. The significance of the increased financial independence that this additional cash income allowed the Mississippians was not lost on Mr. Antoine, who said that he remembered, "Them fellows in Mississippi they would grow cotton, and when they get through getting all their cotton, then they would come to the sugar house and they would give them a job in the sugar house; they'll make them enough money, before they go back, and next summer they'll make their crop *cash*" (Antoine 2001).

These extra jobs allowed African American workers to reduce their financial dependency upon the plantation. Extra income also made it possible for many to save money, which they used to move away from the plantation, purchase property of their own, and achieve other goals such as helping to provide educational opportunities for children and grandchildren.

Self-provisioning to the extent possible was a necessary activity for economic reasons but also was a major source of pride for African Americans at Alma and Riverlake plantations. The first enslaved Africans in Louisiana had to provide food for themselves, using their traditional skills as well as techniques learned from Native Americans and Europeans to feed themselves and their families. This tradition of self-provisioning continued into the Jim Crow era and was supported anew by advocates of racial uplift, particularly Booker T. Washington.

A range of domestic and wild animals and plants were consumed (Table 1). Household-scale animal husbandry and gardening provided domestic food resources, while gathering, hunting, and fishing supplied wild foods. All members of a family could contribute to the self-provisioning effort, building a sense of accomplishment and shared responsibility in the young and maintaining it well into old age.

TABLE 1. Plants and Animals Consumed at Alma
and Riverlake Plantations c. 1870–1940

Plants grown or gathered for food:	Animals raised, hunted, or fished for food:
Okra, snap beans, butter beans, tomatoes, bell peppers, mustard greens, cabbage, sweet potatoes, Irish potatoes, blackberries, dewberries, turnips, peas, corn, squash, plums, peaches, figs, pecans, peanuts, watermelon, garlic, onions, eggplant	Pig, chicken, turkey, cow (milk & meat), sheep, goat, duck, pigeon (squab), catfish, drum, gar, bowfin, sunfish, frog, turtle, tortoise, alligator, opossum, raccoon

Compiled from oral, documentary, and archaeological data.

Most of the foods purchased were staples that were otherwise unobtainable or difficult to produce efficiently at the household scale. These included flour, rice, coffee, and sugar (Cooley 2004, Sambo and Slaughter 2004). The majority of purchases were from the plantation store because of its proximity and their limited access to transportation (Palmer 2005: 158).

Products sold in bulk were packaged in materials that do not preserve well and are missing from the archaeological record at Alma and Riverlake. Tin cans, however, did preserve as fragments. From analysis of the cans present in the assemblages (minimum number of vessels [MNV] based upon diagnostic parts), it appears that African Americans at Alma and Riverlake reduced their purchases of canned foods after 1910, from 14 percent to 9 percent at Riverlake Plantation and from 24 percent to 22 percent at Alma Plantation.

The residents of Alma and Riverlake stored the plant and animal foods they had provided for themselves through salting and canning. Pork, from hogs slaughtered in the late fall, was cured, salted, and put up to store for later use. Hog-killing was a time of community gathering, with neighbors dividing up the tasks of butchering and then sharing the meat of the animals. The exchange and sharing of home-produced foods was another part of the community exchange network, which distributed economic pressure and also reinforced a sense of solidarity and pride in the community. Potatoes and sweet potatoes were a winter crop, but other garden produce needed to be stored after harvesting. "Putting up" produce for the winter months was accomplished through canning. All of the fruits and vegetables grown that were not eaten in season would be preserved in canning jars for later consumption, helping to reduce dependence upon store-purchased produce and canned goods, especially during the winter months.

The archaeologically evident decrease in purchased canned foods after 1910 corresponds with a likewise evident increase in the home canning of foods (from 19 percent to 26 percent at Riverlake and from 10 percent to 18 percent at Alma Plantation). The decline in consumption of this store-bought food at Alma and Riverlake is an example of everyday actions to increase self-sufficiency, reduce dependency and debt, and prepare for a different future.

Using the method devised by George Miller (1980) and values from Susan Henry's (1987) research, I performed ceramic price index analysis on the vessels (MNV from diagnostic sherds) from the Alma and Riverlake assemblages. Both sites showed a decline in value with the post-1910 subassemblages, with Riverlake declining from 1.75 to 1.33 and Alma from 2.47 to 2.10 (Palmer 2005: 194–196).

After about 1910 there was a reduction in the number of higher-priced decorated ceramics in the assemblages at both sites, which lowered the economic value of the ceramic assemblages. No matching ceramics were recovered at either site except for the plain, white-bodied ironstone wares (also known as semivitreous earthenwares). Superficially, a lower value could mean that the residents of Alma and Riverlake were doing worse economically after circa 1910. The lack of matching patterns among these high-value ceramics and the knowledge that it was common for planters and other relatively well-off white people at the time to give ceramics in partial payment

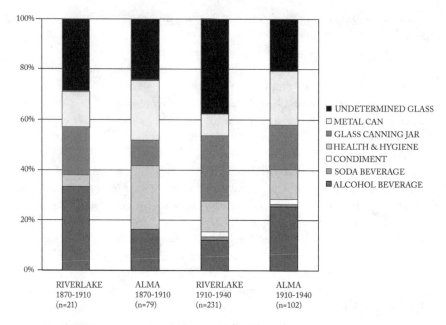

Container types recovered at Alma and Riverlake
plantations (Palmer 2005).

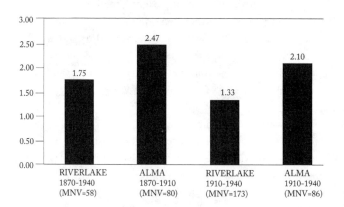

Mean ceramic index values: 1870–1910 and 1910–1940,
Alma and Riverlake Subassemblages (Palmer 2005).

for housework or as gifts, however, led me to a different conclusion. Often these payment or gift ceramics were out of fashion or were from incomplete sets. I strongly suspect that this acquisition of higher-value ceramics as payment or gifts is what many of the higher-value ceramics found at Alma and Riverlake represent. If so, then the reduction of this after 1910 is archaeological evidence of one way in which African Americans rejected racist paternalism and asserted their dignity.

Discussion

Through research combining archaeological, oral, documentary, and ethnographic data, I was able to reconstruct aspects of the everyday lives and activities of late-nineteenth- and early-twentieth-century African American sugar plantation workers at Alma and Riverlake plantations relating to dignity. Although constrained by poverty and racist individuals and institutions, African Americans maintained and asserted their dignity on a daily basis through maximizing their self-sufficiency and limiting debt and dependence. These practices were essential for physical, mental, and spiritual survival but also were a powerful means of asserting dignity and preparing for a better future on a daily basis.

Methodologically, the multiple lines of evidence used in this project were essential; the conclusions reached would have been different if any had been neglected. The use of these different lines of evidence—oral, documentary, ethnoarchaeological, and archaeological data—was necessary to investigate the lives of Alma's and Riverlake's African American residents due to biases and silences of the documentary record but also taphonomic biases that result in the living sites of poorer people and minorities being less well-preserved than those of white elites. Multiple lines of evidence, especially the oral histories that document the voices of African Americans who lived during this time period, are essential for escaping structural biases and forging historical narratives that counter those distorted by endemic racist ideas and structures. A theoretical approach coming out of critical race theory and practice theory-facilitated research that is scholarly and true to the core vindicationist mission of historical archaeology.

This study should encourage other archaeologists to take a second look at late-nineteenth- and early-twentieth-century rural African American sites and to talk to their colleagues in cultural anthropology, geography, and history (especially oral history). Archaeology has the opportunity to provide more insights on how the African American everyday people of the rural South worked toward a second emancipation that led to the civil rights movement as well as how efforts to maintain and assert dignity through daily practices became a route to enfranchisement, reclaiming the vote, education, and civil rights.

References

Antoine, E. 2001. Eddie Antoine interviewed by David Palmer, 6 July. In *Alma Plantation Interviews* on file, T. Harry Williams Center for Oral History, Hill Memorial Library, Louisiana State University, Baton Rouge.

Banning, J. L. 2005. *Feed Sack Fashions in South Louisiana, 1949–1968: The Use of Commodity Bags in Garment Construction.* Ph.D. dissertation, Louisiana State University, Baton Rouge.

Barile, K. S. 2004. Race, The National Register, and Cultural Resource Management: Creating an Historic Context for Postbellum Sites. *Historical Archaeology* 38(1):90–100.

Bauerlein, M. 2004–2005. Booker T. Washington and W. E. B. DuBois: The Origins of a Bitter Intellectual Battle. *The Journal of Blacks in Higher Education* 46 (Winter):106–114.

Blakey, M. L. 2004. Theory: An Ethical Epistemology of Publicly Engaged Biocultural Research. In *Skeletal Biology Final Report,* Vol. I, edited by M. L. Blakey and L. M. Rankin-Hill, pp. 98–115. Report prepared for the United States General Services Administration, Northeastern and Caribbean Region. Howard University, Washington, D.C.

Bourdieu, P. 1977. *Outline of a Theory of Practice.* Cambridge: Cambridge University Press.

Brandon, J. C. 2009. A North American Historical Perspective on Race and Class in Historical Archaeology. In *International Handbook of Historical Archaeology,* edited by T. Majewski and D. Gaimster, pp. 3–15. New York: Springer.

Clark-Lewis, E. 1996. *Living In, Living Out: African American Domestics and the Great Migration.* New York: Kodansha America.

Compact Oxford English Dictionary (Oxford University Press) 2010. Dignity (Definition, Origin). AskOxford.com. Electronic document, http://www.askoxford.com/concise_oed/dignity?view=uk, accessed March 19, 2010.

Conrad, G. R., and R. F. Lucas 1995. *White Gold: A Brief History of the Louisiana Sugar Industry, 1795–1995.* Lafayette: Center for Louisiana Studies, University of Southwestern Louisiana.

Cooley, P. 2004. Percy Cooley interviewed by David Palmer, 13 August. In *Alma Plantation Interviews* on file, T. Harry Williams Center for Oral History, Hill Memorial Library, Louisiana State University, Baton Rouge.

Crenshaw, K. W. 1995. Race, Reform, and Retrenchment: Transformation and Legitimation in Antidiscrimination Law. In *Critical Race Theory: The Key Writing That Formed the Movement,* edited by K. W. Crenshaw, N. Gotanda, G. Peller, and K. Thomas, pp. 103–122. New York: New Press.

De Jong, G. 2002. *A Different Day: African American Struggles for Justice in Rural Louisiana, 1900–1970.* Chapel Hill: University of North Carolina Press.

DuBois, W. E. B. 1989 *The Souls of Black Folk.* New York: Penguin Books.

Dunn, V., and R. Dunn 2004. Viola Dunn with Rosanna Dunn interviewed by David Palmer, 11 August. In *Alma Plantation Interviews* on file, T. Harry Williams Center for Oral History, Hill Memorial Library, Louisiana State University, Baton Rouge.

Epperson, T. W. 2004. Critical Race Theory and the Archaeology of the African Diaspora. *Historical Archaeology* 38(1):101–108.

————. 1999. Constructing Difference: The Social and Spatial Order of the Chesapeake Plantation. In *I, Too, Am America: Archaeological Studies of African-American Life,* edited by T. A. Singleton, pp. 159–172. Charlottesville: University Press of Virginia.

————. 1997. Whiteness in Early Virginia. *Race Traitor* 7:9–20.

Extension Service. United States Department of Agriculture and State Agricultural Colleges Cooperating 1940. A Study of Extension Work with Negroes. Louisiana State University and Agricultural and Mechanical College, Agricultural Extension Division, in University Archives, Special Collections, Louisiana State University Hill Memorial Library, Baton Rouge.

Farnsworth, P. 1993. Current Research, Louisiana: Riverlake Plantation. *Society for Historical Archaeology Newsletter* 26(3):27–28.

Ferguson, K. J. 1998. Caught in "No Man's Land": The Negro Cooperative Demonstration Service and the Ideology of Booker T. Washington, 1900–1918. *Agricultural History* 72(1):33–54.

Ferguson, L. 1992. *Uncommon Ground: Archaeology and Early African America, 1650–1800.* Washington, D.C.: Smithsonian Institution Press.

Flynn, J. P. 1969. Booker T. Washington: Uncle Tom or Trojan Horse. *The Journal of Negro History* 54(3):262–274.

Friedman, L. J. 1974. Life "In the Lion's Mouth": Another Look at Booker T. Washington. *The Journal of Negro History* 59(4):337–351.

Genovese, E. D. 1974. *Roll, Jordan, Roll: The World the Slaves Made.* New York: Pantheon Books.

Giddens, A. 1984 *The Constitution of Society.* Berkeley: University of California Press.

————. 1979. *Central Problems in Social Theory: Action, Structure, and Contradiction in Social Analysis.* Berkeley: University of California Press.

Gotanda, N. 1995. A Critique of "Our Constitution is Color-Blind." In *Critical Race Theory: The Key Writings That Formed the Movement,* edited by K.W. Crenshaw, N. Gotanda, G. Peller, and K. Thomas, pp. 257–275. New York: New Press.

Hall, G. M. 1992. *Africans in Colonial Louisiana: The Development of Afro-Creole Culture in the Eighteenth Century.* Baton Rouge: Louisiana State University Press.

Harlan, L. R. 1971. The Secret Life of Booker T. Washington. *The Journal of Southern History* 37(3):393–416.

————. 1970. Booker T. Washington in Biographical Perspective. *The American Historical Review* 75(6):1581–1599.

Harris, C. I. 1995. Whiteness as Property. In *Critical Race Theory: The Key Writings That Formed the Movement,* edited by K. W. Crenshaw, N. Gotanda, G. Peller, and K. Thomas, pp. 276–291. New York: New Press.

Henige, D. 1982. *Oral Historiography.* London: Longman Group, Ltd.

Henry, S. L. 1987. Factors Influencing Consumer Behavior in Turn-of-the-Century Phoenix, Arizona. In *Consumer Choice in Historical Archaeology,* edited by S. M. Spencer-Wood, pp. 359–381. New York: Plenum Press.

Ignatiev, N. 1995. *How the Irish became White.* New York: Routledge.

Jinks, D. P. 1997. Essays in Refusal: Pre-Theoretical Commitments in Postmodern Anthropology and Critical Race Theory. *The Yale Law Journal* 107(2):499–528.

Joyce, R. A., and J. Lopiparo 2005. PostScript: Doing Agency in Archaeology. *Journal of Archaeological Method and Theory* 12(4):365–374.

LaRoche, C. J., and M. L. Blakey 1997. Seizing Intellectual Power: The Dialogue at the New York African Burial Ground. *Historical Archaeology* 31(3):84–106.

Lawrence, C.R., III 1995. The Id, the Ego, and Equal Protection: Reckoning with Unconscious Racism. In *Critical Race Theory: The Key Writings That Formed the Movement,* edited by K. W. Crenshaw, N. Gotanda, G. Peller, and K. Thomas, pp. 235–257. New York: New Press.

Lightfoot, K., A. Martinez, and A. Schiff 1998. Daily Practice and Material Culture in Pluralistic Social Settings: An Archaeological Study of Culture Change and Persistence from Fort Ross, California. *American Antiquity* 63(2):199–222.

Mack, M. E., and M. L. Blakey 2004. The New York African Burial Ground Project: Past Biases, Current Dilemmas, and Future Research Opportunities. *Historical Archaeology* 38(1):10–17.

Marable, W. M. 1974. Booker T. Washington and African Nationalism. *Phylon* 35(4):398–406.

McKee, L. 1992. The Ideals and Realities behind the Design and Use of 19th Century Virginia Slave Cabins. In *The Art and Mystery of Historical Archaeology: Essays in Honor of James Deetz,* edited by A. E. Yentsch and M. C. Beaudry, 195–214. Boca Raton, Fla.: CRC Press.

Meier, A. 1957. Towards a Reinterpretation of Booker T. Washington. *The Journal of Southern History* 23(2):220–227.

Miller, G. 1980. Classification and Economic Scaling of 19th Century Ceramics. *Historical Archaeology* 13:1–40.

Palmer, D. T. 2005. *Counterpunch the Devil with the Word: African American Daily Life at Alma and Riverlake Plantations, Louisiana, 1870–1940.* Ph.D. dissertation, University of California, Berkeley.

Perry, W., and R. Paynter 1999. Artifacts, Ethnicity, and the Archaeology of African Americans. In *I, Too, Am America: Archaeological Studies of African-American Life,* edited by T. Singleton, pp. 299–310. Charlottesville: University Press of Virginia.

Portelli, A. 1997. *The Battle of Valle Giulia: Oral History and the Art of Dialogue.* Madison: University of Wisconsin Press.

———. 1991. *The Death of Luigi Trastulli: Form and Meaning in Oral History.* Albany: State University of New York Press.

Reeves, W. D. 1999. *Alma Plantation: A History.* Report submitted to David Stewart and family. Lakeland, La.

Ritchie, D. A. 1995 *Doing Oral History.* Twayne's Oral History Series 15. New York: Twayne Publishers.

Rodrigue, J. C. 2001. *Reconstruction in the Cane Fields: From Slavery to Free Labor in Louisiana's Sugar Parishes 1862–1880.* Baton Rouge: Louisiana State University Press.

Roediger, D. R. 1991. *The Wages of Whiteness: Race and the Making of the American Working Class.* London: Verso.

Sambo, P., and N. Slaughter 2004. Peggy Sambo interviewed by David Palmer 16 August. In *Alma Plantation Interviews* on file, T. Harry Williams Center for Oral History, Hill Memorial Library, Louisiana State University, Baton Rouge.

Schiffer, M. B. 1987. *Formation Processes of the Archaeological Record.* Albuquerque: University of New Mexico Press.

Scott, R. 1994. Defining the Boundaries of Freedom in the World of Cane: Cuba, Brazil, and Louisiana after Emancipation. *American Historical Review* 99(1):70–102.

Taylor, E. 1998. A Primer on Critical Race Theory: Who are the critical race theorists and what are they saying? *The Journal of Blacks in Higher Education* (19):122–124.

Thompson, P. 1978 *The Voice of the Past: Oral History.* Oxford: Oxford University Press.

Todorov, T. 2009. Race and Racism. In *Theories of Race and Racism,* edited by L. Back and J. Solomos, pp. 68–74. Translated by C. Porter. New York: Routledge.

Vansina, J. 1985. *Oral Tradition as History.* Madison: University of Wisconsin Press.

Vincent, C. 1981. Booker T. Washington's Tour of Louisiana, April 1915. *Louisiana History: The Journal of the Louisiana Historical Association* 22(2):189–198.

Weik, T. 1997. The Archaeology of Maroon Societies in the Americas: Resistance, Cultural Continuity, and Transformation in the African Diaspora. *Historical Archaeology* 31(2): 81–92.

Whayne, J. M. 1998. Black Farmers and the Agricultural Cooperative Extension Service: The Alabama Experience 1945–1965. *Agricultural History* 72(3):523–551.

Wilkie, L. A. 2000. *Creating Freedom: Material Culture and African American Identity at Oakley Plantation, Louisiana, 1840–1950.* Baton Rouge: Louisiana State University Press.

———. 1996a. Medicinal Teas and Patent Medicines: African-American Women's Consumer Choices and Ethnomedical Traditions at a Louisiana Plantation. *Southeastern Archaeology* 15(2):119–131.

———. 1996b. Glass-Knapping at a Louisiana Plantation: African-American Tools? *Historical Archaeology* 30(4):37–49.

———. 1995. Plantation Archaeology: Where Past and Present Can Collide. *African American Archaeology* 13:2–5.

Wilkie, L. A., P. Farnsworth, and D. T. Palmer 2010. African American Archaeology. In *Archaeology of Louisiana,* edited by M. A. Rees, pp. 307–324. Baton Rouge: Louisiana State University Press.

Williamson, F. W. 1951. *Origin and Growth of Agricultural Extension in Louisiana 1860–1948: How it Opened the Road for Progress in Better Farming and Rural Living.* Baton Rouge: Louisiana State University and Agricultural and Mechanical College, Division of Agricultural Extension.

From Slave to Citizen on James Island

The Archaeology of Freedom at Fort Johnson

For former enslaved laborers, the transition from slave to citizen was not necessarily an easy change. Freedom was experienced differently across the southeastern United States. On James Island, South Carolina, one of the South Carolina and Georgia sea islands that became the heartland of Gullah culture, the archaeology of the "afterlives" (Hicks 2007: 68, see also Wilkie and Farnsworth, "Living Not So Quietly," this volume) of plantations sheds light on how former slaves experienced the transition from slave to citizen. Citizenship is a "political status assigned to individuals by states, as a relation of belonging to specific communities, or as a set of social practices that define the relationships between peoples and states and among peoples within communities" (Canning and Rose 2001: 427). The Fourteenth Amendment reversed the portion of the *Dred Scott vs. Sandford* decision that declared that African Americans were not and could not become citizens of the United States or enjoy the privileges and immunities of it. Archaeology provides a lens through which to examine how former enslaved laborers materially sought citizenship and freedom in postemancipation South Carolina.

Between 1995 and 2000 several archaeological projects were conducted at Fort Johnson, located on Charleston Harbor at the tip of James Island. Research, including large-scale survey, evaluative testing, and a metal detector survey, conducted in advance of the construction of a new marine and environmental research laboratory—the MEHRL project—showed that all of the areas acceptable for a building location contained archaeological remains of one sort or another (Steen 1995; Steen et al. 2002). The area eventually chosen fell primarily in a filled wetland so that relatively little of the intact archaeological remains would be impacted. Excavations and a metal detector survey revealed an occupation that dated primarily to the later nineteenth century. There were no obvious complicated architectural remains, so mitigation plans were made that called for additional hand excavation, topsoil stripping and feature excavation, and long-term monitoring and phased metal detecting.

Because the excavations showed a relatively low artifact density and ephemeral architecture, the occupation appeared to be a fairly typical Low-Country Gullah site.

Army engineer's sketch map of Fort Johnson, 1892. Courtesy of the National Archives, record group 77, drawer 67, sheet 44, Washington, D.C.

Then there is the map that showed six "Negro Cabins" in the area, confirming this impression. At first these cabins were interpreted as the homes of people working on the base, but further research showed that African American squatters occupied the cabins, providing interesting perspective on postemancipation life.

The History of Fort Johnson

Fort Johnson is probably best known as the place where the first shot of the Civil War was fired, but it has a history that is curiously nonmartial. Native Americans occupied it intermittently for at least 10,000 years before the Carolina colony was formed in 1670. The land was claimed by an Englishman named Edward Lacey in the early 1680s, but he quickly died from "country fever" and the land passed through several hands until the threat of war with the French and Spanish in 1704 prompted the legislature to consider the need for fortifications. In 1708 the first Fort Johnson was built (Mustard 1963). Hurricanes and neglect caused it to fall into ruin and be rebuilt in 1737 and 1759. It was rebuilt again during the American Revolution and occupied by both sides but never saw action.

Following the war, Fort Johnson was allowed to degenerate, but it was rebuilt in 1793 under state supervision. The newly formed Army Engineers and Artillerists took control in 1794, and a garrison commanded by a former Charleston militia captain, Michael Kalteissen, manned the fort (Riley 1999). It was destroyed by hurricanes in 1803 and 1806 (Fraser 2006). Both the French and British, who were embroiled in global warfare at the time, threatened to go to war with the fledgling United States, and in 1807 new fortifications were built on higher ground. As the War of 1812 approached, further construction was completed, including a martello tower. But Charleston was never attacked. The hurricane of 1815 destroyed the fortification walls, and they were not rebuilt, as the army's second phase of coastal fortifications focused on other locations around the harbor (Wade 1977). The buildings were repaired, however, and Fort Johnson became headquarters for the army engineers. It served in this capacity until January 1861, when the Confederates took over and refortified it.

For over 150 years, Fort Johnson was a military installation that never saw action. During most of its history, Fort Johnson served a nonmilitary function as well. The harbor's quarantine anchorage was offshore, and incoming captains had to report to the commander or quarantine officer. Although it was an army base, it also served a peaceful and benign function that continues today. Fort Johnson was a place where people from around the world could be found, but it was also on the tip of James Island, a sea island with several large plantations. It was the home of a few hundred white people and a few thousand slaves. The enslaved population, consisting of African, Indian, and mixed-race individuals, provided much of the labor for projects at Fort Johnson and other harbor defenses.

As early as 1831, Fort Johnson took on another role: the planters of James Island began to move their families to a summer resort they called Johnsonville. "Resort" may be a strong word, because the buildings were described as plain and unpretentious. Fever outbreaks were a constant threat during the eighteenth and nineteenth centuries, and the white people who could—along with their households—decamped during the warm months. During the years leading up to the Civil War, Fort Johnson also served as a public landing and passenger steamboat dock. It was a focal point for travelers as well as the people of the island, who passed through often on their way to the market in Charleston.

Johnsonville and Fort Johnson worked together to focus the James Island community in a place that was open and public, allowing residents to see and be seen and to interact with neighbors and relatives. The plantations of the island were spread out, and at times communication among them, especially the enslaved, would have been restricted. As military officers noted in the 1830s, however, the slaves who worked in the households and labored for the army sometimes treated their time here as a visit to a resort, just as their owners did. Officers and residents alike raised complaints about alcohol and noise. This opportunity to socialize was important in building an alternative community over which the white owners had little control.

As tensions mounted in 1860, federal troops abandoned the installation and took refuge at Fort Sumter. The Confederates took over in January 1861 and immediately started building artillery emplacements. The fort was built up considerably during the war. It was bombarded almost daily after the Americans took Morris Island and the surrounding marshes in 1863 but saw a direct land attack on only one occasion. This was easily repulsed, and the Confederates held the fort until their surrender in 1865. Immediately after the war the fort was occupied by federal troops, who inventoried the artillery and dismounted the guns. Soon they were demobilized and sent home.

The period between 1865 and 1872 is poorly documented at Fort Johnson but is of central importance to the people discussed in this essay, as this is the period when they stopped being property—slaves—and became, to a degree at least, American citizens. A list of people treated at the "James Island Hospital" is found in the Freedmen's Bureau papers (National Archives RG 105, entry 2987), but this was likely at the McLeod Plantation headquarters (Rose 1964). Army records mention a Private Samuel Bryant of the 21st USCT Regiment dying at the "small pox hospital Fort Johnson, James Island" in 1865 (National Archives RG 94 7–16–1865), so there is some indication that Fort Johnson continued to serve a public health function.

When the war was under way, most James Islanders, white and black, were evacuated. When the war ended, McLeod Plantation was seized by the Freedmen's Bureau and given to former slaves, but this was quickly rescinded. For years the island had a demographic and social structure quite similar to what had existed before the war. Few were able to obtain land, but most sea island African Americans worked on white-owned farms, living in the old slave settlements, only now for wages or shares. Initially, the work was done under supervised contracts, but with the demise of the Freedmen's Bureau in 1868 individuals negotiated their own deals—for better or worse. The period has been discussed in detail by historians Willie Lee Rose (1964) and Julie Saville (1994).

The postemancipation period was a time of struggle and wrenching poverty for the island's African American residents. In 1872 it was reported that 1,900 of the 4,000 free black people living on James Island died of smallpox (Lebby 1872: 725). Every family probably faced the loss of one or more members.

In 1874 a mortar battery was proposed for Fort Johnson in what would have been a part of the nation's third system of coastal defenses (Wade 1977). In a note accompanying the plans an unnamed author (probably General Quincy Gilmore) stated, "There is nothing left of the old fort at this place except some rough mounds of earth and some Confederate guns which are almost completely buried in the ground" (National Archives RG 77, Drawer 67, Sheet A). He noted the presence of a frame house (70 by 25 feet) and two frame structures (12 by 12 feet), all of which were used for storage. He also said, "There are besides some rough cabins on the reservation occupied by colored people under whose authority is not known, but there seems to be no occasion for disturbing them" (National Archives RG 77, Drawer 67, Sheet A).

The site had been used as a quarantine station intermittently since as early as 1698, but after the Civil War this became its primary purpose (Horlbeck 1891). In 1874 the quarantine station was "near the fort, but outside of the United States Reservation" (National Archives RG 77, Drawer 67, Sheet A). The U.S. reservation was in the center of the peninsula. Dr. Robert Lebby, Sr., of James Island and Charleston had served as the state and city quarantine officer before the war and as a contract surgeon with the army. He and both of his sons served the Confederate government during the war. Robert Lebby, Sr., ran two hospitals in the city, while his sons served in the Confederate army.

With the end of the war, the Lebbys' services went to the new federal occupation government and their private practices. When civil government was restored in 1868, Robert Lebby, Sr., was appointed health officer of the port (Lebby Family Papers 10–14, 1868). A letter thanking him for his "devoted care" was written by a French ship captain in 1870 (Lebby Family Papers 5–7, 1870), so he had obviously been serving in this capacity earlier. Though they had evacuated James Island for the city during the war, in 1872 Robert Lebby, Jr., wrote to his father that he was in the process of building a new house on their old plantation (Lebby Family Papers 3–29, 1872).

Robert Lebby, Sr., was appointed surgeon general of the state by the governor in January 1873 (Lebby Family Papers 1–8, 1873). This is a position with the state militia and may account for a late-nineteenth-century militia button found in 1998. Receipts for his son E. Munroe Lebby's services as assistant health officer for Charleston Harbor in 1873 marked "Fort Johnson" suggest the continued use of, at the least, the docks and boat facilities. Robert Lebby produced detailed reports as health officer in 1872, 1873, and 1874 (Lebby Family Papers n.d.).

Recognizing the dangers of contagious disease, the federal government moved to upgrade quarantine facilities nationwide. In 1880 the National Board of Health provided buildings and facilities, but Dr. Lebby's son Robert Lebby, Jr., administered the operations for the Charleston Board of Health (Ellis 1967). The following year they reported that the quarantine officer was now required to live "at or near" the station. In 1890 it was reported that

> New buildings are now being erected. The Health Officer of the Port, Dr. Robert Lebby Sr., informs me that these buildings consist of a fever hospital thirty five feet six inches by fifty feet six inches; smallpox hospital fifteen by thirty feet six inches; kitchen twelve by sixteen, all one story high; a Keeper's dwelling fifteen feet six inches by thirty six feet, two stories high, lathed and plastered; the others not. The National Board of Health have repaired and strengthened the storehouse to receive cargoes, thirty five feet six inches by seventy feet six inches; have erected two new buildings twelve by twelve by the store house—one for store-keeper's residence, the other for a disinfecting house. Also under order a wharf three hundred and thirty five feet long. (Horlbeck 1891: 75–76)

In 1880 the federal lands were remapped using an 1848 plat as a basis. This outline was used in inspection reports and to show proposed building plans and other modifications until 1906. From that era, several plats have survived that give crucial evidence. In 1880 only three buildings were depicted—an "old buoy shed (not in use)," the health officer's house, and a "negro dwelling." The latter two were on state land, with the former at the point adjacent to the fort. The "negro dwelling" is in the far west of the tract. The same is true in 1883. In 1892 five buildings are shown on the point, two of which are on filled land at the quarantine wharves. Inland eight "negro cabins" and two of "Dr. Lebby's outbuildings" are shown, but not the "health officer's house" or, for that matter, half of the ten buildings mentioned by Dr. H. B. Horlbeck in an 1890 report (Horlbeck 1891). On the other hand, Dr. Horlbeck made no mention of the "negro cabins." A plat drawn in 1906, when the station came back under federal control, accurately depicts the buildings mentioned by Horlbeck and nine "negro cabins."

In 2002 we were forced to conclude that "in 1880 at least one black family was living on state land just off the tract. By 1906 as many as 9 families lived there—perhaps 20 to 30 people. As they were living on government land, there are no land plats or tax records to tell us their names. In all likelihood, some were employed by the quarantine station, but no personnel records remain from the period of state control (Steen et al. 2002: 122).

Historical research conducted at the time failed to identify the residents, so we were forced to rely on historic context and the archaeological record to interpret the remains and the lives of the people. Further work was done at a different part of the site in 2007 in advance of the construction of a laboratory and teaching facility. Historical research focused on the fort's role in the War of 1812 and as a quarantine facility, but there, buried in the midst of a file of land acquisition records, was a two-page document consisting of answers to questions. Unfortunately the questions themselves were not included. It seems a little curious at first, but by reading between the lines it is easy to guess what many of the questions must have been. Answer 17 is pertinent:

> 17: Yes, negro squatters. In my report of September 8, 1892, I say "it appears to me to preserve our title these tenants should either be removed of forced to pay rent."
>
> 17a: Caleb Campbell, wife and daughter; Paul Campbell, wife and five children; Abram Brown, wife and two children; Toney Campbell, wife and four children; Jim Thomas, two daughters and two grand children.
>
> 17b: Respectively 25, 25, 10, 15, 25 approximately.
>
> 17c: Residences and small crops

It was frustrating not to know who lived in the cabins while trying to interpret the remains, but that is not an uncommon state for the archaeologist. Usually, it seems, we are not even fortunate enough to have a convenient map that identifies our subjects by race. Though it was clear from the maps and documents that the site was occupied by African American squatters, that was about all that could be said, at least on a site-specific "particular" level. Attempts to identify potential occupants through the federal census were unsuccessful. We could find some white occupants, but in 1870 and 1880 everyone else in the area was black, and they shared a common occupation (farmer) and economic status (poor). No one was identified as a quarantine worker or nonagricultural wage earner.

Another development was the publication of *James Island: Stories from Slave Descendants* by Eugene Frazier, Sr., in 2006. Frazier is one of those slave descendants and, from his childhood, had an interest in history. His recollections give great insight into the people of the island and their beliefs and customs from a perspective little represented in the historical literature of the Low Country. With this information, we can make generalizations about the people, but with names we can check the interpretations both through documents and through oral history. First I will review the excavations in the squatter settlement and interpretations.

Archaeology at Fort Johnson

Any interpretation at Fort Johnson is difficult because of the interplay of a number of issues. For instance, the later occupation sits on the edge of a relatively dense occupation area that was the home of the base commandant and officers in the 1780s to 1820s. Thus earlier artifacts are mixed in with the later ones. Some artifacts will be used until they will no longer function, which might take many years. Sorting out items with a long-use life from those discarded in the 1820s is sometimes difficult. One example we found was an alkaline-glazed clabber bowl, made near Edgefield between 1849 and 1852. This bowl may have finally been broken and discarded over 50 years later.

Next, during the Civil War an earthwork was built north of the old commandant's house, and troops camped in the area. Numerous tent rings and a camp kitchen were found, along with a number of uniform buttons. But with only a couple of exceptions the buttons were federal, not Confederate. Federal troops were here after the war to dismantle the guns and batteries, which could explain this, but at the same time army surplus clothing was issued by the Freedmen's Bureau. Clothing was also obtained through gifting, trade, purchase, and salvage, so the African American occupants may have owned them.

Finally, and by no means the least important, the entire area has been occupied since the 1950s by medical and marine biology researchers and the state's Department of Natural Resources. Trees have been cleared, roads built, low spots filled, and foundations excavated. Disturbance is widespread and very bad in places. Add in all of the artifacts left behind by those researchers and divide by the fact that the historic occupation is all within the top 30 cm of soil (except in features), and it is not hard to see that this can result in a complicated problem.

The archaeology done at Fort Johnson was spurred by development, but care was taken to do a thorough job, with the active support of the state and federal agencies involved. An earlier survey (Trinkley et al. 1995) had determined that the project area was of "low significance." Questions regarding the accuracy of the "significance" map arose, so further testing was required. It was agreed that the obvious highly sensitive areas should be avoided, and other factors ruled out some areas, so this seemed to be the best place to concentrate. The first step we took in 1995 was to establish a reliable site-wide grid and resurvey the area at a 20–meter interval. The survey showed that even the "low significance" later-nineteenth-century occupation was dense and intact enough to be considered eligible to the National Register of Historic Places and require "mitigation." Fort Johnson as a whole is on the National Register. Individual components are considered contributing elements. If the greater good is served by sacrificing cultural resources, the damage can be mitigated through research and public education.

Documentary research at National Archives at that time revealed that the occupants were free black people, squatters, living there "on whose authority I do not know," as the inspector said in 1874. When correlated with the modern site plan, a series of maps from 1880 to 1906 showed two sets of "negro cabins" in the project area.

There was a time when historical archaeologists mostly concentrated on upper-class white people and the infrastructure that supported them such as taverns and blacksmith shops. But as long as the author has been in the field (1981), an effort has been made to take a more egalitarian, class, and color-blind approach, so the idea that free black squatters were occupying the site was interesting and worth exploring— not something to dismiss as "modern disturbance," as Dan Hicks (2007) discusses. Normally avoidance and preservation is the preferred treatment for contributing properties at Fort Johnson, but this component was on the edge of one of the few areas with relatively little in the way of archaeological remains, and the components were ephemeral and the impact could effectively be mitigated with excavation and research, so plans were made for further work.

In 1998 we tested the entire area with 50–centimeter test units at a 5–meter interval to obtain a statistically meaningful sample and conducted an intensive metal detector survey. We created artifact density maps and excavated larger 2–x–2–meter excavation units to obtain a larger artifact sample and identify cultural features. This quickly established that features such as posts and a well were present, so a combination of hand excavation and topsoil stripping was used to expose the structures that were thought to be the "negro cabins."

Excavations revealed two structures. One structure was clear, and another was hidden in a mess of dozens of posts. By analyzing the depth of these posts, it was possible to suggest a configuration (or configurations). Neither structure had a chimney or brick piers. They were called "rough cabins" in 1874, and later inspectors complained about their shabby appearance. In all likelihood they were built from salvaged lumber. They were probably heated with wood or coal stoves—trash burners, as Eugene Frazier (2006: 102) puts it.

The arrangement of posts and distribution of artifacts told us where the people lived and that their homes were insubstantial, as we might expect. Several expedient barrel wells were found in the area. These were made by digging a large hole down to

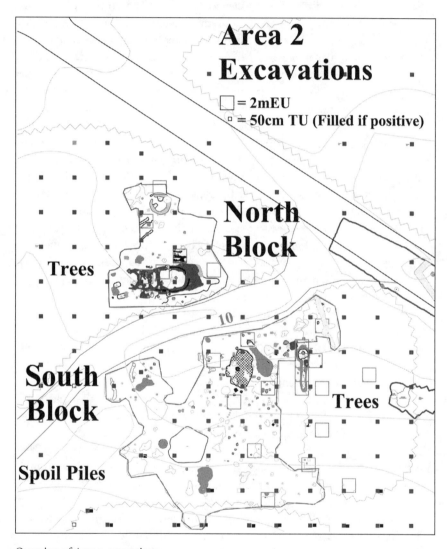

Overview of Area 2 excavations.

Photographs of feature 98-44, a barrel well. Courtesy of the author.

the water table, then sinking another hole into which a barrel was placed. A second barrel was placed on this and the hole backfilled. This provided much of their water supply, though rain barrels were probably also employed. So the excavation process both confirmed historically documented information and revealed new features.

Life on Fort Johnson

Attempts to identify the occupants of these cabins by name were fruitless during the 1998–2002 fieldwork. We tried searching census records by finding known white families and people who had occupations that suggested they worked at the quarantine station, looking to see who their neighbors were. This was fruitless, as all of the black people in the area were listed as farmers and laborers. Further, the quarantine officer, Dr. Robert Lebby, had a family farm/plantation a couple of miles up Fort Johnson Road, so it was hard to say whether he was enumerated there or at the quarantine officer's house at Fort Johnson. The occupants of the cabins remained nameless, faceless people, and archaeology was the only method to extract meaning from the artifacts.

Yet once the identities of the families were discovered, we were able to see what life after emancipation may have been like and how former enslaved laborers sought to become citizens through education, community-building, and creating places of their own. Life during slavery was hard, but life after slavery was not easy either. If and when it was possible, people bought land of their own, but the system was stacked against them in that regard, as working on a share or wage basis on white-owned farms insured that few would ever get far enough ahead to have the capital to become landowners. Eugene Frazier (2006) points to several landowners who were known for their stinginess and for treating workers badly. However, this was the case throughout the South and, indeed is a significant facet of capitalism in general. If labor costs can be kept down, profits are higher.

The path taken by the Campbell, Brown, and Thomas families, squatting on available public land, was an alternative that most people could not take, but it must have been empowering. It was inferred in 2002 that the occupants of the cabins probably worked seasonally at the quarantine station because they had money for ceramics, glass bottles and the contents thereof, multiple firearms (using the minimum number of individual vessels calculation method our "MNG"=8), toys, and other household goods. The same set of documents that provided the people's names provides proof that they were working at the quarantine station seasonally or part-time. In these documents a 1918 letter from the quarantine officer to his superiors in Washington asked for permission to allow two attendants' families to move their houses to Fort Johnson. He stated that they were tenants on the Hinson farm and that Hinson had given them an ultimatum: they must either work in his fields full-time or move out of their houses. In the 1870–1900 census records, the Campbell and Brown families were listed together as if they were indeed neighbors, but in association with the white Grimball family, whose farm was across the island on the Stono River. In these records, they were listed as farmers, not workers such as boatmen or quarantine attendants.

Most of the first generation, the former enslaved laborers, were illiterate and lacked the skills that would allow them to join the industrial workforce. Although the freedmen guarded their status jealously and were free to move, they mostly ended up working on the farms of the former plantation owners and living in what remained of the old slave cabins. This was the only home they knew, after all. It was where their families and friends were; it was where they had created their "place," as Andrew Agha (2004) put it.

Faunal and botanical preservation were bad, and little conclusive analysis could be done. Species identified include the usual cow, pig, and sheep or goats, but also a substantial number of fish, turtles, and shellfish from the surrounding marsh. Lead cast-net weights and copper alloy nails also tell of boat use and maintenance and casting for shrimp and fish. Today many James Island residents still begin every fishing trip by casting for their bait. Shotgun brasses and lead shot tell us also that they were probably hunting for ducks and other birds, though no bird bones were identified.

The documents tell us that the occupants were raising families. Though the desire for literacy was strong among the first freed slaves (Rose 1964), the second generation

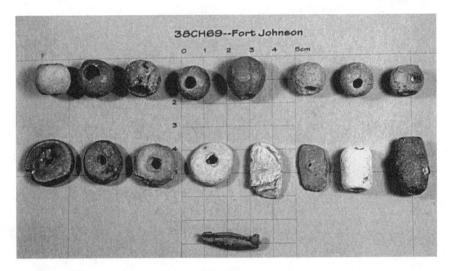

Lead cast-net weights. Courtesy of the author.

was pushed to learn to read and write. Pieces of drawing slate inscribed with lines like a sheet of notebook paper and slate pencils found at the site were interpreted as evidence of this. This is part of a larger pattern that affected poor farm families of all races. During the late nineteenth century, advances in farm machinery and technology led to mechanized plowing and harvesting, scientific crop research led to improved strains, and chemical fertilizers led to higher yields from more marginal soils. Larger farms requiring fewer hands caused people to move to the towns and cities to look for work. Increasingly the jobs required reading, writing, and math skills. For people of color, government help was limited. In many cases schools were based in local churches, and often the teachers were from the community, but a state educational system was finally developed in the 1890s. Four elementary schools for people of color were established on James Island, including one on Fort Johnson Road at the "Three Trees." These landmark live oaks were at the intersection of Fort Johnson and Secessionville roads (Frazier 2006).

Religion and church was an oasis, both physically and mentally, for the enslaved and for the free. Faith in their God was all that kept people going in the hardest of times (Frazier 2006). During antebellum times many slaves attended white churches and camp meetings. When freedom came the African American people of James Island were able to form their own congregations, and these became singularly important for the community. Church was a place where serious cultural negotiations were carried out, where people's place in society was decided. People of all ages were on their best behavior and dressed appropriately. In our excavations we found fancy buttons for ladies' clothing, bone and porcelain collar stays for men's starched-collar

Fancy glass button.
Courtesy of the author.

shirts, and perfume and cologne bottles, all of which add up to pursuing a socially agreed-upon standard of "presentability." A status hierarchy revolving around skin tone, profession, and wealth developed in the black community, and in some cases people doubtlessly used these occasions to display their relative wealth and position, but for everyone cleaning up and dressing in their Sunday best was common practice and an implicitly expected behavior.

In the South at large, the first generations of free African Americans were struggling to become full-fledged citizens in a society that worked to keep them down. The federal government gave them the right to vote, but when state control returned they found they had to fight to exercise that right, and even then they were denied. The dream of equality was quickly buried with Jim Crow and segregation. But within the black community, individuals and families struggled to raise themselves up, and an alternate society developed with professionals, teachers, and workers as its foundation. This is illustrated with the workers at the quarantine station.

The quarantine operation was run by the city and state between the Civil War and 1880, when it was taken over by the National Board of Health. Its operators were still provided by the city, however. In 1906 it was taken over by the Marine Hospital and Public Health Service and was operated by government employees. Among these were local African Americans who worked with both local and "assigned" white people from elsewhere. It is this pattern of enforced interaction in workplaces and school, combined with a web of modern influences including ease of transportation, increased residential mobility, and mass media, that exposed the negative aspects of society while at the same time showing the oppressed that there was another way, which led to the end of legally mandated segregation and the still-imperfect society we live in today. As one who grew up in the lowcountry at the end of the Jim Crow era, the author can testify that many lowcountry white people had to be dragged into the modern era and that the attitudes that allowed segregation are far from extinct (see Heitzler 2006: 183–185). But the development of modern society, as played out at places like Fort Johnson, has resulted in the suppression of such attitudes to a large degree.

Today Fort Johnson is the site of major marine biology and environmental research centers. Students, researchers, and support staff represent most ethnic groups, and many even come from abroad to work and learn there. What happened at Fort Johnson is not unique. Rather it represents larger patterns of culture change. But we are fortunate to be able to chronicle this change using the tools of historical archaeology and to contemplate the process and its ramifications.

References

Agha, A. 2004 Searching for Cabins, Searching for Places: Locating the Living Areas at the James Stobo Plantation, Willtown Bluff, Charleston County, S.C. Unpublished master's thesis, Department of Anthropology, University of South Carolina, Columbia.

Canning, K., and S. O. Rose 2001. Gender, Citizenship and Subjectivity: Some Historical and Theoretical Considerations. *Gender & History* 13(3):427–443.

Ellis, W. D. 1967. *Nathaniel Lebby, Patriot, and Some of His Ancestors.* Unpublished manuscript on file, South Carolina Historical Society, Charleston.

Fraser, W. J. 2006. *Lowcountry Hurricanes.* Athens: University of Georgia Press.

Frazier, E. 2006. *James Island: Stories from Slave Descendants.* Charleston, S.C.: History Press.

Heitzler, M. 2006. *Goose Creek: A Definitive History.* Vol. II. Charleston, S.C.: History Press.

Hicks, D. 2007. *The Garden of the World: A Historical Archaeology of Eastern Caribbean Sugar Plantations, AD 1600–2001.* BAR International Series 1632. British Archaeological Reports, Oxford.

Horlbeck, H. B. 1891. *Maritime Sanitation at Ports of Arrival in the City of Charleston Yearbook, 1890.* Charleston, S.C.: City of Charleston.

Lebby Family Papers n.d.. The Lebby Family Papers. Unpublished manuscript on file, South Caroliniana Library, University of South Carolina, Columbia.

Mustard, H. 1963. On the Building of Fort Johnson. *South Carolina Historical Magazine* 64:129–135.

National Archives n.d.. National Archives Record Groups 77, 92, 94, 105. Washington, D.C.

Riley, H. 1999. Michael Kalteisen and the Founding of the German Friendly Society in Charleston. *South Carolina Historical Magazine* 100(1):29–48.

Rose, W. L. 1964. *Rehearsal for Reconstruction.* Indianapolis, Ind.: Bobbs-Merrill.

Saville, J. 1994. *The Work of Reconstruction: From Slave to Wage Laborer in South Carolina, 1860–1870.* Cambridge: Cambridge University Press.

Steen, C. 1995. *A Report on Archaeological Survey Activities at Fort Johnson, 1995.* South Carolina Department of Natural Resources, Marine Resources Division, Charleston.

Steen, C., J. B. Legg, S. Taylor, and A. Chapman 2002. *The MEHRL Project: Archaeological Investigations at the Hollings Marine Laboratory, Fort Johnson, Charleston, S.C.* Columbia, S.C.: Diachronic Research Foundation.

Trinkley, M., N. Adams, and D. Hacker 1995 *An Intensive Archaeological and Historical Survey at Fort Johnson.* Columbia, S.C.: Chicora Foundation.

Wade, A. P. 1977. *Artillerists and Engineers: The Beginnings of American Seacoast Fortifications 1794–1815.* Manhattan: University of Kansas Press.

CHRISTOPHER C. FENNELL

Examining Structural Racism in Jim Crow–Era Illinois

This chapter examines the contours of racial ideologies and their impacts on social dynamics in the nineteenth and early twentieth centuries in Illinois by undertaking historical, archaeological, and comparative studies of three African American communities. In addition to overt acts of racism and racial violence, African American communities in the nineteenth century combated various forms of structural and aversive racism that diverted economic opportunities away from them and presented challenges for households to overcome (Gaertner and Dovidio 1986; Kleinpenning and Hagendoorn 1993; Kovel 1970). I examine such dynamics using examples from archaeological and historical analysis of three communities in Illinois: New Philadelphia, Brooklyn, and the Equal Rights settlement outside of Galena. The study employs research questions that confront multiple social dynamics that impacted dispositions in the past and continue to influence the present. This project analyzes past multiethnic and racial dynamics using interdisciplinary methods and active engagement with the perspectives expressed by multiple stakeholders, including members of descendant and local communities.

New Philadelphia was the first town in the United States that was planned in advance and legally registered by an African American (Walker 1995 [1983]). It grew as a demographically integrated community from 1836 through the late 1800s. Brooklyn was the first African American town to be incorporated under a state legal system in the United States (Cha-Jua 2000). It was a community started by families escaping Missouri plantations in the late 1820s and grew through the late 1800s. Equal Rights was a rural settlement of several African American households near Galena, started in the 1870s, with residents who utilized church congregation networks and entrepreneurship to overcome racial and economic challenges of the late nineteenth century. Research concerning such communities can expand our understanding of how social networks, racism, and developing markets influenced the ways in which individuals and households made choices in shaping the natural, social, and built environments and in developing social relationships, cultural traditions, and economic strategies.

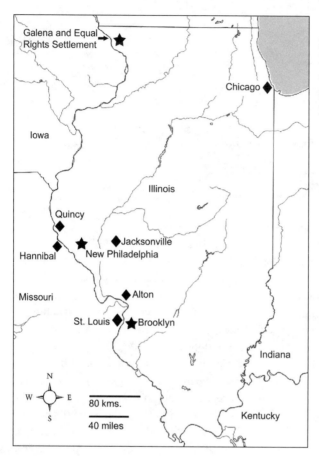

Locations of New Philadelphia, Brooklyn, Galena, and the Equal Rights settlement in Illinois.

In examining such community histories, researchers increasingly focus on the challenges of understanding the full array of overt, de jure, de facto, aversive, and systemic forms of racism that impacted those populations. Incidents of de jure and overt expressions of racial ideologies and discrimination are often apparent in documentary records. Less visible are the workings of aversive and structural racism that result in continuing patterns of de facto discrimination. Periods of overt racism deployed through formal law are often followed by enduring social structures of de facto discrimination and ingrained cognitive biases (Gaertner and Dovidio 1986). Significantly, such enduring structures of racism function at the societal level to channel commercial opportunities away from communities that would otherwise be the economically logical participants in those enterprises in the absence of such distortive ideologies (Dovidio and Gaertner 1998; Kleinpenning and Hagendoorn 1993; Kovel 1970).

New Philadelphia

Investigations of the social history and past racial dynamics affecting New Philadelphia and surrounding regions of Illinois are providing a focus for interdisciplinary engagement. Historical and archaeological research focused on New Philadelphia has been the subject of nationwide media coverage and dialogue, including print news coverage read by millions of Americans. The Public Broadcasting System, National Public Radio, and network news programs have broadcast television and radio coverage of the New Philadelphia Archaeological Project to tens of thousands of viewers and listeners. Such media discussions and public outreach efforts have dramatically increased many Americans' knowledge of the remarkable history of New Philadelphia and the ways in which racializing ideologies unfolded in the past.

Frank McWorter, a formerly enslaved person who purchased his own freedom and moved to western Illinois, founded New Philadelphia in 1830 (Walker 1995 [1983]). Once settled on the Illinois frontier, he established the town of New Philadelphia in 1836 as a money-making venture. The community's development—from an abstract design in a plat drawing, to a growing frontier village, and ultimately to the town's demise after being bypassed by a regional railroad—followed many regional trends.

Frank McWorter, founder of New Philadelphia, Illinois. Sculpture by Shirley McWorter Moss on display at the Abraham Lincoln Presidential Library, Springfield. Courtesy of Sandra McWorter.

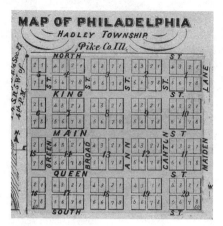

New Philadelphia plat map, excerpt from 1872 *Atlas Map of Pike County.*

Nonetheless, the history of New Philadelphia is remarkable due to the interaction between African Americans and European Americans residing in a community founded by such an exceptional individual during times of extreme racial strife.

New Philadelphia was located in a region marked by racial tensions. Although ostensibly a "free" state, Illinois promulgated laws hostile to the interests of African Americans. Illinois had restricted the rights of free African Americans before becoming a state, and migration of African Americans into Illinois was proscribed in territorial laws passed in 1813. Just 25 miles to the west of New Philadelphia lay the slave state of Missouri and a marketplace in Hannibal for the sale of human lives in bondage. Standing in opposition to these overt acts of enslavement was an abolitionist center in Quincy, Illinois, 40 miles to the northwest of New Philadelphia. Violent conflict erupted across the shore lines of the Mississippi River as pro-slavery interests in Hannibal combated the attempts of Quincy abolitionists to persuade enslaved laborers to flee from Missouri plantations. To the south of New Philadelphia lay Alton, Illinois, where abolitionist Elijah Lovejoy was killed by a pro-slavery mob in 1837. Abolitionist and pro-slavery factions clashed in Griggsville, to the east of New Philadelphia, and nearby Jacksonville hosted a number of homes active in aiding individuals escaping slavery (Doyle 1978: 54). Oral history accounts maintained by McWorter family descendants indicate that the New Philadelphia community was also active in aiding those fleeing bondage during the antebellum period.

Shortly after achieving statehood, the Illinois legislature passed "Black laws" and codified earlier territorial laws that restricted African Americans from entering the state. African American residents of Illinois were required to post a bond of $1,000 as a guarantee against becoming a "charge" of the county in which they resided. An African American could not testify against a European American classified as a "White" under the laws and census. Free African Americans already residing in the state had to file evidence of their free status. Any African American found without a certificate of freedom could be treated as a runaway slave and sold into bondage (Gertz 1963: 454–469). In 1853 the Illinois legislature enacted additional laws restricting the rights of African Americans (Campbell 1970: 51). In spite of these obstacles, western Illinois attracted more African Americans than most of Illinois outside of Chicago in the early and mid–nineteenth century. Notably, the multiracial population of New Philadelphia reached its peak in the mid–nineteenth century and decades after the passage of those discriminatory laws.

In the period up through the Civil War, New Philadelphia grew as a racially integrated community that was economically based on service to the surrounding agricultural community. Both African Americans and European Americans purchased and sold town lots and resided within the town limits during a time immersed in racial discord (Fennell 2008, 2009). The eruption of the Civil War did not deter New Philadelphia's growth. The 1860 federal census lists several businesses within the community and the racial category of the owner of each, including a shoemaker (mulatto), wagon maker (white), blacksmith (mulatto), and carpenter (mulatto).

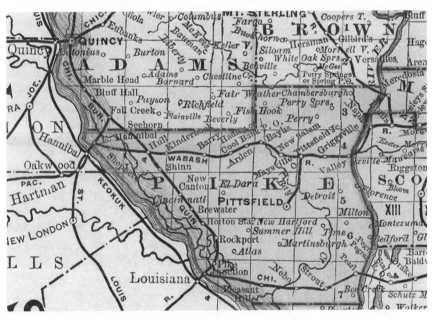

This excerpt from *Rand, McNally & Company's New Business Atlas Map of Illinois,* published in 1897, shows the route of the Hannibal and Naples Railroad, labeled here as the Wabash line, across Pike County, Illinois. The town of New Philadelphia was located between the towns of New Salem and Barry, in an area covered by the letters "de" of the word "Arden" on this map.

Aerial view of New Philadelphia site in 2005 with an overlay depicting the town boundary lines. Courtesy of Tommy Hailey with an overlay by the author.

There was also a physician (white) and a teacher (white). However, New Philadelphia suffered a steady decline in population after the Hannibal and Naples Railroad was routed to the north of the town in 1869 (Fennell 2009). New railroad stops could bolster or hobble frontier towns. Railroads often caused the price of land to increase and "crippled towns they bypassed," and railroad companies were not immune to the influences of corruption, greed, and racism (Davis 1998: 377).

The Hannibal and Naples Railroad Company constructed the railroad across Pike County that bypassed New Philadelphia in 1869, leading to the demise of the town within the following decade or so. The reasons for this bypassing appear to have been shaped by aversive racism. The company that laid the groundwork for that route in the late 1850s was dominated by business interests based in Hannibal, Missouri. The planned route of the railroad lay principally along an east-to-west line that should have run right along the edge of New Philadelphia. However, the course of the railroad track was diverted to arc to the north and bypass the community. The track then turned back south and returned to an east-to-west line level with the location of New Philadelphia but at a considerable distance to the west of that town (Fennell 2009). The typical explanations for why a community was bypassed by a railroad (such as the vagaries of topography or other existing towns having lobbied for the railroad to pass through their communities instead) do not prove persuasive in this case. Aversive racism appears to have led white investors to incur remarkable losses of monetary capital in construction and operation costs in order to bypass New Philadelphia (Fennell 2009).

The town's size had grown to approximately 160 people, 29 households, and several craftspeople and merchants by 1865. After New Philadelphia was bypassed by the railroad, merchants departed for new opportunities, and residential occupation declined steadily, resulting in an order entered in 1885 that dissolved the legal status of the town. A smaller community of neighboring families persisted at the location through the early 1900s. By the mid-1900s the entire town site was abandoned and reverted to prairie and agricultural fields.

In a multiyear archaeological study, we seek to analyze the spatial and chronological distribution of different categories of material culture, faunal, and floral remains as part of analyses that address the primary research questions posed by a team of investigators. The primary research goals of the New Philadelphia Archaeology Project have been articulated in grant proposals approved and funded by the National Science Foundation's Research Experiences for Undergraduates program. The goals of this multiyear study are (1) to understand the town's founding and development as a demographically integrated town, (2) to explore dietary patterns between different households of varying ethnic and regional backgrounds by analyzing faunal and botanical remains, (3) to reconstruct the townscape and lot uses of different households from varying ethnic backgrounds by analyzing archaeological landscape features and botanical data, and (4) to analyze the consumer choices residents of different ethnic backgrounds made in a frontier setting and examine the ways in which household choices changed with increased connections to distant markets and the impacts of changing perceptions of racism.

The archaeology project deploys typical field methods to recover material culture, floral, and faunal remains at the town site. These different data sets provide a basis for analyzing how individual members and families of this integrated community made choices in shaping the natural, social, and built environments and in developing and practicing dietary, agricultural, and consumer strategies and traditions. Our researchers have also focused on understanding the role of consumerism and consumer behavior in a multiracial community. Several previous studies have examined the dynamics in which consumer preferences developed and evolved in frontier and rural communities (Purser 1992; McMurry 1988; Schlereth 1989). Consumption practices varied across regional boundaries as well as across gender, class, and ethnic groups. For example, a study by Paul Mullins (1999) demonstrated the ways in which members of an urban community of African Americans chose to participate in a broad-scale consumer society as a part of a strategy to avoid the racism of local merchants in Maryland. Another archaeological study by Mark Warner (1998) analyzed dietary trends in African American households in Maryland in the late 1800s, finding choices that were notably different from that of many European American residents of the same region. A study of rural consumption patterns in a community like

New Philadelphia promises to reveal new evidence on the ways in which people incorporated mass-produced and mass-advertised products into their daily lifeways. This project also questions the ways in which such consumption patterns were impacted by evolving concepts of racism and the deployment of racial ideologies within the region.

Several observations can be made concerning the results of our archaeological and historical research in the period of 2004–2008 (Fennell et al. 2009; Shackel et al. 2006). Archaeological work through the end of the 2008 field season uncovered over 85,000 artifacts, faunal and floral remains, and the locations of 14 house and business structures, including a grocery and a blacksmith operation. There appears to have been no racial segregation of property locations within the town. The locations of residences and businesses of African Americans and European Americans were spatially interspersed in the town during the nineteenth century. We uncovered no archaeological evidence of violent destruction of properties within the town, even though the community was located within a region sharply impacted by racial strife. Most structures and occupation sites appear to have been concentrated in the landscape covered by the north-central portion of the town plan. Archaeology revealed early house sites not indicated in historic period documents such as deeds, tax ledgers, and census records. Residents enjoyed access to local, regional, and international commodities from the outset of settlement of the town. Ceramic housewares were similar in style, expense levels, and types of assemblages across house sites of both African Americans and European Americans. There may have been some variations in dietary and culinary practices based on the region of origin or ethnic background of particular families who moved to New Philadelphia (Fennell et al. 2009; Shackel et al. 2006).

The railroad detour had the direct effect of bringing New Philadelphia to an end as a town. However, the heritage of the community and the legacies of the McWorter family were not lost. Many descendants of the town's residents and several historians have worked to study, commemorate, and celebrate the heritage of those past lives and accomplishments (for example, Chapman 1880; Ensign 1872; Grimshaw 1876; Matteson 1964; Simpson 1981; Walker 1995 [1983], 1985). These efforts have included publications throughout the nineteenth and twentieth centuries. In addition, Dr. Juliet Walker, a historian and descendant of Frank McWorter, succeeded in placing his grave site, located within the African American cemetery close to New Philadelphia, on the National Register of Historic Places in 1988. In doing so, Walker achieved a remarkable success. Only two other grave sites in Illinois have been recognized by the National Register of Historic Places—those of Abraham Lincoln and Stephen Douglas (Shackel et al. 2006: 2:24).

In 2008 the project team members worked to nominate the New Philadelphia town site for National Historic Landmark (NHL) status. Charlotte King and Paul Shackel, director for the Center of Heritage Studies at the University of Maryland, headed up this effort. The higher degree of significance and evidence for an NHL designation is evident in the fact that over 80,000 properties in the United States have been listed on the National Register of Historic Places, but fewer than 2,500 have received the higher recognition as an NHL. The National Park System Landmarks Committee approved this nomination on October 29, 2008, followed with approval by the National Park System Advisory Board on December 3, 2008. The nomination received official support from U.S. senators Barack Obama and Richard Durbin, among others, and the Secretary of the Interior issued final approval on January 16, 2009. Thus the past incidents of racism that sought to erase the accomplishments of Frank McWorter and the residents of New Philadelphia did not succeed in attaining such an elimination of those accounts within American history.

The active engagement of researchers and community members has enriched the multiple perspectives we draw from the lessons of New Philadelphia's history. For example, we have discussed the lessons that can be conveyed to broad audiences by focusing on the events that led to the railroad's bypassing New Philadelphia. One alternative is to concentrate upon this incident to emphasize that racial ideologies can lead to economically irrational conduct that causes net losses overall (Fennell 2009). By understanding the distortive and irrational conduct generated by racial ideologies, we can heighten public awareness of such past actions in our ongoing struggles against the contours of racism in today's society (Leone et al. 2005; Shackel 2003). Such a lesson can be advanced by concentrating on the racial ideologies that shaped the actions of managers of the railroad company and on the deleterious effects their actions imposed upon the residents of New Philadelphia, leading to the demise of the town.

However, opportunities for learning would be lost if that were the only message advanced by these studies of New Philadelphia's history. Descendant community members raised the concern that such condemnations of racism should avoid singularly emphasizing European Americans as those who had agency and freedom of choice that in turn impacted the lives of African Americans. We can also emphasize lessons from this community's history that concentrate on the choices made by African American families to overcome the adversities and obstacles created by incidents such as a railroad bypassing their town (Leone et al. 2005; Shackel 2003). Researchers are thus working to expand the future scope of the project to follow the histories of families as they departed New Philadelphia and pursued new opportunities elsewhere.

Brooklyn, Also Known As Lovejoy, Illinois

Brooklyn was established as a settlement of free and enslaved African Americans escaping and fighting against bondage. An antislavery activist named "Mother" Priscilla Baltimore encouraged 11 families of free and enslaved African Americans to depart the area of Saint Louis and establish this community across the Mississippi River in 1829. From then until its platting in 1837, the settlement consisted of an all-black community. While it grew as a community of both African Americans and European Americans through the nineteenth century, Brooklyn's population continued to be composed largely of African American residents. Brooklyn included residents engaged as artisans, craftspeople, merchants, farmers, and laborers, and they voted to incorporate the town in 1873 (Cha-Jua 2000: 31–32).

A new, expanded research project will provide a basis for highly valuable data comparisons of Brooklyn, the Equal Rights settlement, and ongoing studies of New Philadelphia. As Sundiata Cha-Jua (2000: 35) has observed: "Perhaps Brooklyn, during the antebellum period, more closely resembled what Free Frank had envisioned" for New Philadelphia. "The communities initiated by Free Frank and 'Mother' Baltimore had much in common; both emerged from African American self-activity, and both became spaces hospitable to Blacks fleeing the fetters of slavery. During this period, Brooklyn differed from New Philadelphia mainly because it was a majority-Black town and offered the opportunities to join organizations and participate in Black-controlled institutions" (Cha-Jua 2000: 35). Both Brooklyn and the New Philadelphia community were active in the "underground railroad" aiding African Americans escaping bondage from the neighboring slave state of Missouri. Brooklyn has also been called Lovejoy, in honor of martyred abolitionist Elijah Lovejoy, killed in Alton in 1837 (Davis 1998: 267; Turner 2001: 77).

Cha-Jua's (2000) study of the history of Brooklyn shows evidence that the community was established and grew with ideals of solidarity and self-determination but that economic opportunities were channeled away from the town over time as a result of racism and political corruption. The town was initially attractive to African Americans escaping slavery who wished to live in a community with a majority of African American residents. In the postbellum period, Brooklyn presented newly arriving African American residents with the promise of participating in the economic growth of industrialization and new jobs in the region surrounding Saint Louis and its transportation hubs of river and rail (Cha-Jua 2000: 44). However, that promise proved fleeting. As new industrial employment grew in the East Saint Louis region of Illinois, those opportunities were not made available to workers living in Brooklyn, likely due to racial prejudices by commercial and industrial operators against such an African American community. Just as New Philadelphia was bypassed in 1869 by the economic advantages that a railroad connection would have provided, Brooklyn was bypassed by railroad, economic, and employment opportunities that were instead channeled to neighboring East Saint Louis (Cha-Jua 2000; Walker 1995 [1983]).

Brooklyn and New Philadelphia both serve as rare examples of early interracial farming and urban communities on the nation's evolving midwestern frontier (Cha-Jua 2000; Walker 1985, 1995 [1983]). Most studies in historical archaeology that

Aerial view of the Brooklyn area today, with the Mississippi River on the left (to the west) and the central residential area of Brooklyn marked by a star. Courtesy of U.S. Geological Survey archive collections, Denver, Colorado, with an overlay by the author.

concentrate on African American subjects have concerned the pre-emancipation era (Leone et al. 2005). Like Brooklyn, the history of New Philadelphia presents very different research potentials. The histories of both communities involve the dynamics of racial uplift and the success of African American families and their abilities to survive and prosper in a racist society in both the pre- and postemancipation eras. The Brooklyn and New Philadelphia stories focus on the struggles for freedom, facing racism, and the efforts of small rural and urban towns to survive.

In this expanding study I am working to participate in an interdisciplinary, collaborative research project that will include University of Illinois (UI) Departments of Anthropology and African American Studies, the Illinois Transportation Archaeological Research Program (ITARP), and the Illinois State Museum, working in coordination with the Historical Society of Brooklyn (HSB) and the local and descendant communities. Among other pending tasks, members of the HSB have recently located new records of town government and family histories from the late nineteenth century that have not been studied previously and will be available for analysis in this project.

Archaeological and surface surveys have established that the archaeological record of Brooklyn lies intact beneath the extensive open spaces of current-day residential parcels. ITARP conducted a recording survey of the Brooklyn cemetery. Excavations at an adjacent site containing the remains of a late prehistoric period deposit have shown that archaeology sites remain intact in this general area, buried beneath layers of twentieth-century fill (Galloy 2003; Koldehoff and Fulton 2005). No archaeological investigations of the community of Brooklyn were conducted before the initiation of this proposed multiyear project (Koldehoff and Fulton 2005).

Researchers working with ITARP, UI, and HSB have gathered deeds, census data, tax records, oral histories, genealogical evidence, and other primary and secondary sources. The earliest deed references have been geo-referenced on the current landscape of the town. Those deed entries were also correlated with census data over the decades of the antebellum and postbellum periods to indicate the most likely locations of the earliest and later households in Brooklyn and changes in residential and business locations over time. Joseph Galloy and a crew of archaeologists with ITARP excavated test units and shovel test pit surveys in several residential lots of the existing town in the summer of 2008. These surveys and test units demonstrated that the archaeological record of Brooklyn's residents from the earliest years of the community onward exists intact beneath the open spaces of current residential properties (Galloy 2008). Future fieldwork should include additional surface surveys, geophysical surveys, and excavations to uncover and fully research the past households and business locations of this remarkable community.

Commemorating the heritage and history of Brooklyn are vital activities in the ongoing efforts of the local and descendant communities to combat the deterioration of their neighborhood by commercial operations that include strip joints and massage parlors. The aversive impacts of past racism have significantly constrained the economic health of this community, isolating it within a tangle of railroad tracks and transport lines that pass it by rather than incorporate it in a viable flow of commerce. One of the elders of the community and a famous member of the American Negro Baseball League, Prince Joe Henry (2007), captured the recent dilemmas facing Brooklyn: "Based upon the number of massage parlors in the community, it is understandable why it was labeled 'Sin City' several years back, but those who labeled it as such [were] unfamiliar with its history. Granted, prior to the strip joints' arrival, the town had undergone several lean years, which basically explains how this materialized. The outcome was cleverly manipulated with a promise of jobs that caught an unsuspecting mayor off guard. Though poverty stricken at the time, Brooklyn is historically rich."

The Historical Society of Brooklyn was formed as a nonprofit organization by local residents committed to combating this declension. Their mission statement included a poignant, powerful charge: "Our land, our legacy was being sold piece by piece. Vice and corruption took over. Our elders fled or hid behind locked doors in fear. The media, local and state officials have forecast our self destruction and demise. They are like vultures circling the wounded, patiently waiting for all signs of life to cease before moving in to consume flesh. They underestimate our resilience and tenacity" (HSB 2008).

This diversity of economic and community interests presents particular challenges for such a collaborative project to enhance and commemorate Brooklyn's heritage. For example, many of the individuals who work in adult entertainment establishments are themselves struggling to navigate the harsh class and economic structures of the day. A project to enhance the pride of Brooklyn's past and present will need to find a way to proceed with tolerance, empathy, and pride in seeking ways to better the lives all of who engage with the community.

Equal Rights Settlement and Galena

Galena, Illinois, is well known for its history as a lead-mining center started in the early 1800s and as the home of Ulysses Grant (for example, Krausse 1970; Owens 1963). While Galena has been largely ignored in popular history accounts, historian

Aerial photograph (1946) of the agricultural landscape in Jo Daviess County, Illinois, on which the Equal Rights settlement site was located. Courtesy of U.S. Geological Survey archive collections, Denver, Colorado.

H. Scott Wolfe (2008) of the Galena Public Library District has worked for years to record and commemorate the rich history of African American residents, entrepreneurs, and church communities in Galena and a nearby settlement called Equal Rights. African American residents of Galena worked as miners, ministers, blacksmiths, educators, cooks, and laborers in the river transport industries (Wild 2008). Those residents also experienced the oppressions of bondage, servitude, and racism within Galena (Wolfe 2004).

In the 1860s, as Galena began to experience an economic downturn, a number of African American families moved out to farmsteads in neighboring Rush Township, where they engaged in entrepreneurial activities such as burning lime in stone kilns to create fertilizer for sale to other farmers in the area and the work of raising crops and livestock. Equal Rights included a church and schoolhouse serving that cluster of African American farms and the surrounding area (Wild 2008; Wolfe 2008). As in the histories of Brooklyn and New Philadelphia, social relationships influenced by church networks played important roles in the founding, location, and development of Equal Rights. Residents were members of the Colored Union Baptist Church in Galena, the Northwestern Association of the Regular Predestinarian Baptists, and later established a new church in Equal Rights as a location halfway between affiliated Baptist congregations spread across the county. By the 1880s Equal Rights included 30 residents on 70 acres of neighboring farmsteads served by the local church and school. Galena experienced a corresponding loss of African American residents in the same period, with census rolls listing 64 in 1870 and 13 in 1880 (Wild 2008; Wolfe 2008).

Racial conflicts within Galena later focused upon Equal Rights. In 1867 members of the Freedman's Aid Society worked to open an African American schoolhouse in Galena. As the school began operations, local European Americans assailed the students, teachers, and school directors with verbal and physical harassment. When a new schoolhouse was constructed in Equal Rights during the 1870s to serve the area's African American families, racial strife again became manifest. Oral histories report that European American residents protested such a school violently and began to refer to the community by the racial epithet of "N——rville." In a remarkable example of the impacts of intergroup conflict, it was apparently this event that motivated the African American residents to adopt the name of "Equal Rights" for their previously unnamed community (Wild 2008; Wolfe 2008).

I am working to launch and participate in an interdisciplinary, collaborative research project on the Equal Rights settlement history that will include the University of Illinois Department of Anthropology working in coordination with H. Scott Wolfe of the Galena Public Library District. This project of historical, oral history, and archaeological research will work to expand our knowledge of African American heritage in Galena and Equal Rights and the impacts of racialization in that region in the nineteenth and twentieth centuries.

Conclusion

Interdisciplinary studies concerning communities such as New Philadelphia, Brooklyn, and Equal Rights help to deepen our understanding of how racial ideologies, social networks, and developing economic structures influenced the ways in which individuals made choices in shaping their social and built environments and in developing economic strategies and cultural practices. Civic engagement in such research projects also significantly aids the members of current-day communities to enhance the recognition and visibility of their African American heritage and accomplishments and to combat facets of structural racism they are experiencing today.

Acknowledgments

Some of the research results discussed in this essay are based upon work supported by the National Science Foundation under Grant Nos. 0353550 and 0752834. Any opinions, findings, conclusions, or recommendations expressed in this chapter are those of the author and do not necessarily reflect the views of the National Science Foundation. I am also very grateful for the very generous funding support of the University of Illinois Research Board.

References

Campbell, S. W. 1970. *The Slave Catchers.* Chapel Hill: University of North Carolina Press.

Cha-Jua, S. 2000. *America's First Black Town, Brooklyn, Illinois, 1830–1915.* Urbana: University of Illinois Press.

Chapman, C. C. 1880. *History of Pike County, Illinois.* Chicago: C. C. Chapman.

Davis, J. E. 1998. *Frontier Illinois.* Bloomington: Indiana University Press.

Dovidio, J. F., and S. L. Gaertner 1998. On the Nature of Contemporary Prejudice: The Causes, Consequences, and Challenges of Aversive Racism. In *Confronting Racism: The Problem and the Response,* edited by J. L. Eberhardt and S. T. Fiske, pp. 3–32. London: Sage.

Doyle, D. H. 1978. *The Social Order of a Frontier Community: Jacksonville, Illinois, 1825–70.* Urbana: University of Illinois Press.

Ensign, D. W. 1872. *Atlas Map of Pike County, Illinois.* Davenport, Iowa: Andreas, Lyter & Co.

Fennell, C. 2009. Combating Attempts of Elision: African American Accomplishments at New Philadelphia, Illinois. In *Intangible Heritage Embodied,* edited by D. F. Ruggles and H. Silverman, pp. 147–168. New York: Springer.

———. 2008. *Historical Landscapes of New Philadelphia.* Urbana: University of Illinois. Electronic document, http://www.anthro.uiuc.edu/faculty/cfennell/NP/, accessed April 19, 2009.

Fennell, C., with contributions from A. Agbe-Davies, M. Bailey, J. Brown, G. Calfas, S. Collins, M. Davila, E. Deetz, K. Fay, T. Hailey, B. Haley, K. Hardcastle, M. Hargrave, C. Martin, T. Martin, A. McCartan, A. Morris, P. Shackel, C. Sumter, E. Sylak, and C.

Valvano 2009. *New Philadelphia 2008 Archaeology Report.* Report on the 2008 excavations sponsored by the National Science Foundation Research Experiences for Undergraduates (Grant No. 0752834). University of Illinois, Urbana. Electronic document, http://www.anthro.uiuc.edu/faculty/cfennell/NP/2008ReportMenu.html, accessed May 13, 2009.

Gaertner, S. L., and J. F. Dovidio (editors) 1986. The Aversive Form of Racism. In *Prejudice, Discrimination, and Racism,* pp. 61–89. Orlando, Fla.: Academic Press.

Galloy, J. 2008. *Reports on Historical and Archaeological Surveys in Brooklyn, Illinois.* Illinois Transportation Archaeological Research Program, Belleville.

Galloy, J. (editor).2003. *Excavations at the Janey B. Goode Site (11S1232), St. Clair County, Illinois: Interim Report, Research Design, and Mitigation Plan.* Research Reports No. 92. Illinois Transportation Archaeological Research Program, University of Illinois, Urbana.

Gertz, E. 1963. The Black Laws of Illinois. *Journal of the Illinois State Historical Society* 56: 454–473.

Grimshaw, W. A. 1876. History of Pike County: A Centennial Address Delivered by Hon. William A. Grimshaw at Pittsfield, Pike County, Illinois, July 4, 1876. Illinois State Historical Society, Springfield.

Henry, P. J. 2007. Rediscovering Brooklyn: Come, Senators, Congressmen, Please Heed Joe's Call. *Riverfront Times,* 6 June. Saint Louis, Mo.

Historical Society of Brooklyn, Illinois (HSB) 2008. *Our Story.* Electronic document, http://www.brooklynillinoisourstory.com/, accessed January 15, 2009.

Kleinpenning, G., and L. Hagendoorn 1993. Forms of Racism and the Cumulative Dimension of Ethnic Attitudes. *Social Psychology Quarterly* 56(1):21–36.

Koldehoff, B., and C. L. Fulton 2005. Constructing Context for African-American Archaeology in the American Bottom Region. *Illinois Antiquity* 40(3):8–11.

Kovel, J. 1970. *White Racism: A Psychohistory.* New York: Pantheon Books.

Krause, G. H. 1970. Galena, Illinois: Urban Land Use Change and Development of a Mid-Western Mining Town (1820–1980). Unpublished master's thesis, Northern Illinois University, DeKalb.

Leone, M. P., C. J. LaRoche, and J. J. Barbiarz 2005. The Archaeology of Black Americans in Recent Times. *Annual Review of Anthropology* 34:575–598.

Matteson, G. 1964. "Free Frank" McWorter and the "Ghost Town" of New Philadelphia, Pike County, Illinois. Pike County Historical Society, Pittsfield, Ill.

McMurry, S. 1988. *Families and Farmhouses in Nineteenth Century America: Vernacular Architecture and Social Change.* New York: Oxford University Press.

McWorter, P. 2008. McWorter Family Statement to National Historic Landmarks Committee, Washington, D.C., October 29, 2008. Electronic document, http://www.anthro.illinois .edu/faculty/cfennell/NP/McWorterNHLstatement.html, accessed April 19, 2009.

Mullins, P. R. 1999. *Race and Affluence: Archaeology of African America and Consumer Culture.* New York: Kluwer Academic/Plenum Publishers.

Owens, K. N. 1963. *Galena, Grant and the Fortunes of War: A History of Galena, Illinois during the Civil War.* DeKalb: Northern Illinois University and the Galena Historical Society.

Purser, M. 1992. Consumption as Communication in Nineteenth Century Paradise Valley, Nevada. In *Meanings and Uses of Material Culture,* thematic issue, edited by B. J. Little and P. A.

Shackel. *Historical Archaeology* 26(3):105–116.

Schlereth, T. J. (editor).1989. *Material Culture Studies in America.* Nashville, Tenn.: Association for State and Local History.

Shackel, P. A. 2003. *Memory in Black and White: Race, Commemoration, and the Post-bellum Landscape.* Walnut Creek, Calif.: AltaMira Press.

Shackel, P. A., with contributions from A. Azzarello, M. Bailey, C. Bauchat, C. Christman, K. Eppler, C. Fennell, M. Hargrave, E. Helton, A. Hsieh, J. Jacoby, C. King, H. Livingston, T. Martin, M. A. N. Colon, E. Pajuelo, M. Schroeder, E. Smith, A. Torvinen, C. Valvano 2006. *New Philadelphia Archaeology: Race, Community, and the Illinois Frontier.* Report on the 2004–2006 excavations sponsored by the National Science Foundation Research Experiences for Undergraduates (Grant No. 0353550). College Park: University of Maryland. Electronic document, http://heritage.umd.edu/chrsweb/New%20Philadelphia/2006report/2006menu.htm, accessed April 19, 2009.

Simpson, H. M. 1981. *Makers of History.* Evansville, Ind.: Laddie B. Warren.

Turner, G. T. 2001. *The Underground Railroad in Illinois.* Glen Ellyn, Ill.: Newman Educational Publishing.

Walker, J. E. K. 1995 [1983]. *Free Frank: A Black Pioneer on the Antebellum Frontier.* Lexington: University Press of Kentucky.

———. 1985. Entrepreneurial Ventures in the Origin of Nineteenth-Century Agricultural Towns: Pike County, 1823–1880. *Illinois Historical Journal* 78(1):45–64.

Warner, M. S. 1998. *Food and the Negotiation of African-American Identities in Annapolis, Maryland and the Chesapeake.* Ph.D. dissertation, University of Virginia, Charlottesville. Proquest, University of Michigan, Ann Arbor.

Wild, M. 2008. Pragmatic Decisions in Equal Rights: History of an African-American Community in Jo Daviess County, Illinois. *African Diaspora Archaeology Newsletter* September. Electronic document, http://www.diaspora.uiuc.edu/news0908/news0908.html#4, accessed April 19, 2009.

Wolfe, H. S. 2008. *A Compilation of Primary Records of the Equal Rights Settlement, Jo Daviess County, Illinois.* Wolfe African American Collection Galena, Illinois.

———. 2004. The Fate of Jerry Boyd: A Case of Kidnapping and Murder in old Galena. *Illinois Heritage* 7(1):10–13.

LELAND FERGUSON

What Means *Gottesacker*?

Leading and Misleading Translations of Salem Records

Early members of the Moravian Church commonly referred to their burial places as *Gottesacker,* a German term for a Christian burial ground (Oxford English Dictionary 1970). Although authorities agree that the most accurate translation of the root words of *Gottesacker* is "God's Field," contemporary English-speaking Moravians translate *Acker* with the homonymic *Acre.* Thus they call their burial sites God's Acre. Nevertheless Moravian historian Daniel Crews (1996) writes that God's Acre "was [and is] thought of as God's Field, where the bodies of believers are sown awaiting the Resurrection." Of course, the phrase carries heavy religious implication, yet a comparison of twentieth-century translations with original German-language Moravian documents from early Salem, North Carolina, shows that in many cases translators have stripped *Gottesacker* of its religious connotation by translating the phrase as "graveyard" or, less frequently, "cemetery." Changes in nineteenth-century Moravian culture and theology explain part of this variability. Other interpretive variations appear to be unfounded overlays of twentieth-century social and racial perceptions on eighteenth- and nineteenth-century Moravian culture.

The Saint Philips Archaeological Project

These inconsistencies came to light during archaeological research at the Saint Philips complex in the Old Salem Historical District of Winston-Salem, North Carolina. This complex occupies two town lots at the lower end of Salem's Church Street.[1] Here, in 1775, the Moravians set up a *Fremdengottesacker,* a Strangers' God's Acre, for non-Moravians who died in or around Salem. It was also called Dobbs Parish *Gottesacker,* for reasons of colonial policy, because the Moravian's land tract of Wachovia also served as a colonial political district and, therefore, as a quasi parish of the

---

1. Lots 248 and 249: E. A. Vogler Map of Salem, 1876, Moravian Archives, Southern Province.

Church of England (Thorp 1989: 155–161).[2] In 1816 Moravians set aside part of this site for an exclusive African American burial ground, and in 1823 African American church members built a log church on an adjacent lot for their, as they called it, "Small Negro Congregation." In 1861 Moravians completed a larger, brick church immediately east of the old Dobbs Parish *Gottesacker* for the African American congregation, and in 1890 they built an addition to this church over a portion of this oldest part of the cemetery. Then in 1913—and for unrecorded and unknown reasons—church leaders decided to pull up and hide the gravestones. "The beautifying and *rearranging of the lawn and surroundings,* the laying of the cement walk, and *the stone steps in front of the church* were accomplished through the generous gift and untiring efforts of Miss Gertrude Siewers" (*Wachovia Moravian* 1914, emphasis added).[3] They then covered all the graves with landscaping fill: what was an old *Gottesacker* with a number of gravestones became the grassy lawn of Saint Philips Church. Thus Salem Moravians obliterated the old *Gottesacker.* In doing so, they severely damaged a fragile landscape record of Salem history, including stone memorials for 29 of Salem's African Americans, seven of whom were either free or owned by non-Moravians. Fifteen were enslaved by Moravian families, and six were owned by the Moravian Church.[4]

North Carolina Moravians first became slaveholders in the 1770s. Church leaders justified the opportunity to buy slaves as an act of providence, providing sorely needed labor for their divinely inspired project. They encouraged slaves to accept Christianity and become part of their community, and in the beginning their relationships with their bondsmen were relatively intimate; church members buried white and black Moravians alike in the congregational *Gottesacker.* Later, in the early

2. Geopolitical subdivisions in colonial North Carolina were coincident with parishes of the state-established Church of England, and law required the Moravians' Wachovia tract be within a parish. Not wanting to be annexed to a nearby parish and thus accountable to an Anglican administration, the Moravians petitioned the colonial assembly to establish a new parish coincident with the boundaries of Wachovia. The government granted their request and created Dobbs Parish. Separate from their Moravian church and governing bodies, the Moravians set up a Dobbs Parish vestry, hired an English-speaking minister, and fulfilled the basic requirements of a parish, which included providing alms for the poor and setting up a parish cemetery.

3. In 1994 and 1996 Old Salem workmen and archaeologists discovered the stones, most of which were for African Americans, hidden beneath the front hallway and steps of the brick church.

4. Incomplete Moravian records indicate at least 20 people were buried in the graveyard at Saint Philips. So far archaeologists have located 87 graves, 25 in the old Dobbs Parish section and 62 in the nineteenth-century African American section. A portion of the southern half of the African American graveyard remains unexcavated.

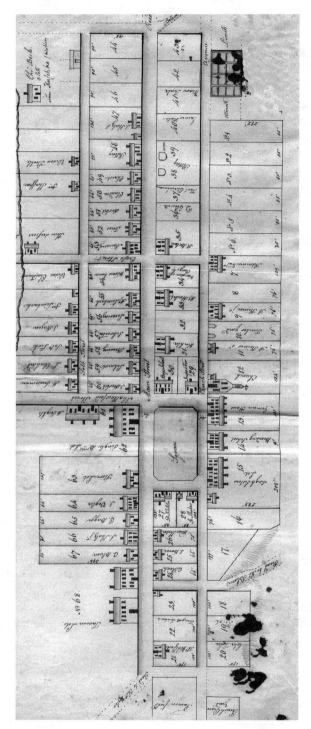

Plan of Salem, September 20, 1822, by F. C. Meinung (Moravian Archives DP f.005.1). The God's Acre of the Salem congregation is on the far left; the "Parish Grave Yard" is on the far right. Courtesy of the *Journal of Moravian History*, Nazareth, Pennsylvania.

nineteenth century, Southern-style racism and racist segregation gained firm foot-ing in Salem and Wachovia, and in 1816 the old Strangers' God's Acre was expanded and designated as the burial place for all local African Americans—Moravian as well as non-Moravian. White, non-Moravian Christians, after 1816, were to be buried in the God's Acre of the Salem Congregation until a suitable cemetery could be set up (Crews 1998; Sensbach 1998).

When archaeological fieldwork began in 1991, the brick church, with the 1890 addition, was the only extant historic feature on the two lots. The 1823 church had been razed and all surface evidence of the graves obliterated (Hartley 1995; Rohrer 1993a, 1993b). Old Salem, Inc., commissioned the archaeological project to find the obscured graves and gravestones and to locate more accurately the 1823 church site. The museum planned to use the results to help interpret the role played by African Americans in the development of Salem. As anthropologists, our archaeological team was not only interested in helping fulfill Old Salem's specific goals but was also keenly interested in the changing character of relationships between Salem's white Moravians (who held the wealth and power within the town) and African Americans (who labored in the town's homes, shops, mills, and fields). Our research joined a rapidly growing body of anthropologically oriented archaeological research aimed at providing new kinds of information and an expanded discussion of African Ameri-can history and American multicultural relations (for example, Blakey and Rankin-Hill 2004; Epperson 2004; Ferguson 1992; Franklin 1997; Leone and Fry 1999; Mullins 1999; Orser 2004; Singleton 1985, 1999).

To aid the investigation, Old Salem provided translations of early German docu-ments held in the Moravian Archives, Southern Province. These translations helped piece together the graveyard layout and the social history of those African Americans buried at the church. And in a surprising way, the varied translations and the grave-yard landscapes displayed the complicated and changing attitudes of white Mora-vians toward not only race and religion but also their own religious community and their historical view of themselves.

The Translations

Translations used in the archaeological project came from two well-known sources: the first 11 volumes of the *Records of the Moravians in North Carolina* and the exten-sive holdings of Old Salem's Museum of Early Southern Decorative Arts (MESDA) (Crews and Bailey 2000, 2006; Fries 1922, 1925, 1926, 1930, 1941, 1943, 1947; Fries and Rights 1954; Hamilton 1966, 1969; Smith 1964). Materials from MESDA included translations by Edmund Schwarze, Douglas L. Rights and Herbert Kant, Erika Huber, Elizabeth Marx, and one or more unidentified translator(s). Schwarze, Rights and Kant, Huber, and the unidentified individual(s) had all translated entries from vari-ous church boards, and transcriptions of their works were held in the MESDA subject card-file for the Wachovia Area, under subject headings: Strangers' Grave-yard; Graveyard, Strangers'; and Graveyard, Parish. Marx translated the entire "Diary of the Small Negro Congregation in and around Salem," dating from 1822 to 1855, after which time entries were made in English. Thus archaeologists worked with translations of several sources by at least eight different scholars.

The early phases of archaeological fieldwork were most involved with finding the location of features. For assistance we turned to early Moravian maps and to specific landscape references in church records such as the placement and boundaries of the burial grounds, the spacing of graves, and the location of the churches. Such refer-ences were most often found in the minutes of the *Aufseher Collegium,* or board of supervisors, the church board responsible for "the material and financial interests of the congregation" (Crews 1996). Other descriptions came from the records of the Helpers Conference *(Helferkonferenz),* the Elders Conference *(Ältestenkonferenz),* and the Congregational Council *(Gemeinrat).*

Right away, archaeologists noticed differences in terminology for Salem's burial places. There was much more variability in terms used for the old burial ground at Saint Philips than the actively used burial place for the Salem congregation. We soon learned that contemporary Salem residents, as well as the guides and staff of Old Salem, spoke of the Salem Moravian burial site at the upper end of Church Street as either "the God's Acre," or sometimes "the graveyard." They were quick to tell us that these were *traditional* Moravian terms and that Moravians did not use the English word *cemetery* for their places of interment. Salem Cemetery, they said, is the public cemetery located immediately east of the oldest part of the Moravian God's Acre.

Although we were working at the lower end of Church Street, the translations we were using contained 18 incidental references to the congregational burial ground at the upper end of the street. In those translations "graveyard" appeared 13 times and "God's Acre" 5 times. "Cemetery" was not used. Thus when referring to the congre-gational plot, the translations were consistent with contemporary terminology with the exception that in contemporary usage "God's Acre" seemed to be more common than "graveyard," whereas "graveyard" was more common in the translations of his-torical documents.

In contrast to this limited terminology for the congregational God's Acre/grave-yard, in the translated records of the church boards, we found eight different names for the burial ground in the Saint Philips complex. Some variation of "graveyard" was used 30 times, "cemetery" 16 times, and "God's Acre" only once when referring to the old parish plot and African American burial ground (see Table 1).

Our impression was that Moravians held to a firm religious and linguistic tradi-tion when referring to the congregational God's Acre/graveyard, whereas they were ambivalent about the association of the plot at Saint Philips with both the Moravian Church and Christianity. Contemporary residents seemed to think of the place as more similar to a potters' field than a God's Acre, and in our archaeological research

TABLE 1. Terms Used by Translators for the
          Burial Ground at the St. Philips Complex

Terms	Frequency
Parish Cemetery	9
Negro Graveyard*	9
Parish Graveyard	8
Graveyard	7
Cemetery for Strangers	6
Strangers' Graveyard**	6
Cemetery	1
Parish God's Acre	1
TOTAL	47

*Counts include "Graveyard for Negroes."
**Counts include "Graveyard for Strangers."

this perception began to color our thinking. We assumed the varied terms were scornful expressions of developing Moravian racism. This impression changed as we began working with Marx's (1985, 1992) translation of the "Diary of the Small Negro Congregation."

White Moravian ministers kept the diary for the mission congregation. In neat German script they wrote about church attendance, baptisms and confirmations, visitations, sermons, marriages, births, deaths, and funerals. As we began using this translated document to help interpret archaeological discoveries, we found a striking difference in terminology for the burial ground at Saint Philips. In Marx's translated diary entries, only two terms were used for this place of burial: "God's Acre" was used exclusively from 1822 until 1838, after which "God's Acre" and "Negro God's Acre" were used with approximately equal frequency. This limited variability and consistent use of religious terminology stood in sharp contrast to the variety of terms for the same place found in the translations of other documents by other translators.

Comparison of the original German diary in the Moravian Archives with Marx's translation revealed that her terminology was consistent with the original text. Of 52 references to the cemetery in the diary, "Parish Gottes Acker" was used once,[5] "Gottes

5. January 7, 1823: Pastor Abraham Steiner wrote: "there was the burial of the seven-month old baby boy of Lewis (Hamilton's) on the local so-called Parish God's Acre." This interment and diary entry were before the construction of the log church and perhaps before the pastor and members of the "Small Negro Congregation" began to consider the plot as *their* God's acre.

Acker" 35 times, and "Neger Gottes Acker" 16 times.[6] For the first 16 years of diary entries, pastors Abraham Steiner and John Renatus Schmidt simply referred to the burial ground adjacent to their church as the *Gottesacker*. In his final diary entry, dated April 1838,[7] Schmidt wrote of praying the Easter Litany on the "Neger Gottes Acker," literally the Black or Negro God's Acre.[8] This was the first use of the racial modifier *"Neger"* for the *Gottesacker* used by the "Small Negro Congregation." Although Schmidt wrote his entry in April 1838, this racial modifier did not become commonly used in the diary until 1843, after which 58 percent of the references were to the *Negergottesacker*. Thus while the diarists used the religious term *"Gottesacker"* throughout the period from 1822 through the end of 1855, there was a clear-cut pattern of intensified racial distinction beginning in the late 1830s and increasing in the following decade.

This transition closely correlates with dramatic social, economic, and political changes in Salem, North Carolina, and the rest of the southern United States. In the 1820s and early 1830s, slave rebellion and threats of rebellion spread fear throughout the region. The abolitionist movement angered slaveholders and encouraged those enslaved. Increasingly state and local governments took steps to restrict the movement of slaves and any opportunities they had for education. In Salem Moravian businessmen pressed the church to allow them to purchase people and employ them as slave labor in their shops. Textile mills began springing up throughout the South, and in 1837 the Salem Manufacturing Company began mass-producing cloth in the Moravian town. This largely church-owned mill was followed in 1840 by the F. and H. Fries Mill, owned by a Moravian family. Both mills employed slave labor in various capacities. Soon the records of church boards show concern about the growing African American presence in Salem. Complaints about "factory Negroes" become common in the minutes of church board meetings,[9] and within the diary ministers began emphasizing that the burial ground at the lower end of Church Street was a particular kind of *Gottesacker*, a *Negergottesacker*. Nevertheless, in their religiously oriented recordkeeping, it remained a *Gottesacker*[10]

6. In contemporary German grammar, *Gottesacker* is one word, meaning *cemetery*. However, in texts reviewed for this chapter, eighteenth- and nineteenth-century Moravian scribes wrote the term as two words: *Gottes Acker*.

7. Schmidt left the African American congregation to serve in the Cherokee Mission.

8. *Neger* (pronounced NAY guer) is the German word for both *black* and *negro*.

9. At the same time there was concern about white factory workers: "... it was suggested and accepted to have a special cemetery laid out for those persons who work at the Factory, since we have to expect from the large number of [white] personnel there most of the applications coming to us for burial in our Salem Graveyard" (*Aufseher Collegium* 1843). A separate cemetery for whites was not set up in Salem until 1857.

10. The church-owned Salem Manufacturing Company began production November 1837. For discussions of this turbulent period of Salem and Wachovia history, see Shirley (1994), Sensbach (1998), and Rohrer (2005).

Other Church Records

After comparing the translated diary with the original text, the remaining translations used in the archaeological project were compared with the archived originals as well. Results were similar. The translated documents ranged from 1753 to 1856 and included references to six different burial sites in the following locations:

Bethabara: Wachovia's small pioneering settlement, founded in 1753, first interment 1757.

Bethabara Mill: A settlement of non-Moravian refugees during the French and Indian War, first burial 1759.

Bethania: A small settlement of Moravians and prospective Moravians a short distance northwest of Bethabara—town founded and *Gottesacker* consecrated in 1759.

Salem, Upper Church Street: Site of the contemporary Salem God's Acre—first grave 1771, five years after Salem's founding in 1766.

Salem, Lower Church Street: Burial ground at the Saint Philips Complex, first grave 1775.

In 93 German-language references to these places of burial, the overwhelming majority of terms used to identify them were religious (see Table 2). *Gottesacker* was used 64 times, most frequently alone but also with modifiers such as *Fremdengottesacker*, Dobbs Parish *Gottesacker*, Parish *Gottesacker*, and *Negergottesacker*. If "parish" is considered a religious rather than political term, then 92 percent of the terms are religious. The terminology implies that Moravians traditionally considered all six of these burial sites to have been consecrated ground, including the *Gottesacker* at Saint Philips.

TABLE 2. Frequency of basic terms for Wachovia burial places in original German-language documents used in St. Philips Archaeological Project

Term	No.
Gottes Acker	64
Begräbnissplatz	3
Hutberg	2
Parish Burrying [*sic*] Ground	1
burial place	1
TOTAL	71

The English terms "Parish Burrying Ground" and "burial place" were used once each in German-language records. Capitalization and spelling as in originals.

"Our Graveyard"

In 1856 the church relinquished economic control of Salem and sold property to individual residents and shopkeepers. They also began keeping records in English rather than German, which coincided with an abrupt change in burial site terminology. Whereas earlier reporters consistently used *"Gottesacker"* for Moravian places of burial, subsequent record keepers dropped the term. Rather than replacing *"Gottesacker"* with the English translation, "God's Acre," Moravian scribes began referring to their burial places as "graveyards" and occasionally" burial grounds." In the "Diary of the Small Negro Congregation" from 1856 to 1876, as well as the recently published volumes XII (1856–1866) and XIII (1867–1876) of *Records of the Moravians,* there is no use of the English phrase "God's Acre."

In 1922 when Moravian archivist Adelaide Fries published the first volume of *Records of the Moravians,* she listed "graveyard" in the index but not "God's Acre." The second volume, published in 1925, had entries for "God's Acre" but no entry for "graveyard." Subsequent volumes included "graveyard" and "God's Acre" with roughly equal frequency. This pattern suggests that in the 1920s Fries and her associates were of two minds: It is likely they had grown up referring to the congregational place of burial as "our graveyard" and understanding that non-Moravians buried their dead in cemeteries. However, as they translated and edited the earliest Moravian records, they discovered their distant ancestors consistently used *"Gottesacker."* Thus in the early twentieth century "graveyard" was the traditional term everyone knew, but *Gottesacker,* translated "God's Acre," must have been an attractive alternative for revivalist historians and preservationists. With poetic power it reinforced images of Wachovia's pioneers as righteous Pietists. In Salem the original Moravians believed they lived as close to God as possible on earth. Furthermore, they trusted that when they "fell asleep" their souls would fly to Jesus's side; and God, as a loving gardener, would care for their buried bodies until the joyous days of their resurrection.

The abrupt change in Moravian records from the phrase *"Gottesacker"* to the religiously neutral "graveyard" appears as an intriguing feature of the Moravian struggle with issues of identity and spirituality in the rapidly changing milieu of nineteenth-century America. Quite likely, the transition occurred in everyday speech long before the dramatic change in official records. There was no German word similar to the Greek-rooted English word "cemetery." However, the German words *"begraben"* (to bury), *"grab"* (grave), and *"grabhof"* (graveyard) were phonetically and alphabetically similar to English "grave" and "graveyard." Thus German-speaking Moravians may have more easily picked up "graveyard" than "cemetery." Perhaps also there was an advantage in maintaining a distinctive Moravian identity. In the middle of the nineteenth century, "graveyard" was a relatively new English word. The *Oxford English Dictionary* (1970) cites 1825 as the first recorded written use of this combination of two old-English nouns. Since "cemetery" was probably used traditionally by English-speaking non-Moravians in the Wachovia vicinity, Moravian use of "graveyard" may have helped maintain their distinctiveness. This is undoubtedly the case in the written record of the 1850s and later: Once they began keeping records in English, Moravian writers consistently referred to Moravian burial places as graveyards and non-Moravian places as cemeteries, for example, Salem Cemetery. Thus it is not difficult to see how Moravians began employing "graveyard" and why they eschewed "cemetery." What is more difficult to understand is why they did not simply begin calling their burial places "God's Acres."

Gottesacker and the Moravian Ideal

The *Oxford English Dictionary* (1970) reports the English use of "God's Acre" as early as 1617 and identifies it as an adaptation of German "*Gottesacker.*" In 1841 American poet Henry Wadsworth Longfellow wrote a poem celebrating the English-language use of this term and crediting its Saxon origin. Thus the term was known in English and was apparently dear to early Moravians; however, in the nineteenth century they stopped using it. Following a recent argument by Moravian historian Craig Atwood (2004), it may have been that nineteenth-century Moravians began to question the appropriateness of either "*Gottesacker*" or the translation "God's Acre" for their burial places.

According to Atwood (2004), the Moravians who founded Salem in 1766 imagined it as a town where every resident personally knew the Savior, Jesus Christ. Choirs—groups based on sex, age, and marital status—worked and worshipped together. Choir members shared individual faith experiences; when they saw fellow members faltering, they encouraged them until they returned to the Savior's fold or were asked to leave the community. Hence pioneering Moravians in Salem felt that not only were individuals saved but also considered their entire town as a harmonious province of true believers as close to heaven as anyone could be on earth. As they approached the end of their lives, Salem residents were surrounded by members of their community, especially their family and choir. Visitors prayed and sang hymns and encouraged the fading person to look joyously toward union with the Savior. When a person passed away and was buried in the row with fellow choir members, the living looked upon their new residence in the *Gottesacker* not as a repository of death but as a resting place for their bodies. Their souls were now joined with Christ, and on the millennial Day of Judgment their souls and bodies would be reunited and resurrected (Atwood 1992; Spangenberg 1959 [1790]).

Not only were the Moravians sure of their own deliverance, they were also filled with optimism for the salvation of others. During the early years of their church they sent legions of evangelists throughout the world as witnesses to those who had never heard of Christ's saving grace. They formed societies to revitalize the sagging faith of Christians in other churches, and they began building congregational towns like

Salem that would serve as centers of faith and temporal testimonials of the harmonious lives of true believers. Through evangelism they anticipated many so-called heathens would be drawn to Christ; with an ecumenical spirit unusual for the eighteenth century, they accepted the faithful confessions of non-Moravian Christians, believing that there were many ways to form a union with the Savior (Freeman 1998; Lewis 1962; Weinlick 1984).

As Moravians in Wachovia and Salem encountered non-Moravians, this hopeful enthusiasm characterized their interactions. When non-Moravians flocked to the shelter of Bethabara during the French and Indian War, the Moravians demonstrated their charity by helping build a fortified settlement for the newcomers. In 1759 when several refugees died during an epidemic of disease, the Moravians set up a *Fremdengottesacker* (Strangers' God's Acre), laid out in Moravian fashion with separate squares based on age, sex, and marital status. This *Gottesacker* seems to have exhibited early Moravian faith that their example would inspire others to follow their pious path.

The consistent use of the religious name for the several Moravian burial places indicates that early Wachovia Moravians believed all of these plots would be the resting places of repentant believers. Through time, however, Atwood argues that Moravians came to be less and less confident about the condition of the souls buried in their *Gottesäcker*, and their exuberant idealism began to wane.

It began, according to evidence on the ground, in the congregational God's Acre. A careful survey of the original square for unmarried females shows a surprising distance between the graves of the first and second unmarried females to die in Salem. In 1777 Anna Münster was the first single sister to die.[11] As would be expected, she was buried in the usual first position in the God's Acre, the southwestern corner of the square for single females. Soon after Münster's death, another of Salem's single women died. Normally she would have been buried next to Münster, but this particular person apparently presented a dilemma: Her name was Kathy (Cathe);[12] she was an enslaved African American who worked in Salem's tavern. Salem's minister wrote that "Until [Kathy] became sick she had not been especially interested in salvation, but finally she became deeply concerned [and] before her end the Saviour showed her grace, and took her to Himself as a poor, redeemed sinner" (Fries 1926: 1163).

Gravediggers did not bury Kathy next to Anna. Rather, they dug her grave at the far end of what would become the second row, a position that separated her from the rest of Salem's single-sister graves for more than 35 years. Archaeologist Geoffrey Hughes, who first noted this disparity, calling it "transient segregation," has considered possible reasons for Kathy's isolation: "Was Cathe's segregated burial a reflection of Moravian attitudes toward the ambiguities of enslavement? Was Cathe simply

11. Identified as Anna Münstern, the feminine spelling of Münster, on her gravestone.
12. Identified as Cathe on her gravestone.

considered too young at 18 to be interred next to Anna, a mature woman or 35 at the time of her death? Was her religious sincerity so in doubt because she was not a communicant member of the church, it seemed an injustice to bury her next to an example of pure Moravian womanhood? All of these reasons and more may have gone into the final decision to segregate Cathe from the rest of Salem's single women" (Hughes 2005: 143).

Skin color and ethnic differences were not likely the principal reasons for Kathy's isolation. In 1797 and 1810, respectively, the African American Moravians Abraham and Peter Oliver were buried right in place with fellow choir members who were white, and four African American children of black Christians were buried with their little choirs. Eighteenth-century Moravians believed Africans suffered slavery as a result of God's curse of Noah's son Ham, but curses were not unusual in the Old Testament. Since Adam and Eve, God had cursed all humans in one way or another, and throughout the world Moravians were living, worshipping, dying, and being buried in close relation to people of color. No, it is more likely that Kathy's transient segregation resulted from Moravian concerns about her fidelity—the purity of her soul—than her race. Hughes may be right that the reasons for Kathy's segregation were complex. Nevertheless eighteenth-century Moravians were very concerned about the sincerity of confessions and participation in ritual. They may have been most uncomfortable burying a young unbaptized, unconfirmed deathbed convert next to a lifelong Moravian sister (McClinton 2007; Sensbach 1998, 2005, n.d.; Zeisberger 2005).

As the community lived into the nineteenth century, race and racism played an ever-increasing role in the development of Salem, including the segregation of their places of burial. Alongside this obvious social schism, the historical record and the colloquial linguistic transition from *"Gottesacker"* to "graveyard" suggest a more subtle issue: Moravians were becoming less and less certain about the souls of people buried in their *Gottesacker.*

Often white non-Moravians requested burial in the congregational *Gottesacker,* and the *Aufseher Collegium* routinely denied these requests. Yet church leaders decided that non-Moravian girls who died in their boarding school should be buried with the single sisters, and this led to questions about family members of the girls should they die while visiting Salem. All the while, race continued to be an entangling social issue.[13]

Finally in 1816 church leaders decided to segregate racially Salem's places of burial. The minutes of the *Aufseher Collegium* record that they intended to lay out a

---

13. "From time to time the request is voiced that the remains of dead persons who did not belong to the community in Salem . . . be buried in our grave yard *[Gottes Acker].* . . . The only permissible exception would be the death of a student from the boarding school" *(Aufseher Collegium* 1815). This quote is an example of an anonymous translator interpreting the congregational *"Gottes Acker"* as *graveyard.*

cemetery exclusively for white non-Moravians who died in their neighborhood and that, "In case such a burial would take place before such an enlargement, we could not do otherwise but to bury the corpse in the row with our Brethren. The so-called Parish cemetery ["*Gottes Acker*"] would then be the resting place for the Negroes" (*Aufseher Collegium* 1816).[14]

The proposed non-Moravian, white-only cemetery—Salem Cemetery—was not set up until 1857, and between 1816 and 1857 several non-Moravians were buried in the congregational *Gottesacker*. No doubt these individuals were nominally Christians, but Moravians could not know the states of their souls, or even the souls of fellow Moravians, in the intimate ways their parents and grandparents had known one another when the community was small and all members shared their confessions of faith daily. Moreover, following the mainstream of American culture, Moravians had become more individualistic and private. Under these circumstances perhaps the congregational burial ground began to seem more like a graveyard than a field sown exclusively with God's faithful.

An Archaeological Contribution

Results of the archaeological investigations at Saint Philips shed light on this complicated story. By combining historical documentation with results of our excavations, we were able to delineate the original *Fremden* or Parish *Gottesacker* and the 1816 expansion for African American burials.

Church records and maps indicate that originally the Parish *Gottesacker* was to be approximately 60 feet square and set back a similar distance from the lane that would later become Church Street. At first they placed burials in five grave rows with no divisions of age, sex, and, presumably, marital status, although the records do not address this particular point. In early church records they also acknowledge that the map of this *Gottesacker* had been lost, that the list of graves was incomplete, that the plot was not well kept, and that the locations of some graves were being lost. The archaeological finds were consistent with their description: Near the center of what would have been the Parish *Gottesacker*, we found five graves in a carefully aligned row. Subsequent burials followed the row pattern, but they were not neatly spaced, and the rows appeared irregular. Wide, uneven spacing suggested gravediggers were not certain of the location of earlier graves and therefore left ample room between graves.

Excavations also confirmed that the 1816 expansion of the Parish *Gottesacker* to form the *Gottesacker* for the "Small Negro Congregation" involved extending the northern and southern boundaries of the old *Gottesacker* square to the street. Labels

14. This quotation is an example of a twentieth-century translator interpreting "*Gottes Acker*" as *cemetery*.

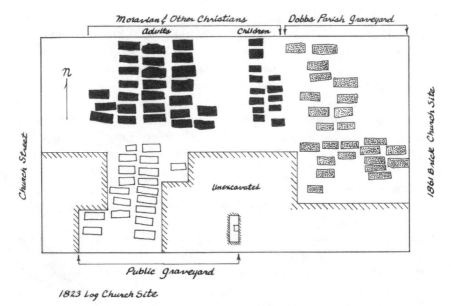

Archaeological schematic of the Saint Philips Complex graveyard.
Courtesy of the *Journal of Moravian History,* Nazareth, Pennsylvania.

on an 1839 map showed the final *Gottesacker,* including the old part to the east and
the new part to the west, to have been a 70– by 120-foot rectangle. The map also
showed bisecting north-south and east-west walkways forming a cruciform pattern;
however, neither this map, nor any other, showed the layout and location of graves.

Over several years, excavators removed topsoil and fill dirt from the entire northern half of this rectangle and from a large portion of the southern half. In addition
to exposing the irregular pattern of graves in the old Parish *Gottesacker,* these excavations revealed a regular pattern of graves in the northwestern quadrant and in
the northeastern quadrant immediately east of the north-south bisecting walkway.
Graves here were reminiscent of a typical Moravian *Gottesacker:* in the northwestern
quadrant were 26 adult-size graves in 5 well-aligned rows. These included 3 complete
rows of 7 graves each. The easternmost and westernmost rows were incomplete,
with 2 and 3 graves respectively. Across the north-south walkway east of these graves
were 13 child-size graves in a complete 8–grave row and an incomplete row with 5
graves.

South across the east-west bisecting walkway, limited excavation showed a striking difference. Here the rows were longer, with nine graves per row. They were not
so neatly aligned as on the northern side, and there were graves of different sizes in
the same row.

Comparing the archaeological pattern with Moravian records, archaeologist Michele Hughes (2005) has concluded that the graves north of the walkway were exclusively those of Christians—Moravian and non-Moravian, adult and child. To the south, she believed, the church buried African Americans who were not Christian. Thus the African American burial place was, in practice, two burial grounds—one consecrated, the other unconsecrated.

Although they make no mention of this division in the "Diary of the Small Negro Congregation," the 1816 relegation of all African American burials in Salem to this one location must have created a problem for church members and the minister. Traditionally, Christians buried their dead in consecrated ground with other believers. This was especially important for Moravians for whom the Easter Litany on the *Gottesacker* became one of their definitive rituals. How could they perform this ritual in a burial ground sullied with nonbelievers? The answer, it appears, was to divide the expanded ground into two parts, a *Gottesacker* to the north and a public cemetery for other African Americans to the south.

The north-south, Christian/non-Christian division in the Saint Philips graveyard shares a structural similarity to the two burial grounds at the upper end of Church Street. Immediately east of the congregational God's Acre is Salem Cemetery, operated by Salem Cemetery Inc. For 40 years church and civic leaders discussed the need for a public, white-only cemetery in Salem; and finally, in 1857, they sold property to a nonprofit commission for the cemetery. Archaeological evidence shows that during the same period guardians of the African American church and burial place must have been dealing with a similar issue—maintaining a Christian *Gottesacker* while providing a burial place for the public, many of whom may have been non-Christians. On a much smaller scale, their solution seems to have been the same as that for the upper end of Church Street. However, their Christian/public division began in the 1820s, more than three decades before the founding of Salem Cemetery.

In the nineteenth century the *Gottesacker* for the African American congregation was much smaller than the *Gottesacker* of the Salem congregation, reflecting the small number of African American Christians in and around Salem. Ironically, in their small size and intimate relationships, Salem's African American Christians of the early nineteenth century were perhaps more similar than their white neighbors to the community of pioneering Moravians who founded Salem in the 1760s.

Disquieting Issues

The translations of *Gottesacker* in documents used in the Saint Philips project appear to represent a complex mix of legitimate Moravian tradition. twentieth-century revivals, and culturally biased distortions. The frequent translation of *Gottesacker* as "graveyard" in the early volumes of the *Records of Moravians* continues a firmly established nineteenth-century transition to religiously neutral terminology for Moravian places of burial. This transition meshes well with Atwood's (2004) conclusion that during this period Moravians became less certain about the salvation of those they buried.

While the interpretation of *Gottesacker* as "graveyard" continues a nineteenth-century tradition, the revival of *Gottesacker* as the English "God's Acre" and the variety and pattern of nonreligious and religious terms for the burial ground at the Saint Philips complex emerge as expressions of twentieth-century values and perceptions. The unstated guidelines for translating the various occurrences of *Gottesacker* closely follow Moravians' changing perceptions of themselves, twentieth-century racial stereotypes, and the upheaval of the civil rights movement. In some cases these overlays appear consistent with legitimate historical meaning: "God's Acre" does seem a more accurate translation of the eighteenth- and early-nineteenth-century usage of "*Gottesacker*" than "graveyard," yet this usage glosses over an unsettled mid-nineteenth-century period of Moravian introspection and questioning.

The increasing popularity of "God's Acre" as a translation of "*Gottesacker*" may be traced from the infrequent occurrence in the earliest volumes of the *Records of Moravians* to more common usage in later publications. This trend corresponds to the growing popularity of early Moravian history in the middle of the twentieth century, which culminated with the restoration of the old congregational village by Old Salem, Inc. While the middle-twentieth-century trend slowly recast the congregational graveyard as a God's Acre, phrasing for the graveyard at Saint Philips moved in the opposite direction. Following what probably became local habit, most translators shied away from religious wording for the site; in spite of records that consistently and specifically referred to the burial ground as a *Gottesacker*, they translated this phrase as simply "graveyard" or the decidedly non-Moravian" cemetery." This treatment correlated with the racism and racist segregation of mid-twentieth-century regional culture, including Moravian Salem.

That Marx translated *Gottesacker* as "God's Acre" in the "Diary of the Small Negro Congregation" is most likely related to the timing of the translation and the reasons for her commission. Other scholars translated most of the nondiary documents in the mid–twentieth century—during the days of rigid statutory segregation. In contrast Marx, working in the 1980s, translated the diary well after Salem Congregation began referring to their graveyard as "God's Acre," after the civil rights movement, and during a period when scholars and community leaders were responding to minority demands for alternatives to traditionally racist historical narratives. Moreover, Old Salem, Inc., commissioned her to translate the diary as they considered exploring the Saint Philips complex and reviving the overlooked story of Salem's African Americans and the "Negro Congregation." Thus it is no surprise that when she encountered the term "*Gottesacker*" in the script of the diarists, she translated it as "God's Acre." It was her straightforward translation that caused us to question our naive acceptance of the common historical account.

The anthropological archaeology at the Saint Philips complex functioned on several levels. On the ground we located, mapped, and interpreted the complex pattern of graves and gravestones found at the site. Beyond this basic level, we were interested in the inextricable association of the Saint Philips story with the rest of Salem and Wachovia and with how our own biases might slant our interpretations. From the earliest days, Moravians have struggled with a variety of issues that included dealing with slavery and race as well as changes within their faith community. Now Old Salem's Saint Philips archaeological project and our anthropological study have become part of this discourse. In the process, all parties involved, including our archaeological team, have faced disquieting issues. Perhaps the most surprising of these issues has been the subtle way the innocent-seeming language of everyday discourse can influence our perceptions of the past. This is a poignant reminder for us not only to be careful with the interpretations we draw from others, but also to think carefully about the ways our own interpretations may be inconsistent with our values and the truth we seek.

Acknowledgments

For their assistance and encouragement in preparing this chapter, the author would like to thank Craig Atwood, Daniel Crews, M. O. and Martha Hartley, Geoffrey and Michele Hughes, John Larson, Paul Peucker, Richard Starbuck, and the staffs of the Moravian Archives, Southern Province, and the library and research room of the Museum of Early Southern Decorative Arts.

References

Atwood, C. 2004. *Community of the Cross: Moravian Piety in Colonial Bethlehem.* University Park: Pennsylvania State University Press.

———. 1992. From Joy to Grief: Changes in Moravian Attitudes toward Death from 1740–1876. Unpublished manuscript on file, Princeton Theological Seminary, Princeton, N.J.

Aufseher Collegium 1843. 22 February. Unpublished manuscript on file, Museum of Early Southern Decorative Arts (MESDA), Old Salem, Inc., Winston-Salem, N.C.

———. 1816. MESDA card file, Wachovia area, translator unknown. 21 October. Unpublished manuscript on file, Museum of Early Southern Decorative Arts (MESDA), Old Salem, Inc., Winston-Salem, N.C.

———. 1815. MESDA card file, Wachovia area, translator unknown. 24 September. Unpublished manuscript on file, Museum of Early Southern Decorative Arts (MESDA), Old Salem, Inc., Winston-Salem, N.C.

Blakey, M. L., and L. M. Rankin-Hill (editors) 2004. *The New York African Burial Ground Skeletal Biology Final Report*, Vol. 1. Washington, D.C.: Howard University.

Crews, D. 1998. *Neither Slave nor Free: Moravians, Slavery, and a Church That Endures.* Winston-Salem, N.C.: Moravian Archives.

———. 1996. *Moravian Meanings: A Glossary of Historical Terms of the Moravian Church, Southern Province.* 2nd ed. Winston-Salem, N.C.: Moravian Archives.

Crews, D., and L. Bailey 2006. *Records of the Moravians in North Carolina, XIII*. Raleigh: North Carolina Department of Cultural Resources, Division of Archives and History.

———. 2000. *Records of the Moravians in North Carolina, XII*. Raleigh: North Carolina Department of Cultural Resources, Division of Archives and History.

Epperson, T. W. 2004. Critical Race Theory and the Archaeology of the African Diaspora. *Historical Archaeology* 38(1):101–108.

Ferguson, L. 1992. *Uncommon Ground: Archaeology and Early African America, 1650–1800*. Washington, D.C.: Smithsonian Institution Press.

Franklin, M. 1997. Power to the People: Sociopolitics and the Archaeology of Black Americans. *Historical Archaeology* 31(3):36–50.

Freeman, A. J. 1998. *An Ecumenical Theology of the Heart: The Theology of Count Nicholas Ludwig von Zinzendorf*. Bethlehem, Pa.: Moravian Church in America.

Fries, A. (editor). 1947. *Records of the Moravians in North Carolina, VII*. Raleigh: North Carolina Historical Commission.

———. 1943. *Records of the Moravians in North Carolina, VI*. Raleigh: North Carolina Historical Commission.

———. 1941. *Records of the Moravians in North Carolina, V*. Raleigh: North Carolina Historical Commission.

———. 1930. *Records of the Moravians in North Carolina, IV*. Raleigh: North Carolina Historical Commission.

———. 1926. *Records of the Moravians in North Carolina, III*. Raleigh: North Carolina Historical Commission.

———. 1925. *Records of the Moravians in North Carolina, II*. Raleigh: North Carolina Historical Commission.

———. 1922. *Records of the Moravians in North Carolina, I*. Raleigh: North Carolina Historical Commission.

Fries, A., and D. L. Rights (editors) 1954. *Records of the Moravians in North Carolina, VIII*. Raleigh: State Department of Archives and History.

Hamilton, K. G. (editor).1969. *Records of the Moravians in North Carolina, X*. Raleigh: State Department of Archives and History.

———. 1966. *Records of the Moravians in North Carolina, IX*. Raleigh: State Department of Archives and History.

Hartley, M. O. 1995. *Explorations in a Church Yard: St. Philip's Field School, Salem, N.C.* Winston-Salem: Old Salem, Inc.

Hughes, G. R. 2005. Salem Asleep: A Discursive Archaeology of God's Acre, 1771–1815. Unpublished master's thesis, University of South Carolina, Columbia.

Hughes, M. A. 2005. The Formation and Development of an Ideology of Racism in Salem, N.C.: 1816–1859. Unpublished master's thesis, University of South Carolina, Columbia.

Leone, M. P., and G. Fry 1999. Conjuring the Big House Kitchen: An Interpretation of African American Belief Systems Based on the Uses of Archaeology and Folklore Sources. *Journal of American Folklore* 112(445):372–403.

Lewis, A. J. 1962. *Zinzendorf: The Ecumenical Pioneer*. Bethlehem, Pa.: Moravian Church in America.

Marx, E. (translator) 1992. Diary of the Small Negro Congregation in and around Salem. Part II: January 1, 1843–December 30, 1855. Winston-Salem: Moravian Archives,

Southern Providence and Old Salem's Museum of Early Southern Decorative Arts (MESDA).

———. 1985. Diary of the Small Negro Congregation in and around Salem. Part I: March 4, 1822–December 25, 1842. Winston-Salem: Moravian Archives, Southern Providence and Old Salem's Museum of Early Southern Decorative Arts (MESDA).

McClinton, R. 2007. *The Moravian Springplace Mission to the Cherokees,* 2 vols. Lincoln: University of Nebraska Press.

Mullins, P. A. 1999. *Race and Affluence: An Archaeology of African America and Consumer Culture.* New York: Kluwer Academic/Plenum.

Orser, C.E., Jr. 2004. *Race and Practice in Archaeological Interpretation* (Philadelphia: University of Pennsylvania Press.

Oxford English Dictionary 1970. *God's Acre* entry. London: Clarendon Press.

Rohrer, S. 2005. *Hope's Promise: Religion and Acculturation in the Southern Backcountry.* Tuscaloosa: University of Alabama Press.

———. 1993a. *Freedmen of the Lord: The Black Moravian Congregation of Salem, N.C., and Its Struggle for Survival, 1856–1890.* Winston-Salem: Ad Hoc Committee for the Preservation of St. Philip's Church.

———. 1993b. *A Mission among the People: The World of St. Philip's Church from 1890–1952.* Winston-Salem: Ad Hoc Committee for the Preservation of St. Philip's Church.

Sensbach, J. 2005. *Rebecca's Revival: Creating Black Christianity in the Atlantic World.* Cambridge, Mass.: Harvard University Press.

———. 1998. A *Separate Canaan: The Making of an Afro-Moravian World in North Carolina, 1763–1840.* Chapel Hill: University of North Carolina Press.

———. (n.d.) *African-Americans in Salem.* Winston-Salem: Old Salem, Inc.

Shirley, M. 1994. *From Congregational Town to Industrial City: Culture and Social Change in a Southern Community.* New York: New York University Press.

Singleton, T. A. (editor).1999. *I, Too, Am America: Archaeological Studies of African American Life.* Charlottesville: University of Virginia Press.

———. 1985. *The Archaeology of Slavery and Plantation Life.* New York: Academic Press.

Spangenberg, A. G. 1959 [1790]. *Idea Fidei Fratrum: An Exposition of Christian Doctrine as Taught in the Protestant Church of the United Brethren or Unitas Fratrum.* Translated and edited by B. Latrobe. 3rd ed. Winston-Salem: Board of Christian Education of the Southern Province of the Moravian Church in America.

Thorp, D. B. 1989. *The Moravian Community in Colonial North Carolina: Pluralism on the Southern Frontier.* Knoxville: University of Tennessee Press.

Weinlick, J. R. 1984. *Count Zinzendorf: The Story of His Life and Leadership in the Renewed Moravian Church.* Bethlehem, Pa.: Moravian Church in America.

Zeisberger, D. 2005. *The Moravian Mission of David Zeisberger, 1772–1781,* edited by H. Wellenreuther and C. Wessel and translated by J. T. Weber. University Park: Pennsylvania State University Press.

KENNETH L. BROWN

BaKongo Cosmograms, Christian Crosses, or None of the Above

An Archaeology of African American Spiritual Adaptations into the 1920s

Enslaved Africans transported to the New World brought with them a wide range of local religious beliefs and practices. The question of whether these African religions were preserved in North America has been the source of much debate in archaeology, since the harsh circumstances under which most enslaved laborers lived—high death rates, the separation of families and tribal groups, and the concerted effort of white owners to eradicate "heathen" (or non-Christian) customs—rendered the preservation of religious traditions difficult. Yet songs, rhythms, movements, and beliefs in the curative powers of roots and the efficacy of a world of spirits and ancestors did survive into the nineteenth century (Maffly-Kipp 2005). These beliefs and practices were increasingly combined in creative ways with the various forms of Christianity to which Europeans and Americans introduced African slaves.

Art historian Robert F. Thompson (1983) first proposed the BaKongo Cosmogram model to help explain a recurring symbol in art of the African diaspora. Leland Ferguson (1992) was the first to employ this model in archaeology in his attempt to explain the meaning of crosses or "X"s often enclosed by circular lines or etched into circular "frames" that he observed on a number of Colonoware vessels recovered in the Low Country of South Carolina. Ferguson noted that the marked vessels had been deposited in a similar fashion and that the marks appeared to have been something more than ceramic decorations or signs of ownership. Employing West Central African ethnographic data, Ferguson built a case for these marks as representations of BaKongo Cosmograms. For BaKongo speakers, a watery barrier separates the world of the living from that of the dead. The sun circles through these worlds in a counterclockwise fashion, providing alternating periods of light and dark, and this daily cycle serves as a metaphor for the continuous cycle of human life. In this model, the horizontal line of the cross represents the "watery" barrier between the two worlds, while the vertical line represents the path of power from the spirit world to that of the living, linking the two across that boundary. The cyclical nature of this belief is symbolized by the placement of the cross within the circular base of a vessel, an annular support, or an etched circular line. In the years since Ferguson's initial formulation of this model, it has been employed by numerous archaeologists and folklorists to explain at least two symbols found on items made and/or utilized by African Americans across the American South (Brown 1994; Fennell 2003, 2007; Franklin 1997; Ruppel et al. 2003; Wahlman 2001; Young 1997). In each of these cases, the investigators generally interpreted the symbol as representing evidence that Africans and African Americans in the New World employed the Bakongo Cosmogram as proposed by Ferguson.

Historians and historical archaeologists have raised at least three problems concerning this model and its utility in explaining the crosses or "X"s. The first problem is the belief that it is unlikely the worldview of any West African culture, or group of cultures, would have been transferred to the New World intact. For example, Chris DeCorse (1999) has argued that in the absence of other data, defined formal similarity is not sufficient evidence to support the presence of a complex worldview, especially given the very simple nature of the symbol. Indeed, as DeCorse (1999: 140) states, "By way of caution, it is important to point out that the ideas involved—African cosmology, division between the living and the dead, and transition—are extremely complex, while the symbols involved are quite simple. Similar, but not identical, marks have been found on ceramics in other cultural and historical

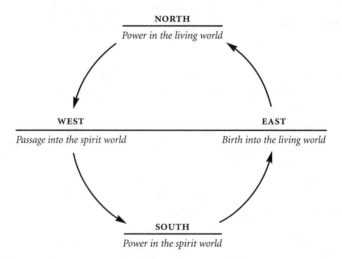

Diagram of the directions and their meaning within the BaKongo Cosmogram. The horizontal line represents water that divides the world of the living from the spirit world, while the vertical line represents the continuity between the two worlds.

settings. . . . In the case of the Kongo and South Carolina marks, it is possible that a symbol was transported but did not retain the same meaning." The large number of "West African" cultural traditions, the rigors of capture, the statuses and roles of those captured and enslaved, the horrors of the Middle Passage, and the circumstances of enslavement in the New World, particularly the requirements of plantation agriculture, are all seen as having operated against the adaptation of any single worldview by African Americans.

A second problem concerns the observed similarity between the cross of the cosmogram and the Christian cross. Beginning in the 1830s, a form of Christianity was actively taught to many of the enslaved across the South in an effort to better control them and to blunt some of the criticisms of abolitionists. The "success" of this conversion, in part, has led at least one archaeologist to comment that for African Americans, "I think the BaKongo cosmogram question is a bunch of nonsense: Where is the evidence that the cross symbol seen in North America is anything but a Christian symbol? South Carolina, at least, was overwhelmingly Protestant Christian, and while evidence exists for the retention of some traditions, the documentary evidence at least points to only a single major religion, Christianity" (Steen 2003: 1). Within this argument, religious symbols should be first related to Christianity, as it was taught to and expressed by African Americans, rather than their being tied to West African cultural traditions. Indeed the apparent lack of the cosmogram in modern African American spirituality can be employed as an argument against its use within the antebellum New World.

Historian Jason Young (2007) has raised a "second variant" of this problem. That is, the visual similarity between the BaKongo Cosmogram and the Christian cross may have permitted it to be a multivocal symbol among the Africans and African Americans who employed them. According to Young's analysis, this shift toward a multivalent symbol occurred as a result of the integration of Christianity and traditional BaKongo religious beliefs that began to occur after the introduction of Catholicism into West-Central Africa during the fifteenth century by the Portuguese (Heywood 2002; Thornton 1983, 1998, 2002; Young 2007). In Young's (2007: 88–89) view, "the cross likely stood as a symbol of dual significance from which participants could draw a variety of meanings, both Christian and non-Christian. . . . Crosses carried multiple interpretations and may be interpreted variously, signifying at one and the same time Kongolese notions of the cycles of life and death, the ring shout, and Christianity."

If the beliefs held by Thompson (1983), Stuckey (1987), Ruppel et al. (2003), Fennell (2003, 2007), and Brown (1994, 2001, 2005) concerning the importance of crossroads for Africans and African Americans are correct, then this raises a third potential interpretation for the Cosmogram/cross symbol among African Americans. For example, Ruppel and co-authors (2003: 329) equate the crossroads symbol with the cosmogram, writing, "The symbolism of the cosmogram or the crossroads appears throughout the African diaspora, and represents a powerful idea found among people primarily from West Central Africa (and in other forms in West Africa) that came to have new life and meaning in the Americas. The crossroads is the meeting place of heaven and earth, the living with the dead, the beginning and the end of life, and a place of magic where life's problems can obtain supernatural solutions. "These authors suggest that for West African cultures outside of the BaKongo area, the symbol of the crossroads is a more important one for social, political, and/or religious beliefs and behaviors. Indeed, as will be presented, the meanings of the sets of crossroads deposits identified beneath certain structures in the Levi-Jordan, Frogmore, Richmond Hill, and, now, the Magnolia quarters suggest that the cosmogram model was not followed during the placement of these features (Brown 2005, 2008a).

Thus the crosses etched on to the Colonoware vessels might have served as a symbol that could have been interpreted in a variety of ways depending on the beliefs of the observer and/or the context in which any cross was embedded. Indeed, it could have had all three (and possibly more) meanings simultaneously. If this was the case, then the cross found archaeologically on small portable objects and/or as deposits placed below cabin floors may represent an example of what Mintz and Price (1992: 15) mean when they state that direct retentions from West Africa were "more the exception than the rule." In this case, the formal similarities of the symbol, simple as the design is, permitted a variety of possible meanings for each viewer, not simply a single meaning. It can also be argued that the study of the problems related to the meaning of the "cross" symbol and the function of artifacts on which it was displayed has suffered from the lack of testing the cosmogram model within its historic, ethnographic, and archaeological contexts within the New World.

The purpose of this essay, however, is not to provide a test of the cosmogram model, but instead I employ the archaeological data obtained during the excavation into four plantation quarters sites across the South in order to demonstrate three points: (1) if the BaKongo Cosmogram was introduced into the New World, it quickly became modified in ways that differentiate it from its original West-Central African meanings, while maintaining the significance of the crossroads; (2) the evolution of the beliefs concerning the crossroads and their material manifestations into the 1920s can be documented in both urban and rural settings; and (3) the evidence related to curing and conjure are seen archaeologically and continue to be practiced today.

The Comparative Project and African American Spirituality, including the BaKongo Cosmogram

As a result of the interpretations of data derived from the Levi-Jordan plantation quarters in 1997, comparative excavations were conducted into three additional plantation quarters sites: Frogmore, on Saint Helena Island, South Carolina; Richmond Hill, in Bryan County, Georgia; and the ongoing investigation of the Magnolia

Plantation, a component of the Cane River Creole National Historical Park in Natchitoches Parish, Louisiana. These excavations have been undertaken to test the hypothesized differences in African American culture caused by the labor regime (gang versus task) imposed on the enslaved (Adams 1987; Berlin and Morgan 1993; Morgan 1982, 1998; Reitz et al. 1985) and to investigate the internal adaptive processes operating within the enslaved/tenant communities of plantations that maintained large enslaved labor forces.

In conducting our investigations into the Magnolia Quarters, we have concluded that at least one set of cardinal direction, crossroads deposits was excavated along with portable objects with crosses carved into them. Here I will briefly summarize the archaeological data related to these crossroads deposits and then turn the focus to the relevant data from the Magnolia Quarters, where occupation of the cabins lasted for nearly 120 years, from 1840 through the late 1950s. To begin this discussion, at least one archaeologist (Weik 2008) has pointed out that it is necessary to demonstrate the contemporaneity of the crossroads deposits that have been identified beneath structures on the Jordan, Frogmore, and Richmond Hill plantations. Since such a demonstration is critical to our interpretation of the features, several factors need to be at least briefly discussed prior to turning to a discussion of the Magnolia data. Unfortunately, short of a time machine, there is no way to conclusively demonstrate that these deposits were placed "at the same time." However, several attributes of the deposits identified within each individual set appear to provide at least circumstantial support for the interpretation of contemporaneity. First, they were all placed beneath wooden floors after the structures were built and are the only nonarchitectural features that were placed beneath their respective structures. Second, the features containing the deposits begin at approximately the same elevation within the subfloor stratigraphy of each structure. Third, in all but one of these cases, these deposits are aligned with the cardinal directions forming a cross with a north-south and an east-west axis. Finally, the deposits form two distinct patterns related to the length of the arms defined, depending on the intended activities conducted in the structures above them. Beneath the church/praise house structures the lines are approximately same length, while for the curers' cabins the north-south axis is approximately half the length of the east-west distance.

The Curers' Crossroads Deposits

Sets of crossroads features, designed to sanctify the cabins utilized for curing/conjuring and probably childbirth were identified from Levi-Jordan and Frogmore quarters (Table 1). These sets of features are interpreted as having elements of the curers' ritual kits on the east, power symbols of the world of the living on the north, protection devices on the west, and a representation of the spirit world on the south. While the actual materials employed in these deposits differ, they appear to have the same

TABLE 1. Cardinal direction deposits found beneath the floors of cabins interpreted as having been occupied and utilized by Curers

NORTH (Worldly Power)

Coin Deposit
(*Jordan*)

Articulated Calf Deposit
(*Frogmore Manor*)

WEST (Protection)	**EAST (Healing/Birth)**
Amula/Iron Deposit	Conjurer's Kit Deposit
(*Jordan*)	(*Jordan*)
Articulated Chicken Deposit	Conjure Bottle Deposit
(*Frogmore Manor*)	(*Frogmore Manor*)

SOUTH (Spirit World)

Ash/Burned Shell/Burned Metal Deposit
(*Jordan*)

Ash/Burned Sand/Burned Metal Deposit
(*Frogmore Manor*)

meaning to those who deposited them. For example, while the eastern deposits consisted of elements of the curers' ritual kits, the western deposit at Frogmore consisted of a fully articulated chicken that had been placed upright into a hole and facing toward the east. The base of a green glass bottle had been placed over the top of the chicken. At Levi-Jordan the western deposit was interpreted as being similar to a Yoruba *amula* (Brown 2001). Here two iron kettles were placed one inside the other, wrapped in chains, and deposited with a bayonet and a large number of artifacts made of iron. The function of both of these western deposits can be interpreted as attempts to protect the space within the cabin by capturing evil as it attempted to enter the cabin. Chickens certainly serve this purpose in a large number of West African cultures (MacDonald 1995), the Gullah (Brown 2004), and among African Americans in other parts of the South, including Brazoria County, Texas (Brewer 1976; Wright 1994). Thus within the BaKongo Cosmogram model the east represents one's birth into the world of the living, and certainly the curers' kits could be employed during childbirth, although curing goes well beyond and continues throughout a person's life. For the BaKongo Cosmogram, the west signifies one's transition from the world of the living to that of the dead. However in these two cases, the western deposits protected those seeking aid along with the practitioners during the rituals associated with curing, childbirth, and, possibly, conjuring. The curers' deposits at Levi-Jordan span the period from 1858 until the abandonment of the quarters in 1887, while at Frogmore they appear to date from around 1830 until the 1860s.

The Church/Praise House Crossroads Deposits

Sets of crossroads deposits have been identified beneath structures that served as churches/praise houses for the occupants of the Jordan and Richmond Hill quarters (Table 2). These sets of features are interpreted as having deposits that signify one's birth into membership within the church/praise house on the east, the power of the community or congregation and its beliefs on the north, transition from life to death on the west, and the power of the community and/or its memory on the south. Again, while these deposits bear some relationship to the meaning of the cardinal directions of the BaKongo Cosmogram, there appear to be a number of significant differences, although not as many as can be interpreted for the curers' deposits. For example, the east appears to have signified one's acceptance into the church community rather than their physical birth into the world of the living (Brown 2005). The south, in both cases, appears to represent an altar to the memory of the ancestors, rather than one's power in that world. The Levi-Jordan church appears to have been converted from a residence shortly after its construction in the 1850s (possibly in 1858) and abandoned as a church in the early 1870s (Anonymous 1979), although it continued to serve as a school until after 1880 (Brown 2005). The Richmond Hill praise house appears to have functioned from the 1830s through the early 1900s.

While not found at Richmond Hill, a second set of cardinal direction crossroads deposits was recovered beneath the floor space of the Levi-Jordan church. As can be

TABLE 2. Cardinal direction crossroads deposits found
beneath the floors of Praise Houses

NORTH (Community's Power)
Coin/Crystal/Household Deposit
(*Jordan*)
Shell Cross Deposit
(*Richmond Hill*)

WEST (Transition/Death)	EAST (Rebirth as an Adult)
Brick Altar/Iron Deposit (*Jordan*)	Brick/Knife Deposit (*Jordan*)
Human Skull/Iron Deposit (*Richmond Hill*)	Mirror Glass Deposit (*Richmond Hill*)

SOUTH (The Community's Past)
Ash Deposit
(*Jordan*)
Plaster "Sankofa" Symbol Deposit
(*Richmond Hill*)

observed, while both sets of crossroads deposits shared the same western deposit, the so-called "brick altar," the second set generally surrounded the "religious crossroads deposits." Indeed, the two sets of crossroads deposits appear to have shared the "knife deposit" as the eastern deposit in the religious crossroads, and as the central deposit of the "political crossroads deposit." (Table 3), and has been interpreted as having functioned more in the political role of the church's congregation than its religious function (Brown 2005). In this case, the plaster "cross" was located near the doorway into the sanctuary of the church as well as the doorway between the sanctuary and the minister's residence. This plaster cross was the only one of the seven deposits that was well protected during its placement, possibly suggesting its importance in the function of the structure. The southern deposit spans the sanctuary, through the minister's residence and into the cabin to the south. An elaborately carved "fly-whisk," a necklace that included the bone spurs from at least two chicken legs, and a number of other artifacts were recovered from the deposits beneath the cabin to the south. This cabin has been interpreted as having been the residence of one of the community's elders (Brown 2005).

The Magnolia Quarters "Crossroads" Deposits

The ongoing investigation into the Magnolia Plantation Quarters began in June 2005. The eight brick cabins that remain in the quarters were likely constructed during the 1840s and continued to be occupied after 1865 by families of tenants and, later, "day laborers" on the plantation through the late 1950s (A. Hertzog, personal communication 2006; B. Hertzog, personal communication 2006; Hunter 2005). These excavations have permitted us to investigate the evolution of a number of beliefs and behaviors that have been defined within the archaeological record of all four of the African American communities included in the larger comparative project (Brown 2008b). For Magnolia the occupation of the cabins continued for over 120 years, with roughly 90 years of occupation after emancipation. The crossroads

TABLE 3. The interpretations of the deposits forming the possible "political" cardinal direction crossroads deposits found beneath the floor of the Jordan Community praise house

NORTH (An Altar to Ogun?)
White over Red Feature Deposit

WEST (Transition)	EAST (Consecration)
Brick Altar/Iron Artifact Deposit	Plaster "Cross"

SOUTH (The Strength of the Ancestors)
Ash/Kettle Base/Household Artifact Deposit

deposits beneath two of the cabins have been extensively investigated to date (cabins no. 1 and no. 4). A number of apparent "conjure tricks" have also been defined beneath and around these cabins. Given the data thus far generated, I will focus on the two possible crossroads deposits with a brief discussion of the conjure tricks.

Both of the hypothesized crossroads deposits are currently known from only three of the required four deposits. Future fieldwork should provide an answer to whether or not at least one of these sets forms a complete cardinal direction crossroads. These deposits have been identified within cabins no. 1 and no. 4. Based on the available stratigraphic data, determination of when the wooden floors were constructed within these cabins has become an important variable in the discussion of these specific deposits, as well as the evolution of the crossroads deposits defined on African American sites in general. Unfortunately, activities related to the preparation of cabin no. 1 for exhibit by the National Park Service (NPS) led to the removal of the original wooden floor and a large portion of the soil and artifact deposits that had built up over the cabin's original dirt floor. This work all but destroyed the stratigraphic relationship between the hypothesized cardinal direction crossroad features. However, for cabin no. 4, other than rodent burrowing activities, the internal stratigraphy appears to have remained relatively intact. Excavation techniques that provide for very tight vertical and horizontal provenance control and that were consistent with techniques employed at the other three sites were implemented to demonstrate that the deposits were placed within the footprint of these cabins during a brief period of time. Based on our investigation, each of the Magnolia cabins tested had dirt floors until sometime after the turn of the 1900s. Limited ethnographic research conducted by Muriel Crespi (2004), along with data on floods that impacted the cabins, supports the interpretation that this also likely occurred around the time the cabins were altered from one-room cabins for two families to two-room cabins for a single family. Crespi's (2004: 44) informants stated that this change began when the population of the quarters "thinned earlier in the 20th century." Limited evidence related to two flood deposits was recovered from beneath the wooden floor of cabin no. 4, with the earliest one probably the result of the famous flood of 1927. As this deposit can be seen to overlay a nearly 0.25-inch-thick deposit above the dirt floor, it suggests that a wooden floor was built sometime shortly before the flood.

On the other hand, several lines of evidence suggest that the construction of the wood frame additions on the east side of the existing cabins occurred at a later date than the placement of the wooden floors inside the two cabins thus far investigated. This evidence, consisting of oral testimony, historic photographs of the quarters, and archaeological data, supports the construction of these rooms around 1930. Photographs taken in 1928 show that while a number of changes had taken place within the community, including the definition of personal space (fences, and so on), and the construction of porches, no rooms had been constructed on the eastern facade of the existing cabins at that time. However, one photograph believed to be of cabin no. 1, taken in 1922, shows that a small wood frame room had been enclosed on the northern end of the porch constructed on the western facade of the cabin. These lines of evidence support the interpretation that in these two cabins the wooden floors were constructed prior to the placement of the frame rooms on the eastern sides of the cabins but likely after each cabin had been converted for occupation by a single family.

Cabin No. 1

At least two conjure tricks appear to have been associated with the occupation of cabin no. 1: the placement of a Hoyt's Nickel Cologne bottle in the north room and the placement of a liquor bottle beneath the southern edge of the porch on the western side of the cabin. While both bottles contain attributes that support their manufacture well after the turn of the 1900s, it is the oral history and the construction of the porch and an eastern frame addition that suggest both the date and the meaning behind the placement of at least one of the conjure tricks. Oral testimony states that the addition to the cabin was employed as a place to gamble, and Hoyt's appears as an important element in conjure tricks connected with success in affairs related to gambling, money, and love. The bottle was found standing upright and buried in a small hole dug into the original dirt floor of the cabin, 1.5 feet from the center of the doorway leading into the frame addition. All those entering the room would have to have passed over the bottle, likely in an attempt to transfer their luck to be held by the bottle while they gambled within the room. The liquor bottle was found upside down in a small hole dug below the southern edge of the porch. Given the location of the gate into the yard of the cabin, this location meant that all those entering the porch from the south would have passed over the bottle. At this point in our research the exact function of this bottle can only be guessed, but an attempt to control someone's habits related to the consumption of alcohol seems likely.

The potential crossroads deposits beneath cabin no. 1 were placed under the wooden floor of the southern room. The eastern deposit consisted of a brass locket and small snail shell placed into a large, square hole centered approximately 2.5 feet from the middle of the window on the eastern wall of the room. Both sides of the locket contained etched designs, at least one of which appears similar to a *gris-gris* symbol employed by Marie Laveau meaning "to take control of one's life" (Canizares 2001: 43). The symbol was etched into the side of the locket that faced toward the east when it was discovered: the direction associated with birth/rebirth in the crossroads deposits that have been identified elsewhere. The southern deposit consisted of a large number of green bottle glass fragments, at least one human deciduous tooth, and a small blue glass bead. Bennie Keel (personal communication 2004; Miller 2004) originally discovered what we have now defined as the western deposit during his 1999 investigation of the cabin for the NPS. The deposit has been described as a large "trash dump" that had been placed approximately 2.5 feet from the center of the western wall. Miller (2004: 126) calculated a mean ceramic date of 1891 for the materials recovered by NPS from this feature, while her mean ceramic date for cabin no. 1 was 1900. During our initial investigation of cabin no. 1, we redefined and cleaned the walls of the units excavated within cabin no. 1's southern room by Keel and his crew. However, our only excavation into this feature occurred when we encountered its northern end in one of our units. Analysis of the stratigraphy associated with this feature suggests that, like the others, this one had been dug into the original dirt floor of the room around the time that the wooden floor was constructed, possibly between 1900 and 1910. Unfortunately, if a northern deposit exists, excavation suggests that it was covered when the NPS reconstructed the floor of the hearth, a location noted by Leone and Fry (2001: 147) as a possible pattern in the placement of ritual caches by African Americans. Currently, we are negotiating with NPS for the removal of the reconstructed hearth in order to excavate the area in an attempt to determine the presence/absence of the northern deposit.

Limited historic and ethnographic evidence suggests that for some of its occupation the Magnolia Community's midwife lived in cabin no. 1 (Brown 2008b; Crespi 2004; Teal 2007: 49). Two of the historic photographs taken within the Magnolia Quarters in 1922 are believed to show cabin no. 1 and one of its longtime residents (Brown 2007, 2008b). The woman in the photograph is named "Aunt Agnes" in a handwritten text next to the photographs. Teal (2007: 49) identified this woman as the midwife noted in Crespi's (2004) ethnography who lived in the Magnolia Quarters until her death in 1922 at the age of 119. As Aunt Agnes has not yet been found

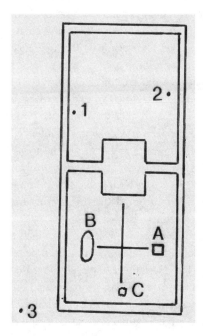

A drawing of six of cabin no. 1's artifact features. (1) The location of the altered gold Miraculous Medal; (2) The location of the Hoyt's Nickel cologne bottle; (3) The location of the liquor bottle; (A) The location of the pit that contained the secondarily carved locket and snail shell; (B) The location of the "trash pit" first identified by Keel (1999); and (C) The bottle glass, deciduous tooth, and ash deposit.

on any of the slave lists known for Magnolia, she may have moved into the community sometime after emancipation. Crespi's (2004: 48) informants stated that a midwife was resident within the quarters at least through 1919 but that no midwife was present within the community by the early 1940s. Thus it is possible that Aunt Agnes's death in 1922 may have caused members of the community to go elsewhere when a midwife was needed. If this evidence has been interpreted correctly, then the historic, oral historic, and archaeological evidence derived for cabin no. 1 further suggests that the frame addition to the cabin and the gambling activities postdate Aunt Agnes's death and that they occurred after the cabin ceased to be occupied by a midwife.

Finally one artifact discovered adjacent to the southern post of the door frame in the north room of the cabin appears to relate to the incorporation of both Catholic beliefs and Voodoo within the community, or at least by a resident of the cabin. The object is a small gold Miraculous Medal, one of two such medals recovered from the Magnolia Quarters that were modified from the original form struck under the auspices of the Catholic Church. These medals were struck by the Catholic Church during 1832 in response to a request made by the Virgin Mary during three apparitions the Virgin Mary had with a novitiate nun, Sister Catherine Laboure in Paris, France. The Catholic Church canonized Sister Catherine Laboure, becoming known as Saint Catherine. The medals were designed with the Virgin Mary standing on the earth and crushing snakes, thus symbolically proclaiming that she was "the Queen of Heaven and Earth" and that "Satan and all of his followers are helpless before her" (Association of the Miraculous Medal 2006). The Virgin Mary is posed with rays of light extending from her fingers. On each of the three Miraculous Medals we have recovered, the figure of the Virgin Mary is surrounded by an inscription, written in French (the gold medal) or English (the white metal and aluminum medals) that reads: "O Mary, conceived without sin, pray for us who have recourse to thee." On the back of the medal, twelve stars, symbolizing Christ's Apostles, are placed around a cross with a bar under it. The cross and bar symbolize Christ, his sacrifice for humankind, and the earth. A capital "M" is intertwined with the bar below the cross and is intended to symbolize the Virgin Mary's role with Christ, the world, and her role "in the salvation of the faithful and as the Mother of the Church" (Association of the Miraculous Medal 2006). Finally, beneath the cross two hearts have been placed to symbolize the love of Jesus and the Virgin for humanity. It is believed that by wearing the Miraculous Medal many "blessings" would be granted to the wearer.

The small gold medal recovered from cabin no. 1 measured just under 0.7 inches in length. In a comparison with a similar medal struck in 1850, a number of alterations appear to have been made to the Virgin Mary. First, the halo placed above Virgin Mary's head was changed so that it appears more as a head wrap. Second, the features of the face, including the shape of the head, the eyes, nose, mouth, chin, and neck were altered. These changes resulted in the "Virgin" figure having large, deep-set eyes, a broad nose, thick lips, and a thin neck. If the original model for the gold medal recovered beneath cabin no. 1 was like that of the Vachette medal, then the "vertical" orientation of the Virgin's head has also been changed slightly. Third, as folklorist Gladys-Marie Frye (personal communication 2007) pointed out, the chest area of this medal "has been augmented," while the neckline of her dress appears to have been significantly lowered. Fourth, the earth that was to be placed beneath the snakes on which the Virgin is standing on all of the medals struck for the Catholic Church has been removed, although the snakes appear to have been left in place.

The alterations to the cabin no. 1 gold medal have been interpreted as demonstrating the incorporation of Christianity and its symbols into African American belief systems (Brown et al. 2006). However, the alterations that were made to the gold Miraculous Medal might suggest that the result had been intended as a representation of "Erzulie Freida" or "Ezili," the Vodou and Voodoo goddess of love (Dorsey 2005:196). Erzulie has been linked with the Virgin Mary by a number of researchers including Rigaud (1971) and Hurston (1990). Although the two are often closely identified, Hurston (1990: 121) states that Erzulie Freida "has been identified with the Blessed Virgin, but this is far from true. Here again the use of the pictures of Catholic saints have confused observers who do not listen long enough. Erzulie is not the passive queen of heaven and mother of anybody. She is the ideal of the love bed. . . . The Virgin Mary and all of the female saints of the Church have been elevated, and celebrated for their abstinence. Erzulie is worshipped for her perfection in giving herself to mortal men." Hurston (1990: 122) also provides a limited physical description, stating that "Erzulie is said to be a beautiful young women of lush appearance. . . . She is represented as having firm, full breasts and other perfect female attributes." Metraux (1972: 110) supports this description when he states that she is the "personification of feminine grace and beauty. She has all the characteristics of a pretty mulatto: she is coquettish, sensual, pleasure-loving and extravagant."

According to Rigaud (1971: 31), Erzulie "is represented as a dark-skinned Ethiopian woman." She represents the moon and was the wife of the sun. Rigaud (1971: 31) also notes that "the Africans call her *Mawu*, but she is best known in Haiti as *Erzulie*. Legba, the origin and the male prototype of Voodoo, is the sun, which presides over the rites while Erzulie, the origin and female prototype, is the moon. Legba is the Christ; Erzulie the Virgin." Rigaud continues his analysis linking Erzulie's role with the lunar serpent and a person's desire to obtain wealth and prosperity:

> The African tradition inherited through the Haitian oum'phors reveals that the female, or lunar, serpent Aida-Wedo seen painted on the oum'phor walls is a *path of seven colors* employed by the divine power as a medium for transmitting his orders from the sky to the earth. This path, which conducts God from the sky to the earth is, of course, the rainbow. As a symbol, the rainbow—like Voodoo—has its origin from the sun. In the oum'phor, then, Erzulie, who in

the form of a rainbow plays the role of the lunar serpent Aida-Wiedo, is the magic principle of wealth and prosperity. She is invoked by all who desire a change of fortune or who wish to become wealthy (Rigaud 1971: 32–33).

In this light, it is interesting that while the earth has been removed from beneath the "Virgin's" feet, the snakes were retained. Thus this tiny medal appears to have been altered in a fashion intended to fit a Catholic material object into the beliefs practiced by at least one member of the Magnolia community in a fashion similar to that found in Haitian voodoo. The medal is small enough that it could have been openly worn on a chain around the neck with relatively little chance the alterations would have been noted by a casual observer. Thus it is possible that the medal and its redefined meaning could have been worn in "plain sight" with a relatively low risk to the wearer.

Cabin No. 4

One conjure trick and two other possible tricks were originally defined during the excavation of cabin no. 4: two in the north room and one in the south. The likely trick in the south room consisted of a large, square hole dug into the dirt floor of the room centered on the window in the east wall. The shape, size, and location of the pit was identical to the one discovered beneath the floor of the southern room of cabin no. 1. Although no artifacts were recovered from this feature in cabin no. 4, the very high organic content of the fill near the base of the feature may suggest that something of a perishable nature had been originally buried within the feature. It is interesting to note that pits in this location have been found in two cabins (cabins no. 1 and no. 4) and one of the areas where a cabin is known to have stood (Ruin B). Thus far, only cabin no. 3 lacks a pit feature in this location. However, only the pit feature in cabin no. 1 has yielded artifacts deposited within the feature.

During 2007 an almost complete chicken egg that had been placed into a small hole dug into the original dirt floor of the cabin was discovered along with a large quartz crystal approximately 1.5 feet from the center of the doorway that had been built into the eastern wall of the north room of cabin no. 4. The feature was initially defined as a possible conjure trick, given the importance of chicken eggs and crystals in conjuring as well as the location of the feature immediately below the center of the doorway (Hyatt 1970–78; Puckett 1926). However, more recent discoveries have somewhat altered the interpretation of these artifacts as forming part of a conjure trick. The egg and crystal appear to form the eastern end of a set of crossroads deposits that were placed into the eastern half of the room. The southern deposit was recovered during excavations conducted in January 2009. This deposit consisted of a small brass box (likely for a rosary) that had been placed, like the chicken egg, into a small hole dug into the original dirt of the cabin. A crucifix had been placed beneath the box, with Christ's head oriented toward the south, placing his body facedown beneath the cross. The figure of Christ was resting on a large fragment of chicken eggshell that, in turn, had been placed on top of a lens of white plaster that covered the base and lower walls of the hole. The western deposit has yet to be excavated, but a small hole has been dug into the dirt floor in the predicted location for a western deposit of a set of crossroads features and will be excavated during the 2009 field season. The small pit was identified beneath a brick that had been placed to provide support for one of the wooden floor joists. While a rodent burrow has clearly impacted the western edge of this feature, portions of its original walls were observed outside of the burrow, suggesting that most of the feature was not disturbed by the rodent activity. This deposit was located within 0.25 feet of the center of the room and the same distance from the crucifix as was the egg. If a northern deposit exists, it has not yet been identified, although the presence of two unaltered Miraculous Medals, discovered approximately halfway between the chicken egg and the hypothesized location of the northern deposit, suggests such a deposit might be present. Interestingly, of the five Miraculous Medals that have been recovered from our investigations of cabins no. 1 and no. 4, these two represent the only ones to have been recovered from the eastern side of a cabin.

If this turns out to be a set of crossroads deposits, it is significant for at least three reasons: (1) for the first time the southern feature of a set of crossroads deposits, and the one hypothesized to be associated with the world of spirits and ancestors, was expressed with Christian artifacts, though still associated with the "West African" color for death and mourning (white); (2) for the first time a set of crossroads deposits has been identified beneath a structure that appears to have functioned solely as a residence rather than one that had been occupied/utilized by a curer or as a church/praise house; and (3) for the first time the deposits have been identified beneath half of the room, rather than set below the entire floor space of a room. Stratigraphic evidence suggests that these deposits were placed around the time that a wooden floor was initially constructed in this room. Based on the appearance of two flood deposits beneath the wooden floor, it appears to predate 1927 by a short period of time. Thus if the planned excavation defines the northern deposit, it suggests that the tradition of the cardinal direction crossroads was still being practiced well into the 1920s in the Magnolia community, if not across the South.

Elsewhere our research has indicated that the tradition of the crossroads continued into the 1920s in at least one urban context: leading into the sanctuary of the Bethel Baptist Church near downtown Houston. In 1923 this historic African American church underwent extensive changes in its architecture during a major reconstruction of the church. These changes included the movement of the pulpit and altar area of the church to the second floor and the construction of a stairway for access to this area on the western side of the newly remodeled entrance to the church (D. Blacklock-Sloan, personal communication 2007). At the time of this reconstruction a crossroads "X" was hidden in a location that required church leaders, especially the minister, to pass over it as they entered the area of the altar and pulpit, in a fashion similar to the plaster "X" identified beneath the entry into the Jordan quarters church. The "X" was rediscovered after a fire completely gutted the structure in March 2004, and the tile into which the "X" had been carved fell. An examination of other tiles that had fallen from the walls of the church during the fire revealed that this tile was the only one that had had an "X" carved into the underside of it prior to its having been fired. When he was shown the "X" after the fire, the pastor of the church was completely unaware of its presence and suggested that it might simply have been the result of an attempt to better seat the tile during the construction activities. Certainly that remains a distinct possibility, but the preparation of the tile prior to its being fired, the shape selected for this "additional edge for seating the tile," the location selected for this specific tile, and the lack of other similarly marked tiles might suggest that this represents a later version of a crossroads.

Other modern practices among members of the Gullah community may actually be the result of the evolution of the crossroads and the beliefs associated with it. For example, the tradition of pouring libations to the ancestors is a practice that involves the pouring of liquid in the four cardinal directions around a central point, in a counterclockwise fashion beginning on the east, while the names of ancestors are spoken in an effort to bring them into the ritual or decision-making process. The placement of conjure tricks, well documented during the 1930s and 1940s, continues today in many communities, not simply African American ones. As I have argued elsewhere (Brown 2004), close collaborative research with members of the Gullah and Geechee, as well as elsewhere in North America and the Caribbean, might lead archaeologists to a far better understanding of the African American past. African ethnography can provide data for testing against the archaeological record of African American sites, but the direct use of this data, as was the case for the original definition of the BaKongo Cosmogram, needs to be avoided. Modern West African cultures have themselves evolved in the 200 years since the ending of the legal slave trade, and they have evolved under different conditions than those experienced by peoples living in the New World.

To conclude, contrary to what has been written, including by myself (Brown 1994), the "X"s etched onto portable objects and the crossroads deposits defined beneath structures utilized by African Americans likely do not represent BaKongo Cosmograms. On the other hand, they cannot be seen solely as Christian crosses. Rather, the uses and meanings of crossroads deposits, and probably the "X"s placed on more portable objects, represent examples of what Fennell (2007) has recently termed "ethnogenic bricolage." In African American communities, West African traditions, including the early adaptation of Christianity into their spiritual beliefs by BaKongo speakers prior to the advent of the slave trade (Thornton 1998), were literally driven underground by the conditions of enslavement, tenancy, sharecropping, and day labor. What is equally clear is that these traditions, as they were originally defined, continued to evolve within the African American communities of North

America. Only gradually did their meaning—and finally even their placement—change and/or become eliminated from the spiritual practices of African Americans. The evolution of these sets of deposits along with the "X"s on portable objects supports the belief that the pace and direction of the changes to their meanings and functions were under the control of the African Americans themselves and not dictated by the dominant European American culture.

References

Adams, W. H. (editor).1987. *Historical Archaeology of Plantations at Kings Bay, Camden County, Georgia.* Reports of Investigations No. 5, Department of Anthropology, University of Florida, Gainesville.

Anonymous 1979. *109th Anniversary Souvenir Book: Grace United Methodist Church, Brazoria, Texas.* Brazoria County, Tex.: Grace United Methodist Church. Manuscript on file, Jordan Project Archives, Department of Anthropology, University of Houston, Tex.

Association of the Miraculous Medal 2006. The Miraculous Medal Story and Its Meaning. Electronic document, www.amm.org/medal.asp, accessed June 10, 2009.

Berlin, I., and P. D. Morgan (editors) (1993) *Cultivation and Culture: Labor and the Shaping of Slave Life in the Americas.* Charlottesville: University of Virginia Press.

Brewer, J. M. 1976. *Dog Ghosts and the Word on the Brazos.* Austin: University of Texas Press.

Brown, K. L. 2008a. Africans in American Material Culture: Does a Pot Hanger Only Function When It Is Used for Cooking? *Bulletin of the Texas Archaeological Society* 79:3–18.

———. 2008b. *A Preliminary Report on the 2008 Excavations into the Quarters Community of the Magnolia Plantation, Cane River Creole National Historical Park, Natchitoches Parish, Louisiana.* Prepared for the National Park Service, Southeastern Archaeological Center, Tallahassee, Fla.

———. 2007. *A Preliminary Report on the 2007 Excavations into the Quarters Community of the Magnolia Plantation, Cane River Creole National Historical Park, Natchitoches Parish, Louisiana.* Prepared for the National Park Service, Southeastern Archaeological Center, Tallahassee, Fla.

———. 2005. *The Archaeology of Cabin I-A-1: The Levi Jordan Plantation Quarters Community's Praise House/Church.* Technical Report Series, Vol. 2, The Levi Jordan Plantation State Historic Site, Brazoria County, Texas. Texas Parks and Wildlife Department, Austin, Tex.

———. 2004. Ethnographic Analogy, Archaeology, and the African Diaspora: Perspectives from a Tenant Community. *Historical Archaeology* 34(1):79–89.

———. 2001. Intertwined Traditions: The Conjurer's Cabins and the African American Cemetery at the Jordan and Frogmore Plantations. In *Places of Cultural Memory: African Reflections on the American Landscape,* pp. 99–114. Washington, D.C.: U.S. Department of the Interior, National Park Service.

———. 1994. Material Culture and Community Structure: The Slave and Tenant Community at Levi Jordan's Plantation. In *Working towards Freedom: Slave Society and Domestic Economy in the American South,* edited by L. E. Hudson, pp. 95–118. Rochester, N.Y.: University of Rochester Press.

Canizares, R. 2001. *The Life and Works of Marie Laveau: Gris-Gris, Cleanings, Charms, Hexes.* Plainview, N.Y.: Original Publication.

Creel, M.W. 1988. *A Peculiar People: Slave Religion and Community-Culture among the Gullahs.* New York: New York University Press.

Crespi, M. 2004. *A Brief Ethnography of Magnolia Plantation: Planning for Cane River Creole National Historical Park.* Studies in Archaeology and Ethnography no. 4. National Park Service, Washington, D.C. Electronic document, http://www.cr.nps.gov/aad/pubs/studies/study04a.htm, accessed May 4, 2009.

DeCorse, C. R. 1999. Oceans Apart: Africanist Perspectives of Diaspora Archaeology. In *I, Too, Am America: Archaeological Studies of African-American Life,* edited by T. A. Singleton, pp. 132–155. Charlottesville: University Press of Virginia.

Dirvin, J. I. 1984. Saint Catherine LaBoure of the Miraculous Medal. TAN Books and Publishing, Inc.

Dorsey, L. 2005. *Voodoo and Afro-Caribbean Paganism.* New York: Citadel Press Books.

Fennell, C. C. 2007. *Crossroads and Cosmograms: Diasporas and Ethnogenesis in the New World.* Gainesville: University of Florida Press.

———. 2003. Group Identity, Individual Creativity, and Symbolic Generation in a BaKongo Diaspora. *International Journal of Historical Archaeology* 7(1):1–31.

Ferguson, L. 1992. *Uncommon Ground: Archaeology and Early African America: 1650–1800.* Washington, D.C.: Smithsonian Institution Press.

Franklin, M. 1997. *Out of Site, Out of Mind: The Archaeology of an Enslaved Virginia Household, ca. 1740–1778.* Ph.D. dissertation, Department of Anthropology, University of California, Berkeley.

Heywood, L. M. (editor). 2002. Portuguese into African: The Eighteenth-Century Central African Background to Atlantic Creole Cultures. In *Central Africans and Cultural Transformations in the American Diaspora,* pp. 91–113. Cambridge: Cambridge University Press.

Hunter, H. A. 2005. *Magnolia Plantation: A Family Farm.* Natchitoches, La.: Northwestern State University Press.

Hurston, Z. N. 1990. *Tell My Horse: Voodoo and Life in Haiti and Jamaica.* New York: Harper & Row.

Hyatt, H. M. 1970–78. *Hoodoo-Conjuration-Witchcraft-Rootwork: Beliefs Accepted by Many Negroes and White Persons, These Being Orally Recorded among Blacks and Whites.* Hannibal, Mo.: Western Publishing.

Leone, M. P., and G. M. Fry 2001. Spirit Management among Americans of African Descent. In *Race and the Archaeology of Identity,* edited by C. E. Orser, pp. 143–157. Salt Lake City: University of Utah Press.

MacDonald, K. C. 1995. Why Chickens? The Centrality of the Domestic Fowl in West African Ritual and Magic. In *MASCA Research Papers in Science and Archaeology, Vol. 12: The Symbolic Role of Animals in Archaeology,* edited by K. Ryan and P. J. Crabtree, pp. 50–56. Philadelphia: University of Pennsylvania Museum.

Maffly-Kipp, L. 2005. African American Religion: To the Civil War, Pt. I. National Humanities Center. Electronic document, http://nationalhumanitiescenter.org/tserve/nineteen/nkeyinfo/aareligion.htm, accessed June 11, 2009.

Metraux, A. 1972. *Voodoo in Haiti.* New York: Schocken Books.

Miller, C. E. 2004. *Slavery and Its Aftermath: Archaeological and Historical Record at Magnolia Plantation.* Ph.D. dissertation, Department of History, Florida State University, Tallahassee.

Mintz, S. W., and R. Price 1992. *The Birth of African American Culture: An Anthropological Perspective.* Boston: Beacon Press.

Morgan, P. D. 1998. *Slave Counterpoint: Black Culture in the Eighteenth-Century Chesapeake and Lowcountry.* Chapel Hill: Omohundro Institute of Early American History and Culture, University of North Carolina Press.

———. 1982. Work and Culture: The Task System in the World of Lowcountry Blacks, 1700–1880. *William and Mary Quarterly* 39(4):563–599.

Puckett, N. N. 1926. *Folk Beliefs of the Southern Negro.* Chapel Hill: University of North Carolina Press.

Reitz, E. J., T. Gibbs, and T. Rathbun 1985. Archaeological Evidence for Subsistence on Coastal Plantations. In *The Archaeology of Slavery and Plantation Life,* edited by T. A. Singleton, pp. 163–191. Orlando, Fla.: Academic Press.

Rigaud, M. 1971. *Secrets of Voodoo.* New York: Pocket Books.

Ruppel, T., J. Neuwirth, M. P. Leone, and G. M. Fry. 2003. Hidden in View: African Spiritual Places in North American Landscapes. *Antiquity* 77:321–335.

Steen, C. 2003. Bakongo Cosmograms or Christian Crosses? *Newsletter, The Council of South Carolina Professional Archaeologists* XXIV(4):2–5.

Stuckey, S. 1987. *Slave Culture: Nationalist Theory and the Foundations of Black America.* Oxford: Oxford University Press.

Teal, R. D. 2007. *Natchitoches Parish.* Charleston, S.C.: Arcadia Publishing.

Thompson, R. F. 1983. *Flash of the Spirit: African and Afro-American Art and Philosophy.* New York: Random House.

Thornton, J. K. 2002. Religious and Ceremonial Life in the Kongo and Mbundu Areas, 1500–1700. In *Central Africans and Cultural Transformations in the American Diaspora,* edited by L. M. Heywood, pp. 91–113. Cambridge: Cambridge University Press.

———. 1998. *The Kongolese Saint Anthony: Dona Beatriz Kimpa Vita and the Antonian Movement, 1684–1706.* Cambridge: Cambridge University Press.

———. 1983. *The Kingdom of Kongo.* Madison: University of Wisconsin Press.

Young, A. L. 1997. Risk Management Strategies among African American Slaves at Locust Grove Plantation. *International Journal of Historical Archaeology* 1(1):5–37.

Young, J. R. 2007. *Rituals of Resistance: African Atlantic Religion in Kongo and the Lowcountry South in the Era of Slavery.* Baton Rouge: Louisiana State University Press.

Wahlman, L. A. 2001. *Signs and Symbols: African Images in African American Quilts.* Revised ed. Atlanta, Ga.: Tinwood Books.

Weik, T. 2008. Discussion: *Archaeologies of Resistance: The Underground Railroad, Maroonage, Armed Struggle, and Beyond.* Paper presented at the Society for Historical Archaeology Annual Meeting, Albuquerque, N.Mex.

Wright, C. L. 1994. I Heard it through the Grapevine: Oral Tradition in a Rural African American Community in Brazoria County, Texas. Unpublished master's thesis, University of Houston, Department of Anthropology, Houston, Tex.

Matthew M. Palus

Infrastructure and African American Achievement in Annapolis, Maryland, during the Twentieth Century

Democracies that cannot protect a citizen's body or produce a just city far outnumber those that do today, even though the promise of these achievements constitute much of democracy's appeal

James Holston (2008: 309)

In 1951 the City of Annapolis in Anne Arundel County, Maryland, annexed nearly five square miles of surrounding land, redesignating the corporate limits for the city to encompass a belt of settlements that had grown up since the Civil War. Included in this annexation of 10,000 people was a community called Eastport, which was platted speculatively in 1868 and was the earliest of several independent villages that grew up around Annapolis in the surrounding county (Warren 1990). Annexation was not a discrete event, such as the 1950 referendum vote that was decided in favor of annexing 14 communities and nearly 5 square miles into the city of Annapolis (*Evening Capital* 1950), but rather it was a long-term historical process that only culminated in annexation, entailing changes in the organization of the city's governance and economy and the appearance of new material forms, specifically the infrastructure that bound together the economy and government in new ways. Furthermore this history of urban expansion overlaps with a history of African American settlement, investment, and wealth accumulation outside of Annapolis. The effort to consolidate the suburb and the city through annexation represents a counter to the trend of African American community-building in relatively independent suburbs. This essay brings together my attempts to use archaeological traces of public services—specifically sewer and water infrastructure—to describe the embeddedness of race within the expanding operations of local government during the early twentieth century. I discuss the establishment of an African American community adjacent to the city of Annapolis in Maryland during later nineteenth and early twentieth centuries within a racially and ethnically mixed village called Eastport and the subsequent outcome of a project to integrate Eastport into a metropolitan sewerage district during the 1930s.

Race and Government

During the first quarter of the twentieth century there was a perceivable change in the conduct of government in the City of Annapolis, which was of consequence to African Americans living both inside and outside of the city limits. The administration of the city was by degrees disarticulated from the established social networks that gave shape to the power of the city council throughout the nineteenth century. People in Annapolis contacted the city government more and more through the mediation of bureaucracy, and the city government was felt materially through municipal services as, for instance, municipal water and sewers introduced new routines and embedded people within new relationships of administration, surveillance, and power (Palus 2009).

This historical process, which Foucault (1991) would call governmentalization, was by no means completed in Annapolis; rather patronage was driven into the back rooms of city government and existed there as a sort of open secret until the Sunshine Laws and indictments that were handed down in Maryland during the 1970s (Brugger 1988: 643–654). But during the early twentieth century, government slowly acquired this new basis that was separate from the influence of the city's "men of affairs" (Hannah 2000: 56). Policy, regulation, and the more *impersonal* operation of bureaucracy began to replace patronage as the guiding principle of government. And the utilities that were set in place during the later nineteenth and early twentieth centuries are a material trace of the ongoing "governmentalization of government" (Dean 1999: 193) in Annapolis. In this frame services like sanitary sewers and clean water are extensions of the security that is provided by police, health officials, and other agents of state power and inspection. Sanitary infrastructure is part of the instrumentation of government, no different from police power, even though its action is subtle, literally buried, and much more easily overlooked.

These constructions parallel the processes that Foucault and other writers on governmentality have described. Governmentality can be defined as a style of government that emphasizes the increasingly detailed management of the economy, which more and more relies on representations of the population under governance, particularly social statistics. Foucault (1991: 95) writes, "the finality of government resides in the things it manages and in the pursuit of the perfection and intensification of the processes which it directs; and the instruments of government, instead of being laws, now come to be a range of multiform tactics." Termed the apparatus of security, these multiform tactics and their sustaining discourses and materialities reflect "the dramatic expansion in the scope of government, featuring an increase in the number and size of the governmental calculation mechanisms" (Hunt and

Wickham 1994: 76), an intensification of relations of power, and a flourishing of operations that make families and individuals more and more the subject of governmental authority while seeming to act through the liberties of the governed. Thus Colin Gordon (1991: 5) suggests that "what Foucault finds most fascinating and disturbing in the history of Western governmental practices and its rationalities is the idea of a kind of power which takes freedom itself . . . as in some sense the correlative object of its own suasive capacity."

A governmentality framework means suspending the functional interpretation of water and sewer lines in the context of public health and sanitation and interpreting them instead as the material culture of government, a sprawling archaeological record of government's expansion. Public services like water and sewers introduced new materialities that changed the way people organized their daily lives, not simply to discipline them but more broadly to govern them. I propose that people were more intensively governed as an outcome of large-scale sanitation projects and that governing itself was carried out through these new material cultures. The archaeological record of well and privy abandonment in Annapolis, and arguably in many other contexts (Carnes-McNaughton and Harper 2000; Ford 1994; McCarthy and Ward 2000; Rosenswig 1999; Stottman 1995, 2000), narrates the connection of people into networks made to operate systemically through the application of authority at a picayune scale in everyday practice. By the end of the nineteenth century, city ordinances compelled Annapolis residents to connect with municipal sewers on streets where sewer lines were in place rather than build new privies or vaults, and this ordinance was extended in 1913 such that all existing privies had to be connected to municipal sewers wherever this was possible. All archaeologically known wells and privies in Annapolis seem to be abandoned by 1910 (Aiello and Seidel 1995; Cochran et al. 2008; Dent and Ford 1983; Doyel-Read 1990; Goodwin et al. 1993; Larsen 2002; Mullins and Warner 1993; O'Reilly 1994; Shackel 1986). In 1936 the state legislature enacted a law making it a misdemeanor to fail to connect with existing sewers after receiving notice from health authorities, and this law applied throughout Annapolis and its metropolitan sewerage district (Maryland 1936; McWilliams 2009).

Infrastructure articulated population with government in new ways during the early twentieth century, and it reveals how communities were discovered and enclosed as population in the first place. Perhaps more important, the archaeological traces of infrastructure can reveal the limitations of governmental power and inconsistencies within the governmentalized state. Despite the efforts of reformers and lawmakers, some residences in Annapolis remained disconnected from sanitary sewers into the mid–twentieth century, and in Eastport a proportion of both African American– and white-identified households were clearly disconnected from municipal water and sewer infrastructure. A study completed by the Annapolis Housing Authority in 1938 determined that 27 percent of all homes in the city were without indoor plumbing (Mullins 1999: 15), a figure that presumably excludes areas within the Annapolis Metropolitan Sewerage District that were outside of the Annapolis city limits and therefore beyond the oversight of the city's housing authority.

Racial differences embedded in certain public services in Eastport can yield an account of African American agency, resistance, and ultimately the achievement of a measure of autonomy and self-determination, rather than yielding only an account of structural, race-based discrimination. Structural racism is a frame for recognizing the subtle yet pervasive action of racial discrimination that is broadly cultural as well as economic and legal, "the hidden ways in which racism is extended into every facet of life by virtue of the fact that it informs the institutional rules and regulations, the ordering conceptions, of work and play, economic and political arrangements and cultural conceptions" (Goldberg and Essed 2002: 6). Its genealogy (following Goldberg and Essed 2002: 6–7) runs from Franz Fanon (2004, 2008) to the formulation of institutional racism in Stokely Carmichael (Kwame Ture) and Charles V. Hamilton's manifesto *Black Power* (1967), to the work of historians such as Winthrop Jordan (1977) and the broader engagement with critical race theory in the social sciences (for example, Crenshaw et al. 1995; also see Epperson 2004), much of it emerging from within recent feminism (for example, Stoler 1995; Weinbaum 2004). Structural racism relates to the overt and legalistic forms of discrimination that arose during the Jim Crow era, so described by Manning Marable: "The Jim Crow system of racial exploitation was, like slavery, both a caste/social order for regimenting cultural and political relations, and an economic structure which facilitated the superexploitation of blacks' labor power, [a system that was] dependent upon the omnipresence of violence or coercion. . . . For all practical purposes, the black American was proscribed by the state from any meaningful political and social activity for two generations. Behind this powerful proscription, as always, was the use of force" (Marable 2007: 10–11). If Jim Crow designates a specific episode of struggle over the rights and enfranchisements of African Americans, structural racism refers to a broader formation that spans the struggle for civil rights in the second half of the twentieth century and also manifests with innumerable race-based inequalities in contemporary America. It is an idea that is far less fixed in historical terms and in its manifestations.

The understanding of race promoted by the notion of structural racism has been expanded in recent scholarship by "a recognition of race as socially constructed, as being *made* in the process of history, culture, and social relationships . . . This shift has enabled an understanding of race and racial identities as changing and complex, as a product of culture rather than nature, produced and sustained through power and subject to resistance, reappropriation and subversion" (Alexander and Knowles 2005: 1). The recognition that racial formations (Omi and Winant 2002) are vulnerable to appropriation and subversion, that the production of racial identities and meanings is also at the hands of the consumers of racial meanings, plays against a rigid sociological read of structural racism and invites discussions of racial ideology as hegemony and race itself as a historical accretion of overlapping meanings, as well as a field of practice. Thus "race is *performed* in mundane encounters between individuals as well as at the interface between people and structures" (Alexander and Knowles 2005: 2).

In this essay, I am promoting Foucault's theory of governmentality as an analytic that can expose the operations of structural racism and the historical embedding of racial difference in the applications of and engagements with governmental power that expanded in everyday life during the twentieth century. By 1930 African American families in Eastport had achieved the same rate of homeownership as neighboring white people within the community; however, a far greater proportion of African American households were not connected to municipal sewer and water infrastructure that was installed in Eastport around the same time. Race-based inequalities in housing and in access to public services can be seen as aspects of structural racism both in this historical context and also in contemporary America. However, the outcome of African Americans' struggle with these systematic disadvantages in the Eastport neighborhood during the first half of the twentieth century reads as fractious and textured rather than uniform. I attempt to read the disparity in access to public services in the light of African American economic achievements represented by homeownership and interpret the racialization of public services in the Eastport neighborhood as a measure of this community's enclosure under this new apparatus of government.

I argue that the partiality of these new public services is tantamount to a racialization of government (cf., Goldberg 2002; Nobles 2000; Poole 2006). If, to paraphrase Foucault (1991), the finality of modern liberal government is in the perfection of the processes that it directs, is the racial identification of people one such process? Are racial identities brought into focus through the action of government in the early twentieth century? This is a certainty. But through what tactics, what instrumentation, is this accomplished? The designation of a metropolitan sewerage district around the city of Annapolis during the 1930s provides the setting for a case study of the way in which one neighboring African American community was governed. The degree to which the neighborhoods, homes, and bodies of African Americans were integrated into new apparatuses of government—both the technologies of infrastructure themselves and the administrative apparatuses attached to them—reveals the racialization of the project of government in Annapolis during this period.

Homeownership in Eastport's African American Community

Shortly after the Civil War, speculators in the city of Annapolis and the surrounding county chartered a corporation called the Mutual Building Association of Annapolis to purchase and plat a 100-acre parcel of land, which grew into the Eastport neighborhood. The small home lots that were created on the next peninsula south of Annapolis represented a crucial historical opportunity for working and middle-class people to own land, among them African Americans. Family lines founded during the early development of the Eastport community created a legacy in land, and land is a significant material trace of the accomplishments of the African American families who made a community in Eastport.

While African Americans began to settle in Eastport during the 1880s—Mount Zion Methodist Episcopal Church, a visible anchor for black settlement in the neighborhood at the end of the nineteenth century, was founded during this time—they did not seem to acquire title to land from the Mutual Building Association to any great degree. Examination of grantor records indicates that the Mutual Building Association transferred all land in Eastport to other ownership by the end of the nineteenth century. In all, 90 deed instruments record these transactions, registered with the county between 1868 and 1900. Comparison of the grantees on these records with the 1880 and 1910 censuses indicate that of those 90 deeds, only 4 represent the likely sale of land to African Americans, 8 parcels out of the 256 parcels that were initially platted (Palus 2009: Appendix B). This reads as the patent exclusion of African Americans from the speculative moment that turned unplatted farmland into substantial profits and shows that African Americans who did acquire title to land in Eastport did so through intermediaries between the building association and themselves; several "rounds" of profit were extracted from the land before African Americans obtained it, but they obtained it nonetheless and in spite of such obstacles.

How did African Americans in Eastport prosper when, to quote W. E. B. DuBois (1906: 220), "economic society refused to admit the Black applicant on his merits to any place of authority or advantage"? Homes comprised an extremely important form of heritable wealth for Eastport's African American community, just as they do for working people in the United States today. Census records from 1910 to 1930 reveal that a substantial proportion of African American households in Eastport

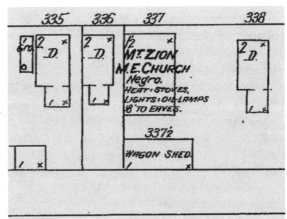

Detail of sheet 19 of Sanborn Map Company's 1908 Insurance Map of Annapolis and Eastport, Maryland, which depicts Mount Zion A.M.E. Church in Eastport. Courtesy of Library of Congress.

either owned or were working toward ownership of the homes that they occupied. Annapolis was home to a significant population of free African Americans during the early and middle nineteenth century, and at mid-century there were a number of free African Americans in the city who owned property. By the end of the Civil War, there were 41 African Americans in Annapolis who owned land within the city, comprising nearly 25 percent of African American families and 10 percent of all individuals owning property in Annapolis. Surrounding Anne Arundel County was home to 900 African American families after the Civil War, and while most heads of these households were farmhands or laborers, there were 80 farms in the county that were operated independently by African Americans. Fifty of these independent farms were black-owned, and the remaining farms were operated by tenants to white landowners (Calderhead 1977: 16–17). By 1900 rural Anne Arundel County had over 1,800 African American families and approximately 300 farms that were operated independently by African Americans, with from 5 to 150 acres under tillage. Approximately 200 of those farms were black-owned, and the other hundred farms were operated under tenancy agreements or some other arrangement (Calderhead 1977: 21).

These successes at landowning were eroded after the turn of the twentieth century, as African Americans in Maryland and throughout the United States faced increasing disenfranchisement, and white supremacy became doctrine. The resurgence of the Ku Klux Klan during the 1920s found membership in Maryland, particularly between 1922 and 1925 (Brugger 1988: 476–477; Mullins 1999: 70). The "new Klan" visited Eastport at the end of the summer of 1922. In September of that year the Annapolis paper reported that "Several hundred persons from Annapolis and vicinity witnessed the initiation of about twenty-five candidates into the Ku Klux Klan last night, the initiation being held in the field at Horn Point, Eastport. Members of the Klan appeared in the official regalia of the order, and with about seventy-five automobiles lined up in a circle around the spot where the initiation was held, the headlights of the cars flashed on the fiery cross erected in the center of the circle, the scene presented was a spectacular one" (*Evening Capital* 1922a). Not 10 days later, the paper reported that "Five men, wearing the white robes of the Ku Klux Klan . . . made a visit to the Church at Eastport last night in connection with a special service which was addressed by Rev. John G. Ford" (*Evening Capital* 1922b), who was pastor at a Baptist church in Anne Arundel County. "The church was crowded by a congregation of men, women, and children, for the nature of the service had been heralded in advance and incidentally it was announced that Rev. John Howard Eager, of Baltimore, acting pastor of the church [in Eastport], had become a Klansman. At the close of the service, about 30 men, all residents of Eastport, advanced to the pulpit upon invitation of Rev. Ford to become members of the Klan, or at least to learn more of the principles of the *new* organization" (emphasis added, *Evening Capital* 1922b).

In between these two events, marking a surge in Klan participation and membership among white men in Anne Arundel County and in particular Eastport, the Eastport Volunteer Fire Department (VFD) held a weeklong carnival at a lot on Horn Point, potentially the same ground where seven days earlier the Klan had initiated 25 new members. That Klan parading and recruitment coincided with other festivities organized by the VFD is probably not coincidental; rather this may represent fairly general support for the white supremacist message of the New Klan. In October 1922, in an event described as a "Spectacular Pageant" by the *Evening Capital*, as many as 2,000 robed members of the Ku Klux Klan attending from all over Maryland paraded through Annapolis. "The visiting K.K.'s were the guests of those of Annapolis and Anne Arundel County, of whom there are reported to be in the neighborhood of 1,000, and [the] street parade had its finale in an oyster roast and feast at Horn Point" (quoted in Mullins 1999: 70). Perhaps this cycle of parades and celebrations marks summer's end as Klan rally and carnival season in Eastport and Annapolis for a period during the Klan's resurgence during the mid-1920s.

It was precisely in this climate of overt, public, and widespread celebration of white supremacy that a stable population of African American families in Eastport underwent an important transition, from renting to owning their homes. The U.S. Census of Population between 1910 and 1930 presents almost a house-to-house directory of the Eastport neighborhood, and indications of property ownership along with reported values of homes narrate the development of a community that secured its future with land in spite of expanding measures confirming white supremacy (U.S. Census 1910, 1920, 1930). Census records from 1910 to 1930 reveal that a substantial proportion of African American households in Eastport either owned the homes that they occupied or were working to remove encumbrances to ownership, such as a mortgage on the house and property (Table 1). In Eastport 37 percent of African American households in 1910 were either paying off a mortgage on their land and home or owned these free and clear. This rate of homeownership far exceeds the baseline rate of African American homeownership reported for the Upper South at the time of the 1910 census, which settled out at around 20 percent (Schweninger 1990: 180). Black homeownership in Eastport in 1910 was also proportionally higher when compared with local and regional contexts. A bulletin published by the U.S. Bureau of the Census in 1915 presented data on changing rates of African American homeownership throughout the United States and reported that 21 percent of African American families throughout the Southern Atlantic region, stretching from Delaware to Florida, owned their homes. In Maryland 25.6 percent of African American families owned the homes that they occupied in 1910, including farm and nonfarm homes owned free and those that were encumbered by mortgages, compared with a much lower rate of 11.4 percent in Washington, D.C. (Harris 1915: 29).

TABLE 1. Rates of Homeownership among African American
and White Households in Eastport, 1910–1930

1910 Census

	Home Owned		Mortgaged		Rented		Total	
	n	Percent	n	Percent	n	Percent	n	Percent
African American Households	11	14.1%	18	23.1%	49	62.8%	78	100.0%
White Households	47	18.3%	59	23.0%	146	56.8%	257	100.0%

1920 Census

	Home Owned		Mortgaged		Rented		Total	
	n	Percent	n	Percent	n	Percent	n	Percent
African American Households	25	30.9%	12	14.8%	43	53.1%	81	100.0%
White Households	102	29.3%	93	26.7%	149	42.8%	348	100.0%

1930 Census

	Home Owned		Mortgaged		Rented		Total	
	n	Percent	n	Percent	n	Percent	n	Percent
African American Households	52	60.5%	n.d.	—	33	38.4%	86	100.0%
White Households	318	62.7%	n.d.	—	182	35.9%	507	100.0%

Source: U.S. Census 1910, 1920, 1930.

In Maryland in 1910, homeownership was more common among rural and small-town African Americans than those living in large cities. In Maryland cities having more than 5,000 African American inhabitants, a set that excludes Annapolis, there was a very high ratio of African American individuals to identified black-owned homes. This measure divides the number of African American residents by the number of black-owned homes to produce an index of black homeownership. In Maryland cities with more than 5,000 African American residents had one black-owned home for every 91 African American residents, while cities with fewer than 5,000 showed a much higher rate, with one black-owned home for every 13 African American residents. This pattern generally holds true throughout the South, though these indices reflecting rates of black homeownership in large cities versus rural and small-town contexts are less exaggerated in Virginia and Delaware (Harris 1915: 30).

Census data is available to compare the rate of African American homeownership in 1910 for nonfarm homes throughout the state of Maryland, in Anne Arundel County, in Annapolis, and in the village of Eastport (Rogers 1918: 466–501). Rates of homeownership are similar among African Americans throughout the state and in Anne Arundel County, at approximately 20 percent, including homes owned free and homes that are encumbered. The rate of ownership without encumbrance is actually very similar among African Americans considered throughout the state of Maryland, in Anne Arundel County, and in Eastport, varying from 13.3 to 14.5 percent. However a little more than 5 percent of African American families throughout the state and county had mortgaged their homes, while in Eastport the rate of mortgages among African Americans was 23.1 percent. Less than 4 percent of African American households in Annapolis had mortgages on their homes in 1910, and the vast preponderance, 86.6 percent, were renters.

The fact that more African Americans in Eastport were living in homes that were mortgaged than owned their homes free and clear may represent the economic vulnerability of this group; homeownership and its financing is a vector for economic discrimination, but it is also a site for struggle in which some African Americans prevailed. Homeownership rates climb dramatically among African Americans in Eastport from 1910 to 1930. This suggests instead that these earlier mortgages represent economic leverage. This observation has bearing on the consideration of economic and noneconomic factors in the connection of African American homes to municipal sewer and water services. In reviewing this data I mean to suggest that obstacles overcome by African American families to acquire home and land—not all of them economic—may represent the agency and capability to also provide for those homes to be plumbed and sewered.

In 1920 and 1930 rates of homeownership reported in the census for African American and white-identified households in Eastport rose together. African American homeownership in Eastport slightly exceeded the rate of white homeownership in 1920, at approximately 31 percent, and adding together homes that were owned free and homes that were mortgaged, this rises to approximately 46 percent of African American households. Ten years later, around 60 percent of each group owned or had mortgaged their home. In sum by 1930 African Americans had matched the rate of homeownership among their white neighbors in the Eastport community (U.S. Census 1920, 1930).

The rate of African American homeownership in Eastport compares very favorably with reported rates of homeownership throughout the state in 1920 and 1930 (Steuart 1922: 1282–1283, 1933: 573). In 1920 African Americans in Eastport exceeded the rate of homeownership for African Americans throughout Maryland at nearly double the proportion of homes owned (30.9 percent) and homes under mortgage (14.8 percent) compared with figures for the state (15.7 percent of homes owned and 7.8 percent of homes mortgaged among African Americans statewide). The decennial census of 1930 did not distinguish homes owned from homes encumbered, but African Americans in Eastport again doubled the statewide rate of African American homeownership, approximately matching the rate of ownership reported for white people in Eastport and across Maryland. Tenure data reported for farm and nonfarm homes are similar in 1930.

Comparing 1930 census data on homeownership for Eastport, Annapolis, and surrounding Anne Arundel County (Steuart 1933: 585–589) establishes firmly that black homeownership in Eastport was exceptionally high. Black homeownership rates for Annapolis and Anne Arundel County reflect the continuing pattern of homeownership among rural or suburban African Americans exceeding those in urban contexts. This may indicate the degree to which suburban growth around cities like Annapolis created opportunities for African Americans to acquire homes. In Eastport slightly more than 60 percent (n=52) of African Americans' homes were owned by their occupants, with or without encumbrance of a mortgage, compared with just 22 percent (n=186) of African American households in Annapolis and nearly 44 percent (n=1,214) of those throughout Anne Arundel County. Census figures for the county would include those families residing in Eastport in 1930.

Sanitary Infrastructure and the Production of Race

By the turn of the twentieth century a fundamental utilities infrastructure was in place in Annapolis, including systems for distributing water, gas, and electricity, and a far less-sophisticated and less-complete network of sewers that drained into surrounding waterways. It is not certain that any such utilities were installed anywhere in the Eastport community except perhaps a small number of electric streetlights paid for by the county. Of the Annapolis utilities, sewers were the one area that was entirely maintained and administered by the city government. The water utility also came under municipal authority in 1911 when the City of Annapolis purchased all stock in the utility from the State of Maryland and any private stockholders. The other utilities were each in their own way the product of governmental intervention. For instance the local electrical utility was created on the basis of a contract to provide street lighting in the city, but it was profit-oriented in a way that sewer service could never be (Palus 2005).

Given these relationships between each utility and the city government, it should not be surprising that the corporate limits of Annapolis also was a limit on the extent of some public services. Water and sewer services extended to the limit of the city council's political interests, and this left some sections within Annapolis without these services, to say nothing of the population that came to reside in the surrounding county.

Three issues developed together in Annapolis during the 1920s. Dumping of sewage in waterways around the city created a terrible pollution problem that the half-measures taken to contain municipal sewage could not resolve. Also the quality of water from the city's reservoir grew worse and worse, described as murky, cloudy, and odorous. This decline in water quality resulted from a series of expansions at the city's nineteenth-century waterworks, established four miles outside of Annapolis during the late 1860s. The problem—and the agitation that surrounded it—ultimately called for the city's waterworks to be overhauled in order to provide for filtration of water pumped into the city. Faced with this expensive prospect, the president of the Annapolis Water Company (Smith 1925: 17) asked, "Is Annapolis ever going to be called on to furnish water to the U.S. Naval Academy, Eastport, West Annapolis, and all suburban sections? If so, when and on what terms?" He essentially anticipated expansion of service to the metropolitan area around Annapolis, if not in-fact annexation.

In 1927 the Annapolis water utility added to its capacity by building a million-gallon standpipe in the western part of the city. At that time the utility laid new water mains throughout Annapolis and introduced this service to Eastport for the first time, running a 12-inch main underneath the bridge connecting Eastport to Annapolis. Municipal water lines and fire hydrants first appear on Sanborn maps of Eastport published in 1930. While the last public wells in Annapolis seem to go out of use by circa 1900–1910, wells and cisterns continued to be used in Eastport well into the twentieth century, as can be demonstrated archaeologically (Gibb 2001; Palus 2009).

In the same year that the Annapolis reservoir and distribution system was overhauled and municipal water was first made available in Eastport, a petition was brought before the Annapolis city council "stating that it represented 20 percent of the legally qualified voters of Eastport requesting that the City hold an election to determine whether or not Eastport shall become a part of the City of Annapolis" (Annapolis 1927: 101). The petition was not acted upon, but the act of petitioning contrasts with earlier modes of interaction between the governing body for the city and the persons they governed. For Foucault and others who work with the idea of governmentality, population is the object of government, and government is executed upon representations of population. With this petition, residents in Eastport seem to organize themselves as a population and offer the petition as their representation. They invited the city council to address them as a population, self-described as "legally qualified voters," seemingly in anticipation of the essential quality of citizenship in the governmentalized state: to be simply counted and thus accounted for.

The question remains: *Which segment of Eastport had organized themselves in this way and fled toward annexation?* The answer cannot be simple, lacking the original petition itself. But I propose that looking at the incorporation of municipal services into everyday routines in Eastport households is one way to answer it.

A further step in the provision of municipal services to neighboring communities in the county was accompanied by a revision of governmental authority in and around the city of Annapolis. The vehicle for this revision, this governmentalization of the city's operation, was the creation of a large sewerage district during the early 1930s. This special-purpose district designated a new authority that straddled the jurisdictions and the traditional roles of the city and the county governments.

The actual extent of municipal sewers into Eastport is revealed in a series of as-built plans drawn in 1933 and updated thereafter. The photographs that documented the work suggest that main sewer lines were buried under Eastport streets in 1934, while individual house connections may have been added more gradually. Because the Annapolis Water Company and the Annapolis Metropolitan Sanitation Commission shared the services of one sanitary engineer, the plans include details of the water infrastructure installed in Eastport after 1927 as well as sewer infrastructure. The Department of Public Works in Annapolis maintains that the plans used in my study were redrawn in 1954, so rather than depicting the initial state of the water and sewer infrastructure they may show what it looked like 20 years after the metropolitan sewerage district was created. For this reason, the absence of service and the voids in these plans speak more loudly than the connections they depict. There are 132 homes without service, around 16 percent of the homes depicted on the as-built plans throughout Eastport.

Public services like those I have described in Eastport were ostensibly provided for the improvement of public health and welfare or, as I have framed it, to embed Eastport residents within an "apparatus of security" that was an extension of the

Sewer construction on Chester Avenue in Eastport, November 5, 1934. Courtesy of Tom and Pamela Dawson, Stevensville, Maryland.

security enjoyed by many residents in Annapolis. Water clean enough to drink and ample enough to combat house fires was made available by this apparatus throughout the Eastport community in 1927. This is clear from Sanborn fire insurance maps that show the locations of hydrants at street corners throughout the neighborhood, irrespective of who lived where. It is also seen in the detailed plans of Eastport's water and sewer infrastructure, created through the authority of the Annapolis Metropolitan Sewerage District. However, detailed study of the plans, which also depict the Annapolis Water Company's distribution system within the Eastport community, show that inequalities arose from how these services were accessed and utilized. Water and sewer lines extended down Eastport streets, but they did not always connect with African American homes.

The 1930 U.S. Census potentially introduces demographic information to this data, to put households in the dwellings that are shown on the utility plans (U.S. Census 1930). In all, 594 households were enumerated in Eastport during the 1930 census, and many households are identified by their street address. A proportion of these equaling 243 households could be linked across these two records. Cross-tabulating data from the sewer and water plans with the race variable in the 1930 census draws out some relevant patterns in how these services and the populations that they serviced may have been racialized. The 243 households in the sample include 66 African American families and 177 households coded as "white" during the 1930 census, which included a number of European immigrants or persons who may have identified with some European ethnicity. African American households are particularly well represented in this sample; the 66 African American households matched from the census to the utility plans comprise over 75 percent of African American households enumerated during the 1930 census and close to 90 percent of all African American persons living in Eastport in that year. Municipal utility plans show that at least *one-third* of these African American households were not connected to municipal sewer or water. A much smaller proportion of white households was without service: 8.5 percent were not connected to city sewer, and a little more than 12 percent did not use city water (see Tables 2–4).

TABLE 2. Water and Sewer Service to Identified African American Households in Eastport, by Tenure

	Water and Sewer Service Present		No Service Present		Totals	
	n	percent	n	percent	n	percent
Home owned	28	66.7%	14	33.3%	42	100.0%
Home rented	15	65.2%	8	34.8%	23	100.0%
Total Households	43	66.2%	22	33.8%	65	100.0%

TABLE 3. Water Service to Identified White Households in Eastport, by Tenure

	Water Service Present		No Service Present		Totals	
	n	*percent*	*n*	*percent*	*n*	*percent*
Home owned	89	89.0%	11	11.0%	100	100.0%
Home rented	64	85.3%	11	14.7%	75	100.0%
Total Households	153	87.4%	22	12.6%	175	100.0%

TABLE 4. Sewer Service to Identified White Households in Eastport, by Tenure

	Sewer Service Present		No Water Present		Totals	
	n	*percent*	*n*	*percent*	*n*	*percent*
Home owned	94	94.0%	6	6.0%	100	100.0%
Home rented	66	88.0%	9	12.0%	75	100.0%
Total Households	160	91.4%	15	8.6%	175	100.0%

Further, the proportion of African American households that were not connected to city services is the same for families that owned or had mortgaged their homes and for African American families who rented their homes. For these families, home-ownership does not predict whether their homes were connected to city services, whereas among white households dwellings that were occupied by renters were more frequently disconnected from city sewer and water. I suggest that the relatively high rate of homeownership among African Americans in Eastport is a key to interpreting the racialization of public utilities and, by extension, the racialization of the nascent governmental form in Annapolis during the early twentieth century. It is possible that African American households sometimes postponed receiving these services through inaction, again to paraphrase Foucault (1991), preventing the "perfection of the processes" that provide for the security of population, as a reflection of agency that today is difficult to recognize. Why would a homeowner not connect their home to municipal services if service was available? This question confounds interpretations premised in the notion that sewers are about the improvement of public health.

The inequalities created between black and white households during the installation of sanitation infrastructure in Eastport, specifically municipal water in 1927 and sanitary sewers after 1934, show that access to these services broke down upon racial lines. Access to sanitary services in Eastport could even be termed a white privilege and placed among those other privileges that convinced working-class white people that they were different from their economic peers who were black people. DuBois (1935) described these privileges as a supplemental psychological wage paid particularly to working-class white people to compensate them for sharing the labor market with African Americans and to differentiate them from African Americans as such (Kelley 1994: 30–31). The wages, and in this context the services provided by the state, promote racial identification of people rather than merely identifying *a priori* raced people. As Mary Poole (2006: 3) has written, "the founding legislation that created the American welfare state discriminated on the basis of race," in that it "related to some citizens as workers and others only on the basis of their proven poverty. . . . public policy has contributed most to inequality through the belief of policymakers that race is real, that human beings really are 'black' or 'white.'"

At least one-third of African American homes in Eastport were not connected to this infrastructure, but as many as two-thirds did connect to municipal water and sewer networks by 1954, when the utility plans examined during this study were archived. If the preponderance of African Americans in Eastport lived in "modern" sanitary houses by the mid–twentieth century, does this fact represent an achievement to be celebrated? Is it a mode of resistance to the discrimination that seems embedded within the projects of a patriarchical city government, government that continually struggled to achieve rationality in the application of its power? The truth is that the systematic exclusion of African Americans from this one privilege of citizenship—an exclusion that was overcome by the majority of African Americans in Eastport—is multiplied endlessly by slights and insults that together amounted to the persistent denial of the security that was provided freely to neighboring white people. Governmentality in Annapolis was racial governmentality, a possibility that Foucault did not truly allow room for but which is suggested by other writers on race and American government (for example, Balibar and Wallerstein 1991; Goldberg 2002; Kazanjian 2003).

This interpretation connects obliquely with the plan for economic emancipation that DuBois mapped out in several essays on black separatism, particularly in *Black Reconstruction in America* (1935). However the idea that African Americans might be disposed to abstain from services is one that needs to be substantiated more carefully through firsthand accounts and oral histories of modernization in Eastport and Annapolis. Paul Mullins's book *Race and Affluence* (1999) shows quite clearly that African Americans in Annapolis strove to attain the same consumer privileges as white citizens and to enter the public spaces of consumption. This alone intimates the desires of African Americans to have the same modern conveniences as white people. Outdoor privies are a powerful symbol of the inequalities that African Americans suffered before the "Second Reconstruction" of the civil rights era (Marable 2007). Privies probably conjure up other inadequacies in the services that were provided to African Americans under segregation. Only a subtle read of the relationship between African Americans and the racial state would support the interpretation that privies were curated, as a tactic for delaying engagement with the apparatus of security for Annapolis, when presumably privies would also be despised.

The rate of homeownership among African Americans in Eastport *is,* demonstrably, a considerable accomplishment. By 1930, amidst Eastport's enclosure within the sanitary system for metropolitan Annapolis, African Americans in this neighborhood had attained the same rate of homeownership as neighboring white people, breaking with the pattern of black tenure seen throughout Maryland, Anne Arundel County, and by the greatest margin in the city of Annapolis. If African Americans in Eastport could match the rate of homeownership among white people, why should access to public services fall beyond their reach? This question calls for consideration of the importance of homes to African Americans in Eastport, the role that homes played in the overall accumulation of wealth and the relative prosperity of African American families across generations, and also the relationship of African Americans in Eastport—figured as labor—to governmental power that grew to surround homes and bodies during the 1920s and 1930s. I suggest that this expression of black economic power in Eastport would predict equal access to municipal services if access were predicated upon economic factors alone. Clearly it is not. Access is a matter as complicated as the persons that it touches. Racial exclusion from access to public services, the state's apparatus of security, is partly accomplished by the structural racism of the state, but I also suggest that disconnection expresses African American autonomy and "slippage" from state power. Disconnection presents the clear possibility that African Americans are governed differently from white people in early-twentieth-century America, who are more completely citizens and more completely articulated with this and other apparatuses of government.

Because infrastructure like municipal water and sewers defines the color line so clearly, we can consider these technologies as racial materialities, as race-in-process, by looking at how municipal services were apportioned and how these services identified people more clearly to their racial types. The sanitary system as an apparatus of security becomes a part of the ongoing construction of race even as the sanitary system emerges from the changes in how Annapolis was governed at the end of the nineteenth century and early in the twentieth. Furthermore, if services like municipal sewers can be described as the material culture of government, what does the relative rate of connection and disconnection signal about how communities of different races in Eastport were governed? How is the relationship between each household and the municipal infrastructure the work of agency?

This last consideration is my central concern in this essay. If a far greater proportion of African American households were not accessing municipal services from Annapolis, does this mark them as victims of systematic disinvestment, victims of the economic violence that constrained opportunities for African Americans after Reconstruction and promoted their continuing poverty? Or can it also (not instead of) mark them as resistors to their own incorporation as a governable population, resistors to the terms of their governance being suddenly changed, and ultimately as resistors to their annexation into the city of Annapolis? To answer this question and to dispel purely economic explanations for the relatively high rate of disconnection among African Americans in Eastport, I explore black homeownership in this community as a relative measure of wealth. By 1930 African Americans in Eastport had achieved an especially high rate of homeownership, and throughout the years from 1910 to 1930 African Americans in Eastport far exceeded homeownership rates among people of color in Annapolis, in Anne Arundel County, and throughout the state. While there is not parity in wealth between African Americans and their white neighbors in Eastport, by 1930 there is approximately the same proportion of home-owning families in each group. In this way homeownership can be seen as an alternative source of security for African Americans in Eastport and as a measure of what they could accomplish economically, ultimately to suggest that where African Americans were not connected with municipal services, it was not solely because they lacked the means to make a connection. Rather I take this to represent a negative disposition toward the new material forms describing the action of liberal government that is characteristic of African Americans in Eastport.

To conclude, I outline some possibilities. One interpretation of these patterns sees race as a factor in the designs of civic projects, which it inarguably is. The disparity in provision of services to African American– and white-occupied homes intensifies the meaning of racial identification and subjection. Another interpretation, which does not exclude this first one, suggests African American households that are through their own agency independent of the city-owned infrastructure and a community that is arguably governed to a lesser degree than their neighbors.

Acknowledgments

I am very grateful to Jodi Barnes for encouraging me to participate in this volume and for her patience as I completed my contribution. I am also indebted to Jennifer Babiarz, Hannah Jopling, Cheryl LaRoche, Mark Leone, Christopher Matthews, Carol McDavid, and Paul Mullins for their advice and encouragement, which is ongoing. Jane McWilliams provided me with excerpts from her historical research on public utilities in Annapolis, and Ginger Doyel also contributed generously from research for her book on the Eastport neighborhood. Plans of municipal water and sewer infrastructure in Eastport were provided by Paul Lackey of the Annapolis Department of Public Works. Finally, research presented in this chapter was completed as part of my doctoral dissertation at Columbia University, under Nan Rothschild's sponsorship and guidance.

References

Aiello, E., and J. L. Seidel 1995. Three Hundred Years of Annapolis: Phase III Archaeological Investigations of the Anne Arundel County Courthouse Site (18AP63), Annapolis,

Maryland. Draft report on file, Archaeology in Annapolis Laboratory, University of Maryland College Park.

Alexander, C., and C. Knowles (editors) 2005. Introduction. In *Making Race Matter: Bodies, Space and Identity,* pp. 1–16. Hampshire, UK: Palgrave Macmillan.

Annapolis, Mayor and City Council of 1927. Proceedings of the Mayor and Aldermen of Annapolis, Volume 23. MSA M49–23 (1/22/2/5) Original Municipal Records, Mayor and City Council of Annapolis. Maryland State Archive, Annapolis.

Balibar, E., and I. Wallerstein 1991. *Race, Nation, Class: Ambiguous Identities.* London: Verso Press.

Brugger, R. J. 1988. *Maryland: A Middle Temperament, 1634–1980.* Baltimore, Md.: Johns Hopkins University Press and the Maryland Historical Society.

Calderhead, W. L. 1977. Anne Arundel Blacks: Three Centuries of Change. In *Anne Arundel County: Three Centuries of Change,* edited by J. C. Bradford, pp. 11–25. Annapolis, Md.: Anne Arundel County and Annapolis Bicentennial Committee.

Carmichael, S. 1967. *Black Power: The Politics of Liberation in America.* New York: Vintage Books.

Carnes-McNaughton, L. F., and T. M. Harper 2000. The Parity of Privies: Summary of Research on Privies in North America. *Historical Archaeology* 34(1):97–110.

Cochran, M. D., M. M. Palus, S. N. Duensin, J. E. Blair, Jr., J. E. Knauf, and J. L. Mundt 2008. Phase II Archaeological Testing on Fleet Street (18AP111), Cornhill Street (18AP112), and 26 Market Space (18AP109), Annapolis, Maryland. Review draft prepared for the City of Annapolis, Public Works Bureau of Engineering and Construction. Report on file, Archaeology in Annapolis Laboratory, University of Maryland College Park.

Crenshaw, K., N. Gotanda, G. Peller, and K. Thomas (editors) 1995. *Critical Race Theory: The Key Writings That Formed the Movement.* New York: New Press.

Dean, M. 1999. *Governmentality: Power and Rule in Modern Society.* London: Sage Publications.

Dent, R. J., and B. Ford 1983. Interim Report on Reynolds Tavern Excavations. Report prepared by Historic Annapolis Foundation for the Maryland Historical Trust. On file, Archaeology in Annapolis Laboratory, University of Maryland College Park.

Doyel-Read, E. 1990. Archaeological Excavations at State Circle. Report prepared by Archaeology in Annapolis. On file, Archaeology in Annapolis Laboratory, University of Maryland College Park.

DuBois, W. E. B. 1935. *Black Reconstruction in America.* Cleveland: Harcourt Brace.

———. 1906. The Economic Future of the Negro. *Publications of the American Economic Association* 7(1):219–242.

Epperson, T. W. 2004. Critical Race Theory and the Archaeology of the African Diaspora. *Historical Archaeology* 38(1):107–131.

Evening Capital 1950. Greater Annapolis Voted; City to Become Fourth Largest in Maryland. 24 May. Annapolis, Md.

———. 1922a. 25 Inducted in Klan Last Night at Horn Point. 9 September. Annapolis, Md.

———. 1922b. Five Klansman in Robes Visit Church; Bearing Emblazoned Cross They Present Token to Eastport Baptist Pastor; Address by Reverend Ford. 18 September. Annapolis, Md.

Fanon, F. 2008. *Black Skin, White Masks.* New York: Grove Press; Berkeley, Calif.: Publishers Group West.

———. 2004. *The Wretched of the Earth.* New York: Grove Press.

Ford, B. 1994. Health and Sanitation in Postbellum Harpers Ferry. *Historical Archaeology* 28(4):49–61.

Foucault, M. 1991. Governmentality. In *The Foucault Effect: Studies in Governmentality,* edited by G. Burchell, C. Gordon, and P. Miller, pp. 87–104. Chicago: University of Chicago Press.

Gibb, J. G. 2001. Memorandum to Chair and Members of the Annapolis Historic Preservation Committee regarding 111/113 Chester Avenue, November 26, 2001. On file, Department of Planning and Zoning, City of Annapolis, Md.

Goldberg, D. T. 2002. *The Racial State.* Oxford: Blackwell Publishers.

Goldberg, D. T., and P. Essed 2002. Introduction: From Racial Demarcations to Multiple Identifications. In *Race Critical Theories,* edited by P. Essed and D. T. Goldberg. Oxford: Blackwell Publishers.

Goodwin, R. C., S. L. Sanders, M. T. Moran, and D. Landon 1993 Phase II/III Archeological Investigations of the Gott's Court Parking Facility, Annapolis, Maryland, Vol. 1. Frederick, Md.: R. Christopher Goodwin & Associates, Inc.

Gordon, C. 1991. Governmental Rationality: An Introduction. In *The Foucault Effect: Studies in Governmentality,* edited by G. Burchell, C. Gordon, and P. Miller, pp. 1–51. Chicago: University of Chicago Press.

Hannah, M. G. 2000. *Governmentality and the Mastery of Territory in Nineteenth Century America.* Cambridge: Cambridge University Press.

Harris, W. J. 1915. *Negroes in the United States.* U.S. Department of Commerce, Bureau of the Census, Bulletin 129. Washington, D.C.: Government Printing Office.

Holston, J. 2008. *Insurgent Citizenship: Disjunctions of Democracy and Modernity in Brazil.* Princeton: Princeton University Press.

Hunt, A., and G. Wickham 1994. *Foucault and Law: Towards a Sociology of Law as Governance.* London: Pluto Press.

Jordan, W. 1977. *White over Black: American Attitudes toward the Negro, 1550–1812.* New York: Norton.

Kazanjian, D. 2003. *The Colonizing Trick: National Culture and Imperial Citizenship in Early America.* Minneapolis: University of Minnesota Press.

Kelley, R. D. G. 1994. *Race Rebels: Culture, Politics, and the Black Working Class.* New York: Free Press.

Larsen, E. L. 2002. Phase III Archaeological Investigations for the Banneker-Douglass Museum Expansion, The Courthouse Site (18AP63), 86–90 Franklin Street, Annapolis, Maryland, 2001. Report prepared for the Maryland Commission on African American History and Culture and the Maryland Department of Housing and Community Development. Report on file, Archaeology in Annapolis Laboratory, University of Maryland College Park.

Marable, M. 2007. *Race, Reform, and Rebellion: The Second Reconstruction and Beyond in Black America, 1945–2006.* Jackson: University of Mississippi Press.

Maryland, State of 1936. Laws of Maryland, Special Section 1936, Chapter 158. Annapolis, Md.

McCarthy, J. P., and J. A. Ward 2000. Sanitation Practices, Depositional Processes, and Interpretive Contexts of Minneapolis Privies. *Historical Archaeology* 34(1):111–129.

McWilliams, J. W. 2009. Annapolis History Chronology. Electronic file, Maryland State Archives, Annapolis.

Mullins, P. R. 1999. *Race and Affluence: An Archaeology of African America and Consumer Culture.* New York: Kluwer Academic/Plenum Publishers.

Mullins, P. R., and M. S. Warner 1993. Final Archaeological Investigations at the Maynard-Burgess House (18AP64), an 1850–1980 African-American Household in Annapolis, Maryland. Report on file, Archaeology in Annapolis Laboratory, University of Maryland College Park.

Nobles, M. 2000. *Shades of Citizenship: Race and the Census in Modern Politics.* Stanford, Calif.: Stanford University Press.

Omi, M., and H. Winant 2002. Racial Formation. In *Race Critical Theories,* edited by P. Essed and D. T. Goldberg, pp. 123–145. Oxford: Blackwell Publishers.

O'Reilly, C. 1994. Archaeological Excavations at 18AP44: 193 Main Street, Annapolis, Maryland, 1985–1987. Report on file, Archaeology in Annapolis Laboratory, University of Maryland College Park.

Palus, M. M. 2009. *Materialities of Government: A Historical Archaeology of Infrastructure in Annapolis and Eastport, 1865–1951.* Ph.D. dissertation, Columbia University, New York.

———. 2005. Building an Architecture of Power: Electricity in Annapolis, Maryland in the 19th and 20th Centuries. In *Archaeologies of Materiality,* edited by L. M. Meskell, pp. 162–189. Oxford: Blackwell Publishing.

Poole, M. 2006. *The Segregated Origins of Social Security: African Americans and the Welfare State.* Chapel Hill: University of North Carolina Press.

Rogers, S. L. 1918. *Negro Population, 1790–1915.* U.S. Department of Commerce, Bureau of the Census. Washington, D.C.: Government Printing Office.

Rosenswig, R. M. 1999. Nineteenth Century Urbanism and Public Health: The Evidence of Twelve Privies in Albany, New York. *Northeast Anthropology* 58:27–45.

Schweninger, L. 1990. Black Property Owners in the South, 1790–1915. *Blacks in the New World.* Urbana: University of Illinois Press.

Shackel, P. A. 1986. Archaeological Testing at the 193 Main St. Site, 18AP44, Annapolis, Maryland. With contributions by Patricia Secreto. Report on file, Archaeology in Annapolis Laboratory, University of Maryland College Park.

Smith, C. W. 1925. Report of the Mayor of Annapolis on the State of the City's Finances from July 1, 1924 to June 30, 1925, with Statement of the Sinking Fund. Charles W. Smith, Mayor. On file, Maryland State Archive M102–2 (1/22/4/26) City of Annapolis, Annapolis Mayor & Aldermen, Reports and Minutes (Mayor's Report, 1894–1959), Annapolis.

Steuart, W. M. 1933 *Fifteenth Census of the United States: 1930, Population, Volume V.I.: Families* (Reports by States, Giving Statistics for Families, Dwellings and Homes, by Counties, for Urban and Rural Areas and for Urban Places of 2,500 or More). Washington, D.C.: Government Printing Office.

———. 1922. *Fourteenth Census of the United States Taken in the Year 1920, Volume II: Population 1920, General Report and Analytical Tables.* U.S. Department of Commerce, Bureau of the Census. Washington, D.C.: Government Printing Office.

Stoler, A. L. 1995. *Race and the Education of Desire: Foucault's History of Sexuality and the Colonial Order of Things.* Durham, N.C.: Duke University Press.

Stottman, M. J. 2000. Out of Sight, Out of Mind: Privy Architecture and the Perception of Sanitation. *Historical Archaeology* 34(1):39–61.

———. 1995. Towards a Greater Understanding of Privy Vault Architecture. In *Historical Archaeology in Kentucky,* edited by K. A. McBride, S. W. McBride, and D. Pollack. Frankfort: Kentucky Heritage Council.

United States Bureau of the Census 1930. Fifteenth Census of the United States: 1930, Population Schedule. Anne Arundel County, Enumeration District 2–37. Special Collections. University of Maryland College Park.

———. 1920. Fourteenth Census of the United States: 1920–Census. Anne Arundel County, Maryland. Special Collections. University of Maryland College Park.

———. 1910. Thirteenth Census of the United States: 1910 Population. Anne Arundel County, Maryland. Special Collections. University of Maryland College Park.

Warren, M. 1990. *Then Again . . . Annapolis, 1900–1965.* Annapolis, Md.: Time Exposures Ltd.

Weinbaum, A. E. 2004. *Wayward Reproductions: Genealogies of Race and Nation in Transatlantic Modern Thought.* Durham, N.C.: Duke University Press.

PAUL R. MULLINS AND LEWIS C. JONES

Race, Displacement, and Twentieth-Century University Landscapes

An Archaeology of Urban Renewal and Urban Universities

The stereotype of an idyllic college town lingers in the minds of many contemporary observers, but in the wake of World War II federal urban renewal legislation radically reshaped higher education, rewriting the relationship between race, place, and universities. Supported by state slum clearance funding from the 1940s onward, a host of city universities grew or were born almost uniformly in what were once African American neighborhoods. Urban renewal legislation extended a lengthy heritage of state monitoring and surveillance of urban impoverishment and the color line, but its marriage to university planning and expansion was a significant new postwar mechanism that radically reshaped the American city.

The effects of such expansion hang over many contemporary universities that are consciously troubled by a heritage of mass displacement and eager to address community heritage, yet many of the same institutions continue to seek space for future growth. In the late 1950s Indiana University eyed expansion of its Indianapolis Medical School campus and proposed an adjoining undergraduate campus that would be built in a densely settled, predominantly African American neighborhood surrounding the medical school. The University Medical Center had annexed modest slices of the surrounding neighborhoods as early as the 1920s, but by the 1950s federal funding made rapid expansion possible for many comparably ambitious institutions. Some municipalities seeking federal funds partnered quite aggressively with universities, and in some cases those institutions rapidly leveled broad swaths of neighboring communities and targeted other spaces for eventual growth. In 1959, for example, the *New York Times* concluded that after such wholesale removals the communities surrounding much of the University of Chicago "resemble German cities just after World War II" (Wehrwein 1959: 61). Indianapolis's city government, though, was driven by a distinctive Hoosier devotion to the free market and a professed reluctance to turn over redevelopment to federal funders and external parties. Consequently the real estate acquired to assemble what became Indiana University-Purdue University Indianapolis (IUPUI) came through piecemeal property purchases that took more than 20 years. The gradual rate of this development effectively minimized the scope of displacement, but the change was no less profound than in communities that eliminated whole neighborhoods in one fell swoop.

Today hundreds of acres of homes that stood in the neighborhood in 1960 are all gone, their heritage is often completely unrecognized, and the vast scope of the transformation and the university's complicity in that transformation is ignored or inelegantly remembered. A retelling of this story of urban transformation and the color line is exceptionally well suited to archaeology. Over the space of a century, the current-day IUPUI campus spent moments as a thriving African American business district; hosted myriad churches, schools, and leisure spaces; and witnessed the affluent lives of African American gentility and impoverished working-class folks alike, sometimes at the exact same moments. Rapid demolition episodes left behind distinct material deposits. Decades of recurrent parking lot paving and landscaping ironically provide exceptional preservation, and the university's ownership of the property provides unparalleled access to sites.

Research on urban campuses provides a powerful opportunity to conduct truly engaged scholarship and make unrecognized but deep-seated privileges visible. Much of the archaeological story to be told on such campuses revolves around the racial and class privileges that made university expansion possible and now have rendered it rather invisible, even as many of these institutions now experience a tension between the willingness to face up to their institutional complicity in urban renewal and simultaneously continue spatial expansion. Archaeology provides some insight into the development of such communities over the long periods leading up to urban displacement, which inevitably complicates the transparent claims many ideologues made to rationalize mass removals. Nevertheless archaeology does not provide a transparently nostalgic mechanism to recast the lives of many profoundly impoverished people, although it can very soberly underscore the genuine material and social challenges of poverty along the color line, and it reflects how structural racism and classism ensured a twentieth-century material decline that cities were compelled to address by the 1950s.

Archaeology on a university campus is an especially public discourse that invites a vast range of stakeholders beyond former residents and descendants alone. The ways in which descendants, former residents, and various campus constituencies stake claims to the century-and-a-half heritage of these now-dispersed spatial and social neighborhoods in Indianapolis provides a complicated picture of how heritage can be claimed based on archaeological insight. It also illuminates the strategically unrecognized privileges that made mass displacement possible and confronts the ways many universities continue to clumsily negotiate their complicity in mass removals while they aspire to grow further. The challenge is to connect the relatively recent heritage of urban renewal and campus originations to longer histories of the same landscapes, examining persistent inequalities and transformation that continue into the present without lapsing into romanticized histories, failing to circumspectly interrogate a host of heritage claims, or ignoring the link between historical injustices and contemporary inequalities.

Blight and the Urban University

A vast range of legislation had taken aim on "blighted" urban spaces from the nineteenth century onward, typically introducing codes to regulate housing deficiencies and contain the spatial expansion of slums, but by World War II many planners backed by state ideologues turned to wholesale slum clearance to transform the American city. Universities profited from much of this displacement as early as the 1930s, but they were not firmly married to such codes until the Federal Housing Act was amended in 1959 to expressly direct federal aid for "urban renewal areas involving colleges and universities" (Hechinger 1961: E7). Higher education subsequently became a significant civic partner leveraging federal funds and reshaping urban America.

Like many communities that targeted urban "blight," the neighborhoods targeted by Indiana University and the city had deteriorated significantly by the 1950s. In 1953 the *Indianapolis Star* lamented that 20 percent of the city was in need of slum clearance, and the newspaper found a vast number of homes with dirt floors, no plumbing or electricity, and significant rat populations (Connor 1959a). Nearly 1,000 Indianapolis dwellings had no access to indoor plumbing at all, more than 12,000 shared a flush toilet with another household, and nearly 21,000 had no indoor shower or bathtub (Connor 1959b: 1). Nevertheless that physical condition often was not restricted to particular neighborhoods or even single blocks, and it belied the near-Westside's rich heritage and residents' deep connections to the space. Much of the Indianapolis community neighboring the hospital had been settled by African Americans and European newcomers from the 1870s onward, and by the turn of the century it was the center of African-America life in central Indiana, though pockets of mostly European immigrants continued to live in the area into the 1960s. Migration waves at the turn of the century and again during World War II significantly expanded the population density of the neighborhood and included increasingly more impoverished residents in deteriorating conditions.

In 1961 the *New York Times* recognized the dramatic conflicts between urban campus growth and existing communities, arguing that such institutions "must simultaneously plan their own development and clear actual and potential slums" (Hechinger 1961: E7). Urban renewal legislation expanded the power of eminent domain to secure properties in the service of slum clearance, and for some newly born universities and their expanding peers, such codes allowed administrators and city leaders

to engineer surrounding communities in ways that conformed to their own preconceptions of an appropriate university climate. Yet in 1963 education scholar Kermit
Parsons (1963: 208) recognized that since "the urban university's ideas about the
right kind of neighborhood environment are likely to vary from those of residents,
some bitter battles have been fought." In 1953, for instance, the Illinois Urban Community Conservation Act targeted "conservation areas" that were likely to become
slums, a code that helped the University of Chicago reshape much of the surrounding Hyde Park–Kenwood community (cf. Hirsch 2000; Proudfoot 1954: 418; Teaford
2000: 452–453). The project rehabilitated much of the historic architecture in the
community, but it displaced many of its African American residents who could not
make a claim to "middle-class" standing. In 1949 Columbia University president
Dwight D. Eisenhower likened the growth of the university to the nation's wartime
resolve, arguing that "nothing can defeat Columbia" (*New York Times* 1949: 50).
Eisenhower foresaw the university's expansion "right down to the Harlem river." By
1964, though, that growth had resulted in a suit accusing the university of singling
out African Americans and Puerto Ricans for eviction, complaining that Columbia
aspired to make the neighborhood "lily white" (Schanberg 1964: 15). Throughout the
rest of the 1960s Columbia continually faced accusations that it failed to consult
neighbors or displaced residents as it expanded into Morningside Heights (for example, Axel-Lute 2008; Bird 1968; Millones 1968; Roberts 1966).

In 1921 the Indiana University Medical Center took its first aim on the neighboring community when it developed a plan for a convalescent park adjoining the Riley
Hospital then under construction. African American physician Sumner Furniss questioned whether the facility would serve any of the black residents it intended to
remove, and he warned that "he did not think it wise to throw from 1500 to 2000 persons out of their homes" (*Indianapolis Star* 1921a: 5). During the construction of the
park, one of the homes was identified as the oldest dwelling in Indianapolis, and its
yard was dotted with the graves of the city's earliest European settlers, including a
Revolutionary War veteran. The hospital association was reluctant to uproot such a
history and resolved in September 1921 to "preserve the dwelling as a landmark"
(*Indianapolis Star* 1921b: 8). Nevertheless the home was soon thereafter razed, and a
boulder was used to mark the place of the graves; they too were finally bulldozed
without comment or removal in about 1958.

Like many urban universities, Indiana expanded somewhat opportunistically, seizing land when it became available in the absence of particularly clear plans for its use
and routinely failing to measure up in practice to the grandiose master plans. In 1958
the Indianapolis Redevelopment Commission produced what would become one of
numerous master designs for the near-Westside, and they alluded to the development of an undergraduate campus that would occupy three buildings adjoining the
hospital—and in a somewhat different configuration those three buildings did appear
in 1969. But the plan also aspired to place dental and medical school students in new

dormitories, leave most of the neighborhood untouched, build a shopping center, and rehabilitate the city canal to turn its mouth into a serene paddleboat and leisure space, though the canal had been an open sewer for over a century. That plan did not address how the land would be acquired, but in the 1950s two major urban renewal projects directed by the Indianapolis Redevelopment Commission clearly benefited Indiana University. One 19-acre 1956 project referred to as Project F razed 104 homes, citing the significant deterioration of the neighborhood that qualified it as a blighted neighborhood, and Project D cleared a roughly 18-acre neighborhood immediately adjoining the University Medical Center (*Indianapolis Star* 1956; Indianapolis Redevelopment Commission 1959). In each case the city purchased the individual parcels and relocated residents before clearing the land and selling both tracts back to the university at whatever cost the city first absorbed.

In the early 1960s the city and its influential Chamber of Commerce became leery of dependence on external funding and surprised the university by rejecting federal urban renewal financing. This left the university compelled to determine how it could expand into the densely settled neighborhoods around the medical center (cf., Hardy 1989: 27; Wood 1996: 21). By about 1964 the university began to purchase individual properties, and through the late 1960s the university typically acquired between 10 and 20 properties each month. One such space was the 400 block of Agnes Street, which had been residential since about the Civil War and included the Bowers Building, a former department store that became a stationery supply office before its

Homes on Beauty Street targeted for slum removal near the Indiana University Dental School. Courtesy of IUPUI University Library Special Collections and Archives, Indianapolis.

purchase by the university in the summer of 1967 (Indiana University Board of Trustees 1967). By 1970 the university had acquired all but one of the properties on the block, which included about 34 residences in the decades following World War II. A circa 1956 assemblage at 458–460 Agnes Street included a dense assemblage from these last moments of the neighborhood. Some of the material culture hints at the complex ways in which racism and the color line shaped everyday materiality. For instance, the assemblage includes a significant volume of rubber clearly identifiable as bicycle tires that would normally be consigned to an artifact catalog or simply discarded in the field. Indianapolis has always had a special affection for car culture, and in 1953 the city discontinued service on its last electric streetcar, with a local trolley bus service ending four years later (Taggart 1994: 1305). Modest bus service remained in place, but public transportation had always been patrolled through a variety of mostly de facto mechanisms. A rich range of photographs from twentieth-century Indianapolis confirms that some African Americans negotiating the confluence of race and space had been riding bikes for a long time. For the many Indianapolis residents who remained without reliable transportation in the 1950s, bikes negotiated structural inequalities and reflect the subtle ways city spaces were structured along color and class lines. Those who did have cars were often exceptionally attached to them and recognized the class standing and self-determination they symbolized. One proud car owner on California Street, for instance, joined the Goodrich Silvertown Safety League and likely displayed an excavated emblem on the household car. These reflectors were available from Goodrich dealers in a campaign that launched in 1931 for those consumers who signed a safe-driving statement.

Like most Cold War households, the Agnes Street assemblages are dominated by standard mass-produced goods that reflect the American immersion in consumer culture that cut across class and color lines. Nevertheless that immersion took various forms, and there are some trinkets that reflect cultural distinctions even as they mirror the extension of consumer culture into everyday life. The most interesting example is a mass-produced good-luck coin, which was manufactured by King Novelty. Morton Neumann ran several firms, including King Novelty and its sister companies Valmor and Famous Products, that marketed a vast range of cosmetics and curios to African Americans from the Depression until the late 1950s (Yronwode 2003). Neumann's products were advertised in the most prominent African American newspapers and sold throughout the South and Midwest by agents who were often beauticians or root workers, since many of these goods were rooted in hoodoo folk practices (Yronwode 2003). The Agnes Street coin was laden with 21 "good luck" symbols, including John the Conqueror root, lodestone, a Mo-Jo Head, a four-leaf clover, and a burning candle, all of which were invoked in hoodoo practices. Similar practices reaching into the earliest moments of captivity are now well known in archaeological circles, since many hoodoo deposits were intentionally buried to fix spells. Lodestone, for example, was sometimes buried to draw money to a home, and

Advertisement in the King Novelty catalog for a Lucky Mo-Jo Coin like the one recovered on Agnes Street. Courtesy of Paul Mullins.

The coin recovered on Agnes Street. Courtesy of Paul Mullins.

lucky tokens were sometimes used in the same manner, though the coin on Agnes Street was in an undifferentiated context and certainly not in the sort of feature or location that would be used to seal a spell. Lucky tokens have a heritage that reaches beyond hoodoo, but unlike the generalized lucky tokens mass-produced in the 1930s, the Agnes Street coin included distinctive African hoodoo symbols that would have passed unnoticed by most white consumers, and King Novelty sold herb bags, oils, and raw materials like red flannel and lodestone that routinely appeared in conjure assemblages. The token was simultaneously a mass commodity even as it acknowledged cultural distinctions and the dynamism of diasporan practice.

Urban renewal displacements were routinely driven by transparent slum ideology that linked race and poverty. Consequently contemporary scholars hoping to undo such misrepresentation often use material culture and historical texts to demonstrate how residents lived symbolically rich lives and even adhered to many dominant standards despite the appearance of utter destitution. Yet in Indianapolis this risks ignoring the genuine impoverishment that racism created over more than a century, leading to a truly deteriorated neighborhood that was indeed in need of systematic redress, even though displacement was not necessarily the most appropriate mechanism. Archaeology delivers a predictably complicated picture of indigence in the houses along Agnes Street; material culture underscores the residents' material marginalization even as it reveals the range of ways consumers thoughtfully negotiated poverty and were not defined by economic circumstance. For instance, the faunal assemblages from two sites on Agnes Street provide some clues to a diverse range of food consumption tactics. Agnes Street sits a quarter mile from the White River, and residents have fished in the river since the earliest settlers arrived. The home is nearly as close to the Central Canal, an aborted 1839 transportation artery that cuts through the city for nine miles. Fishing often was saddled by racist and class caricatures like that wielded by Edward King (1875: 427), who indicated that African Americans in Georgia "love hunting and fishing; they revel in the idleness which they never knew until after the war." Traveler Julian Ralph (1896: 376) witnessed African Americans fishing throughout the South, noting that "the Southern colored people . . . seem to be eternally at it wherever they and any piece of water, no matter how small, are thrown together." He noted that African Americans even "fish in the canals and open sewers in the streets. . . . It is delightful to see them." For many poor Americans fishing was not a leisure activity but a significant foodway, yet observers like Ralph cast fishing as an aesthetic reflecting essential racial inferiority. But the more pressing challenge in Indianapolis was that the White River was a profoundly polluted waterway. For over 150 years the river has had raw sewage piped into it from the city's sewer system, overflows that continue even today, and upriver farms and local factories continually introduced a vast range of pollutants into the river. The canal had served as a makeshift sewer for more than 100 years and was an equally unpleasant space. Consequently fishing has long provided a charitably problematic food source. A dense assemblage at 458–460 Agnes Street included no fish remains, suggesting that at least those mid-1950s households were avoiding local waterways. A contemporary deposit at 444 Agnes Street had a more modest assemblage of 278 bones, and it included 11 fish elements indicating some modest fishing, alongside six rabbit bones, a raccoon mandible, and a groundhog femur that suggest the residents still did some opportunistic household hunting—or were exterminating pests—in the heart of the Cold War city. Still, the 444 Agnes Street assemblage was dominated by pork and to a lesser extent beef and chicken, as many contemporary assemblages would have been as well. Of the 278 bones in the assemblage, 62 were pork (22 percent), 37 were beef (13 percent), and 41 were chicken (14 percent). That broad-based consumption strategy contrasted to that of the neighbors at 458–460 Agnes Street. The home at 458–460 Agnes Street had a much more overwhelming dominance of pork; 756 of the 1042 elements in that feature were pork (73 percent), 92 were chicken (8 percent) and only four elements were beef (0.3 percent). While pork is a commonplace food on African American tables, the home at 458–460 was home to several residents who worked at the massive pork-packing plant, Kingans, directly across the river. It seems likely they were bringing home some food that had been discarded, and they may also have been furtively pilfering food from their workplace. Such tactical consumption was likely most common among marginalized laborers, which included the men on Kingans' factory line as well as the many domestics and food service laborers who brought food home from their workplaces. Such consumption is very challenging to "see" archaeologically, but clearly many African American households developed a rich range of consumption tactics negotiating consumer space and workplace racism.

The comparison of the bottle assemblage at 458–460 with a neighborhood corner store suggests the decline of the neighborhood retailing that had once supported black consumers' staple needs. By the turn of the twentieth century, modest corner stores were dotted all over the near-Westside, including a typical store at 800 Camp Street that likely hawked canned and bottled goods, some fresh foods, and basic goods like coal and ice. Similar stores dotted almost every corner of the near-Westside into the Depression, and some continued in business into the 1960s. In the early twentieth century, the store was appointed with a rich range of household decorative material culture and includes a large assemblage of toys that suggest it was a common neighborhood gathering space until around World War II. Many such stores began to disappear in the 1930s, hit first by the invasion of chains, then by an exodus of many residents in the wake of World War II, and finally by urban renewal's nearly complete removal of remaining customers. When the Camp Street proprietors filled their backyard privy around 1960, they discarded a toilet and then followed it with a range of goods including 135 bottles (Rosenberg 2008: 56). The functional range of products the store was selling in its final days appears to have been quite restricted: one-third of the assemblage was liquor bottles, another 23 percent were soda, and another 15 percent were wine vessels, which together accounts for 95 of the 135 vessels. Like many eroding retailers, the store appears to have focused on a handful of goods and hoped that convenience would continue to provide some modest but steady income. Yet in 1960 the store appeared in the city directory simply as an ice dealer, and it closed soon afterward (Polk 1960: 172). In comparison the assemblage at 458–460 Agnes Street was composed of 42 percent liquor bottles, an even higher percentage than the corner store, but only 2.5 percent of that assemblage was soda vessels, and no wine bottles were included. The Agnes Street assemblage was even more restricted in its functional diversity than the neighborhood store, which likely reflects the decline of community consumption spaces as well as household poverty. The clearest distinction between the assemblages is that the Agnes Street household had 31 preserving jars, which made it the second-most-common vessel form. Alongside the opportunistically consumed pork remains, the residents appear to have developed a range of market tactics that included household food preservation and tactical reappropriation in addition to conventional retail space.

A Campus and Its Neighbors

Like many urban campuses, IUPUI was torn over how it could effectively marry an existing neighborhood and a working university landscape, and the union of historical residences, campus architecture, and the logistical demands of a university was an unwieldy fit. In September 1966 the university and Indianapolis's Redevelopment Commission hired Victor Gruen Associates to develop a master plan for the campus landscape, adding to a series of broader city plans executed in the 1950s and many more to follow. Gruen was best known as a shopping mall designer who popularized regional shopping centers, designing the world's first enclosed shopping mall, the Southdale Center in Edina, Minnesota, in 1956 and Indianapolis's own Glendale Shopping Center in 1958. In 1953 Gruen likened malls to medieval markets and rural New England towns in which citizens gathered in a space that melded civic and retail dimensions, but he concluded that contemporary "Western civilization, especially the growth of big cities, tended to wipe out a lot of that" (Palmer 1953: 37, 39). Gruen's firm had designed retail centers and pedestrian-friendly urban landscapes in other communities using urban renewal funds and included a university campus plan as part of at least one renewal project prior to its master plan for IUPUI (for example, *New York Times* 1959, 1961). Yet like many emerging urban campuses the Indianapolis administrators had no especially clear sense of the ultimate scope their institution hoped to reach. When the university's intent to build became public, a rush of landlords was eager to sell, and in 1974 the university acknowledged that a "substantial backlog of property owners wanting to sell endangers the University's commitment to the immediate campus neighborhood" (IUPUI Master Plan 1974: 65). The initial 1958 plan of three buildings surrounded by neighbors quickly became hundreds of acres as a law school, administrative spaces, parking dilemmas, and a host of programs gradually emerged. Even today the university has developed another master campus plan that ironically makes many of the same suggestions made by a host of planners over more than 50 years.

A significant amount of resistance to university expansion was rooted in the perception that the university might grow unchecked for decades, a sentiment that persists even today. In the 1960s, for instance, there was some apprehension from residents of the exclusively black public housing Lockefield Gardens that opened in 1938 and sat alongside the medical center. Lockefield had itself displaced 383 homes in 1935 as the city's first urban renewal project, but these had made way for an exceptionally

Photograph (1971) of the new campus of IUPUI and the homes across Blake Street. Courtesy of IUPUI University Library Special Collections and Archives, Indianapolis.

well-appointed, exclusively African American community. In a 1973 university plan, the authors hoped to assuage concerns that the university's eyes were trained on Lockefield, underscoring that "THE COMMITTEE RECOMMENDS THAT THE UNI-VERSITY SHOULD ENCOURAGE THE MAINTENANCE OF LOCKEFIELD GARDENS AS A DESIRABLE HOUSING AREA FOR LOCAL CITIZENS AND REAFFIRM PUBLICLY THE UNI-VERSITY'S POSITION OF NOT ACQUIRING THAT PROPERTY" (IUPUI Goals and Objectives Committee 1973: 82). The university never acquired the complex, but in the late 1970s the residents were all expelled when the city closed the development. In 1983, 17 of the complex's original 24 buildings were razed.

Just as the twentieth-century city is an artifact of racist and classist policies, urban campuses are profoundly shaped by more than a half century of state mechanisms that aspired to reshape racial and political landscapes. IUPUI is perhaps typical of the institutions that struggle with practical needs like ever-more parking, declining and insufficient academic and office space, and an apparent desire to measure up to the models of a stereotypical college campus—and such problems extend well beyond the youthful urban campus to many well-established state universities. Like many institutions born in the second half of the twentieth century, IUPUI was crafted opportunistically. In terms of its spatial scale and ambitions, the institution has spent 40 years determining its role and in turn creating a space that satisfies those ambitions, and the process of acquiring these spaces has been somewhat haphazard and even today witnesses the university's growth into nonresidential neighborhoods north of campus. The degree to which displacement was intentional social engineering by university administrators and their civic government partners may be irrelevant, and apologists are inclined to point to the economic benefits of such universities to rationalize their social effects (for example, Cummings et al. 2005: 156–157). The mechanics of displacement as wholesale clearance or more gradual removals have quite comparable material and social effects, so efforts to rationalize such histories inevitably ring hollow or sound socially uninformed. Archaeology provides one mechanism to simply have public discussions on inequality and landscape transformation that are geared less toward confirming the university's guilt or exonerating urban renewal than they are intended to soberly confront the conditions that made the institution's very existence possible. The long-term effects of such discourse remain to be determined, but archaeology aspires to begin placing questions of heritage and privilege in public discussion.

References

Axel-Lute, M. 2008. Will Columbia Take Manhattanville? *Shelterforce* 22 March. Electronic document, http://www.shelterforce.org/article/print/213, accessed February 2, 2009.

Bird, D. 1968. 300 Protesting Columbia Students Barricade Office of College Dean. *New York Times,* 24 April, pp. 1, 30.

Connor, L. 1959a. Slums Blight 20 Pct. of City. *Indianapolis Star,* 17 August, pp. 1, 14.

———. 1959b Bad Sanitation, Water in Slums Take Heavy Toil of Infants. *Indianapolis Star,* 19 August, pp. 1, 3.

Cummings, S., M. Rosentraub, M. Domahidy, and S. Coffin 2005. University Involvement in Downtown Revitalization: Managing Political and Financial Risks. In *The University as Urban Developer: Case Studies and Analysis,* edited by D. C. Perry and W. Wiewel, pp. 147–174. New York: M. E. Sharpe, Armonk.

Hardy, C. 1989. Interview with Charles Hardy conducted by Philip Scarpino and Sheila Goodenough, 17 October. Unpublished manuscript on file, Indiana University-Purdue University, Indianapolis Archives, Indianapolis.

Hechinger, F. M. 1961. Campus vs. Slums: Urban Universities Join Battle for Neighborhood Renewal. *New York Times,* 1 October, p. E7.

Hirsch, A. R. 2000. Searching for a "Sound Negro Policy": A Racial Agenda for the Housing Acts of 1949 and 1954. *Housing Policy Debate* 11(2):393–441.

Indiana University Board of Trustees 1967. Minutes of the Board of Trustees, 22 September. Unpublished manuscript on file, Indiana University–Purdue University Indianapolis Archives, Indianapolis.

Indianapolis Redevelopment Commission 1959. Progress Report. Indianapolis Redevelopment Commission, Indianapolis, Indiana. Electronic document, http://images.indiana history.org/cdm4/document.php?CISOROOT=/dc018&CISOPTR=4344&REC=7, accessed April 7, 2009.

Indianapolis Star 1921a. Urge Plan for Hospital Park. 1 September, p. 5.

———. 1921b. May Preserve Landmark. 21 September, p. 8.

———. 1956. Medical Center to Build on Slum Cleared Acres. 4 October, pp. 1, 9.

IUPUI Goals and Objectives Committee 1973. Preliminary Report. Unpublished manuscript on file, Indiana University–Purdue University Indianapolis Archives, Indianapolis.

IUPUI 1974. IUPUI Master Plan. Unpublished manuscript on file, Indiana University–Purdue University Indianapolis Archives, Indianapolis.

King, E. 1875. *The Great South.* Hartford, Conn.: American Publishing Company.

Millones, P. 1968. Community Discontent and an Increase in Protests Sow the Seeds of Concern at Columbia University. *New York Times,* 3 March, p. 51.

New York Times 1949. Eisenhower Sees Columbia Growing. 9 October, p. 50.

———. 1959. Newark Unveils Renewal Plans. 13 September, p. 36.

———. 1961. Town Gets a Plan for Model Living. 19 February, p. 338.

Palmer, C. B. 1953. The Shopping Center Goes to the Shopper. 29 November, pp. SM-14–15, 37–42, 44.

Parsons, K. C. 1963. Universities and Cities: The Terms of the Truce between Them. *The Journal of Higher Education* 34(4):205–216.

Polk, R. L. 1960 *Polk's Indianapolis City Directory.* Indianapolis, Ind.: R.L. Polk and Company.

Proudfoot, M. J. 1954. Public Regulation of Urban Development in the United States. *Geographical Review* 44(3):415–419.

Ralph, J. 1896. *Dixie, or Southern Scenes and Sketches.* New York: Harper and Brothers.

Roberts, S. V. 1966. Columbia's Expansion to Uproot Area Residents. *New York Times,* 2 November, p. 47.

Rosenberg, S. A. 2008. *Corner Stores and Bottles: African-American Consumption in Indianapolis.* Unpublished master's thesis, Department of Anthropology, Ball State University, Muncie, Ind.

Schanberg, S. H. 1964. Columbia Named in Rights Inquiry. *New York Times,* 28 February, p. 15.

Taggart, C. J. 1994. Streetcars. In *The Encyclopedia of Indianapolis,* edited by D. J. Bodenhamer and R. G. Barrows, pp. 1305–1306. Bloomington: Indiana University Press.

Teaford, J. C. (2000). Urban Renewal and Its Aftermath. *Housing Policy Debate* 11(2):443–463.

Wehrwein, A. C. 1959. Chicago U. Spurs Renewal Project. *New York Times,* 1 November, p. 61.

Wood, C. 1996. Interview with Richard Pierce, 28 November. Indiana Historical Society. Electronic document, http://images.indianahistory.org/cdm4/document.php?CISOROOT=/dc018&CISOPTR=3680&REC=7, accessed January 27, 2009.

Yronwode, C. 2003. Hoodoo: African-American Magic. Electronic document, http://www .luckymojo.com/hoodoohistory.html, accessed February 2, 2009.

DOUGLAS ARMSTRONG

Excavating Inspiration

Archaeology at the Harriet Tubman Home, Auburn, New York

H arriet Tubman's service to others reached out to many quarters. She helped persons from her birthplace in Maryland to freedom, she nursed people back to health in South Carolina during the Civil War, she surrounded people with the security of freedom in Canada, and she lived, served, and inspired people in Auburn, New York, her place of residence from 1859 to her death in 1913. The heroic acts of Harriet Tubman, as an Underground Railroad conductor and leader within the abolition movement, have secured her an honored place in American history and more broadly for the world as a champion of freedom remembered with the iconic designation "Moses of Her People" or more informally and humbly as "Aunt Harriet" (Bradford 1897, 1993 [1886]). Tubman helped liberate more than 70 individuals during at least 12 trips escorting refugees from slavery out of the southern states, north, and into Canada. She was a Union soldier, a spy, and a nurse during the American Civil War (Larson 2003; Sernett 2007). In 1903 she founded and operated the Harriet Tubman Home for the Aged. However, details of her life and the multifaceted nature of her legacy after the Civil War have been obscured by time and social conditions.

Archaeology provides a lens through which to explore aspects of Harriet Tubman's life in Auburn/Fleming, New York. Archaeological investigations of Harriet Tubman's two farmsteads have helped renew interest in Harriet Tubman's life (Armstrong 2003a, 2003b; Clinton and Baker 2003; Larson 2003; Ryan and Armstrong 1999; Sernett 2007). The act of uncovering the archaeological sites and the material record of Harriet Tubman and her associates has encouraged a greater understanding of the importance of Tubman's properties in projecting the rich texture and humanistic value of her legacy.

The Tubman study involves two farmsteads. The first, a seven-acre farm, includes a standing house and barn and ruins of outbuildings and related features. This farm was acquired by Tubman in 1859 from United States senator William Seward, a strong advocate of abolition. This farmstead was Tubman's home and primary residence until her death in 1913. The property was then sold to settle her estate.

The second farmstead was a 25-acre parcel immediately north of Tubman's original farm. Tubman purchased this property in 1896 with the objective of opening a home for aging African Americans. She deeded this property over to the A.M.E. Zion Church, along with its mortgage, in 1903. The church and its not-for-profit subsidiary, the Harriet Tubman Home for the Aged, has held the property for more than 100 years. In 1990 the A.M.E. Zion Church purchased Tubman's original farmstead, so now the two properties, a total of 32 acres, have been united within the Harriet Tubman Home for the Aged.

Though held in trust by the A.M.E. Zion Church and opened to the public 15 years ago, much of the historical value of the property and its material components were lost, forgotten, misrepresented, or are unknown. Archaeology has helped demonstrate the ability of the property to serve as an interpretive tool. This change has been brought about through the combined efforts of its long-term caretaker the A.M.E. Zion Church, the National Park Service, and a group of interested scholars, descendants, and advocates, who are collectively bringing the detailed texture and richness of Harriet Tubman's legacy back to life (Armstrong 2003b; National Park Service 2008).

On my first visit to the property with a group of students visiting abolitionist sites in central New York in 1994, I was stunned by how little was known about Tubman or the property or Tubman's life in Auburn. On the wall there was a photograph of "John Brown Hall," named in honor of John Brown, whom Tubman considered to be the great martyr of the cause for abolition and freedom, yet the building was no longer visible on the landscape. The woods obscured the location of the building. I challenged the students to find the ruins. The stone-and-brick foundation walls of the ruin were located, and Rev. Paul Carter, manager of the property, was notified. Reverend Carter's excitement was inspirational, and soon we were exploring the ruins and exchanging ideas concerning the potential for future archaeological investigations of the site. This emotionally charged exchange on the ruins of John Brown Hall would turn into a formal cooperative agreement for archaeological research, which began in 1999.

Harriet Tubman's Material Legacy

The story of the Tubman House combines perseverance with a form of forced, society-driven neglect. As the nineteenth century came to a close, Tubman found herself called upon to take in aging African Americans and persons in need.[1] In fact, she had

---

1. At the time that Tubman established the home for the aged, there was another home in Auburn, The Home. The Home was originally created as a home for widows and orphans of the Civil War and did not formally exclude blacks, but by the end of the nineteenth century admission required a significant donation. Hence the cost of entry and maintenance at

chartered a home for the aged in her own home before purchasing the adjacent farmstead. Tubman's idea was to create a self-sufficient cooperative farm on which the goods and products of the farm were used to sustain its inmates and generate funds for its management (*Auburn Citizen* 1907; *Auburn Weekly Bulletin* 1906; *Syracuse Post Standard* 1914). Therefore, when the neighboring farmstead came up at auction, she bid until she was the owner and had to solicit support to cover the down payment and assume a personal mortgage on the balance.[2]

Tubman received a lump sum pension payment of about $500 in 1895, which helped with the purchase. The pension resulted from her petition for Civil War widow's benefits ($8) and nurse's pension ($12). An effort to gain a pension of $25 rather than the $20 that she received was ultimately turned down in 1899 (see Sernett 2007: 99). Tubman's farmstead produced potatoes, fruit (apples and pears), and grain, along with hogs and chickens. Occasionally, there was surplus milk and butter. It was also part of a network of brickworks that produced brick for residential and commercial use. Unfortunately, the type of mixed farming done on this relatively small farm was in the process of being usurped by larger-scale farming with more capital-intensive and, in theory, more productive farms best illustrated by the growing dairy farms in the region, as demonstrated by archaeological studies of the Porter Farm in Chenango County, New York (Rafferty 2000).

The combination of decreased viability for small, mixed-product farms and the cost of caring for elderly residents put a burden on an aging Harriet Tubman that more than once left her behind on the mortgage and on the verge of foreclosure. While Harriet worked the farm and later traveled to solicit funds for her home, her husband, Nelson Davis, worked in the brickyards, and her brother, John Stewart, worked as a teamster for D. M. Osborne & Co. Most of the major businesses and industries of Auburn in the late nineteenth and early twentieth century were owned by former advocates of abolition; hence, employment opportunities were available even if salaries and advancement opportunities were relatively limited.

In 1903 the A.M.E. Zion Church took over the 25-acre property by accepting a gift of the deed and assumed the mortgage. The board of trustees for the home intensified its efforts to raise funds, particularly from within the African American community, and The Harriet Tubman Home for the Aged finally formally opened in 1908, more than 12 years after Tubman purchased the land. In 1911 Tubman became an

The Home was beyond the means of most people of color in the Auburn area. It was founded in 1865 by a group of Presbyterian women of the Auburn Female Bible Society, and the board and sponsors included many families associated with abolition and women's rights issues, including succeeding generations of the Seward family.

2. In addition we have conducted excavations at a brick kiln and in 2008 began excavations of structural features associated with outbuildings adjacent to the surviving wood frame structure on the Home for the Aged property.

inmate of the home that she had founded. An article in the *New York Age* (1911) reported that Harriet Tubman "was taken to the home last Thursday ill and penniless." On March 10, 1913, Harriet Tubman died. Her funeral and the memorial service the following year, in which Booker T. Washington presided as orator, were well attended and widely published (for example, *Auburn Citizen* 1913a, 1913b, 1913c, 1913d, 1914; *Auburn Daily Advertiser* 1913; *New York Times* 1913; *Syracuse Post-Standard* 1913a, 1913b).

The operation of the home was a drain on the church's finances, but they kept their promise to keep the home operating and to care for all of those whom Tubman had taken in, which at its peak was eight to ten individuals. In 1918 the A.M.E. Zion Church paid off the mortgage and celebrated with a party in which the mortgage papers were burned. The home continued to care for those taken in but did not have the financial resources to take on new inmates. The home closed when the last inmate died in the 1920s.

The decline of the property corresponded with its discontinuance as a care facility and the ongoing financial strains on the church. At the same time, there was a general lessening of interest in Harriet Tubman and a shift in the social landscape that created a greater distance between what had once been established intersections and interactions between the black and white communities of Auburn. The wood frame house on the Harriet Tubman Home for the Aged property was vacant from the late 1920s. It had fallen into such disrepair that it and John Brown Hall were ordered to be demolished by the City of Auburn in 1944. A.M.E. Zion bishop William J. Walls organized an effort to save the structures but not soon enough for John Brown Hall, which was bulldozed by the city. Ultimately, funds were raised for the restoration of the wood frame farmhouse, which was rededicated on April 13, 1953. In the late 1920s through 1940s, the buildings on the home for the aged farmstead gradually fell into disrepair. John Brown Hall was declared unsafe and bulldozed by the City of Auburn in the late 1940s, and the wood frame house on the Harriet Tubman Home property was only a shell by 1947. Meanwhile, the owners of Tubman's personal farm modified the house and converted the grounds into a bus company. In essence the once-popular figure was gradually forgotten by all but a few. In this there is a close parallel with W. E. B. DuBois's Homestead in Massachusetts (Harlow and Diffley 2008; Muller 1994; Paynter et al. 1996). Aside from the fact that the State of New York Department of Education and Cayuga County each took action to recognize the property in 1932 with historical markers, for much of the rest of the twentieth century there was little interest in Tubman as a public figure and less interest in her residence or the home that she had created. Earl Conrad, Tubman's mid-twentieth-century biographer, documented this lack of interest, as he repeatedly failed to get the attention of publishers.[3] Finally, through sheer perseverance and the

---

3. Earl Conrad, a young writer and former teamster and Communist sympathizer, was a New York correspondent for the *Chicago Defender*. Conrad began researching his Tubman

finding of a likeminded soul in Carter Woodson, an African American who was also a publisher, Conrad's book of remembrance of Tubman was finally published in 1943 (Conrad 1943; Sernett 2007). Through the efforts of A.M.E. Zion bishop Wall, funds were raised to rebuild the white wood frame house on the Home for the Aged property in 1953, but only after the demolition of John Brown Hall in the late 1940s.

A reawakening in regard to the importance of Harriet Tubman and African American history more generally began in the 1960s with the social history movement, but until the end of the century much of what was written about Tubman was simply a rehashing of Bradford (1897, 1993 [1886]) and Conrad (1943) in literally dozens and dozens of children's books. As Milton Sernett (2007) points out, these books tended to describe Tubman in mythical proportions by overemphasizing the price on her head by slave hunters ($40,000) and the vast number of refugees she escorted to freedom (400 or more). It was not until a new crop of scholars began to take a close and critical look at the historic records and the archaeological sites that a more historically accurate and powerful picture of Tubman begin to emerge. Modern historical scholarship places more reasonable numbers of $200–$400 for her capture and 70–80 refugees brought to freedom (Larson 2003; Sernett 2007). They, along with the current archaeological investigations, provide an abundance of more definitively substantiated details of her life and contributions (Armstrong 2003b; National Park Service 2008).

Studies of Harriet Tubman are thus in the process of a physical and interpretive renewal and revival, and archaeological studies are a part of this resurgence. The Tubman properties are now listed as a National Landmark, and the Tubman sites will soon be recommended for designation as a national park, the first honoring an African American woman in the United States. The new national park will be operated as a joint effort by the Harriet Tubman Home, Inc., a not-for-profit established by the A.M.E. Zion Church and by the National Park Service. The objective is to do more than just restore the historic sites but to present and interpret the materials of her life and honor of the legacy of Tubman by utilizing the site and the data to assist, challenge, engage, and inspire.

Harriet Tubman in the Interplay of Race and Social Relations

Exploration of the site and of records relating to Tubman provide a basis for gaining a better understanding of the unique interplay of race and social relations revolving around Tubman and her farm and care facility in Auburn. Harriet Tubman was not without means but used what she had to serve others. She held a place of special

biography in 1938 and was met with fairly stiff resistance from publishers who were not interested in publishing a book on an "obscure" African American woman (see detailed discussion in Sernett 2007).

recognition in her community, be it sitting at the front of the audience dressed in flags at a gathering commemorating the centennial of Lincoln's birth or entertaining or caring for a bi-modal stream of visitors: one group who made their way to her farm on the outskirts of town to pay homage to her for her deeds; the other who came to her doorstep in need and at times desperation. She was a landowner, but she had many relying on her for support, which in her later years derived in part from rents, pensions, produce, and gifts. She always struggled to balance the need of paying off her mortgage with her desire to distribute whatever resources she had to those in need.

Certainly race, her lack of formal education and training, and, later in life, her position as a female head of household served as limiting factors financially. On the other hand, she was known to all as "Aunt Tubman," and the Auburn community regularly responded with monetary gifts and baskets of goods and supplies. In the late nineteenth century, long after most of her core abolitionist supporters had died, Tubman retained support and special status based on her contributions and ideals. Financial support for Tubman and her envisioned care facility came from both the African American community and Anglo American communities. Most specifically her efforts of establishing a home for the aged were assisted by leaders and congregants of the A.M.E. Zion Church. Tubman was a founding member of the Thompson Road A.M.E. Zion Church, and it was to this church that she turned in order to achieve her goals for the home for the aged. She turned her 25-acre farm over to the church, and finally in 1908, 12 years after chartering and maintaining a less formal home in her house, the Harriet Tubman Home was finally opened in a building called John Brown Hall.

Tubman was not shy about reaching out to anyone who might provide support, and she had strong and long-term supporters in the Anglo American communities of Auburn and Fleming (and central New York in general). Much of this support was tied to her special place in history and mutual bonds felt by people throughout the region. Individuals from Auburn's white community, like women's rights advocate Elizabeth Wright Osborne, befriended and provided a margin of material and financial support to Harriet. Elizabeth Wright Osborne and her husband, David, owned D. M. Osborne & Co. Elizabeth Wright Osborne frequently visited the Tubman household.[4] In one of her letters Elizabeth Wright Osborne describes bringing a Mrs.

4. Several members of the Osborne family had a long and supportive relationship with Tubman. Elizabeth Wright Osborne had Tubman for teas at her home and provided support to Tubman including sending workmen to Tubman's residence, building her a new cistern, and paying medical bills. The detailed manuscript records of the Osborne Family Papers, which are part of Syracuse University's Special Collections, provide an interesting sisterly relationship between the two women. Elizabeth's personal letters, often to others engaged in the late-nineteenth-century and early-twentieth-century women's movement, like

Walling to visit to pay homage to Tubman. Osborne tells how Mrs. Walling brought $2 for a book and then paid another 50 cents for a photograph (Osborne 1906: 1). Osborne's most telling words are in response to the visitor's inquiry about Tubman's financial condition. Osborne indicates that she assured Mrs. Walling that Tubman "had not anything but what people give her." Later in the letter she states: "she does not starve, but she lives very simple and cares for a great many people." Tubman told Osborne that she "wished she could paper her room over, so I suppose she wants me to do it for her. I don't know if I shall or not." Then Osborne goes on to provide a lengthy description that provides both details of Tubman's house and a special relationship and basis for ongoing support: "I fixed her house up last fall, so that it would be comfortable for the winter. I sent a carpenter, who stuck in shingles here and there, fitted the doors, had glass put in where it was out, and he charged me one hundred dollars, when he got through. He also put in a new cistern but did not put in the pipe to carry the water to the cistern, the pig, as I found out afterwards. I gave her a new stove; hers was in pieces, so she was quite comfortable off. I don't mean she shall want while she lives. She certainly has done enough in helping others and has earned the necessities of life, at any rate" (Osborne 1906: 2–3).

This account describes details of the conditions of life at Tubman's farmhouse in the early twentieth century. The information corresponds with the specifics of material findings from broken window glass (perhaps some of which were replaced by Osborne's workman), the replacement of a broken stove (some stove fragments were found at the site), and the replacement of the water cistern (a water cistern was discovered on the east side of the house). However, for this letter, it is the statement of responsibility for Tubman, a bond between Tubman and Osborne relating to a common calling to address social problems that is to me most striking.

In another letter dated February 14, 1911, Elizabeth Wright Osborne writes to her daughters. Amid discussion of a possible trip to the West Indies, Osborne describes being charged an exorbitant rate for hospital care for Harriet Tubman. Though upset about the cost ($8 per week for four weeks), Osborne indicates that she agreed to pay half of the hospital bill if the Town of Fleming agrees to pay the other half. She goes on to bemoan how much "poor folks are charged for health care" and ponders why providers charge "other than they figure I will pay." Osborne concludes her discussion of Tubman by saying, "Dear me, she is one of the people who are living beyond all possibility, it is such a pity. She has been so wonderful in all the days she was helpful" (Osborne 1906: 2).

Emily Howland (who was also a supporter of Tubman), are personal in nature and detailed in social content and commentary. They also project the duality of respect interlaced with condescension and use of pejorative terms that probably relate to the economic, social, and ethnic gulf that existed between these two friends. (An example of correspondence relating to Tubman can be found in Osborne 1906).

The Value of Archaeology: Findings at Harriet Tubman's Brick Residence

Archaeological studies on the property began in 1998. Initial efforts were focused on John Brown Hall, and the success of this study demonstrated the value of archaeological reconnaissance and the potential of heritage-based interpretation for the site (Ryan and Armstrong 1999). This project included public dig days involving more than 300 people from local schools and the Auburn community in 1999 and 2000. The timing of the project also allowed the more than 600 people coming to the annual Tubman Pilgrimage over the Memorial Day weekend to see the see active excavations of John Brown Hall. The timing was important because the A.M.E. Zion Church was in the process of trying to find a way to better utilize the property and fulfill what they felt to be their dual mission to make the site relevant to the African American community and to protect the historic legacy of Harriet Tubman. The realization that the John Brown Hall site contained valuable material remains with which to illuminate the legacy of Harriet Tubman's Home for the Aged, combined with a national movement calling for the reexamination of the Underground Railroad and the black experience in New York, encouraged the A.M.E. Zion Church to renew their efforts to learn more about their property and the material record of Tubman's legacy. It also caused the A.M.E. Zion board to realize the value of the historical components on their property, both standing and in ruins.

The product of our archaeological investigations included not only the positive identification of spaces and places associated with the life of Harriet Tubman but a collection of definitive material remains that project "the intimate and unheralded details of day to day life" (Beaudry 1996: 496). There is a growing body of literature dealing with the archaeological investigation of late-nineteenth-century farms and farmsteads (Groover 2008; Hart and Fisher 2000). This research can be viewed through several lenses, including the cultural landscape (Adams 1990; Armstrong 2003b), the dynamics of the material cultural associated with the household and housework (Barile and Brandon 2004), structures and the *habitus* that look within and beyond the local site (Bourdieu 1977), and the material residue of the created memory associated with sites relating to popular figures or events (Shackel 2000). The Tubman site is of particular interest in relation to her role as a leader in the African American community and her role as a woman who was also a head of household from the mid–nineteenth century (Beaudry 2004; Mullins 1999; Stone and McKee 1998; Suzanne Spencer-Wood 2004). The Tubman site is a reminder that it is necessary "to avoid adopting a single or monolithic definition of 'the household,'" since there are "so many different sorts of domestic arrangements that there is simply not a one size fits all definition that can be of use" (Beaudry 2004: 255).

Clark Pierce, who leased land and operated a brickyard on the property, originally built John Brown Hall as a residence and perhaps a workers' barracks in the

1870s (Auburn City Directory 1874, 1875; Ryan and Armstrong 1999). The nine-room building served as a dormitory and infirmary. Archaeological investigation confirmed the presence of seven rooms including a kitchen and storeroom on the ground floor, leaving the probability that the upper floor was divided into two rooms for male and female inmates.

The vast majority of materials encountered relate to habitation just before and after the turn of the twentieth century. Among the most prevalent type of glass was window glass and pharmaceutical bottles. The window glass is consistent with the photographic record, which documents large six-over-six windows consistent with mid-nineteenth-century construction. The prevalence of pharmaceutical bottles is consistent with the use of the property for the care of the elderly. Canning jars, which were also found in relatively high frequency, reflect the practice of putting up farm fruits and produce and, quite possibly, given the diversity of the types of jars, reflect a pattern of gifting of canned foods to the home. The extremely low volume of alcohol-related bottles, unusual for a site of this time period, probably reflected the temperance philosophy of Harriet Tubman and the A.M.E. Zion Church. The majority of the ceramics found at the John Brown Hall site were flatware such as plates and tea ware, and fewer bowls or other hollowware. The emphasis on plates and tea ware may have been a reflection of the time period of the Tubman Home, the late nineteenth to early twentieth centuries. The large amount of ceramic stoneware storage vessels corresponds with their glass storage jar counterparts and attests to harvesting and preservation practices of homegrown foods by the residents of the home.

Small finds, such as metal pillboxes, in concert with artifact types such as the large number of pharmaceutical bottles, provide more evidence of health-related material use. A recovered heart-shaped pillbox has been taken on by the Harriet Tubman Home as a symbol of the home's intent and Tubman's care for others. The archaeological record demonstrates that health and hygiene were an important part of the daily life of those who resided at the home. Among the items found were toothbrushes, toothpaste tubes, and a metal bedpan. A more complete explanation of the archaeological record at this site can be found in Ryan and Armstrong (1999).

Following the excavations of John Brown Hall, we joined with preservation architects and landscape architects from Crawford and Stearns and conducted a survey of the entire property (Armstrong 2003a, 2003b). While the architects generated detailed analysis and treatment plans for Harriet Tubman's farmhouse, barn, and a wood-frame structure associated with the home for the aged, we walked the entire site and documented structures, ruins, and features and carried out remote sensing in three key areas in order to define subsurface remains and to set and communicate priorities for investigation and preservation (Armstrong 2003a, 2003b). Based on this survey and the fact that Tubman's brick residence was slated for restoration, we determined that Harriet Tubman's farmstead, including her house, yard, barns, and outbuildings, was in need of immediate investigation.[5]

Since 2002 Tubman's farmstead has been the focus of our excavations and research activities.[6] Almost immediately, we identified well-stratified deposits that shed significant light on the history of the property. A definitive layer of burned wood ash, combined with burned artifacts, indicated the presence of a house fire circa 1880–1882, later confirmed through a newspaper account as occurring on February 10, 1880 (*Auburn News and Bulletin* 1880).[7] Excavation also showed that a field-stone foundation was capped off with a new cut-stone foundation upon which the current brick residence was constructed. Evidence of this construction sequence was further demonstrated by a builder's trench with broken bricks at its base. Having once identified this pattern, we were able to recover the same pattern of deposits along the north side of the house by the front door (the front door is actually on the side of the house; we worked under a porch built in the 1920s) and west side of the house. The definitive nature of a well-stratified site with an abundance of material remains at Tubman's residence, linked to the period leading up to a house fire (1859–1880), the period of the fire and reconstruction (1880–1882), and the era following the construction of her brick house (1883–1913) provide an unusually rich source of data for interpretation.[8]

5. While hundreds of thousands of dollars have been generated for the restoration of this property, Syracuse University has maintained a strategy of pro bono contribution. The archaeological effort has been assisted by a grant from Syracuse University's chancellor, and the public interpretation component has been assisted by funds from the New York State Department of Parks and Historic Preservation.

6. In addition we have conducted excavations at a brick kiln and in 2008 began excavations of structural features associated with outbuildings adjacent to the surviving wood frame structure on the Home for the Aged property.

7. Tax and census records show a shift from wood frame to brick construction and the tax records indicate a doubling of property value associated with the new construction in the 1883 tax lists, confirming the completion of the new house by the beginning of 1883 (Cayuga County Tax records 1860–1890; United States Census 1890).

8. While not as clearly demarcated as the definitive ash layers of the fire and building episodes at the site, the period following the sale of the property by Tubman's estate to the Norris family can be tied to episodes of remodeling and further deposition which constitute the upper 10 to 20 centimeters of deposits. These more recent deposits cap the older remains. However, several Norris-era intrusions were encountered in areas associated with the construction of a septic tank, underground gas tank for their bus company, and finally municipal gas, water, and sewer systems that were added between the 1930s and 1960s.

The builder's trench associated with the reconstruction of the foundation and construction of the brick house contained not only well-preserved stratified remains but an amazing deposit of personal artifacts dating to the fire that had been back-filled into the builder's trench when the house was completed (probably 1882). This cache of artifacts includes a collection of pottery, glassware, and personal items from Tubman's household, which appears to have been the contents of Tubman's medicine cabinet. Many of the items show evidence of burning, and all are probably in this builder's trench because they were broken during the fire. Among the materials are an array of stemware including a fluted flower bud vase and many stemware dessert and drinking vessels. The most common ceramics present were oval ironstone plates made prior to 1880 by Onondaga Pottery (now Syracuse China). The materials dating to the 1880 fire are primarily plain, white ironstone, though a range of pottery is present. Dozens of buttons, many burned, provide indices of clothing. The assemblage includes everything from musical instruments to fragments of toys such as porcelain dolls and teacups. Material dating to the early-twentieth-century including coffee or tea ware made by L. Straus and Sons (Macy's, New York) with a teal blue "Imperial Design," supplemented by a similar floral design of the same color (maker unknown), shards from more than 10 cups and 7 saucers were found at seven locations across the site. This suggests that a rather substantial set was acquired, probably by gift to the Harriet Tubman home by an affluent donor or directly from the company. An Ontario Canadian Bank of Toronto trade token dated 1859 was found just outside Tubman's door. Perhaps this is by coincidence but not only does this coincide with the return of Tubman and her parents from Saint Catherine, Canada, but it is also has the same date as her purchase of the property from William Seward. Finally, in addition to excavated materials, a brace plate was found behind a foot rail in the house. The plate reads "Harriet Tubman Davis." This type of plate was used to print calling cards to communicate with friends and neighbors in response to invitations.

Archaeological excavations have demonstrated the value of the archaeological resources at the Harriet Tubman Home and will be of significance to public interpretation of the sites. Harriet Tubman is well known for her heroic acts in liberating African Americans from slavery and fighting for emancipation. She has been described as "America's Joan of Arc" and "the Moses of her people." Yet the full story of her life is little known, and her continued, lifelong commitment to social causes and reform has not found its way into the pages of history—*until now*—and archaeology is contributing significantly to this renewed interest and depth of knowledge regarding Harriet Tubman's life and legacy.

References

Adams, W. H. 1990. Landscape Archaeology, Landscape History, and the American Farmstead. *Historical Archaeology* 24(4):92–101.

Armstrong, D. V. 2003a. Patterns in the Snow. *Dig* 5(1):28–30.

———. 2003b. Preliminary Archaeological Survey and Reconnaissance at the Harriet Tubman Home, Auburn and Fleming, New York. Syracuse University Archaeological Research Center, Anthropology Department, Maxwell School, Syracuse University, N.Y.

Auburn Citizen 1907. Annual Meeting of the Harriet Tubman Home and School. 8 June.

———. 1913a. Harriet Tubman is Dead. 11 March.

———. 1913b. At Church of Zion: Body of Harriet Tubman Davis Will Lie in State. 12 March.

———. 1913c. To Aunt Harriet: Hundreds Pay Tribute at Funeral Services. 13 March.

———. 1913d. A Race of Harriets Would Secure the Future of the Negro, Says Bishop Blackwell. 14 March.

———. 1914. Fitting Memorial of Harriet Tubman Davis Is Appropriately Unveiled: Booker T. Washington Was the Orator. 13 June.

Auburn Daily Advertiser 1913. Goodbye: Death of Aunt Harriet. 11 March.

Auburn City Directory, 1874–1890. Auburn, N.Y.

Auburn News and Bulletin 1880. Charlott [sic] Tubman Burned Out. 9 February.

Auburn Weekly Bulletin 1906. The Tubman Home: Plans for More Effective Work for Colored People in a Businesslike Manner. Affairs Will Henceforth Be Run—Much Has Already Been Accomplished. 12 September.

Barile, K. S., and J. C. Brandon (editors) 2004. *Household Chores and Household Choices: Theorizing the Domestic Sphere in Historical Archaeology.* Tuscaloosa: University of Alabama Press.

Beaudry, M. C. 2004. Doing the Housework: New Approaches to the Archaeology of the Household. In *Household Chores and Household Choices: Theorizing the Domestic Sphere in Historical Archaeology,* edited by K. S. Barile and J. C. Brandon, pp. 254–262. Tuscaloosa: University of Alabama Press.

———. 1996. Reinventing Historical Archaeology. In *Historical Archaeology and the Study of Material Culture,* edited by L. A. DeCunzo and B. L. Herman, pp. 473–497. Winterthur, Del.: Henry Francis du Pont Winterthur Museum.

Bourdieu, P. 1977. Structures and the Habitus. In *Outline of a Theory of Practice,* translated by R. Nice, pp. 72–95. Cambridge: Cambridge University Press.

Bradford, S. 1993 [1886]. *Harriet Tubman: The Moses of Her People.* Bedford, Mass.: Applewood Books.

———. 1897. *Harriet Tubman: Moses of Her People.* New York: Corinth Books.

Cayuga County Tax Records 1855–1890. Cayuga County Tax Records, Town of Fleming, New York. Cayuga County Clerk's Office, Auburn, N.Y.

Clinton, C., and D. Baker (editors) 2003. *Harriet Tubman: The Road to Freedom.* New York: Little Brown and Company.

Conrad, E. 1943. *Harriet Tubman.* Washington D.C.: Associated Publishers.

Harlow, E., and J. Diffley 2008. W. E. B. DuBois Boyhood Homesite. University of Massachusetts, Amherst, Special Collections and University Archives. Electronic document, http://www.library.umass.edu/spcoll/duboishome/duboishouse.htm, accessed June 11, 2009.

Hart, J. P., and C. L. Fisher (editors) 2000 *Nineteenth- and Early Twentieth-Century Domestics Sites Archaeology in New York State*. New York State Museum Bulletin No 495. Albany, N.Y.: University of the State of New York, New York State Education Department.

Groover, M. D. 2008. *The Archaeology of North American Farmsteads*. Gainesville: University Press of Florida.

Larson, K. C. 2003. *Bound for the Promised Land: Harriet Tubman Portrait of an American Hero*. New York: Ballantine Books.

Mullens, P. R. 1999. *Race and Affluence: An Archaeology of African American Consumer Choice*. New York: Kluwer Academic/Plenum Publications.

Muller, N. L. 1994. The House of the Black Burghardts: An Investigation of Race, Gender, and Class at the W. E. B. DuBois Boyhood Homesite. In *Those of Little Note: Gender, Race and Class in Historical Archaeology*, edited by E. Scott, pp. 81–94. Tucson: University of Arizona Press.

National Park Service 2008. Harriet Tubman Special Resource Study: Environmental Assessment. National Park Service, Northeastern Region, Boston.

New York Age 1911. Untitled. 8 June.

New York Times 1913. Harriet Tubman Davis. 14 March.

Osborne Papers 1906. Letter EWO to HOS, Box 60, June 15, 1906. Osborne Papers, Special Collections, Syracuse University Byrd Library. Syracuse, N.Y.

Osborne Papers 1906. Letter EWO to my daughters, Box 87, February 14, 1911. Osborne Papers, Special Collections Syracuse University Byrd Library, Syracuse, New York.

Paynter, R., S. Hautaniemi, and N. Muller 1996. The Landscapes of the W. E. B. DuBois Boyhood Homesite: An Agenda for an Archaeology of the Color Line. In *Race*, edited by S. Gregory and R. Sanjek, pp. 285–318. New Brunswick, N.J.: Rutgers University Press.

Rafferty, S. M. 2000. A Farmhouse View: The Porter Site. In *Nineteenth- and Early Twentieth-Century Domestics Sites Archaeology in New York State*, edited by J. P. Hart and C. L. Fisher, pp. 125–147. New York State Museum Bulletin No. 495. University of the State of New York, New York State Education Department, Albany, N.Y.

Ryan, B. C., and D. V. Armstrong 2001. *Archaeology of John Brown Hall, Harriet Tubman Home, Auburn, New York*. Syracuse University Archaeological Research Center Report, Syracuse University.

Sernett, M. 2007. *Harriet Tubman: Myth, Memory, and History*. Durham N.C.: Duke University Press.

Shackel, P. 2000. *Archaeology and Created Memory: A Public History in a National Park*. Contributions to Global Historical Archaeology. New York: Kluwer Academic/Plenum Publishers.

Spencer-Wood, S. 2004. What Difference Does Feminist Theory Make in Researching Households?: A Commentary. In *Household Chores and Household Choices: Theorizing the Domestic Sphere in Historical Archaeology*, edited by K. S. Barile and J. C. Brandon, pp. 235–253. Tuscaloosa: University of Alabama Press.

Stone, L., and N. P. McKee 1998. *Gender and Culture in America*. Upper Saddle River, N.J.: Prentice Hall.

Syracuse Post-Standard 1913a. Harriet Tubman Davis, 98, Dead after a Brief Illness. 11 March.

————. 1913b. Mrs. Harriet Tubman Davis Laid to Rest in Auburn. 14 March.

————. 1914. Tubman Home Managers Make Appeal for Aid. 23 October.

Toulouse, J. H. 1971. *Bottle Makers and Their Marks.* Caldwell, N.J.: Blackbourn Press.

United States Census Bureau 1890. United States Census Records. Cayuga County Clerk's Office, Auburn, N.Y.

THERESA A. SINGLETON

Epilogue

Reflections on Archaeologies of Postemancipation
from a Student of Slavery

It is indeed exciting to see this collection of essays that focus on African American life after emancipation. Although studies of postemancipation sites (Atkins 1985; Geismer 1982) were among some of the earliest African American sites investigated, the focus on ethnicity, poverty, or social inequalities overshadowed pointed analyses of postemancipation developments in African American life as distinct from those occurring during the time of slavery (this includes not only slave sites but free black, slave runaway, and other black-occupied sites). The predominant focus of slavery in the archaeology of the African diaspora has in many ways set the research agenda and, perhaps, our understanding of life after slavery. Mainstream society often frames present-day race relations in the United States as developing from slavery rather than the aftermath of slavery. An example that illustrates this point was captured in an interview with Barrack Obama, after the election but before his inauguration, when a journalist asked him how he feels about living in the White House— an edifice built by slaves. Obama responded by saying that we do not have to go back to slavery to understand the oppression of black people in this country.[1]

Obama's statement highlights an important and recurrent theme of each chapter in this collection—the forgetting and silencing of the recent African American past. Archaeologists, historical preservationists, and cultural resource managers reinforce this silencing when they dismiss late-nineteenth- and twentieth-century African American sites as too recent, too ephemeral, or not worthy of archaeological documentation and investigation. This volume demonstrates that such characterizations are not only misguided but overlook the potential contributions postemancipation research brings to archaeological perspectives of the African diaspora as a whole. These studies combine discussions of archaeological findings with examinations of archaeological *praxis*, reminding us to be self-critical of our own intentions and goals

---

1. I am paraphrasing this exchange, which I heard on National Public Radio shortly after the presidential election in 2008.

(Babiarz, "White Privilege and Silencing"), to reexamine the sociopolitical context within which scholarly knowledge (including translations) is produced (Ferguson, "Gottesacker"), and to recognize that racism continues to play a significant role in present-day efforts to preserve and memorialize the African American past (Matthews and Larsen, "Black History as Property").

What is particularly refreshing about these essays is that postemancipation is not simply seen as the sequel to slavery. Rather, the authors conceptualize postemancipation life by identifying issues pertinent to its investigation. In doing so they are developing new directions and themes for this research that, on one hand, complement slavery studies but, on the other hand, elucidate the distinctive character of postemancipation life within diverse settings. I briefly comment on a few of these themes below organized around the following topics: Perceptions of Freedom, Afterlives of Plantations, Archaeologies of Jim Crow, and Civil Rights Era and Beyond.

Perceptions of Freedom

According to the *Merriam-Webster on-line Dictionary,* the term "emancipation" means freedom from bondage or control. While legally free from bondage, African Americans found their lives and livelihoods subjected to the control of former slaveholders, military officers, government agents, or other paternalists constraining their access to freedom. African American pursuit of the benefits deriving from emancipation was a never-ending quest. Agbe-Davies ("Reaching for Freedom") examines the meanings of freedom among second- and third-generation African Americans born after emancipation who migrated to Chicago from the Deep South (Mississippi, Louisiana, or Alabama) in search of their freedoms. These Chicago transplants equated freedom with opportunities, equality, privileges, and living in peace, among many other advantages. Her study shows that archaeologists should not presume for their archaeological subjects how they perceived freedom or what were the material manifestations of their freedom. Freedom, like any abstraction, is contingent upon the context and needs to be defined and analyzed, not assumed.

Agbe-Davies's study of freedom has important implications for slavery studies because archaeologists often interpret enslaved laborers' independent production or consumption of particular items as evidence that slaveholders bestowed limited amounts of autonomy on enslaved people. The association of freedom with particular artifacts, however, may well be misleading. One only need to consider the very sparse deposits of artifacts recovered from slave runaway sites that served as temporary refuges from slavery (see, for example, La Rosa Corzo 2005). The occupants of these sites risked everything to obtain only a fleeting prospect of freedom. In a similar vein, postemancipation so-called "squatter" sites (see Steen, "From Slave to Citizen"; Wilkie and Farnsworth, "Living Not So Quietly") are also examples of this quest for freedom that supports John Dewey's notion that a free person would rather take his/her chances in an open world than a guaranteed one in a closed world (see Agbe-Davis, "Reaching for Freedom"). The materiality of freedom varies from setting to setting and site to site. Understanding its complexity and nuances poses significant challenges to archaeological inquiry.

Afterlives of Plantations

Slave plantations usually contain occupational deposits dating after emancipation. These occupations vary considerably from the reoccupation of slave quarters and other outbuildings visible in only a few postemancipation artifacts to substantial artifact deposits, reordering of slave quarters (Brown and Cooper 1990), or relocation of living spaces (Orser and Nekola 1985) to form tenant farmer or wage-labor operations. The ephemeral quality of many postemancipation occupations on plantations is a common characteristic (Palmer, "Archaeology of Jim Crow"; Wilkie and Farnsworth, "Living Not So Quietly"). In some cases these ephemeral deposits contribute to documenting the occupational histories of former plantations that deed searches often fail to provide.

Many years ago I located and excavated two undocumented structures consisting only of crudely made chimney hearths at the site of an antebellum cotton plantation on the Georgia coast. An 1867 coin found at the base of one of the hearths established a postemancipation construction date (Singleton 1985). I was particularly struck by the ephemeral quality of the site compared to the substantial remains of antebellum slave quarters located on surrounding plantations. The postemancipation date, along with correspondence suggesting that newly emancipated African Americans were forming their own unauthorized settlements (squatting) on plantations in the area, encouraged me to interpret the site as a temporary settlement of newly emancipated African Americans. I believed then, as I do now, that the site provided insights into the transitory nature of African American life during the early days of emancipation.

Laurie Wilkie and Paul Farnsworth's ("Living Not So Quietly") study of a twentieth-century Bahamian household archaeologically documents a household undocumented in deed and tax records. Distinct differences, they observe, in the use of domestic space between the earlier slave occupation and the later postemancipation occupation is a beginning effort to bridge the gap in understanding everyday life during the period beginning after emancipation and extending to the present day in the Bahamas.

Archaeologies of Jim Crow

Jim Crow—the era of legalized racial segregation and the second-class citizenry of African Americans—emerged after the end of Reconstruction in 1877 and officially ended with the landmark Supreme Court case of *Brown vs. the Board of Education* in 1954, which reversed the separate-but-equal doctrine of *Plessey vs. Ferguson* established in 1896 (Chafe et al. 2001: xxvi-xviii). Jim Crow, however, was more than a legal decree but was a social environment. My use of the term refers to social practices resulting in racial discrimination, segregation, and other efforts to subordinate African Americans during the late nineteenth and twentieth centuries. In this sense, Jim Crow extended well beyond the borders of the southern United States (Dixon, "Place of Recreation"; Fennell, "Examining Structural Racism") and persisted long after 1954, giving rise to the 1960s civil rights movement. Even today the legacy of Jim Crow is visible throughout the American landscape in racially segregated cities, rural communities, neighborhoods, schools, and many other institutions. Some of the best scholarship in postemancipation archaeology has focused on the Jim Crow era (Mullins 1999; Orser 1988; Wilkie 2000).

The occupational histories of the vast majority of the sites studied in this volume include the Jim Crow era, although only a few chapters specifically address issues pertaining to Jim Crow such as structural racism (Fennell, "Examining Structural Racism"; Palus, "Infrastructure"), blatant inequalities (Palmer, "Archaeology of Jim Crow"), or segregation (Ferguson, *"Gottesacker"*). Other studies focus on the institutions African Americans established during the Jim Crow era (Armstrong, "Excavating Inspiration"). Kelly Dixon's ("Place of Recreation") study of the Boston saloon in Virginia City, Nevada, technically predates Jim Crow but provides a rare glimpse into a black-owned recreational business that catered to an African American clientele. As Dixon insightfully observes, William Brown, the owner of the Boston saloon, would have been denied the opportunity to own and operate a drinking establishment in his native Boston, Massachusetts, because of Boston's discriminatory practices concerning the ownership of drinking houses. Perhaps Brown named the saloon Boston to critique the city's discrimination. Her investigation dispelled racist descriptions suggesting the saloon was a low-class drinking house. When compared with other excavated saloons in Virginia City, the Boston saloon site yielded more upscale decorative items, furnishings, glass, and tableware than some of the other saloons.

The archaeology of Jim Crow holds a great promise for explicating everyday life and cultural practices of the era. Historians of Jim Crow now rely heavily upon oral histories to gain access to the experiences and perspectives of people who lived during Jim Crow as they came to realize that traditional written sources of this era produced static historiographies of oppression rather than ones that explored African American creativity (Chafe et al. 2001: xxvii-xxviii). Archaeological studies of Jim Crow, on the other hand, yield abundant evidence on African American creativity and the lives of ordinary people (Armstrong, "Excavating Inspiration"; Brown, "BaKongo Cosmograms"; Palmer, "Archaeology of Jim Crow"). Analysis of how Jim Crow impacted everyday life or cultural practices is often lacking, however, in some of the archaeological ethnographies of the era. To interpret everyday life without any regard for the social context under which these lives were lived is comparable to the ethnographies written on indigenous peoples during European colonialism that ignored the structural changes colonialism wrought on those communities. At the same time, archaeologists need not follow the flawed path of historians producing archaeological ethnographies of oppression. Archaeological studies of the Jim Crow—or any—era should aim for a balanced approach incorporating both perspectives.

Civil Rights Era and Beyond

Paul Mullins and Lewis Jones's ("Race, Displacement") study of an African American neighborhood lost to urban renewal examines the tremendous potential of undertaking archaeological research on African American sites dating after the 1950s. Urban renewal, the post–World War II public effort to rid cities of slums and rehabilitate them, displaced large numbers of African Americans. In Chicago, where urban renewal was dubbed "Negro removal," old neighborhoods disappeared, new ones faced rising racial pressures, and segregation became public policy (Hirsh 2005). Urban-based universities greatly benefited from these programs, expanding their campuses and completely changing the cultural landscape with little regard for the communities affected by these changes. The use of the university campus as both research site and site for the public discourse of African American displacement is bold and brilliant. It also demonstrates the kinds of innovative scholarship archaeological study of the recent past offers.

In the 1990s a major issue confronting archaeologists undertaking research on the African diaspora was how to develop public engagement with African American communities (for example, McDavid and Babson 1997). For the contributors of this volume, this is a nonissue because all or most of them have engaged with descendant communities and other stakeholders in pursuing their research. An issue still in need of examination concerns the question of how archaeologists develop anti-racist positions in their public engagement. Jennifer Babiarz ("White Privilege and Silencing") and Christopher Matthews and Eric Larsen ("Black History as Property") approach this thorny question from two different perspectives. Babiarz points directly to the need for white archaeologists to acknowledge white privilege and reposition themselves, noting that collaboration with African American communities will never work unless there is an understanding on the part of white archaeologists about their own white privilege. Matthews and Larsen direct their criticism to racist practices used in developing two historic sites, one in Alexandria, Virginia, the other in Jamaica, New York. In both cases, the sites were memorialized erasing documented, but unofficial, memories associated with these sites. Their critique reminds us silencing of the past is an active, ongoing process requiring our close scrutiny.

This volume demonstrates along with other publications (Mullins 1999; Leone et al. 2005) that archaeology of postemancipation is a well-established part of the archaeology of the African diaspora. This scholarship no longer needs to look toward slavery studies for its direction, nor should the end of slavery continue to define it. Postemancipation is an appropriate term for the first twenty years following emancipation, but should it continue to be used to define the entire 145 years following the end of slavery in the United States? I envision future volumes will focus on the archaeologies of particular themes or particular time periods within the 145-year period since emancipation. I look forward to seeing what the future has in store for this growing area of archaeological research.

References

Atkins, W. 1985. Material Culture and Expressions of Group Identity in Sandy Ground, New York. *American Archaeology* 5:209–218.

Brown, K. L., and D. Cooper 1990. Structural Continuity in an African-American Slave and Tenant Community. *Historical Archaeology* 24(4):7–19.

Chafe, W. H., R. Gavins, and R. Korstad (editors) 2001. *Remembering Jim Crow: African Americans Tell about Life in the Segregated South.* New York: New Press.

Geismar, J. H. 1982. *The Archaeology of Social Disintegration in Skunk Hollow: A Nineteenth-Century Rural Black Community.* New York: Academic Press.

Hirsch, A. 2005. Urban Renewal. In *The Electronic Encyclopedia of Chicago,* edited by J. L. Reiff, D. Keeting, and J. R. Grossman. Chicago: Chicago Historical Society. Electronic document, http://www.encyclopedia.chicagohistory.org/pages/1295.html, accessed April 2, 2010.

La Rosa Corzo, G. 2005. Subsistence of Cimarrones: An Archaeological Study. In *Dialogues in Cuban Archaeology,* edited by L. A. Curet, S. L. Dawdy, and G. La Rossa Corzo, pp. 163–180. Tuscaloosa: University Press of Alabama.

Leone, M. P., C. LaRoche, and J. J. Babiarz 2005. The Archaeology of Black Americans in Recent Times. *Annual Review of Anthropology* 34:575–598.

McDavid, C., and D. W. Babson (editors) 1997. Thematic issue: In the Realm of Politics: Prospects for Public Participation in African-American and Plantation Archaeology. *Historical Archaeology* 31(3).

Mullins, P. R. 1999. *Race and Affluence: An Archaeology of African America and Consumer Culture.* New York: Kluwer Academic/Plenum Publishers.

Orser, C.E., Jr. 1988. *The Material Basis of the Postbellum Tenant Plantation: Historical Archaeology in the South Carolina Piedmont.* Athens: University of Georgia Press.

Orser, C.E., Jr., and A. M. Nekola 1985. Plantation Settlement from Slavery Tenancy: An Example from a Piedmont Plantation in South Carolina. In *The Archaeology of Slavery and Plantation Life,* edited by T. A. Singleton, pp. 67–94. Orlando, Fla.: Academic Press.

Singleton, T. A. (editor).1985. Archaeological Implications for Changing Labor Conditions. In *The Archaeology of Slavery and Plantation Life,* pp. 291–304. Orlando, Fla.: Academic Press.

Wilkie, L. A. 2000. *Creating Freedom: Material Culture and African American Identity at Oakley Plantation, 1840–1950.* Baton Rouge: Louisiana State University Press.

CONTRIBUTORS

Anna S. Agbe-Davies is an assistant professor in the Department of Anthropology at the University of North Carolina at Chapel Hill. She received her Ph.D. from the University of Pennsylvania. Agbe-Davies is the coeditor of *Social Archaeologies of Trade and Exchange: Exploring Relationships among People, Places, and Things.*

Douglas Armstrong is a professor in the Department of Anthropology at Syracuse University. He received his Ph.D. from the University of California, Los Angeles. Armstrong is the author of *Creole Transformation from Slavery to Freedom: Historical Archaeology of the East End Community, St. John, Virgin Islands.*

Jennifer J. Babiarz is a Ph.D. candidate in the Department of Anthropology at the University of Texas at Austin and is an associate director of Archaeology in ihe Community. She received her B.A. from the University of Massachusetts Amherst and her master's in applied anthropology from the University of Maryland at College Park.

Jodi A. Barnes is the staff archaeologist at the South Carolina Department of Archives and History in Columbia, South Carolina. She received her Ph.D. in anthropology from American University in Washington, D.C. Barnes is the coeditor of *Managing Archaeological Resources: Global Context, National Programs, Local Action.*

Kenneth L. Brown is an assistant professor in the Department of Anthropology at the University of Houston. He received his Ph.D. in anthropology from Pennsylvania State University. Brown is the co-author of "Structural Continuity in an African-American Slave and Tenant Community," published in *Historical Archaeology.*

Charles R. Cobb is the director of the South Carolina Institute of Archaeology and Anthropology and a professor in the Department of Anthropology at the University of South Carolina, Columbia. He received his Ph.D. from Southern Illinois University Carbondale. Cobb is the author of *From Quarry to Cornfield: The Political Economy of Mississippian Hoe Production.*

James M. Davidson is an assistant professor in the Department of Anthropology at the University of Florida in Gainesville. He received his Ph.D. from the University of Texas at Austin. Davidson is the author of "Rituals Captured in Context and Time: Charm Use in North Dallas Freedman's Town (1869–1907), Dallas, Texas," published in the journal *Historical Archaeology.*

Kelly J. Dixon is an associate professor in the Department of Anthropology at the University of Montana in Missoula. She received her Ph.D. from the University of Nevada. Dixon is the author of *Boomtown Saloons: Archaeology and History in Virginia City.*

Paul Farnsworth is a project director for William Self Associates and a research affiliate of the Archaeological Research Facility at the University of California, Berkeley. Farnsworth is the co-author of *Sampling Many Pots: An Archaeology of Memory and Tradition at a Bahamian Plantation.*

Christopher C. Fennell is an associate professor in the Department of Anthropology at the University of Illinois at Champaign-Urbana. He received his Ph.D. in anthropology from the University of Virginia and Charlottesville. He is the author of *Crossroads and Cosmologies: Diasporas and Ethnogenesis in the New World.*

Leland Ferguson is professor emeritus in the Department of Anthropology in the University of South Carolina, Columbia. He received his Ph.D. from the University of North Carolina at Chapel Hill. He is the author of *Uncommon Ground: Archaeology and Early African America, 1650–1800.*

Lewis C. Jones is a Ph.D. candidate in the Department of Anthropology at Indiana University in Bloomington. He received his B.A. in history and B.S. in secondary education from Indiana University-Purdue University Indianapolis and his M.A. in anthropology from Indiana University Bloomington. He is co-author of "Archaeologies of Race and Urban Poverty: The Politics of Slumming, Engagement, and the Color Line," published in the journal *Historical Archaeology.*

Eric L. Larsen is a research associate for the Center for Heritage Studies in the Department of Anthropology at the University of Maryland at College Park. He received his Ph.D. from the State University of New York at Buffalo. He is the author of "Integrating Segregated Urban Landscapes of the Late-Nineteenth and Early-Twentieth Centuries," published in the journal *Historical Archaeology.*

Christopher N. Matthews is an associate professor in the Department of Anthropology at Hofstra University. He received his Ph.D. in anthropology from Columbia University. Matthews is the author of *The Archaeology of American Capitalism.*

Paul R. Mullins is a professor in the Department of Anthropology at the Indiana University-Purdue University Indianapolis. He received his Ph.D. in anthropology from the University of Maryland at College Park. Mullins is the author of *The Archaeology of Consumer Culture* and *Race and Affluence: An Archaeology of African America and Consumer Culture.*

David T. Palmer is an regional archaeologist for the Archaeology Program and adjunct assistant professor in the Department of Sociology and Anthropology at the University of Louisiana at Lafayette. He earned his Ph.D. in anthropology from the University of California, Berkeley. Palmer is a contributor to *Archaeology of Louisiana.*

Matthew M. Palus is a lecturer in the Department of Anthropology at the University of Maryland at College Park. He received his Ph.D. in anthropology from Columbia University. He is co-author of *They Worked Regular: Craft, Labor, and Family in the Industrial Community of Virginius Island.*

Theresa A. Singleton is an associate professor in the Department of Anthropology at Syracuse University in New York. She received her Ph.D. from the University of Florida. Singleton is the editor of two volumes on the archaeology of the African Diaspora: *The Archaeology of Slavery and Plantation Life* and *I, Too, Am America: Archaeological Studies of African-American Life.*

Carl Steen is the president of Diachronic Research Foundation in Columbia, South Carolina. He received his M.A. from the College of William and Mary. Steen is the author of articles and reports on the archaeology of South Carolina.

Megan Ann Teague is a Ph.D. candidate in the Department of Anthropology at the University of Florida. Currently she is an adjunct professor at Kennesaw State University.

Laurie A. Wilkie is a professor in the Department of Anthropology at the University of California, Berkeley. She received her Ph.D. from the University of California, Los Angeles. Wilkie is the author of *The Lost Boys of Zeta Psi: A Historical Archaeology of Masculinity in a University Fraternity* and *The Archaeology of Mothering: An African-American Midwife's Tale.*

INDEX